Letters of Lady Anne Barnard to Henry Dundas

Lady Anne Barnard in later life. Artist unknown.

THE LETTERS OF LADY ANNE BARNARD TO HENRY DUNDAS

FROM THE CAPE AND ELSEWHERE / 1793-1803

TOGETHER WITH HER

JOURNAL OF A TOUR INTO THE INTERIOR

AND CERTAIN OTHER LETTERS

Newly edited with an introduction and notes by

A. M. LEWIN ROBINSON

B.A., Ph.D., F.L.A.

A. A. BALKEMA / CAPE TOWN / 1973

ISBN 0 86961 024 4

Contents

Henry Dundas, 1st Viscount Melville, by Henry Raeburn

Andrew Barnard, by Sir Thomas Lawrence

Illustrations

The source of each illustration in the list is given in brackets: the following code has been used (refer to Introduction, page 5) : (F) indicates reproduction from Fairbridge's *Lady Anne Barnard at the Cape*; (L) from originals in the S.A. Library; (C) from originals in the William Fehr Collection, The Castle, Cape Town; and (B) from the collection of Lord Crawford at Balcarres, Scotland.

The Lutheran Church, Cape Town. The house on the left is now the Netherlands Embassy, while on the right is the Martin Melk House.

Acknowledgements

The assistance of the following is gratefully acknowledged: Mr. José Burman; Dr. Mary A. Cook, Swellendam; the Rt. Hon. Lord Crawford; Miss Joan H. Davies, Cape Archives; the City & County Librarian of Dublin Public Libraries; Mr. Mervyn Emms, Bergvliet, Cape; Miss A.D. Kilgour, Johannesburg Public Library; Mr. D.D. Murison, Scottish National Dictionary; Mme. H. de Puyfontaine via Dr. J.W. Louw, Cape Town; Dr. M.W.B. Sanderson, National Maritime Museum, Greenwich.

INTRODUCTION

The Historical Background

It was in June 1795 that nine British warships under the command of Admiral Sir G.K. Elphinstone with 1 500 troops on board, came to anchor in Simon's Bay on the eastern side of the Cape Peninsula. The purpose of this visit was to take possession of the Cape of Good Hope in the name of the Prince of Orange, at that time a refugee in England, to prevent it falling into the hands of the French revolutionary forces, and on the understanding that it would be returned to the Netherlands when peace was restored. A.J. Sluysken, the governor, however, who might have been expected to admit the British occupational force without opposition, was adversely swayed by the news just received that the new Batavian Republic was to ally itself with France. He was therefore determined to defend his settlement with such resources as were at his disposal. The British forces landed however under General J.H. Craig and advanced to Muizenberg where a motley army of mercenaries and burgers awaited them. The mercenaries fled and the Cape was surrendered, although there was some uncertainty until the articles of capitulation were signed at Rustenburg House on September 16th. In view of the Anglo-Dutch alliance, possession was now taken in the name of King George.

General Craig remained in command of the Cape settlement for eighteen months and more, but during 1796, Henry Dundas, Secretary for War and the Colonies, moved to have a civil governor appointed and the experienced Earl Macartney was chosen for the post. He sailed from Portsmouth on February 3rd 1797, and in the same fleet but on a different ship, went the newly appointed secretary of the Colony, Andrew Barnard, with his charming and noble wife Lady Anne, the intimate friend of Dundas, of the Prince of Wales, William Windham and other well-known members of London society. This same lady, who in the absence of Lady Macartney was to be the first lady of the Colony, became the authoress of a unique collection of letters which not only have no equal in giving us a graphic picture of the Colony at the turn of the century, but were a valuable source of information about Cape affairs for Secretary Dundas.

The Writer

How did such a distinguished lady come to make the perilous voyage to this outlandish place – three months distant from the centre of civilization? Her story is well known to many from the introductions to previous editions of her letters, to Dundas by W.H. Wilkins in 1901, and to Macartney by Dorothea Fairbridge in 1924, as well as other accounts, but this foreword would be incomplete without a short resumé of the life of this remarkable woman.

Lady Anne Lindsay was born on December 8th 1750, the eldest child of James, 5th Earl of Balcarres, who was 60 at the time of her birth, and his young wife Anne Dalrymple, a woman of strong character who ruled her family, which grew to eleven during the next eighteen years, with an iron hand. The more than customary severity however appears to have caused no permanent injury to the young Lindsays, and Anne and her beautiful sister Margaret, to whom she was greatly attached, grew up to be women more than usually accomplished for their day. In 1771 Lady Margaret departed to marry Alexander Fordyce of Roehampton, and, left much to her own devices, Lady Anne developed her literary bent. The ballad, *Auld Robin Gray* dates from this period. When set to music, this became very popular, although she did not admit its authorship for many years.

After the Earl, who had spent many years striving to recoup the family fortunes much reduced by the Jacobite Rebellion, died in 1768, the Lindsays spent some time in Edinburgh where they met Dr Samuel Johnson on his visit there, as well as the brilliant young Scottish lawyer, Henry Dundas, who came to have such an influence on Lady Anne's life.

Lady Margaret's husband died all too soon and Anne went to live with her in Berkeley Square. Here came those prominent figures of London society already mentioned, not the least being Henry Dundas, now well launched on a political career that was to make him a power in the land and far beyond its shores. Many expected him and Anne to marry, but it was not to be, though his first marriage ended in divorce. She indeed after nearly twenty years as a London hostess surprised all her acquaintances by marrying the impecunious but honourable Andrew Barnard, son of Thomas, Bishop of Killaloe and Kilfenora, one of Doctor Johnson's circle. Andrew had been in the army, rising to the rank of captain in the Inniskilling Regiment, but service in the West Indies had undermined his health and he had been on half-pay for ten years. To begin with Lady Anne was sorry for him when he begged her to save him from being obliged to marry a rich elderly widow, but that she came in time to love him deeply and sincerely there is no doubt. They were married in St. George's, Hanover Square, on October 31st 1793, and it was soon after this that the series of letters written by Lady

Anne to Henry Dundas began. This will carry on the Barnards' story.

The Letters

The great majority of the letters here published were originally among the Melville papers preserved at Melville Castle, Midlothian, until 1926 when they were put up for sale and bought by Sir Leicester Harmsworth, brother of Lord Northcliffe. To him we owe the beautiful, tooled leather binding in which they now are. Sir Leicester died in 1937, but not until mid-1948 did the letters again appear on the market when they were offered by the London firm of Francis Edwards for the sum of £450 – by no means an excessive price, even in those days. Nevertheless, though the South African Library naturally felt that Cape Town was the rightful place for the letters to find a lasting abode, the price was beyond its means. Fortunately the South African National Society came forward and through the generosity of the late Captain W.D. Hare, formerly M.P. for Mowbray, was able to secure them and place them on permanent loan in the Library.

These letters consist of 34 addressed to Henry Dundas by Lady Anne – 21 from the Cape and 13 from England and Ireland, being those numbered below: 1 – 30 and 36 – 39. Three letters are included in the hand of her husband, one from her brother, Alexander, 6th Earl of Balcarres, to Lady Anne, and one (11a) from W.S. van Rijneveld, the Fiscal, who proved such a good friend to the Barnards at the Cape. In addition there is one letter (87a) *from* Dundas to Lady Anne, dated 11-9-1800 and replying to hers of 14-5-1800.

As the letters begin from Ireland, so do they end, the four last (36 – 39) being from Dublin and Holyhead, 10-8-1803 to 21-9-1803, being written during and immediately after a visit to the Earl of Hardwicke, the Lord Lieutenant, and his wife the former Lady Elizabeth Lindsay.

Two other letters from Lady Anne to Dundas have been traced in other collections and transcriptions and are included here with kind permission. These are no. 32 of 24-4-1801, which is in the Cape Archives and no. 33 of 23-5-1801, in the Africana Museum, Johannesburg.

Lady Anne was a prolific correspondent and in addition to her writing to Henry Dundas she was of course in communication with other friends. After Lord Macartney, the first civil governor, left the Cape, she wrote at length to him, this series of letters being capably edited by Dorothea Fairbridge and published in 1924 under the title *Lady Anne Barnard at the Cape of Good Hope*. In the case of her sisters she found it most satisfactory to send them an account of her experiences in journal form, and since the important letter to Dundas describing the Barnards' journey inland in May 1798 was removed from the collection before it came to the South African Library, it has been thought fit to include here the account of this journey given in Lady Anne's *Journal of a residence at the Cape of Good Hope and a short tour into the interior, addressed to her sisters in England*, part of which was published in *Lives of the Lindsays*, vol. 3, 1849. Inevitably the taking of a secondary, printed source must allow for misreadings in the transcription by the first printer and the rendering of proper names may not always be what Lady Anne herself intended, and this must be accepted, but there is no doubt that this journal version of the journey is the most detailed one that she left behind.

Letters of Lady Anne to other persons are also to be found in the British Museum, particularly those to her old friend William ("Weathercock") Windham, Secretary at War, 1794-1801, who was once a suitor for her hand, and to the Earl of Mornington, later Marquis Wellesley, governor-general of India, who spent some time at the Cape en route for that country in February 1798. These letters have not been given here in extenso unless there are no others for the same period, as their contents would seem redundant. Other letters have been quoted in notes. One thing that does emerge from a comparison of these letters however is the writer's ability to change her style according to the person she is addressing. To Dundas she writes as to a dear friend – her equal, even if a public figure, and one she can importune, or on occasion even plead with, if the situation warrants. Lord Macartney she addresses as a friend but is never familiar, while to Windham, as befits a rejected but not despised suitor, she is affectionately personal. To the old reprobate Wellesley, on the other hand, she can be light of touch, flippant and well-nigh scandalous.

In the Melville Castle collection there is also a letter to Lady Anne from her eldest brother, Alexander, the 6th Earl of Balcarres, dated Jamaica, April 20th 1796. He was governor of the island and was apparently one of the first people to whom Lady Anne appealed for a post for her husband. In an execrable hand he writes that there is little chance of his being able to be of assistance in this direction. This letter was enclosed in one to Henry Dundas (see Letter 7). Three letters from Andrew Barnard to Dundas, dated 23-8-1797, 29-9-1798 and 9-3-1800, are of a formal nature, as one would expect, and only the first has been printed here. It is not suggested that they are the only letters he wrote to Dundas from the Cape, though we do have Lady Anne's word that he saw little need for it. In her letter of 29-11-1797 (no. 14) she writes: "I have been enquiring if Mr. B. wrote to you, he says 'My dear Anne what between Lord Macartney & you, upon my soul I pity poor Mr Dundas too much for all he has to read to plague him with more – Lord M. very properly takes the business part, and the accounts of everything upon himself & you write all the lighter parts, so what is left for me?' "

Other short letters in the collection are those included for the information of Henry Dundas. That from the Fiscal, Willem Stephanus van Rijneveld (no. 11a) is in French and in his own hand, while others are copies, by herself in the case of the interchange of letters between Andrew and General Francis Dundas on the latter's ignoring him in matters of business (nos. 23a & b), Nos. 26a – e, on the other hand, between Andrew, General Dundas and Sir George Yonge, are in a formal secretarial hand.

As already mentioned, one letter (no. 27a) is a copy of one by Henry Dundas *to* Lady Anne, dated September 11th 1800. Why this alone of those Dundas must have written her should have survived in this collection is not known. One can only surmise that it was due to its importance, being one at least in which he felt constrained to put Lady Anne right on certain matters, in this case her views regarding the administration and capabilities of his nephew Francis as acting governor.

Lady Anne's handwriting is full of character. It varies from the fairly neat to the definitely untidy, as for instance when she wrote in haste because the ship lying off Plymouth was about to sail. Rarely however can her hand be regarded as above reproach. It is nevertheless remarkable that she found so much time for letter-writing in a busy life. It is fortunate that she used such good materials, for all her letters are in an excellent state of preservation and unfaded. The majority are on strong laid quarto 22,5 cms. x 19 cms., while a few are on foolscap 32 cms. x 19,5 cms. On May 4th 1799 (Letter 22) she apoligised for using such bad paper as she was away in the country. This "bad" paper, while having a poor surface, is very durable.

Earlier Publications

As mentioned above, the majority of these letters to Dundas were first published in 1901 under the title *South Africa a century ago*, edited with a memoir, by William Henry Wilkins, M.A., F.S.A. (1861-1905) who was at one time private secretary to Lord Dunraven when Under-Secretary of State for the Colonies. He also edited the manuscripts of Sir Richard Burton and was the author of various other historical works. This edition was published by Smith Elder & Co. An edition based on the foregoing, with the same title, was published in Cape Town by Maskew Miller in 1924, under the editorship of Hector James Anderson, an inspector of schools, with an introduction by A.C.G. Lloyd, Librarian of the South African Library, in addition to Wilkins's memoir. This edition includes extracts from the journal addressed to her sisters and some illustrations. The introductory matter in these editions is very good but the editing of the letters leaves a great deal to be desired by modern standards of scholarship. Apart from the almost total absence of annotation, Wilkins exceeded an editor's licence by correcting grammar and spelling, altering words, extending abbreviations and omitting considerable passages, including nearly all postscripts. Eleven letters have been ignored altogether while frequently he runs two letters into one or even makes one long one into two.* It is these errors and omissions which encouraged the preparation of this new edition.

The Sketches

Letter no. 11 contains a few rough sketches from Lady Anne's own hand, done first in pencil and then emphasized in ink. These are a rear view of General James Hartley of the Bombay Army (who was a fellow

*two**
For an analysis of these shortcomings see *Quarterly bulletin of the S. Afr. Library*, 4(1): 7-11, Sept. 1949.

passenger on the ship), a view of Simon's Bay and a view of the Hottentots Holland Mountains from Muizenberg. There are also some amusing attempts to illustrate the shadows cast by the human form at the equator. Here and there in the text a few small sketches will also be found. This edition however is also illustrated by sketches from a small collection presented to the South African Library by the 27th Lord Crawford in 1923, and by a number of more finished sketches which are preserved at Balcarres, and which are here reproduced by courtesy of the present Lord Crawford, to whom we are most grateful.

Many of these were published in Dorothea Fairbridge's edition of Lady Anne's letters to Lord Macartney, *Lady Anne Barnard at the Cape of Good Hope* (Oxford, 1924), from which a large selection has been made to bring as many pertinent sketches together as possible. Finally, by courtesy of the Officer Commanding, Western Province Command, a small number of original sketches from the William Fehr Collection at the Castle, Cape Town, are also reproduced.

Lady Anne begins her journal

Letter 1

Just forty days after the Barnards' wedding, Lady Anne was writing to her old friend from the home of her parents-in-law near Dublin where she had been taken to meet old Mrs. Barnard – the Bishop she must have known in London. Ireland was for the time-being peaceful but revolt simmered beneath the surface.

St Wolstans near Dublin*
Decr 10 – 1793

almost the last words which you used to me on parting in Brook St were, – "let me hear from you I pray when you are comfortably settled" – long e're now I shoud have wrote to you coud I have said as much for the good Health of Mr Barnard as for my own, but the remains of his severe illness renderd it necessary for us to travel so slow that we were long on the road, and I prefered delaying giving you some account of myself till I was settled here – we had a vile passage. – I thought I shoud have been drownd & food for fishes instead of being alive & merry in this Hospitable (& now) *quiet* region. – on reaching this place I found myself welcomed as the Queen of Sheba might have expected to have been, all the inhabitants opening their arms to receive me, the old servants grinning with satisfaction and every dog wagging his tail, the kind partiality of the Bishop & his wife to me*, the satisfaction which all their friends & connections express here in getting me amongst them cannot fail to impress with gratitude a heart that I feel knows both how to value & to return such kind Testymonys. – St Wolstans is a very beautifull place the house commodious in all respects – the grounds well laid out – a river runs within a hundred yards of the windows which are cut down to it, with a fine bank of wood & Mr Connollys seat* on the other side, I look upon it as a great perfection in any place to present one with its best view without putting my Lazyness to the trouble of going out to poak after it, & that is exactly the case here as I have the bank the river the cascades the summerhouses all before me as I sit at my work, not the sleepy, dull, old, river called Father Thames, not the Drunken, boisterous, galloping, rivers of our Scottish mountains but a pretty sort of cantering river which sports without roaring & contains plenty of good Salmon & other fish – this place originaly was a monastry & was inhabited by some hundred monks, the ruins of the Abbey remain in detached pieces & form fine objects, but the finest object in the ruins woud

*Dublin**
St. Wolston's Priory (founded 1202) is situated on the banks of the Liffey, some 10 miles from Dublin, near the village of Celbridge, and was formerly the seat of the Alen family. Bishop Barnard acquired it from the estate of Bishop Robert Clayton (d. 1758), his wife's uncle, whose executor he was. See *J. Roy. Soc. Antiquar. Ireland* 49(1):55-59,1919.

*to me**
Thomas Barnard, D.D. (1728-1806) was at this time bishop of Killaloe and Kilfenora. His first wife, who died not long after this, was Anne Browne.

*seat**
Thomas Connolly (1738-1803), Irish politician, M.P. for Malmesbury and champion of legislative union with Britain, lived at Castletown House, Celbridge, adjoining St. Wolston's.

be to be able to find out some treasures which tradition says the monks hid *somewhere*, but which are still undiscoverd – I am willing to believe the father & son when they hint that I am the treasure which they have found, but I am unwilling to date my origin from the days of the monks how much soever those gentlemen are supposed to have known what was good – I congratulate you and all his Majestys ministers on the peacefull state of this country – I am told that last year there reignd Disaffection & allarm in every ones mind, or rather, the first in the minds of many, the allarm has partly cured the disaffection & the judicious steps we have all taken as well as the Horrible events of france have united to conciliate all partys into the Hearty intention of supporting Government in its own plans of what is best – . I can judge a little of this by the language of Mr Connolly, who is at present a good citizen & a most keen officer. – perhaps I have no business to give my thoughts which are mine only & may be very unfounded, but inspite of the partiality which his natural connections with Fox* & that party give him to all their measures & ways & inspite of his keeping up a talking from time to time to this effect, I shoud think that if the next Lord Lieut is judicious, & will take Mr Connolly up as a publick spirited man who he woud wish to gain over as a friend, by shewing himself a little attention & confidence that he may be won & with him many others, but this cannot be the case under the present Lord Lieut.* – I hear his spirits are better but his nerves still affected, I was told that he had had an hours conversation with LyW: the day before her death, & when he left her was deeply affected, saying that she was an angel & regreting that he had not known it sooner. – had he been a good husband I shoud have been sorry for him, but as he was not so I am *very* sorry for him at present; as I believe there is no rack so severe as that which chief Justice Conscience condemns the criminal to who has trespassed & who sees it too late to amend. – people form conjectures you know, as those at a distance from the fountain head will do, about who is to be secretary* – I have heard Riders both named, Bushes both, father & son, Tom Steel, but the youngest Rider appears to be the most believd of any – pelham* too – he has been mentiond – by the bye I wish you Joy of the five ships which it appears by the papers of today that Lord Howe has taken,* I wish there were *more of them*, but for a beginning we will be content – if Lord Moiras* expedition succeeds that will be a blessed matter we *have done all we coud* to aid it by stuffing 20 of Col Lenoxs* soldiers as full as we coud of good beef, ale & whisky tother night when they arrived here on their march, some of the young recruits seemd low spirited but all said they woud lay down their life for their Col – . I gave each of them a sh: poor souls as they departed, to be laid out *4* times under their sacred promise that 3 pence each time (only shoud be spent) on whisky on their march – just as they were going my Scots servant came up – "*O my Leddi*, here is a man who was with Lord Balcarres* as he was taken prisoner in america" – this of course was a half crown business – but in five minutes he returnd – My *Leddi* my Leddi here is a woman who comes from *Fife*, & she is the only Soldiers wife *amongst all the twenty* – the argument of *Fife* was conclusive to the tune of a crown, & as the hint of there being no more soldiers wives to come for-

*Fox**
Charles James Fox (1749-1806), the Whig leader.

*Lieut**
John Fane, 10th earl of Westmoreland, lord-lieutenant or viceroy of Ireland, 1790-95. He was succeeded by Lord Fitzwilliam. Sarah Countess of Westmoreland d. 9-11-1793.

*secretary**
The Chief Secretary to the Government, Lord Hobart (see below) was resigning on his appointment as Governor of Madras. The next Secretary was Sylvester Douglas, afterwards Baron Glenbervie, who held office 16-12-1793 to 12-12-1794.

*pelham**
The Bushes were Charles Kendal, a brilliant young lawyer, and Gervase, an M.P. – *not* father and son. Thomas Steele, M.P. for Chichester, was joint paymaster-general of the forces. Thomas Pelham, later 2nd earl of Chichester, was Chief Secretary under Lord Camden, 1795-98.

*taken,**
A rumour only. Howe was at sea constantly during 1793 but had no successes.

*Moiras**
Major-General Francis Rawdon-Hastings, 1st marquess of Hastings, 2nd earl of Moira, was sent to Brittany with an expedition to aid the French royalists but achieved nothing.

ward was a good one, he carryd off the money to his dear country-woman rejoicing. – about this part of the country all the lower class of people are catholicks, in accidental conversation with these sort of folks one sometimes hears more truth than is to be met with in the more regular accounts of their betters – I find that the Catholics in Ireland are more allarmd at the french doings & more apprehensive of any attack here from such wretches than the protestants are, a low woman said to me that the *foreigners* had all the prayers of the poor with them for their success – I feard she meant the french, but I found that *French* are *french* [,] foreigners is the united armys, "they are fighting for us all said she & till they gain the day we shall have three meagre days a week" – all the catholicks it seems restrict themselves to fast three times a week at present & have prayers for the success of our troops – there certainly is amongst them a few plotting turbulent men who from self Interest may be glad to create the appearance & perhaps the reality of little local disorder but every body agrees in saying that it is not the *people* who are so disposed –

*Lenoxs**
Most probably Lt.-Col. Charles Lennox (1764-1819), 35th Foot, who succeeded his uncle as 4th duke of Richmond in 1806 and was viceroy of Ireland, 1807-13. It was his duchess's ball that took place in Brussels on the eve of Quatre Bras (1815). His aunt, Lady Louisa, was the wife of Thomas Connolly.

But it is time for me to conclude – let me ere I do, say a little of my own motions, Hopes and wishes – you bid me do so, and I know you Must ever feel *that* for me which makes me certain, that kind & friendly words are not words of course, – I shall not return to England for these six weeks or two months I believe – and on that account shall not be in the way of hearing of any vacancy such as I might solicit from Your friendship to me, for Mr Barnard – I have not forgot what you hinted to me in confidence, respecting the possibility of his deriving a benefit from a situation, austensibly [sic] given to another, and to be sure, this woud be a very eligible favour for *our interests*, & one I shoud most gratefully thank you for; but *till* such a thing occurs, will you contrive to place him in *Any* office, no matter of *how little* salary, in which he may have *something to do* & prove himself *usefull*. – he wishes to be a man of business & wishes to attach *himself* to *yourself*, this is his *own* Idea & you may be sure I have patted it on the back; he was pleased with your manners to him when you talkd to him of a matter I once recommended him for to you, said, he "never talkd to a great man who had so much the power of making a man who was *asking a favor* feel at ease with him" as yourself, & that if you coud place him in your own board or anywhere, where he might gain your friendship by deserving it & by being *connected with yourself* he shoud be glad; that as to the dignity or advantage of the situation he shoud not much mind either, as in a little time he hoped you coud add to these –

*Balcarres**
Alexander, 6th earl of Balcarres and 23rd earl of Crawford (1752 1825), a general in the army and Governor of Jamaica. He was Lady Anne's eldest brother. As a battallion commander of the 53rd Foot during the American War of Independence he was obliged to surrender in 1777 and was a prisoner until 1779.

In a word into your hands I put the matter & leave it, *you* will find out a mode of serving him, the sooner you can in any shape the better as I *greatly wish* on my return that he may *at once* begin a life of *occupation abroad* & of comfort at *Home*, both of which advantages to *My own Happiness*, I prefer owing to you [than] to any other person, because I never can cease to have for you sentiments, which make the feeling of gratitude sit easy on the heart –

*Leinsters**
William Fitzgerald, 2nd duke of Leinster (1749-1804). His eldest daughters were Lady Mary and Lady Emily. His eldest son, b. 21-8-1791, was Augustus, Marquess of Kildare.

I must now leave You to dress, We dine at the Duke of Leinsters* one of our nearest neighbours, the two eldest daughters are grown up & are fine young women with a mixture of simplicity & dignity which bespeaks good dispositions & noble blood – the young Heir is but two years of age and resembles nothing so much as the Infant Hercules which Sir Joshua painted for the Empress of Russia in the act of Strangling two serpents,* I hope the young Kildare will not grow up to look upon England & Scotland as those serpents & try to strangle them for the benefit of Ireland – there is a neighbourhood here close studded with many of the familys of the first distinction, they have all been to wait on me as the Bishops new daughter, which I shoud be *Happy* to impute to *my own merits* but must not in Justice, as had I been a less tolerable daughter he is such a favorite here with his neighbours that they woud have been eager to shew me civilitys. – I have not yet been in Dublin exept for one day to dine with the Hobarts,* I shall see a little of it before my return I suppose, but there is not any thing to be met with in it, so new or interesting to you as woud justify me for troubling you with another stupid letter, unless you desire to hear again from me while there in which case I shall give you a sheet of Irish news & Irish accounts as far as I see, or as I hear from those wiser than myself. – Margaret does not mention your name to me in any of her letters, so I shoud presume she has not seen any thing of you – in conversation with Lord Hobart I shoud be much obliged if you woud mention my Brother John* now commanding the Fort of permacoil opposite to pondecherrie as an officer whose chances in life have been hard, being still a captain poor fellow after all his imprisonments & wounds, & as one you shoud be glad coud he serve – I have already named him to Lord H: but your two words will be of more use than a whole Dictionary of mine. – once more Adieu & god Bless you, when you find three minutes leisure (if such a thing can be found) you may give me a page to tell me that you are well, & resolved *not* to retire from any of your departments *till* you inroll Mr B: somewhere, or somehow which you perceive is a *very modest* reason for forcing you to remain Secretary of State – I coud give you a better if I chose it, that I doubt if your Successor with All his time at his command will get thro the Business with half the dispatch or effect that you do with ten mens work on your hands. – once more posatively Adieu for the last time of saying it –

*serpents**
Sir Joshua Reynold's painting "The infant Hercules" is now in the Hermitage, Leningrad.

*Hobarts**
Robert, Lord Hobart, later 4th earl of Buckinghamshire (1760-1816), was appointed Governor of Madras in Oct. 1793.

*John**
The Hon. John Lindsay (1762-1826), 7th son of the 5th Earl of Balcarres and an officer in the 71st Highlanders. He was engaged in the war against Tippoo Sultan, Napoleon's ally in Mysore. A word in Hobart's ear may perhaps have born fruit as he obtained his majority the following March and was Lt.-Col. in Jan. 1798. Permacoil was about 15 m. north of Pondicherry.

Letter 2

In spite of Lady Anne's assertion that they would only be staying in Ireland for two months at the most, they were still at St. Wolston's after three and likely to remain for several more.

Dublin
March 10 1794

with the certainty that by the publick papers themselves I *must* know how you do long before this coud receive any answer, yet the vexation & anxiety I feel about your Illness (which can be no trifling one if it renders your strong mind & constitution unfit for publick business) leads me to write now, tho I am conscious of the above & that your life & Health is too precious to this country as well as to your private friends for the papers to remain silent on the nature & progress of your Malady. – A putrid sore throat I have known you have; a complaint also in the stomach & bowels, I shall be better pleased to hear it has been one of these Ills, than owing to the oppression of business, as the necessitys of the times will constantly expose you to be their victim, while a load rests on your shoulders little Inferior to that which we see Atlas bending under – Oh how ardently do I not long to see that calm restored to the world that we have once seen it in, at present we are all playing a game, but too anxious an one, from the desperation of the stake, & playing under the sad disadvantage which in a degree every country I suppose in the world is exposed to, of having danger doubled thro the infection of principles which coincide too much with the private interests of the basest parts of the community. – some little time ago an idea of Invasion here, prevailed very much, at present I hear no more of it, but much of turbulent doings in distant parts of the country, I fear much that the loyalty of the inferior ranks of the Kingdom will much depend on the success of the French arms. – when things go ill with them all seems quiet & one hopes the Horror of their Systems have partly produced that effect, but from some late talkings I much doubt whether they woud not find many more partizans here than I at first thought on coming into this land. – the wise men who I hear reasoning on the matter seemd to apprehend much more danger of an attack in this country than in England, & the quarter, near to Dublin. – they also seemd to think it probable from there being a better chance here of assistance from ill affected natives, & some boldly maintained that after leaving the necessary guards to the different magazines & posts together with a sufficient force to awe Internal insurrection that the military on this spot was not sufficient to send out two thousand men to oppose the enemy. – all this woud have frightend me very compleatly had I not that confidence in your knowing better than any one here *can, what* to apprehend & *where* to re-inforce that it tranquilized me for my head. – I heard some general officers lately in conversation expressing great fears of being sent to cork in order as they said to guard a coast not half so much in Danger as the bay of Dublin – I *prate* like a *parrot* remember, by repeating such things to you but tis not perfectly useless to know the sentiments of professional men when they are given unguardedly in private conversation. – I am sure if the people here have any fears, they are at least resolved not to die with empty stomachs, for the sound of dinners is such & the abundance of good things given so great, that I have some thoughts of Hanging on a tin pocket as old pig Wharton used to do* that I may steal a few good dinners for Berkley Square when I return to my Home & mutton chops – I have about 24 feasts to receive before I visit you in London, will you give me the best of all feasts, better than the stalled ox, a friends cordial welcome, glad to see me again. – you shoud. – Margaret told me that tho I had not heard from you (w^c considering what you have to do I did not think extraordinary) that you had frequently thought of writing to me, & sent me this assurance as an antidote to any mortification I might feel at your silence, & all I shall say is that you need not write to me for the *forms sake* of the matter, I let you off from that, shoud occupation be ever so much suspended as to let you follow inclination *easily* I shall wellcome yr letter, short, or long & whatever you may choose to say, shall be to me only, as Mr B: & I have very right & well judged rules on every thing that respects correspondence, which cannot be spontaneous & easy if four eyes are for certain to read what two has wrote; – I believe neither of us, will be disposed to put a rule implying so much mutual *confidence* to any improper purpose. – his Health is perfectly restored at present, tho his four years residence in the West Indies has certainly laid into his constitution a bilious tendency which makes it not much to be depended on, it does not however affect his humour which is I think the gentlest & kindest I ever saw & without the ostentation of it the most *attach-able* if that may be called a word; – where such a quality is found, it certainly shoud be attach-*ing* –

You will be pleased to hear How much satisfied the people here are with the new Secretary* – at first the Idea of his being a professional man, frightend the gay people & awed the grave, but the grave upon searching into his private character for ability & firmness, being also a good many of them of the same *cloth*, determined to Hold him up instead of badgering him in the House of Commons, while on the other hand, his own unaffected manners & good sense, backd by the *Internal eloquence* of a *most excellent cook* have now so fully gaind the point of general good will that I dare say you have accounts here from every one to tally with mine. – Lord Westmoreland goes about – & every thing goes on as usual which is saying All that the *Delicacy* & *prudency* of my

*to do**
Possibly Dr. Thomas Warton (1728-1790), professor of poetry and Camden professor of history at Oxford, and one of Johnson's circle.

*Secretary**
Sylvester Douglas (1745-1823) assumed office on Dec. 16 1793. A distinguished barrister, he was M.P. from 1795 to 1806 and created Baron Glenbervie on Nov. 11 1800 when he was offered the governorship of the Cape of Good Hope, a post which he never took up however.

Scottish pen will allow me to say of Irish doings. – whatever they are, the world seems to be in no *blunder* about them, & in good truth I think the sin & shame much lightend instead of *aggravated* as the *addle pates* here will convince me it is, by there being no longer a wife to vex with the flirtation. – I saw Corry* tother day who told me he had dined with you all, a pleasant & jolly party – May you have many such & a little more time to enjoy them – God Bless you & preserve you – I will not add more at present as I grudge the time w[c] my stuff takes you to read. – Adieu then & believe me to remain what I ever have been & shall be – most affectionately Yours –

I will take advantage of your cover to enclose a letter to Hardwicke* a measure not respectfull – but pardonable

*Corry**
Armar Lowry-Corry, created Baron Belmore in 1781, viscount in 1789 and earl in 1797.

*Hardwicke**
Philip Yorke, 3rd earl of Hardwicke (1757-1834), married Lady Elizabeth Lindsay, Lady A.'s sister, in 1782. He was Lord Lieutenant of Ireland 1801-04.

Letter 3

Though still in Dublin in July Lady Anne was again broaching the subject of her husband's future career, Dundas having in that month become Secretary for War and the Colonies in Pitt's administration.

Dublin
July 12th 1794

more reasons than one, at present lead me to write to you my dear friend; the news papers and the melancholy event it contains is one that I shoud not have been silent on, had I had no other motive. – poor good Henry Drummond! * – I was in hopes the former report of his death being contradicted, that he might have recoverd and enjoyd many happy years, but all is now over, I see and he has left only those tyes which must be a great comfort to a woman on such an occasion; your daughter has allways conducted herself with a degree of prudence & domestic tenderness so exemplary that she has every thing to look back on with satisfaction I am sure, and nothing to grieve over that she coud have helpd. –

the papers for the last two or three days have been full of your intentions to retire from being Secretary of State, whatever loss I may think this to the country for your own sake I am heartily glad of it, I am convinced it (along with other things) was too much for you, and to spend the good life before you with the prodigality you was obliged to do while overstretching your powers, was contrary to the duty you owe yourself, your wife, and family. – on an occasion so important as this however, I think it right for me to remind you of myself, and by laying open to you my Hopes, wishes, and the way they have regulated my conduct *here*, ingage you still more to assist me in discharging the very esential Duty I am come under. – depending on your kindness so many proofs of which I have experienced on former occasions and almost certain that distance woud not make you forget the Hearty assurance you gave me of serving my husband, I have never teased you about it, because I committed my interests wholy into your hands, while I have formd all my councils here upon the confidence I had in you. – In consequence of what passed between you & me the last time I saw you, which I naturaly reported to Mr Barnard, I prevailed on him to give up the army, tho considerable advantages were offerd to him by the Lord Leut, as he has been seventeen years in the army and has served many

*Drummond**
Henry Drummond (1762-4.7.1794), grandson of 4th Viscount Strathallan, was a London banker. He married Anne, 2nd daughter of Henry Dundas in 1786. She married again, see Letter 36.

years abroad,* but he paid that compliment to my comfort, and to his expectations thro me of being fixed in some civil line at Home by an employment under yourself if possible. – I have also to establish ourselves more permanently in England prevailed on him and on his family to consent to our letting St Wolstans for a term of years almost the prettiest place in Ireland, but one which our Income did not render it eligible to keep and to have a House in London also. – to indulge me these things have been done, am I not therefore doubly bound my dear friend to use every exertion which Zeal, duty, & gratitude can use with the friend who has long been mine, who knows our situation and who I trust will not on this occasion *desert me*, to replace to him the pleasures I have deprived him of in order to secure my own comfort amongst my own friends. – he was fond of his country house & fond of his profession, but he is more attachd to me than to both put together; or to any thing else in this world & I am certain that from various motives you will have real pleasure in learning from me the truth, that nothing can exceed the gentle, consistent, & daily attention with which he endeavours in every thing to make me Happy his dispositions are quite as amiable as I expected them to be, and his activity, parts and conduct rather beyond my expectations from them tho they were not inconsiderable – his knowledge of the languages (while at present it is but an accomplishment) may be usefull, & his eagerness to have something to employ his mind "business – business Anne" is decided – I really feel so pledged to procure him what may have that effect, and to his father & mother who might not else have consented to his giving up this country, that my whole thoughts have been bent on this for some time, yet I shoud not have said a word more on the subject till I saw you had not the present talk of your resigning one of the departments which gives you the power of serving those you protect led me to think that I ought on this occasion to remind you of us, and to entreat it of you, to place him ere you retire in some line of business if possible, or emolument, which need not afterwards preclude your taking him more immediately into your own department

I will not add more – I thro myself at you with Earnestness & Hope – *You owe me some Happiness* – in *Truth you do* – pay me by making me the means of serving a man who has rebuilt in a considerable degree what tumbled to its foundation, who makes mine his study & whose prospects in this country have been given up for me –

I shall be in England soon, and shall let you know as soon as I arrive – mean time – *God Bless you* and as the Ghosts say – "*Remember me*" –

*abroad**
Barnard was commissioned in the 27th (Inniskilling) Foot in 1777 and served in America and the West Indies where he attained the rank of captain. His health however was undermined and he went on half-pay when the regiment was reduced in 1783. He resigned his commission in 1794 as Lady A. indicated. (See *Army lists*.)

Letter 4

Only towards the close of the year 1794 did the Barnards return to London, to the house in Berkeley Square which Lady Anne used to share with her widowed sister Margaret Fordyce. Her repeated requests to Dundas for preferment for her husband met with no success however until after the Cape of Good Hope fell to the British on August 7th 1795. Lord Macartney, an experienced administrator, was to be sent out as Governor and Andrew Barnard was invited to accompany him as Colonial Secretary.

april 30 – 1796

Since I saw you last my dear friend I repeated to my husband what passed between us relating to him – he was much pleasd by your assurances to me that you had not ceasd to think of a situation for him, and that what was *delayd* was not *forgotten* by you. – I found in him the same anxious desire of *employment*, and the same readyness to embrace any mode of proving by his activity and Zeal that he was not unworthy of your patronage – so far from starting at the idea of the cape, he seemd to be animated with a portion of your own enthusiasm about it, and bid me say that if you chose to send him there you shoud find him doubly anxious to perform his dutys well, that the whole was plannd by you. – but while I see him delighted with the idea of this new Territory over which I have little doubt of *your* presiding I cannot help saying, that *I* shoud be much better contented with a very inferior employment at home to that which your friendship might give him there, or any where abroad – much is not necessary to content me with respect to emolument, but that which I feel him most interested in, is to see him launchd into a life of active employment, after which he pants so much; an ambition so laudable for a young man & so much the *wisdom* as well as *duty* of every wife to encourage in her husband, that I certainly woud do every thing in my power to accomplish his views at whatever Sacrifice – from this cause after a little reflection I find myself at no loss to determine on what is best; if you find that you have no situation fit to occupy him respectably with a certain portion of advantage annexd to it in *this* country, and if you find that you have the conferring of what you please in your own *New* Kingdom, give him an employment at once important and beneficial and I will accompany him there – perhaps some use might be derived from my being there to those very plans which you will have a pride & pleasure in seeing carried into execution in the best manner, & possibly the respectability attending his carrying out with him his family might justify you for any degree of importance or advantage annexed to the situation you bestowd on him as apparently calculated to tempt me also to the measures. – you said that you coud scarce propose any such plan as the cape to me for *him*, as it woud imply separation, (for you probably did not suppose I coud think of accompanying him); Separation woud certainly be painfull, but to me it woud be chiefly so from the opinion that when things are all well & people living comfortably together in confidence & Harmony those long absences which teach them to feel Independent of each other are bad, and seldom produce a re-union equally perfect with what woud have continued without the interruption – this being the case, the sick at sea, cowardly, and not quite young enough to think a new climate very safe, I am ready to put on my cork Jacket for his advantage, and I think I may very safely say, that I know no man more fitted for such an undertaking than himself as his extreme activity, Judicious good sense & excellent conciliatory temper woud render him a person equal to any quantity of business – perfectly capable of improving on ideas given to him & of carrying them into execution, while he has none of that presumptuous conceit of ability which instead of cooperating with the views of his masters might sett itself up to judge for them –

if Lord Macartney* shoud be the man to go, I fancy he woud be pleasd to have the son of his old friend, one of his government, as he used to know the bishop well –

april 10 – since I begun this letter I have heard that he is in Italy, but coming home, I will not therefore lose more time in sending it off to you, and at the same time to beg of you earnestly to let me see you sometimes at this Juncture either at this house or at your own, as communication & consultation may be of esential use to us in starting & getting ideas – a month hence (if you detain us by no good) I shall return to Ireland to remain for six months at least, dispirited I own when I have to tell the Bishop & Mrs Barnard that the flattering hopes I gave them for their son, from the kind promises you made me previous to our marriage three years ago, was not (from I will suppose a variety of good reasons) realized – I then explaind myself fully to you my dear friend & refer it once more to your own mind whether you ought not to feel yourself doubly bound to make my heart & situation comfortable to what you are to any other woman in this world – to a man generous as well as just how many motives are there not in the strong tho defeated regards which have subsisted between us, for you to take my husband by the hand & make Me thro him as Happy as you can! to pay me All you have, & still owe me, you never *can*, but what you can you shoud & you have yet before you the pleasure of obliging me, I have paid you tears of gratitude for the Hearty manner in which you pledged yourself to serve us, & while I have any memory I must depend on your doing so – but Hope deferred maketh the Heart sick – God Bless you – this letter is too long but I forgot myself at the top of the page else it woud have been shorter by every thing exept the business part – Adieu – evr yours –

*Macartney**
George, Earl Macartney (1737-1806). He had been Governor of Madras, 1781-85, and Ambassador Extraordinary to Pekin in 1792-93. His appointment as Governor of the Cape was dated 30 Dec. 1796.

Letter 5

The next two letters are undated but must have been written a few weeks later than that of April 30th. Andrew, it appears, was prepared to accept the appointment but hardly expected his wife would wish to go with him to such a distant and uncivilized spot. Lady Anne's reaction was quite different and clearly Dundas must have reprimanded her in no uncertain terms.

Sunday – [1796]

I mentiond to you at Wimbledon about a fortnight ago my dear friend that I greatly wishd to see you again more at leisure to ask many questions I coud not then ask, but I woud not intrude myself on you lately, surrounded as you have been with people on business – let me however before I enter on the subject of my present letter tell you more fully than I have yet had the opportunity of doing how strongly & gratefully we feel the friendship you are shewing us and the desire you have to serve us, it shall be impresst on us both as long as we live, & will give alacrity to every endeavour of Mr Barnards to prove himself deserving of your protection. – but while we feel this compleatly and warmly, let me acknowledge privately to yourself that within these few days some things have ocurd to mortify me in a way that you only can dispell; and you will dispell it, either in one way or another I have not a doubt – You so compleatly restricted me from mentioning the offer you made thro me to Mr Barnard to any person capable of giving me information on similar matters that I was of course without the possibility of gaining any; the conversation I had with you at Wimbledon* was hurried, & you may know that I never possess myself when talking over any matter of business with you in publick, in such a manner as to be sure I have not misapprehended some point; however I believd I had not: I had by letter professd myself ready to go to the cape with Mr Barnard if you woud make our situation there as respectable in point of rank & as beneficial as you had it in your power to do – you mentiond the Secretary to the council, as the office next to Lord M^c^cartney in power, patronage & business, you may remember that the word *Secretary* made me pause & that I earnestly askd the question of you along with an apology for my ignorance if it was above or below the members of the council, to which you replied that tho its nominal rank was not so high, its real consequence was greater as it was on the same footing as Mr

*Wimbledon**
Dundas had acquired a villa at Wimbledon in 1786.

Rose* at the treasury or Mr Nepean* at the admiralty, and is in short, you added the prettiest appointment I ever had it in my power to give a young man – elated & pleased I saw that the Mr B^s. rank was inferior in council to its meriting that his consideration thro his patronage & Salary like that of Mr *Rose* & Mr *Nepean* was greater, & that his exertions and close attention to business while the others of the council had less to do woud like *theirs* be rewarded with a larger salary in order to make up by Emolument & respectability of Living, for any other inferiority which might render the situation less flattering to me – possessd of this opinion I askd for no information besides your own which I had perhaps not sufficiently obtaind – of late I have been in the way of hearing the governments of Madrass & Bengal talkd over, of hearing the department of Secretary to the council mentiond & it was with feelings of anxiety & vexation I heard it talkd of as one of so much inferiority to the council, sitting as clerk only to their instructions, without vote, not even corresponding under his own name with you – my sister told me on her return that the salary also was inferior by 1,000 pr an. to the others, being the lowest of the whole, she said that when you mentiond this to her she had a greater desire to say something on it & also to ask you some questions, but Mr Barnard had taken her word so expressly that she woud ask no questions whatsoever that regarded emolument, but leave it to you to say of yourself what you thought fit, that she felt herself absolutely tyed up from it – as to me I give you my sacred word that I have not & woud not for a great deal tell Mr Barnard that I am now writing to you as I do not believe he woud let me send this letter, *he* has no claims on you beyond what your friendship to *me* gives *us*, is extremely gratefull for things as they are, without reference to others & feels ready to serve you to the end of the world in whatever way you chalk out for him, but *I* feel that with these arrangements still open & nothing so finally settled that a degree of change may not be made by you, that it is best for me to speak out frankly how things strike me – I understand from Marg that you wish to have Douglas* first in council, I mean after Lord M^c:, & that you think of offering the other place to Mr Wallace*. – will you grant me a suspension of that offer till we shall talk it & the secretaryship a little more fully over; – Mr Wallace is a single man; I do not know what his claims on you are, but he is perhaps not less qualified than Mr Barnard for the office of Secretary while Mr Barnard woud equally co-operate with yr views & Lord Macartneys in council – to be Inferior to any person but Mr Douglas or a man of equal eminence & standing I own woud give me very sensible mortification, to come next to him or, for Mr Barnard to have *the liberty of choosing* between the one situation & the other woud fulfill my wishes and give me that *equality* at least (if not superiority) of situation which I have mentiond is the bribe to take me there & the comfort while I *am there* separated from my friends; with a family & servants, living on a Hospitable plan to *conciliate every body*, as is our wish, to have a *smaller Salary to support it* as well as a *smaller rank in Society* woud in a great degree defeat *my object* & in a less degree that which you might have in my going; – if Mr Douglas accepts as I before said, of course we shoud & ought to be placed behind him, but to have

*Rose**
George Rose, Secretary to the Treasury, 1782-1801.

*Nepean**
(Sir) Evan Nepean, created a baronet in 1802, Secretary of the Admiralty, 1795-1804.

*Douglas**
Presumably Sylvester Douglas. See note to Letter 2.

*Wallace**
Probably Thomas Wallace (1768-1844) of Lincoln's Inn, M.P. for Crampound, 1790-96; Lord of Admiralty, 1797-1800, created Baron Wallace of Knaresdale, 1828. He married Dundas's widow in 1814. Neither he nor Douglas were appointed to the Council.

the next best situation to his woud be desirable, shoud he not accept, two members of the council will then be to be found, in which case I flatter myself you woud give Mr Barnard the option of being next to Lord Macartney – to be the inferior my dear friend of young men without the pretension of Douglas woud grieve me – while I have thus opend my mind to you let me tell you at the same time that I throw the consideration before you, for *YOU not me* to determine on, you have but to send Mr Barnard & me *Where* you please *Whatever* situation you offer & in whatever line it may present itself inferior to my hopes, we shall accept, & *follow up your views in it* to the best of our powers, – I say *we* for if Mr Barnard as Secretary at the cape finds his situation less consequential or beneficial than he expected it woud be he will stand the more in need of me to keep up his spirits, but on the other hand I shall go with satisfaction & alacrity if I feel our consequence & condition, but with depression in the other –

When can I see you for half an hour? if you cannot say *when to-night*, let me know in the course of tomorrow – oh how much trouble & vexation woud be saved by a little more power of communication on points, but hurried moments snatchd, send every thing fit to be said or askd out of ones head –

evr gratefully & sincerely yours

Anne Barnard

"Moonlight before we saild" (Portsmouth)

Letter 6

wed: night – [1796]

I have let two days elapse in the hope that I might feel less miserable before I answerd yours, which did not simply make me unhappy, every word of it made me feel a degree of bodily pain that I did not think words coud have conveyd – if I was unreasonable from misapprehending some things it is not unnatural for me to be ignorant on, or if I too sanguinely pressd you to place Mr B, too much above what his pretensions justified you for, in your own eyes, or in those of others, why coud you not have *Scolded* me – but scolded me kindly, telling me how abominably in the wrong I was, without writing me this cruel letter as if you hated me all the time the pen was in your hand, – you know very well when you told me your kind intentions to Mr B, at Wimbledon how Gratefully I felt, and had you told me of something not *quarter* so good at home, you woud have found me equally gratefull tho Happier. – I believe the great sacrifice I felt myself making in leaving so much that I held dear behind made me anxious to find as ample a recompense as I coud in Mr B^{s} advancement; – lately the conversation of some Indian people led me to suppose that I might find the situation of Secretary less flattering than I had been supposing it, and thinking it possible that my having *dwelt so much* to you on his earnest wish for *Business*, might have induced you to give him this situation instead of making him one of the council where I apprehended there was less to do I thought I might venture without reserve to lay open my feelings to you on the subject thinking it possible that you might make a change without any strong inconvenience & not being aware that I coud be thought unreasonable for Hazarding the request, but the Event came down like thunder on my head, for I find I have like the poor foolish dervise in the arabian nights intertainments askd the Genie for the Rocks egg – "wretch, said he it is my SON that thou presumest to ask for" – but woe is me I am not ready to jest about this yet – we must have a little word of forgiveness and oblivion and a shake of the hand [one line obliterated] before I can jest – I believe I shoud say something in answer to yours about *two words* of mine which it will cost me no difficulty to recant because ten to one I have not used the right ones according to the proper meaning of them in what may be calld a political negociation – I will venture now to look into your terrible letter for them that I may not misquote you – "patronage & Rank' – hang them both – by patronage I certainly meant *there*, Importance or consequence, for as to patronage at the cape I fancy unless we were to patronize the Ostriches & Elephants and by the bye the first I am much disposed to patronize, we shoud find few Natives else to look up to us as yet – by Rank, I meant the 1st, 2^{d}, 3^{d} 4th or 5th place in society, and being the fifth I wishd to be the third if asking you to make me so woud do it – with respect to Mr B. and his feelings about all this, this is the point I must enlarge on the most fully – but a very few words will do it, I have only to tell you as an honest woman who never in her recollection told a lye, that there is not in the whole inside of his beard or head one feeling on the situation you have placed him in that you woud wish to change if you had the power of looking in and planting as you pleasd – he is a compleatly gratified-satisfied man, ready to go to the poles and back again with Jealous gratitude to you – calculating upon nothing but how he shall best prove it and as to rank – patronage – salary or any of these concomitants I believe they do not enter his head further than that there is quite enough to maintain us there very well, & the funds at home will go to pay any little old scores – these general thoughts of contentment and satisfaction, with two dutch masters a dutch valet de chambre, a short hand writer grammars – maps of the country & a strong desire of getting on in whatever may improve him in his department fill his head & heart nor has there ever a single word passd between him and me on the subject of my last letter to you, nor did there ever an Idea of the sort which I expressd to you ever pass his lips – I might equally say rise in his mind, else I shoud have known it. – the only time when either Income or the office of Secretary being below or above the council was talkd among us, was when my sister was going to Wimbleton, [sic] & then he said "Margaret remember that I take your word that no anxiety to know any particulars regarding the appointment Mr Dundas is so good as to think of for me may lead you to ask any questions about the Salary or any particular respecting it, it woud appear distrustfull and greedy". – Marg^{t} a little hurt said, 'not so when the anxiety is for another,' – ["] true said he but *we* are allmost one & I woud rather you did not, be the Salary little or large I feel myself gratefull for his goodness in thinking of me and shall certainly accept of it, well pleasd to be so distinguishd at first setting off in life & upon my soul M: I am convinced that Lord M: and I will go on uncommonly well" – a point of which to say the truth I have no doubt – but I believe I told you all this before – . when your Horrible letter arrived as Mr B. was present I opend it only, and saying it was not for me gave it to Marg^{t} who read it as if it was for herself and put it in her pocket, but I saw by her face she knew what I was to suffer from it – and indeed I have not till now *dared* to read it again it had such an effect on me, now I have, because I have made up a sort of mental reconciliation between us in which I make you as affectionate, friendly & kind as I coud wish – the castle of Ideas is one in which each Individual is omnipotent, and There you never art [sic] but as I woud have you, you never *there* end with dear *Madam* or sign yourself at full length Henry Dundas – But – to leave ideas for realitys to which we must allways come down at last, Forgive me pray, and shake hands – do – I wish I had not vexed you – I am sure I have vexed myself more – but now that it is *past*, at some future day I may say to myself, it being so, 'Well on that occasion I nobly dared, as the woman *I am*, and a good wife to the very amiable good man whose wife I am, I lookd high to be sure and aimd high – I faild – ' but he that fights and runs away may live to fight a future day when he has more pretensions – but dont you suppose for my thus quoting Hudibrass* that I am laying in *a claim* when I am only singing a couplet –

My dear friend, my heart feels lighter – yet after all, does it not require All Lord Mcartneys smiles – a prosperous voyage & *Your* approbation of Mr B. in his department & all things running smooth to make amends for so long a separation from all those one loves – give me a kind thought now and then when absent at least – I hope when there to establish myself with chearfull alacrity and Zeal to the general cause, to *Be* very comfortable & to make comfort grow up all around me – God Bless you – half a time will do & you will not delay it long – pray put my last letter and this in the fire –

*Hudibrass**
In Samuel Butler's *Hudibras* the correct reading is:
"For those that fly may
fight again
Which he can never do
thats slain."
Lady A. was more likely remembering the epigram in *The Art of Poetry on a new Plan*, 1761:
"For he who fights and
runs away
May live to fight another
day."

Departure for Portsmouth

And so it was that January of 1797 found the Barnards at Portsmouth awaiting a favourable wind to sail for the Cape in the Sir Edward Hughes, *ship of the Hon. East India Company's service. Their immediate entourage consisted of the young Ann Barnard, Andrew's cousin, their superior "upper servant" Samuel Eusebius Hudson who had travelled down before them to prepare the cabins, Mrs. Davies (presumably Lady Anne's maid) and another servant, Mrs. Wright. There was also a small boy, Hervey, a Barnard relation, Dorothea Fairbridge tells us, though there is no mention of him in the letters.*

begun the 28 of Jan:
[1797] [At Portsmouth]
sealed 31 of Jan: –

Here we are and have been since last wednesday waiting for a wind – but the weathercock continues to crow the wrong way – Today there is some little hope of its coming round, we all anxiously pray for it and as we are all Godly people I hope we shall have some effect – we found Lord Macartney well & in spirits, Sir William Pitt* the same . – are told that we are to see Lord Cornwallis* at the cape ere long on his way to India, if so – we shall not see you soon there as I know the confidence you have in his wisdom & good conduct – Happiness attend you & dear Lady Jane* whereever you are – I visited our Ship yesterday & found my garden well, all my plants alive – in the place of Mr Barnards Horse I have substituted a Cow, I thought it a pity that we coud not have tyed Horns on the Horse and voted to be A cow, but I feard the gentlemen who were hard hearted woud not have pardond its Masquerade dress – it is eighty guineas vexatiously placed, I fear lost, but we may get out of the scrape somehow, tho I know not how – Captain Urmston* is much hurt with his own want of thought, he had not dreamt of having any horse when he was at the Indiahouse, got his accidentally at portsmouth & never was struck with its being an impropriety his taking it – as to us poor Souls we were Ignorant, & ignorance includes Innocence, it is a pity it shoud include punishment too –

I left Margaret tolerably well, tho low, I had had a letter from my brother Balcarres, and I bid her shew it to you if she chanced to see you, if not that she might enclose it with the one I shoud write to you from portsmouth – I am glad that all goes on now so very smooth –

*Pitt**
General Sir William Augustus Pitt (1728-1809), Governor of Portsmouth, 1794-1809.

*Cornwallis**
Charles, 2nd earl, later 1st marquis Cornwallis, Governor-general of India, 1786-1793, and C. in C. Bengal Army. He defeated Tippoo Sultan at Arikera, 1791. Master-general of the Ordnance, 1795. In fact he only returned to India in 1805, dying soon after.

*Jane**
Lady Jane (more correctly Jean) Dundas, 6th daughter of the Earl of Hopetoun, married Dundas as his second wife, 2.4.1793.

*Urmston**
James Brabazon Urmston, master of *Sir Edward Hughes.* He was knighted in 1824 and became President of the Supercargoes at Canton.

adieu my dear friend – present my kind love to your wife & to Miss Maria* and believe me to be your obliged & affectionate –

Anne Barnard

(*In Andrew Barnard's hand*)

I am truly sorry my Dear Sir that you shoud have had any trouble about my Unfortunate Horse but I had no Idea that the Gentlemen of the Committee of Shipping were so Decided in their Resolutions I must confess it has been a Considerable Vexation, and Disappointment to me, as I had flattered myself with the Hopes of obtaining your Approbation for the Steps I was taking to procure a Breed of Horses at the Cape, fully equal to Mount our Cavalry there, or to be Carried to India for that purpose, and am Sorry that a Little Private Pique, shoud so considerably hurt the Publick Service – We are looking out most Anxiously for a change of Wind, which we hope will be the case after the very hard Gale which Blew last Night, we mean to Sail with the very first Spirt of a Northerly wind, I am Happy to say that Lord Macartney is much better since he left Town, I beg my Respectfull Regards to Lady Jane, and Assure you Sir that I am your Obliged

and Faithfull serv[t]

Barnard

*Maria**
Presumably a sister of Dundas's.

H.M.S. 'Trusty' springs a leak

Letter 8

The convoy sailed from Portsmouth on February 5th, arriving at Plymouth on the 7th.

[On Board HMEICS *Sir Edward Hughes*]
Feb. 7 1797 – laying before plymouth

this is a most unlucky accident my dear friend! – I little thought when I bid you adieu with a fair wind fine view – good ship & apparent prosperity & hope of a speedy voyage that we were likely to be baffled in it by any other chances than the Elements or the Enemy; but so it is – I told you we had passd the needles in safety [see the sketch above] leaving them on our left, our pilot a good one of the name of Francis – on passing thro them there is never any respect paid to a commodore, each one getting over that dangerous pass the best way he can under the express protection of the pilot who it seems is Master & commander in chief while he is on board, but past this danger, then the Etiquettes of the sea begin & we of course lay to till our commodore & Lord Macartney came up & took the lead of us* – this they did before evening – soon after Day break we saw them pumping hard on board & Capt Urmston said he did not like the look of the *clear water* which was coming from the pump – the commodore put out a signal for him to come on board w^{c} he did & found to the Desolation of all our best Hopes, that the ship had had the misfortune of having run on one of the sharp rocks w^{c} are hidden by the tide and had got a leak in her bottom which admitted water at the well in *such quantity* as to shew that the matter was of very serious consequence – some of the officers had taken notice at the time that the ship had struck with three little shocks upon something, but it passd over, & they hoped the best, at the *time* there was 5 fathom water on *each side*, therefore it seems to have been *bad fortune* that of meeting with this rock rather than misconduct – it is said this morning that the pilot had left it *before* this Happened – as having conducted it over the dangerous points – if so I shoud be apt to think his anxiety to get back to portsmouth with the tide & before night came on, had led him away rather too soon – but on board here the circumstace of the 5 fathom water on each side is considered as a

*us**
In H.M.S. Trusty, 4th rate, 50 guns, built 1782.

proof that there was not any fault in the method of navigating the vessel – the misfortune however is a sad one – it is absolutely necessary it seems for the ship to put in to plymouth & to go to dock – and docks are full! I fancy Lord Macartney will entreat another ship of the admiralty – all heads on board have been at work to think *what* ship he can get – we left the Leander ready at Spithead, if you coud send or spare any thing a little bigger than it with the regiments for portugal – there is a sixty guns here which I hear coud be immediately got ready – all being compleat but the rigging – or if Lord M: coud think of going in M^c^intoshes India man.* – but I suppose I ought not for self security to breath an Idea of this kind even to myself – I never heard any one suppose it possible – but I want to get off now we are embarked, Oh what a gallant voyage we shoud have had! the wind so fair – our crew so fine – Now our poor Captain looks with a face a yard long & says he cannot depend on it that his tars may not play him a dogs trick for the sake of new Bounty money* – this will be a sad disappointment in point of interest to this Honest East India captain who however seems to unite a *seamans spirit* with a landmans prudence – he & Mr B: are slipping on board the boat to go to know Lord Macartneys intentions & the commodores pleasure – I have wrote you these Hasty lines in half a minutes time pardon their incorrectness & believe me ever truly yours –

Anne Barnard

the gentlemen have gone – we returnd all but Mr B. who waits capt U.^s^ return from shore & the boat is taking off some ladys for shore –

they are I find to try to get the *trusty repaird* & hope they will be able to do it sooner than capt campbell seems to think *possible* – if there is *only* a hole in her bottom forced by the above accident she *may* they think be a float again in a fortnight but some fear that she is not quite sound – a few days will shew this when they have seen the misfortune – but Mr Campbell shakes his head & says, that it will take double the time to put her to right that those on board the trusty expect – this moment while I was taking a view of the ship she dropd her flag half down & the capt called out good God poor Montgomery is dead – he told me that that disposition of the flag showd he had that moment departed this life – I knew him a very good young man a brother of D pembrokes* –

this is a very hurried & vile letter full of ills – at plymouth letters directed to the port House will find me so pray give me a line to say you are all well – God Bless you

*man.**
H.E.I.C.S. *Hindostan* (Capt. W. Mackintosh), headed the next East India Co.'s fleet which sailed on March 18th. (*Lloyd's Register*, 1797.)

*money**
A gratuity was paid to recruits to the army or navy. By putting in to a naval port the Captain was running the risk that his men might for this reason desert in order to sign on in a ship of war.

*pembrokes**
Not identified. Possibly a relation of the Earl of Pembroke and Montgomery, though the latter's surname was Herbert.

Getting the cow on board
'Sir Edward Hughes'

Letter 9

The convoy finally sailed for the Cape on February 22nd. How the following letter, written at sea, came back to England we do not know. As Lady Anne recounts, it was handed to the Captain of the Britannia, *one of the convoy, who had decided to part company with them as his ship was so much slower.*

2·30 South latitude
17-west longitude –
March 9 – 1797 –

Mrs. Saul, a fellow passenger

I seize the present opportunity to write a few lines my dear friend, more than a few I shall not attempt at present as I shall reserve the general account of our passage till I can add that of our arrival at the cape, which we hope will take place in five weeks from this time, – we shoud have been some hundred miles farther on our way had it not been for the Brittania* who is so slow a sailor that no Day has passd that the Trusty & ourselves were not obliged to lay to for her, but she has this moment let us understand that she means to part company with us tomorrow, and I assure you that we say *Bon voyage* from the bottom of our Hearts in *all* senses of the word. – we have this day got the South trade wind, we passd the line last sunday, and endured much the last ten days from the heat, the thermometer being at 84 & 85 but after some Heavy rains since Sunday, we have fallen on the Trade, and there is a fresh breeze now blowing, which if it was fair woud send us on at 8 knots an hour but being only half in our favour we do not reach five; we have had in *general* fine weather, all but ten terrible days, during which Time altho we never were in positive danger as we had not lost masts nor suffered esentially in our rigging as the Britannia did, yet it was a very anxious time even for the stoutest Sailor on board partly owing to the immense Rolling of the Ship which was such as to dip the upper guns more than once in water, and this with 271 heavy Guns on board which you know far better than I can tell you we are taking out to India with us, was rather a dangerous Circumstance in such gales as we have had – thank god However they seem to be over, and I woud fain Hope that we shall not have more of the same sort at least till we get into the neighbourhood of the cape where I must expect to be all frightend again before we land – about 5 weeks hence we flatter ourselves with getting there if all goes smooth, but this letter I suppose will reach you a month before you are likely to receive any dated from cape Town – all on board

*Brittania**
Another East Indiaman (770 tons) in the convoy.

have been well, not a sick man, partly owing to the dry weather, & partly to the attentions of the captains who you very justly reported to me was one of the civilest & most Liberal men that can be met with – there is of our mess mates, I may say about 24 including two or three of the ships officers that the cuddy* cannot contain – we all go on like *Lambs*, exept two that I shoud say nothing of was it not that you must hear of them from other quarters – I mean the Campbells – I did not mention them in my two last letters to you as I hoped they woud improve in civility & good Humour but I now fear there is no chance for that, as the gentlemen have all been obliged to drop common conversation beyond the necessitys of society with Mr Campbell* he contradicts all round him in a manner so unlike a person used to civilized Society – and as to Mrs C: after every fair attention on the part of the ladys on board which are five besides herself, she, it seems is resolved to keep apart from all, & from the acquaintance of any *English* woman, reserving herself as Genl: Hartley* tells me to be the Head of the Dutch *party* instead of one of the English & finding much fault with government for sending as she says "a parcell of people who cannot please the dutch or be likely to adopt their manners" – . Major Baynes* tells me that her calculation will not to herself prove a good one, as the dutch appeard to him, eager to be well with the English, and will not (at present at least) be likely to back her intention of setting up a separate party from them – Mr Barnard & I mean all that lyes in our power to fulfill your wishes, and the plan of temperate good sense by endeavouring to make *all* around us as comfortable as we can, and Meeting every reasonable Habit or custom of the place half way to conciliate all – but I own from what I see & others tell me they hear of the unreserved opinions of these people (when they do talk wc is seldom,) which are very different from what you have probably heard fall from them, we shoud imagine them much too democratic in their principles to be friends any longer than it appears for their own Interest to be so – this I say to you freely because I think it *right* in consequence of the great power they conceive themselves to be invested with, to let you know in what light they appear to every individual on board of this ship *None* exeptd. I had heard Mrs C: was violent before I came on board, and that she was not very literal, I suspect that she does talk a little wide as she frequently mentions that Lady Jane is so fond of her that she makes it a point to spend three mornings every week at Mrs C:s lodgings for the sake of undisturbed conversation – I have now to wish you Joy of the late Brilliant Success of Sir John Jervis* – I wish he had lickd the french instead of the spaniards – here is the captain of the Britannia* come on board for our letters so I must conclude this Hurried Epistle Lord Macartney I this moment learn has got a fit of the gout but he was perfectly well till within these few days – adieu my dearest friend – make my kindest & best love to your wife who I hope is long ere this time in good Health & to your two young Ladys – & believe me Your ever affectionate & gratefull friend Anne Barnard

Mr B: has been very well till within these few Days when he has had a little bilious attack – you shall hear from me in a less Hurried & more particular manner when we arrive if it please God to send us there safe –

*cuddy**
Ship's saloon.

*Campbell**
Presumably Capt. Donald Campbell, port captain of Table Bay. His wife was of Cape Dutch descent.

*Hartley**
Major-Gen. James Hartley (1745-1799), of the Bombay Army. He was going out as supervisor and magistrate of the Malabar Province and was second-in-command of the Bombay Army against Tippoo in 1799.

*Baynes**
Major Edward Baynes, 32nd Regt. He had been a.d.c. to Major General Sir James Craig at the Cape.

*Jervis**
Jervis, created Earl St. Vincent in the following May, was C. in C. Mediterranean and defeated the Spanish fleet off Cape St. Vincent on 14.2.1797.

*Brittania**
Capt. T. Barrow.

Through a stern window

Moonlight at sea

Letter 10

Table Bay was eventually reached on May 4th, seventy-one days after leaving Plymouth.

Cape of Good Hope
May 11 1797

I cannot let any opportunity escape my dearest friend of writing to you tho at the present I must confine myself to a few lines only – they shall Simply say, that we are *here safe* & well – that I ought not as yet to send you any opinion, of the place which I have hardly seen or the society which till last night, (at a ball at Sir James Craigs*) I have had no opportunity in the few days I have been Here of Judging of – an extensive & general (as well as particular account) of everything *past* & *present* is coming to you by the next ship along with the chart of our voyage which I have not Quite finishd & a few little drawings of things which it fell in my way to take in a very hurried way but which amused me during the voyage, & I am now going on with – in that packet you shall find every thing you can wish to know from the *Honestest pen* & *pencil* I will venture to say in the world (for I must not confine myself to saying *in Europe*) – I never exagerate either with the one or the other, sometimes I may extenuate but I sett down nought in Malice. – *we* feel ourselves much disposed to like the place – the air is exhilerating & climate delightfull – we are busied & harassd at present but that will be soon over – Lord Macartney is *perfectly kind* to us, and I shoud think by the very little I can Judge will please *generally* in a society which has of late been languishing for a governor to settle its *Interests* (w^{c} is the first thing to a Dutchman) & its pleasures & benefits – I see *great dispositions* in him to conciliate as far as the little I can as yet judge – he has been so kind as to give us the government House* in the Castle which Genl: Dundas* I thought woud have taken, but the General was in one which he said (as a batchelor) he thought suited him better, the very next door to ours, & that in his opinion the married folks had better live in the largest – N: B: he looks better than I ever saw him, is in excellent spirits & *he* likes the place, – I do not think – the other officers who I have talkd with have done so as *yet*, but, I trust that this will be a different place in many respects soon – this same House which they both have so kindly granted to us, is certainly *too good* – & that is its fault: has too much representation with it, requires too many serv-

*Craigs**
Major-General Sir James Craig, joint commander of the British forces which took the Cape in 1795, and commandant until Macartney's arrival.

*House**
This was built on the south end of the Kat, the wall across the main castle courtyard.

*Dundas**
Major-General Francis Dundas, Henry Dundas's nephew and O.C. British forces at the Cape.

ants – & a little more will be expected from private folks living in it (such as ourselves) than is quite to be wishd, but *being there*, Nothing shall be wanting on our part that ought to be done. – I wish I coud say that nothing will be wanting In the country; but till next Harvest I fear there will be considerable inconvenience & a *great dearness* as well as Scarcity of every thing experienced; from the quantity of corn w^c has been exported (as I hear) to England during our English scarcity which has left the granarys Empty here w^c woud otherwise have had enough to maintain the country & *even* the many additional mouths – I shall roar loudly on the subject of pottatoes – carrots & all sorts of things on which cattle can be fed – these two articles grow *very* well in this sandy soil – but are not sufficiently adopted by the lower classes, & never tasted by the animals – inshort they are only to be met with (& there we have them in quantitys) at the best tables – I am convinced there is much ground that cannot be *pasture* for want of water which coud raise them well, & that very near the cape – . Mr B. & I find the *houses – Horses* & *wine* better than we expected – but every article in life (*beef* & *mutton only* exepted) which is 2½ pr lib) *about* twice as dear as in London, this I hope is only for the present – Labour is *very* dear – & tradespeople of all descriptions in a moderate number are necessary – particularly carpenters – a couple of shoemakers I shoud think coud live well – as there are No shops here, a few people, to unite in a retailing way a good many different branches, woud succeed, & make a fortune to themselves, but the place wont bear a great many of each description. Mr B: has purchased a boat from our excellent captain to try to judge of the coast & means of getting at wood &cc – how far he will be able to effect many little trips at this season of the Year I know not, I have *heard* that the only thing against many things coming by sea conveyance is the danger of the navigation the want of safe Harbouring for boats & the chance of the crew being kept where they land for days or weeks by the winds which kept up in a moment – but I am called & orderd to seal else I shall lose the opportunity – this comes by Young Wortley* a young man beloved & respected by all here who know him, for good understanding Heart – & *principles* – he has disliked the place much, but he has had all the worst of it – I hope in my next to say a great deal more & to apologize better for this very hurried Scrawl – *Sir James Craig* is well & as Happy – no – Happier than any king I know – I will not say a word of any other friend as I am already on the verge of being too late – Doctor Gillans friends* are *excessively* kind to us – & are good people – I long *very much* to hear of you & L^y Jane – neither were well when I was at plymouth – God Bless you my dear friend & preserve you – to us all & to yr ever affect

Anne Barnard

Mr Barnard bids me say that he will not by *this* conveyance trouble you with any letter as it coud give a very imperfect account of every thing exept of his own sentiments of gratitude & attachment to you –

I wrote a few lines by the Britannia bound to st Helena to be forwarded by the governor there – just after we had passed the line –

*Wortley**
James Stuart-Wortley-Mackenzie – he dropped the last name – (1776-1845), was a captain in the 72nd Highlanders commissioned to carry the Governor's dispatches. He entered Parliament later that year and in 1826 was created Baron Wharncliffe.

*friends**
These friends were the Stromboms, *vide infra*, Letter 11.

Looking northwest from Lady Anne's window in the Castle

Cape Town, Cape of Good Hope

Mr. Barnard

To Walker, Robertson & Co. Dr.

1798		Rd	
Jan.y	1 Soup Spoon	2	-
	2 Butter do	2	-
	1 Jar Linseed Oil	9	-
	2 pr. Ladies Shoes	6	-
	2 Whips	4	-
	1 ditto	3	-
	5 pr. Ladies Shoes	15	-
	1 lb twine	1	-
	3 yds. Blue Cloth	9	-
	1 dressing Glass	12	-
February	1 Sett Harness	120	-
	1 Tin Case	10	-
March	6 lb Nails @ 3/	2	2
April	~~2 Rings~~ Miss Barnard	~~2~~	-
	2 pens	2	-
	1½ Ells Blue Cloth	4	4
May	4 Salt Stands	2	-
	1 ~~doz Knives & forks~~	6	-
	6 ~~Bottles Bitters~~	3	-
	3 lb Tobacco	1	7
	2 Doz. Knives	2	-
	2000 Needles	6	-
	6 Scissars	1	4
	4 do	1	4
	1 lb thread	4	-
	6 Knives	-	6
	Carried Over Rd	232	3

Andrew Barnard's account with Ms. Walker & Robertson, January- May, 1798

Letter 11

The Barnards lost no time in becoming thoroughly involved in the life of the Cape, as the following letter amply shows. Enclosed with it were two other letters, the first a revealing letter in French to Lady Anne from the Fiscal, Willem Stephanus van Ryneveld, to which she refers on p.57, and the second one to Dundas by Andrew Barnard. This was clearly a personal letter and in no way official.

Also enclosed were three sketches, the first of General Hartley (see Letter 9, note 4) made on shipboard, the second of Simonstown and the third of the Hottentots Holland Mountains. With them was a semi-humorous depiction of the small shadows cast by General Hartley and the younger Ann Barnard at the Equator, stated to be the work of Andrew Barnard.

Cape of Good Hope
July 10 1797

From the Castle of good Hope, situated in the inside of the garrison, over which rises the Table mountain at a considerable *real* distance the close apparent vicinity from the effects of its height, & from the window of my bedchamber which overlooks the offices, built in a colonade round a spacious square pond of water supplyd from the head & tail of a spouting dophin, I begin this letter to my dearest friend, firmly convinced that he will be as much interested in its contents from private affection to the writer as from curiosity to know every point however minute which regards a publick concern — . I am perfectly convinced also however that you must receive along with this such numberless letters from others so *much better* qualified to give you an account of every thing worth your knowing, that it woud seem allmost *conceited folly* in me to describe things as they appear around me, or still more to give my miserable *female notions* on any thing, was it not for the above reason, that your friendship for me will contrive a general apology for every thing silly or erroneous & while all seems yellow to the jaundiced eye, all will seem rose color & interesting to that partial pair of *black sparklers* with which you read the Epistels of your female friends, but to land us here properly, let us first return to the ship & bring up matters with a little regularity. — our voyage on the whole was a prosperous one, we sailed from plymouth the 23^{d} of Febr: and landed at the cape

The Great Barracks and Lion's Head on a stormy day, viewed from the Castle.

the 5th of may; – we had but few calms, & no storm such as to endanger the ship, the ten days of weather so very rough as to give sufficient apology to a coward for being afraid; particularly from the rolling of the ship in which you know we had 272 great guns for Bengal which often brought our upper guns under water & renderd the Beautys in their various cabins, black & blue from the rolling & pitching they produced – we met with but few occurances of consequence – the heat between the tropics was excessive, but not beyond or equal to what I expected, as the thermometer was never above 83, or 4 We passd the line exactly at 12 °clock, the sun in his meridian, & on his way from his country seat of capricorn to that of cancer – I enclose to you something which it struck me to take, because I had been told there was *no such thing* to be seen as a *shadow* when the sun was immediately above our heads, & as I think general Hartly one of the best men *under the Sun* I made him stand for his vertical shadow along with my cousin Miss Barnard – you will perceive that he appears a *turbot* & she a *star-fish* which is all much as it ought to be. – I made a few little drawings of sharks – dolphins – flying fish hardly worth your looking at, which I shall send to Margaret, the only merit of which consists in their being *literally just,* I Hate all exageration whether in the pencil or the pen, or the conversation, also a chart of the voyage out, our tract w^c is nearly finished, the heat decreased as we passd the tropic of cancer, & after having quitted our blankets, & cloth Habits we all took to them again. – our course was pretty direct by the chart from the time we passd the Maderas (where *you* made us go into a *fine scollop* to avoid certain cruisers which we have since heard you had intelligence of) till we got into the latitude of the cape, where contrary winds vexed us much, & blew us very nearly into the latitude where the Guardian was lost by mountains of Ice, however, five or six days produced a favourable change and the joyfull news of *land* being seen was announced, tho it was enveloped in such fogs as did not permit us to enjoy its appearance till we were exactly placed in the Bay opposite to cape Town. – then, as if by one consent the Lions rump whisked off the vapours with its tail; the lions Head untyed, and dropd, the necklace of clouds w^c surrounded its erect throat, & table mountain over which a white damask table cloth had been spread half way down shewd its broad face & smiled, while guns from the garrison & from all the batterys, wellcomed his Majestys government, & the distant hills who coud not step forward to declare their allegiance, by the awefull thunders of their acquiescing echos, informed us that they were not ignorant of the arrival of the governor who was at that moment putting his foot on Land. – nothing coud be finer than the coup D'eoul, [sic] yet nothing can have so little affinity with each other as the bold perpendicular mountains bare & rocky & the Low white card houses which from the Bay seem less, from their contrast & scarce large enough to hold an ant, – but this is *not* the case, for they are excellent. – I fear I shall not have time to send a drawing of this scene, but it shall come at a future time. – the Stromboms* having heard of our arrival, sent us an invitation to come to their house w^c was a Blessing of no *moderate sort*, every place being crowded. – Lord Macartney preferrd going to one of the Lodging

*Stromboms**
Mr J. Strombom was a merchant, believed to be of Danish origin, with a house at 28 Heeregragt and a store in Berg St. (now St. George's St.). (*C.T. Gazette*, 13-9-1800).

houses (indeed all the private houses half a dozen exepted are such) to incommoding Sir James Craig by going to his abode. – we walked from the Key to Mr Stromboms, tho his carriage was sent to meet us, but we preferd the feeling of *Hard land* under our feet, to all artificial conveyances – the first thing that struck me strongly & disagreeably, was a very offensive smell in the air w^c I afterwards found in some of the houses, & which I was told proceeded from the oil with w^c the slaves grease their Hair. – waggons of wood next appeard, drove by one man, eight, and ten horses moving with perfect docility to the crack of his whip. – next appeard more melancholy evidences of the far distant classes amongst Human creatures, slaves returning from a 7 or 8 miles distance, loaded each with two bundles of sticks slung across his bare shoulders, it made one sigh at first, the only comfort in looking at the weight of the bundles, was, that one of them *only* was for the master the other was for the private benefit of the slave – we walkd up the town which I found much superior in appearance, in size & in the size of accommodation of the Houses to what I had expected & were kindly wellcomed by the Stromboms who made their house our Home during ten days & much unlike the Dutch systems woud accept of no repayment. – but she is an English woman he is a Dane & both the intimate friends of our sweet Doctor Gillan, who I hope is at this moment as well as we wish him. – long looked for as Lord Macartney had been, his arrival seemd to give new life to languid spirits, even the Dutch who had fairly flatterd them-selves till a governor came, that a governor never woud come, & that the place woud somehow or another fall back into the old Hands or be ceded to the french, seemd to have got a cold bath first, but revived Health & alacrity of mind thro *certainty* of the worst, & the *necessity of beginning business* again on an *acertaind footing*, which had not been the case during the procrastinated decisions of Sir James Craig who had not acted *contrary to Human nature* by delaying all unpleasant rules to the commencement of the *new* governors administration. – mean time, thro his eagerness to conciliate, & to keep well with the *natives* we found that every article of life had been permitted to rise to an immoderate price, uncheckd by any scheme of abatement by competition, or by prevailing on the natives to bring down their stock, & that there was an actual scarcity of grain in the place; the number of mouths to be fed being three times doubled, while that granary w^c the dutch policy had always kept filled with *one* or two *years* grain before hand, & which woud *now* have stood us in good stead, had loaded a few ships, to be a *breakfast* for London, & to prove the abundance of this place – bread of course was raised, but not very esentially as grain was ground all thro, & brown bread of a coarser quality than what you have usually seen, of w^c I send you a bit, but I think good was universally used, much to the annoyance of the dutch who reckon themselves undone if without the finest, *they* I believe however, sustained but little of this inconvenience as they are too provident not to have a private *stock* of every thing, which is kept up till an opportunity is found of selling to advantage, nor is there *one* house at the cape where *any article* may not be bought in a clandestine manner if a tempting price is paid – but the master pretends to know nothing

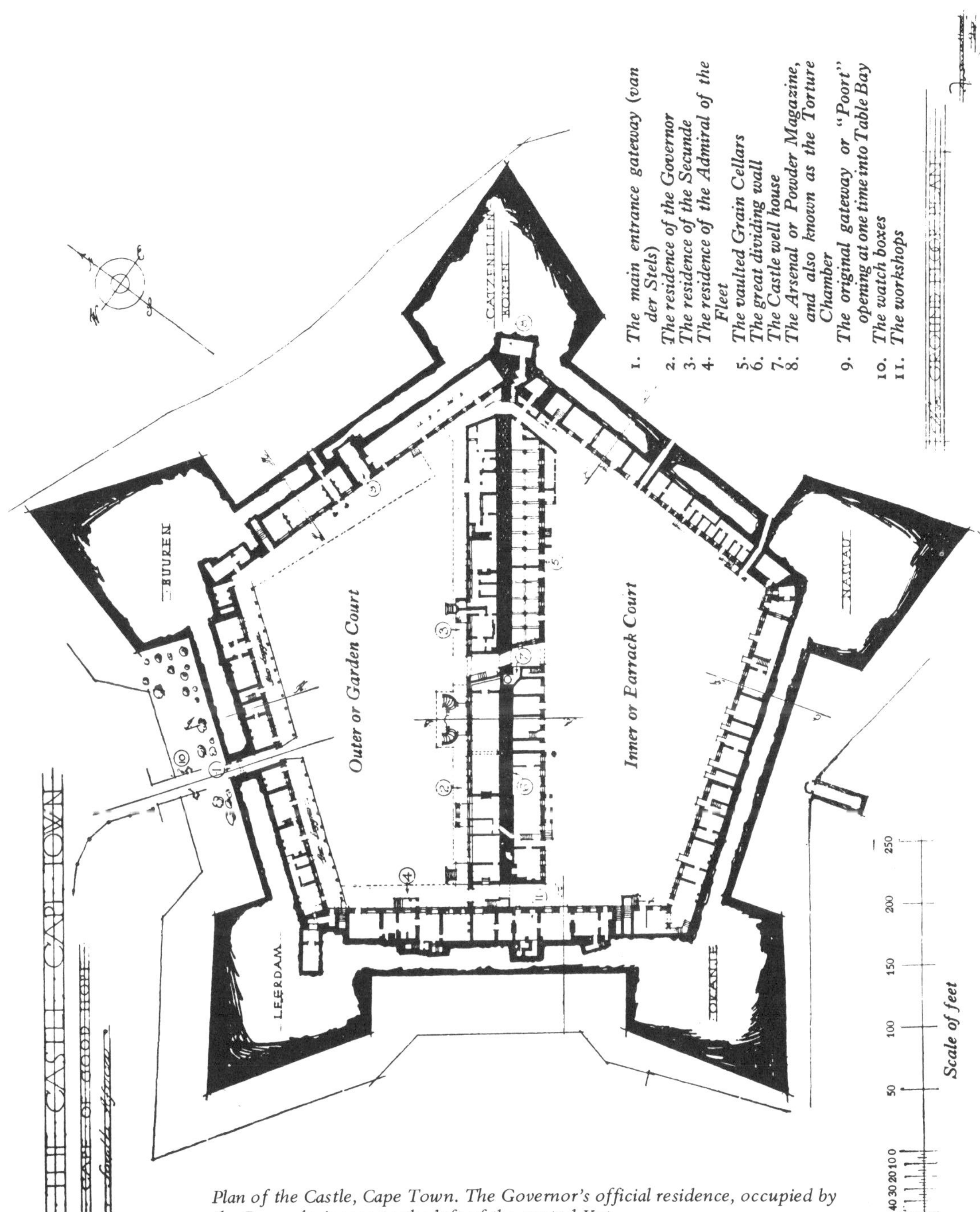

Plan of the Castle, Cape Town. The Governor's official residence, occupied by the Barnards, is seen to the left of the central Kat.

"Vertical shadows" – the young Ann Barnar
and General Hartley in the tropics

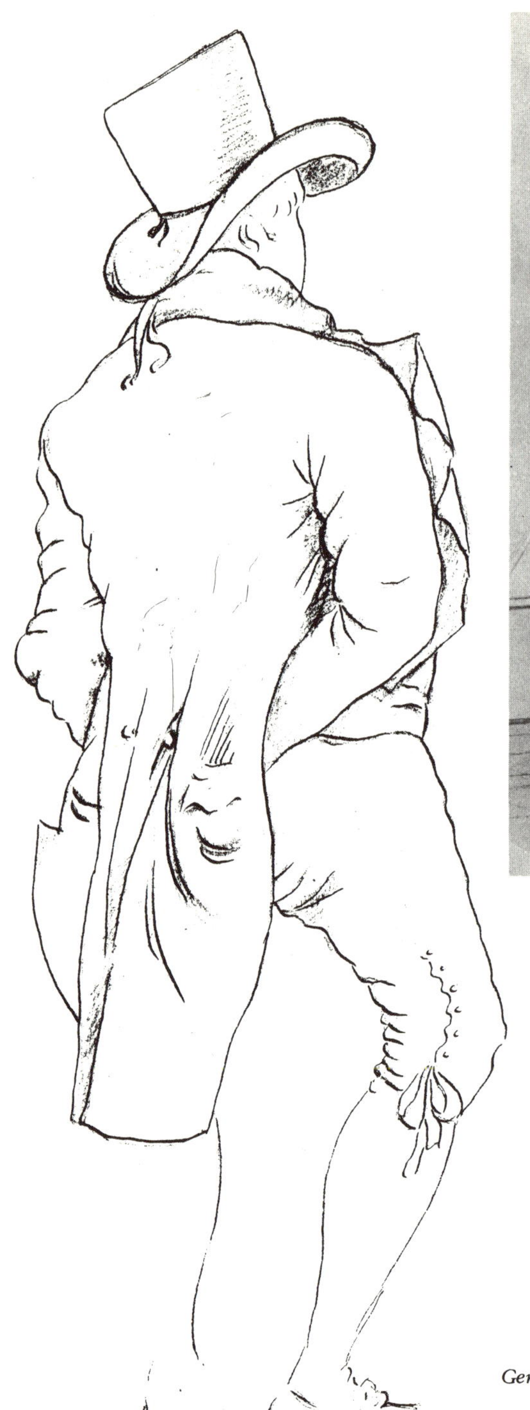

General Hartley – standing under the Sun

of the matter, as there is a great degree of false pride amongst them, no one choosing to confess he does the things, which all *do*, all know *are done.* – immediately on our arrival Mr Stromboms House was filled with scarlet & blew coats, who came to visit us & to rejoyce on our arrival – I shoud have been sorry to have listend to the dislike every individual expressd of the place without reserve, had I not hoped that many *favourable changes* woud soon take place from Lord M:s wisdom, & from the acquisition society was making in a few good humoured people thrown into the leaven tub which at that moment appeard to have too much of *acid* in it. – I plainly saw by Genl Craig, that he had been disappointed at not remaining there himself, but since he was not to do so, that it was very agreeable to him to go to India. – he appeard however to be much less sanguine in his expectations from the benefits arising to us from the cape, or from its possibility of its being renderd flourishing & comfortable or *any real acquisition* to us than I had imagined him to have been. – he boldly said that the expectations formd *from it* & *of it* were too high. – one coud only listen to this, with a portion of pausing regret, mixed with another little portion of distrust of a judgement, which tho a very tolerable one as I imagine in many respects, is not so extensive in its views or powers as some others I know of – admiral pringle* however backd this with six & thirty pounder corroborations – he said it was the worst nautical situation of a country, that it was possible for the Devil himself to contrive, fewer possibilitys of Harbourings & Landing places than it was possible to conceive. – no rivers – no water – torrents in plenty from the mountains tops, but nothing in the bosom of the earth – he conceived also the dutch policy to have been a sound one, when they checkd all population or improvemt as the place improved & peopled he thought woud to *us* only prove a second america, & woud be more likely to rob us of India, than to secure it for us, in time – he held all establishment of manufacture to be dangerous & foolish, & that no pains shoud be taken with the interior of the country, but merely with the skirting of it, which coud produce comforts to our people after their long passages to & fro – All this he laid down much more cleverly, god knows, than I repeat it, but as he added that it was the "cussedest place" that ever was found, nothing good in it & that even the hens did not lay fresh eggs, so vile was every animal that inhabited it, There appear'd to be no small mixture of prejudice along with some reasonable causes of dislike of this place; – I coud only pause here *also*, and wait to hear the *other side* of the question; but this I was not likely to have from the *military* who all to a man have disliked their quarters: nor is that much to be wonderd at, as every thing since the first capture of the place has been so extravagantly dear that the poor subalterns are both starved & undone – the private soldiers live well, & cheap, as the articles: Beef, mutton & bread are still reasonable, the first being only 2½ per pound, raised to 4 p p *now* & I suppose bread is not more, or so much as in London, as our house bills for it amount to nearly the same sum, it costs us there – at first there was much drinking amongst the private men from the cheapness of wine which coud then be procured for about 3 pence a bottle, but now I have heard there are wise taxes laid on it or

*pringle**
Rear-Admiral Thomas Pringle succeeded Admiral Elphinstone in command of the Cape Station on 7-10-1796. He was succeeded by Sir Hugh Christian in March 1798.

some way is contrivd to render its attainment less easy & counteract its pernicious effects in the *garrison*, it being now, not under 6 pence a bottle – every other article of life (the four above exepted, wine bread, & butchers meat) is extraordinarly dear and an officer who comforts himself on going to this distant destination by the thoughts of his living within his pay, is therefore disappointed in the extreme to find that he is obliged to spend more than if he were in London. – and this by no means owing to purchasing of *English articles*, as the articles of the country are equally expensive – garden stuff – fruit – eggs – butter three pence & a pound of pottatoes 6 pence – a dish of colly flower 1-6 – milk about a shilling pr quart the washing of a shirt 6 pence – oranges about the same price as in London, almonds, raisins, walnuts nearly the same, & every assistance of labour three prices – this circumstance together with the high price of horses (an ordinary one being thirty & fourty pounds) & fodder enormous & not to be attaind & the want of amusement of every kind, has made the military sick of this situation, vexed with scarcity & poverty & Hippd with *Ennui*. – perhaps their distance from the fountain of *promotion* may add to this, and the very little notice taken of the subaltern officers (which has come to a point Mr B & I think very cruel, & wish to mend as far as *we* can) has renderd them still more dispirited, no man here beneath a Col. or Major at *least*, being invited to any thing. – in this position we found things – I have certainly heard that (from want of better society we shall suppose it) the garrison were much given to drinking & gaming, every day this prevails *less & less* Genl. Dundas does *not* encourage *either*, indeed in my opinion considerably the *contrary*. at review dinners & on such publick occasions he pushes about the bottle in a manly way but you woud be pleasd to see how wisely, temperately & aqueably [sic] he conducts himself in his situation, how till he & Lord M: are together, on what comfortable terms he is with *all* around him. – I dwell the more on this, as there was a time when I remember hearing him called Hot & Haughty, if such things, have been or are in his temper they are at present checked and *laid aside*, he is a most pleasant member of society, & well liked by man and woman. – I see also great satisfaction in every one with the manners of our Lord, who was expected to be cold & dignified; fond of his own opinion & stiff in maintaining it, such was the publick notion of him. He certainly has wishd to impress it differently & has suceeded; he promotes society, & is markedly attentive in it to the individuals who compose it, respects those inferior to himself in their departments lays down rules with wise firmness, but no mixture of pride & (I may say) as far as things have come, Beloved; I shall only quote you the words of *one smallish man*, as it contains *more* than his own feelings – "I am *so* glad said he to find myself a gentleman now! I had begun to fancy myself a blackguard, but I look up to myself now from the manner Lord M: treats me". – Lord M: immediately on his arrival declared his intention of living in the government House in the garden*, which he apprehended coud not be too cold in winter, and which is certainly cooler than any other here in summer; Genl: Dundas was next to make his Election, he prefered remaining in the second sized house within the castle,* being fixed there

*garden**
The present Government House in the Gardens, begun in 1674. It underwent considerable improvements during the Barnards' time and further alterations under Lord Charles Somerset.

*castle**
Presumably the former Secunde's house, to the left of the archway in the Kat, as the Admiral's house, at right angles to the Governor's house, was naturally already assigned.

with "proper Batchelor establishment, to occupying the great government house w^{c} required more furniture, servants & was fitter for a *Family*; this he gave up to us, partly from good humour & partly from the above reasons; it is a pallace, containing such a suite of apartments, as makes me fancy myself a princess when in it, but not an *Indian* or *Hottentot* princess as I have fitted all up in the stile of a comfortable plain English house, Scotch carpets English linnen & rush bottom chairs with plenty of lolling sophas which I have had made by Regimental carpenters & stuffd by Regimental Taylors; in a week or two, I shall invite all who wish to be merry without cards, or dice, but who can talk or *hop* to half a dozzen black fiddlers, to come & see me on my publick day which shall be once a fortnight, when the Dutch Ladys (all of whom love dancing or *flirting* still more) shall be kindly welcomed & the poor Ensigns & cornets shall have an opportunity of stretching their legs as well as the generals. – I shall not be stinted for *room*; as I have a Holl of 60 feet, a drawing room of 40, a dancing room of 20, a tea room of 30, & three supper rooms – one of which only I shall have supper in, & that cold & disultory [sic] – with side boards & no chairs, as I wish to make others Happy without being ruined by their drinking half a Hogshead of Claret *every party* – Ducks & chickens &cc they shall have, but as turkeys are one pound *a piece*, I shall not *fly* at any of their Excellencys. – Rondebosh the pleasantest country house belonging to Government* at 4 miles distance from the cape, being occupied by Genl: Campbell, Lord M: begd him & his wife to remain in it, which they have done: I like our house in the garrison better however than any one *we* coud have had elsewhere, as it is close by the office, where Mr B: is from ten in the morning to three or four, & sometimes part of the evening. – I shoud perhaps leave it to Lord M: to say how he is pleased with the secretary, but to *You* I cannot resist expressing the great satisfaction I feel in seeing Mr B: get thro the business of his situation in a manner which I perceive is so compleatly satisfactory to Lord M:, & so conciliating to every one round him. – I allways knew that his abilitys woud be found equal to any demand that coud be made on them, but I feel this conjecture established into a very *pleasant certainty*, by having on more occasions than one, seen Lord M: throwing on him very consequential decisions w^{c} have been *invariably approved of*, & even adopting from time to time *alterations* which Mr B; has ventured to make in papers, after Lord M: has approved of them, Mr B: having no reserve with him in *Ingenuosly* giving his opinion, Lord M: on the other hand seems posatively *fond* & most *companoniable* with Mr B:, who appears & is as happy in his department as a man can be, who thirsted after imployment, had it bestowed on him by a friend, he is glad to be obliged to, & in it feels himself equal to it. – with such reasons for being Happy, if I tell you that *I* am Happy & that *I like the cape*, & see much of the disgust with w^{c} it is talkd of by others, as arising out of their own acid humours, but half supported by the fact, you will not be surprised – you must however read *My* account of its merits, when I begin to expatiate on them with some grains of allowance, as well as those opinions *against* on the *other side*, as I know that I have a natural disposition to pick out flowers amongst weeds if I can, & to make the best

*Government** Rustenburg House, Rondebosch, where the capitulation of the Cape was signed on 6-9-1795. There were five Generals Campbell listed in the *Army List* of this day but the one mentioned here was presumably Brigadier General Campbell who was appointed member of a commission to examine paper money and to destroy publicly old and defaced money on 26-8-1797. (Cape Archives BO 56/143).

of all "existing circumstances". – but independant of this being the turn of my mind, let us look at the facts – here is a *divine climate*, at least I have found it so as yet no fog – no damp – no variations to check the perspirations & to fall on the Lungs, but a clear pure, yet not sharp air, full of Health & exhilaration to the spirits – here *is* scarcity, but here *will be plenty*, I am convinced when the Harvest comes round, which quickly follows the sowing here, at least a 3^d quicker than in England. – the farmers saw no *certain* market before for their grain, nor woud venture to sow what was in their granarys for fear of its being reapd by they knew not *Who*; now here is a fixed government & a certain utterance for all they can send down to this shore; less will probably be raised *this year* than will be necessary, to make things *very* cheap, but industry will be doubled next year more slaves will be got, more cattle taken into the yoke & plenty I think will ensue. – the town is clean one or two dirty circumstances attending the Killing of animals exepted. – the features upon natures face magnificently strong. – I love these bold strokes with w^c the almighty has separated the dry land from the sea in his chaos. – the Bay opens beautifully at the foot of the mountains, while the Hottentot hills* at 20 miles distance rise in forms so stupendously excentric that I look at them with admiration every time I see them – it is in the power of activity & taste to make this the finest scene in the world by planting & I have but little of either but little as I have, if I was only sure of living a couple of hundred years, to see the effect of my labour I woud begin to plant tomorrow with alacrity those grounds round the town which from their want of water cannot be applied to any purpose save that of rearing wood w^c I think they woud do in plenty for the use of the town, the silver tree & *Scotch fir* particularly growing to *perfection* "and join the gentle to the rude" the marriage of Miss Silver tree, or the Yonge frow Silver tree,* with Donald firtop is exactly what I quote, the lady being coverd with leaves of grey sattin & the fir, stout, of a fresh bold green, & hardy as its countrymen. – I hear you say, & you speak it like a *great* man, like a *good* man – like a man of a mind far more extensive than any country is, "but why must you live to 200 years to plant? cant you plant tho you shoud live only 20, some one in the future will have the benefit of it & thank you?" – I can to be sure – & I *will* that is more, I will do as much as my *private* purse can fairly do, for *publick* spirit, but a great deal I cant, unless I can persuade others to do so too, as the grounds so planted must be enclosed else the little tender sticks, woud be torn up by the slaves for fire wood in a twelve months time. – there is a plan (I am not sure by whom suggested) Mr Barrow* mentioned it to me on the top of the table mountain, of making a sort of navigable cannal or connection by water, & by the Bergh river between the sea at false Bay, or Simons Bay (as they call it here) to fall into the Salt river at the foot of the table mountain (Ill have this drawn on my little chart if I can, before I send off my letter for fear of my making mistakes) if this coud be done it woud be a great thing for this place – the expence was talkd of as great, but Lord Bless me, if we keep this place John Bull woud fill the subscription of 2,00000 in the course of a morning on change. – by the bye I must tell you a little about this same expedition of mine – having

*hills**
Hottentots Holland Mts., a range on the east side of False Bay.

*tree**
Leucadendron argenteum, almost entirely confined to the Cape Peninsula.

*Barrow**
Afterwards Sir John Barrow, bt. (1764-1848), private secretary to Lord Macartney. He travelled widely through the Colony to obtain more accurate topographical information than was then known. He published *Account of travels into the interior of Southern Africa*, 18-1-04. He was 2nd Secretary of the Admiralty, 1804-45, and was the founder of the Royal Geographical Society.

Earl Macartney, Governor of the Cape 1797-98, by Mather Brown

Mentor, Table Mountain guide

been told that no woman had ever been on the top of it Table mountain (N.B. this was not *literally* true one or two having been so) & being able to get no account of it from either the inhabitants of this town, all of whom wishd it to be considered as next to an impossible matter to get to the top of it, as an *excuse for their own want of curiosity*, and having found the officers all willing to believe the natives for *ditto reason* Lazyness, there was some ambition as a motive for climbing as well as curiosity: and as Mr Barrow is just one of the pleasantest & best informed & eager minded young men in the world about every thing curious or worth attention I paid my adresses to him, to mount the hill along with me. – we were joined in the plan by two of my ship mates officers. – & my maid chose to be of the party, I had a couple of servants, & a couple of slaves with cold meat & wine,* Mr Barrow & I each slinging round our shoulders a tin case for plants, of w^c^ we were told we shoud get great variety on the top of the mountain – it is three thousand five hundred feet in heigth, & reckond about three miles to the top of it from the beginning of its great ascent, the road being – (or rather the conjectured path for there is no road) necessarily squinted in the zig zag Z way w^c^ much increases the measurement of the walk – at 8 oclock Mr Barrow & I with our followers set off – we reachd the foot of the mountain on horseback & dismounted when we coud ride no more – indeed nothing but a Human creature or an *antilope* coud ascend such a path. – we first had to scramble up a pretty perpendicular cascade of a hundred feet or two, the falls of which must be very fine after rains & the sides of which were shaded with myrtles, sugartrees & geraneums* – we continued our progress thro a low foliage of all sorts of pretty Heaths & ever greens, the sun at last beginning to beat with much force down on our heads, but the heat was not, tho great, oppresive, wherever we saw questionable stone or ore Mr Barrow attackd it with a Hammer I had luckily brought for the purpose, but he found the mountain thro all its stratas, of which there are inumerable, composed of *Iron stone** & that at least to the quantity of 50 per cent – it made me smile to see the marks of the Human footstep in the great quantity of *old soles & heels of shoes* W^c^ I saw every here & there, I suppose these *relicks* have lain Time immemorial, as leather I believe never decays, at least not for a great while; it proved that the dutch men told fibs when they said that few people had tried to get up this Hill – that & fatigue obliged me frequently to sit down & as I had an umbrella with me, a few minutes allways recruited me, – at least about 12 oclock the sun begun to be so very hot, that I rejoyced at the turn of the mountain which I saw woud soon bring us into the shaddow, before we Reachd the great gully by w^c^ we were to get *out* on the top.* – redoubling my activity, at last we made the turn, but it is wonderfull the sudden chill which instantaneously came over us, we lookd at our thermometers & in a second, they had fallen under the shadow 15 degrees; being now 55, & before on the brow of the hill they were 70 – we had now come to a fine spring of water which fell from the top of the Rock, or near it over our heads, we drank some of it with port wine, but it was too cold to have been safe had we not had more way to climb. – I saved a bottle of it for you, cher ami – opposite there was a cave cut in the rock which is

*wine**
In her Journal Lady A. says she was accompanied by Col. Lloyd, (Lt. Col. James Phillips Lloyd, 86th Ft) Barrow, Dr. Pattison, and other gentlemen, with the slave Mentor as guide.

*geraneums**
Sugar tree (obsolete) = Suikerbos, i.e. *Protea mellifera*. Geraneum = Pelargonium.

*stone**
Table Mountain is principally sandstone.

*top**
Platteklip Gorge.

Platteklip Gorge, Table Mountain

View of the Town and the Bay when descending the Mountain

occasionally inhabited by run away negroes, of which there were traces; once more we sett off and in three hours from the bottom of the hill reachd the very tip top, of this great rock, looking down on the town (allmost out of sight below) with much conscious superiority – and smiling at the formal meanness of its appearance, which woud have led us to suppose it built by children out of half a dozen packs of cards. – I was glad on this pinacle to have a *birds eye view* of the country – the Bays the distant & near mountains – the coup d'oeul brought to my awed rememberance, the Saviour of the world presented from the top of "an exceeding high mountain" with all the Kingdoms of the Earth, by the Devil, nothing short of *such* a view was *this* – but it was not the garden of the world that appeard all around; on the contrary there was no denying the circle bounded only by the Heavens & Sea to be a wide *desart* – bare – uncultivated – uninhabited – but Noble in its bareness & (as we had reason to know) capable of cultivation from its soil which submits easily to the spade & gratefully repays its attention; – on the top of the mountain there was nothing of that luxuriancy of verdure, & foliage flowers or Herbage, described by travellers, there were roots & some flowers & beautifull Heaths on the *edge* of the rocks, but the soil was cold, swampy, mossy, coverd in general with half an inch of water, rushes growing in it & sprinkled all over with little white pebbles, some dozens of which I gatherd to make *table mountain earings* to my fair *European* friends. – we now produced our cold meat – our port – madeira & capewine, we made a splendid & Happy dinner after our fatigues, when I proposed a song to be sung in full chorus, not doubting that all the Hills around woud Join us, God save the King – God save great George our King, roard I, & my troop – God save – God save God save – god save – god save – god save – god save – god GREAT GEORGE OUR KING – great George our King – great George – great George – great George – repeated the loyal mountains – the impression is very fine said Mr Barrow with his eyes glistening – I coud not say *yes*, because I felt more than I chose to trust my voice with, Just then, but I wishd great George our King to have stood beside me at the moment, & to have thrown his eye over his new possessions, which we were thus (his Humble viceroys) taking possession of, in his name. – my servants shot a few pretty birds which you shall see by & bye & we found it time to return home, w^{c} we coud not reach [,] we saw, before 6 oclock at night – nothing was more singular than to look down far – far below, on the flag raised on the top of the lions head, a rock perpendicular, of some hundred feet, on the top of a *great North Berwick Law.** [Sketch] – it is round this rock that there is a constant *necklace* of clouds playing; but this day all was clear – the person who keeps guard on this rock is drawn up by ropes fixed in a particular manner – it was difficult to ascend the hill, it was much more so to *descend* – the *ladys* were *dressd* for the occasion, else I need not say more after the word *else* – the only way to get down was to sit down, & slip from rock to rock the best way one coud. – my shoes I had tyed with some yards of tape w^{c} had been a good scheme, & at last we reachd Home not more tired than I expected we shoud have been, & more than ever convinced that there are few things *impossible* when

*Law**
A conical hill near North Berwick, East Lothian.

there is, in man or woman a decided & spirited wish of attainment. – Doctor pattison* (a very amiable, sensible & Humane man sent out by admiralty as physician to the navy Hospital) told me there was *no sum* he coud not have won at the cape against my ever reaching the top of table mountain – he said he woud not take them *in*, for he knew I woud do it if it was possible, for any body to do it, if I said I woud I had found however no further gratification from having been there, than the pleasure of being able to say "I have seen it" – for my fancy coud have painted the same very pretty without going up – since that time I rode round to Camps Bay, the road to which is finer than any scene I ever saw in my life, or coud have seen – that is to say fine from mountains & sea – I must make some sketches of this road. – but my time has been *as yet* wholly occupied with *domestic cares*; I am a Martha with the full intention of being twenty better things by & bye; mean time as we have a great many people who eat & drink with us in a family way, & as it is extremely difficult to get many things or servants to do them properly I am obliged to be more of an *usefull* than an *accomplishd* female; if I can in any way make things comfortable to my kind Husband & his friends I am well employd. – I see a great deal of yr friends the Campbells – I mean the general & his wife – she is a good humoured, pleasant, good looking creature with a very good heart, & is much calculated to render society pleasant & easy. – the general you know to be a respectable & gentleman like man. – of the other Campbells* I cannot say so much; in a former letter I mentioned how much they had endeavored to make themselves disagreable in their various ways on board of ship; I had really been afraid from what genl: Hartley said, (and from her own manners) that she woud endeavour to sett up a dutch party against the English women going out; but I am glad to find that nothing is in her power: she is very much disliked here, even by her countrywomen, & he equally so, nor woud she be at all on the fore ground of society, was she not tempted (which I will suppose is by a love of receiving *notice*) to go to rather too great lengths with most of the gentlemen to obtain it, her character has not yet had time to be *very naughty* but three or four flirtations going on at present, is making it rather equivocal; amongst the *dutch* women this is *nothing* each one has her lover, & if more, it only the more proves her charms. – I have blushd to hear one of her sisters make her child count up mamas sweethearts on its little fingers when some of the sweethearts *present* knew it to be no *Joke* & some others in England coud have corroborated. – capt Campbell was very Haughty at first to every body but I believe he has [been] taken down some pegs by Ad: pringle. – we had them to dine here lately, we wish to have *no* quarrels no miffs* – they wishd to miff with us, but we are so civil without familiarity that they cannot *make it out*, so now they eat our mutton & gulp. – amongst a few gentlemen who augur more from this place than others, is Mr Strombom, he thinks highly of its powers & fertility – Mr Barrow also is of this party, both of these however, think that *this* is not the best situation for the capital, but that simons bay woud, had it water & water I dare say might be found if dug for skillfully – I wish the King woud send out his friend Mrs Milbanke* with her *hazel wand*, she woud poke up and

*pattison**
Dr. W. Pattison, described in official records as chief surgeon to the naval hospital at Simonstown.

*Campbells**
See note on p.29.

*miffs**
Miff, *n.* = a petty quarrel; *v.* = take offence. O.E.D. quotes this very passage.

*Milbanke**
Undoubtedly the Hon. Mrs. Judith Milbanke (1751-1822), daughter of Sir Edward Noel, bt., 1st viscount Wentworth. Her husband Sir Ralph Milbanke, succeeded as 6th bt. in Jan. 1798. No other allusion to her water-divining powers has been discovered, though quite a lot is known about her as her only daughter, Anne Isabella, had the ill fortune to marry Lord Byron. Lady A. and Judith Milbanke were well acquainted and in the 1780's it was thought possible that the former might marry Judith's brother the 2nd viscount Wentworth. The allusion to the Duke of Manchester's is not explicable though coincidentally it was at his seat, Kimbolton Castle, that the Milbankes first met. (See Elwin (Malcolm) *Lord Byron's wife*, Macdonald, 1962, ch.2.). She is referred to again in Letter 29.

The Barnards' under-cook

Malagasy slave girl and a chameleon

The Society House, a seaside hotel for members only, on the slopes above Bantry Bay

down till she found plenty, & we shoud have a second Judiths well, as at the duke of Manchesters. – it is thought that Hemp might be raised here with benefit to our mother country & with success. – there is no barley here – that is a grain, which shoud also be brought; – they have only bean. – Beef is certainly inferior to what it is in England, & *so is mutton* which is not thought on tother side of the water – the fat of the first is too yellow & of the last too white – but neither are at present well fed; – the tails are very usefull for every thing lard coud be used for, as they are much purer than it is, & far better than the butter here. – at first one has a prejudice against them, but now I have them used & say nothing. – poultry is about as good as in England but milk & butter inferior, & the cape cows good for nothing, the half breed along with the English ones are better & sell very high – there is a dutch cow here at Simmons bay, that clears her master in milk & Butter w^c he sells to the ships that put in there [,] £200 pr an – her calfs sell for 50 each – but this is a wonder – I had an English cow, but she is *no more* she died of Rheumatisme & a liver complaint – I had no good fare for her, poor cow & a long walk every day to pick up her grass did not agree with her – I soon hope to have poultry & vegetables of our own, as there is a little government cottage at the bottom of the mountain, called paradice, which Lord M: has given us to be rural in – it has not enough of ground uncleard to have a cow, but it will at least raise us chickens & *pottatoes*. – there is no road to it, or rather a road practicable only on horse back, but as it is only a place to hide our heads in, in the shade when the sun gets sulky, we dont much care about that. – the roof is thatchd & old, admitting the rain which rots the timbers but a new roof of reeds w^c the place will furnish, will not cost much, there is a little hasty stream of water, a clump of firs – a good many old orchard trees, a few orange trees – a perpendicular Rock behind & a far extended view of mountains & sea before, the intermediate space uncultivated heath or short stubbd wood, good for little but the oven – of a Saturday John & Joan & Jane the cousin will Noddy it down, leaving the carriage at the bottom of the hill to walk it up, & will there hide themselves till monday, visited only by a few Monkeys from the mount ains – perhaps a wolf – possibly some runaway negroes, but all these (exept the monkeys who are frequent in their visits) are rather bug bears than *realitys* a few scarlet coated aid du camps Messieurs Collier & Crawfurd* part of the number are more likely to break up our retirement & possibly my lord himself in his mornings ride, but he shakes his head when I talk of a bed – alas – it was at paradise that I may allmost say I last saw poor – Anguish –* that was a good humoured very easy temperd young man who we were all disposed to love & who promised fair to contribute to the pleasures of society, I askd him to go with me to look at this cottage at the time that we saw it was attainable – I never saw him in better spirits – he & I used often laugh with each other at the Malcontents as we called them he finding noveltys & amusements every where as I did & as Barrow did. – I think said he if the comptroller of the customs was to be master of this little place w^c some folks woud call miserable he woud be contented to give up London & remain here quietly & Lazyly all his days – he then went on to say how much more

*Crawfurd**
The Hon. William Colyear (1776-1833), captain, Duke of York's Dragoons and 2nd son of 3rd Earl of Portmore; Lt. Col. James Catlin Craufurd, 98th Foot.

*Anguish**
Comptroller of customs. He apparantly committed suicide.

comfortable he now was than he ever had been, that his income was fixed equal to his best hopes thro yrs & Lord Ms kindness & that from its date he even now possessd a little matter to make him clear with the world – inshort I thought him rather a happy man, he was not however altogether in good Health, as I afterwards heard, & had been taking I believe some physical prescriptions – I thought by a transient glance I had of him one day after that his countinance seemd heated & confused, but I never saw him again – he left universal regret behind him & the full conviction that mental malady had been produced by bodily malady only; for he had done nothing to reproach himself with – I never cease thinking of him when I drive past his grave which must be passd, on going to the review ground – talking of reviews – the troops here I fancy are esteemd to be in fine order – to me they appear well dressd – well matchd men & better looking than any of the lately raised Reg^{ts} that I saw in England – I hear of no disturbances & sleep secure every night in the garrison with 700 men – desertion is over & many of those that had deserted is returned since the proclamation – amongst others a man who has been absent above a year, who bears an unletterd testymony to a matter which had been doubted [,] the existence of the unicorn in the interior parts of Africa – some years ago, some of the natives had expressd their surprize at seeing it in the Kings armes & when they were askd if they coud procure such an animal for a sum of money they had shudderd saying 'aye to be sure' but he was 'their god'' – this soldiers evidence corroborates this, he describes him to be much larger than a horse tho less than a small Elephant – about as high he said as the room – he had on shoes made of the hide of one, they are of immoderate strength & the skin more of the horse hide sort than of any other* – Mr Barrow who went up the country to the Boshemens Land* will may be see something of this animal but he will be chiefly in quest of a still better thing a good silver or gold mine, of the first there is no doubt of there being several & containing a much greater quantity of silver than is to be found in any of the mines we have in England, I hear there is also gold mines* – if we coud pay off *our paper debt* with some of this & hand you over some to pay off your national it woud be pretty; he is to bring me down a little girl from a particular country, far – far in the inner parts of this wide continent where the people do not exceed four feet in stature & females have little pads or footboards behind which serve for a seat for their children, instead of carrying them on their shoulders – *they are clever & faithfull

I hear the day before yesterday a sad incident happend or rather a wicke act, the son of our Butcher being killd by his slave, a Malisse* in revenge fo having been refused liberty to go out on Sunday, tho it was *not* his turn to do so – after he had stabbd him he attempted to murder his mistress, & stabbd one of her slaves, I suppose the unfortunate wretch woud have *run Muck* as is the term in this country of Frenzy from despair & the certainty of death, when they kill every one they meet, it is some years since an instance of this kind has happend, the unfortunate man had been wounded in his attempts & must have died, but life was abridged by the gallows an hour after the affair happend, to deter others – but thank god the days of Torture are over, & the sad evidences of what

*other**
The rhinoceros. The white rhino was identified by Burchell in the Cape interior in 1817.

*Land**
Bushman Land, just south of the Orange River.

*mines**
Although the early Dutch governors spent much time searching for precious metals there is no proof that silver was actually discovered at the Cape. South Africa's present output is from the Witwatersrand. Gold was said to have been mined south of the Limpopo in ancient times but its discovery by white men dates only from 1867 in Matabeleland.

*shoulders–**
Clearly a description of a Bushman girl with her enlarged posterior. The Dutch settlers first came in contact with Bushmen in 1655.

*Malisse**
i.e. Malice.

Above: A modern reconstruction of Paradise, Newlands

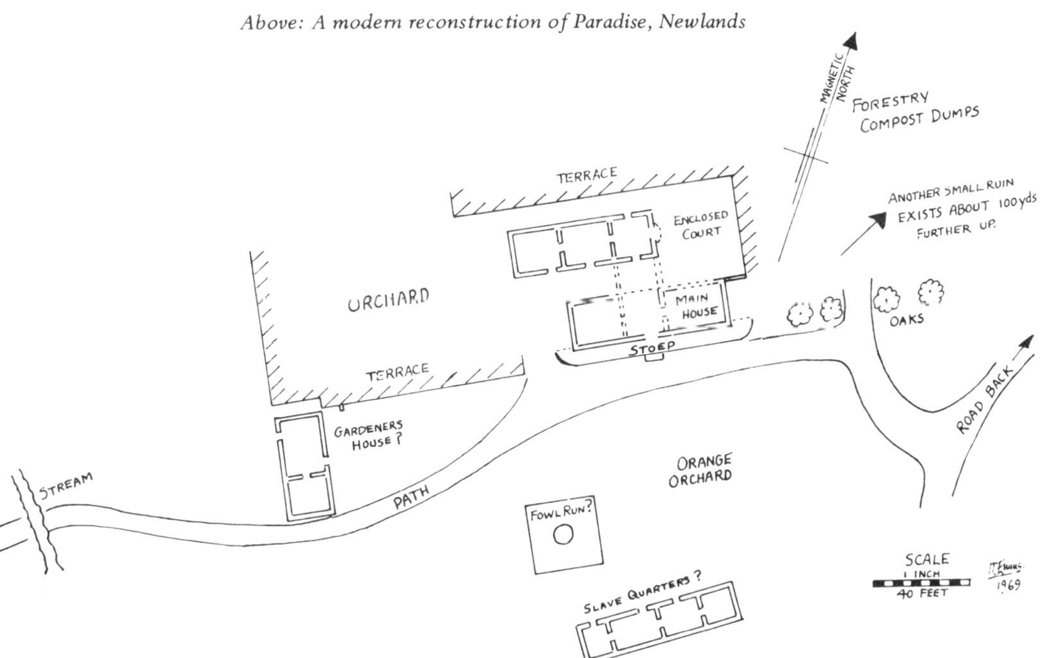

Plan of Paradise, Newlands, based on surviving ruins. (Both sketch and plan are by Mr Mervyn Emms.)

was practised in the dutch government only remain, on a high ground hard by the entrance to the castle, it froze my blood at first, but Habit hardens the nerves, I hope without hardening the heart – I had a visit at the castle from one of the caffre chiefs with his train of wives & dogs, he was as fine a morsel of Bronze as I ever saw & there ought to have been a pair of them with candlesticks in their hands – nothing coud exceed the savages notes which accompanied their uncouth Gestures in their warlike dances. I gave them many trifles & the captain a cap which pleased him so much that with the gallantry of nature he came forward on receiving it from the Balcony in the court yard kissed my finger respectfully – I had prepared some dinner for them, but found they coud eat nothing but beef or mutton – pyes – fouls & still more particularly *fish* they seemd to have no taste for, indeed till they reachd the cape they had never seen a fish, Hooks & lines being unknown to them & the fish therefore in their rivers live unmollested by the wiles of creations Lords – wine they liked, but rum transported them – I have tried but at present vainly to get fine feathers, all have been bought up to send to Europe before they reachd the cape, at least since I have arrived. – apropos – shoud you have any friends coming here, I give you & them this general advice to bring every thing from London that is necessary for the consumption of *one year*, Indian goods as well as other things. – nothing is of the best quality & most things are, by tacit perhaps private agreement of the posessors kept up to an immoderate price – there is a man at Simons Town one Trail* in some of the publick departments (a great rogue) who buys up every thing the moment the ships come in & then puts his own price on the goods

N.B. by his office he is debard from what he practises to the necessity of others – Mr B: wrote to beg he woud ask a little lump sugar from one of the captains of the ships lately arrived & that Mr Green* woud pay for it – Mr Trail was "fortunate enough" he said to have obtaind some "already", at only =4=6 per pound – Mr Green wisely declined this precious sugar. – coud coals be brought out they woud answer well also some grates & portable Kitchens – whover means to settle here shoud bring *every thing* – furniture in particular but it shoud come out packd in little compass – I brought all my chairs in pieces close tyed up – viz windsor & rush bottom chairs – carpets & blankets are necessary, for winter is winter here & nothing but avarice prevents all from having fires this 11th day of July, but a fire is a serious matter – this day signals have appeared of the arrival of 6 more ships – 3 india men are at present at Simons town & I hope this new fleet contains my brother Hugh* – it will be a Joyfull meeting! – I shall leave this letter open for what else may occur – it is a long long one already – & yet I have still much to say – I have not mentiond the arrival of Mr & Ly Anne Dashwood* – she is sister to Lord Lauderdale a sweet good girl who has performed a very heavy duty in my opinion tho it does not seem to strike her as much in following or rather accompanying here a husband whose dreadfull countinance bears awefull Testymony to a vitiated mind & person, thank god he has contrived to give her such an account of the *How* he happens to be in this state as renders it less shocking to her, but in my opinion his ugly face is more tolerable than the unprincipled

*Trail**
Donald Trail, harbour master, Simonstown, and master attendant of the Navy.

*Green**
John Hooke Greene, collector of customs.

*Hugh**
The Hon. Hugh Lindsay (1765-1844), 8th son of the 5th Earl of Balcarres, director of the East India Co., marshal of the Court of Admiralty.

*Dashwood**
Lady Isabel Anne Dashwood, daughter of 7th Earl of Lauderdale, married Francis Dashwood of Hall Place, Bexley, Kent, and died 1858. Although the description might fit, there is no evidence that Dashwood was related to the notorious Francis Dashwood, Lord le Despenser (1708-1781), described by Sir Herbert Croft as "the most careless and perhaps the most facetious Libertine of his age."

The Panorama of Cape Town

The following panorama was drawn from the roof of the Kat, or curtain wall of the Castle, and its accompanying buildings (see p.39). In the first section one looks to the south across the Cape Flats; sections 2 to 5 follow in a clockwise direction.

Section 1

On the extreme left, beyond the Nassau bastion of the Castle, is the Stellenbosch road and leading round to the right is the road to Rondebosch. The Hottentots Holland Mountains are in the distance.

Section 2

Devil's Peak. The farm Zonnebloem in the middle distance.

Section 3

Table Mountain, beyond the Oranje bastion.

Section 4

Lion's Head. The Great Barracks. In the foreground is the Keizersgracht (now Darling St).

Section 5

Beyond the Leerdam bastion is the Grand Parade with the Heerengracht (now Adderley St) on the further side. From left to right the streets looked down are: Keizersgracht leading into Shortmarket St, Castle St, and Strand St. The buildings on the Bay front include the Hon. East India Co.'s warehouse, the Custom House and the Commissariat.

Section 6

The main gateway to the Castle. The Buren bastion on the right.

Section 7

Looking straight along the Kat, the Catzenellenbogen bastion is obscured. On the right one looks toward Fort Knokke and the mouth of the Salt River. Across Table Bay are Blouberg and the Tygerberg.

Panorama 7

democratic & free maxims which fall from his lips & which prevent pity from alleviating the natural disgust the man inspires — . it has been necessary to hint to him that some of his doctrines here are better kept to himself & I believe he has said less of late —

August — 10th — my brother was in it, in the fleet I mean & has spent a month with us much, much to our satisfaction, I wish that Margaret had been of the party — & I wish you coud all at wimbledon by a wishing cap take a dinner with us in the garrison — I have given a most capital party, the 3^{d} of this month & shall have one the first thursday of every month for dutch Ladys particularly but cannot have my publick days oftener as every thing is so very-very dear that I shoud be ruined, you will easily believe this when I tell you that amongst other things my thirsty friends drank me up Ten dozzen of porter a little stock of which I had brought with me but not enough to stand many such attacks,* I had about a third part of the Ladys Dutch, but not so many of the men, the Fiscal is a warm friend & the late Secretary Mr Goetz a very obliging man they were here — next time I expect to have a more numerous dutch collection as they will then better understand that they may come without invitation, it woud make you smile to tell you that many of the Dutch women declined paying me the first visit because *I was not of high enough Rank* to receive it — I find they used to visit the governors wife & the councellors wives, but not the secretarys wife *first* & tho the *only* woman belonging to the government yet I am but Madam Le Secretaire you know to *them*, as I looked on this rather as an *evasion* to keep off from visiting in the castle *at all* (as they supposed I might stand on the ceremony of putting myself on the footing of the *governors Lady* there being no Lady but myself) I took it quite easily on *another plan*, and said that tho it was the custom in England for natives allways to visit Strangers first, yet visiting the natives first woud be considerd by them as any conciliatory mark of respect on my part I was perfectly ready to do so, & off I sett with a volley of visits to some of the first people declaring myself an enemy to all forms which in a small society kept respectable people at a distance from each other I fortunately visited only two or three who from sickness were confined at home or who from little circumstances that had passd I *ought* to have called on to return my thanks for having put their daughters under my protection at my party & Hop, for In return to a few lines I wrote the Fiscal on this subject begging to know *his* opinion of what I find [,] by his reply [,] w^{c} I enclose* as it is sensibly & prettily expressd [,] that I shall do best to let it alone & a little time & my now *well known* disposition to be well with them, will effect the matter as far as it need to be effected —

amongst the English who have arrived in the fleet is Capt & Mrs Gardner — the daughter to the late Lady Hobart* — & *very* pretty, young, — brilliant. — but a flower that blows but to fall shortly — shortly — it is malancholy to look at an innocent pretty face when one sees the fate it must have, for never did I know or hear of any person of her age being so perdue already in point of conduct — Capt Gardner does not *choose* to see any thing; as I conclude he has formd his decision in his own mind & will at home on some other occasion take the steps w^{c} it might be inconvenient to take here. — you will admire *her as* far as mere

*attacks**
cf. Baxter (W.T.) "Lady Anne goes shopping" in Q. *Bull. S. Afr. Libr.* 1(2): 33-36, regarding prices at the Cape.

*enclose**
See p.62.

*Hobart**
Mrs. Gardner's father would have been Thomas Adderley of Innishannon, co. Cork.

youthfull looks go, for she has no conversation – of course this must be entre nous – they sail in my brothers ship, but Capt Gardner is *safe* there – *perfectly so* – there is another Lady in the ship a pleasing handsome modest woman a Mrs Orr, who I like much married to a col Orr she has left there, as she has come home for her Health – she is a friend of the Bristols, & was a Miss Daniel – they know her family well –

General Dundas & some officers with him have been up the country for ten days & I have just seen one of them he tells me that at a distance from this place there is by no means the scarcity there is at the cape & that they bought grain for 3 dollars a sack which here costs 11 dollars – this leads one to hope that time & the confidence of the natives in finding a market may render every thing cheaper this ensueing year – Ill let this remain open till the last day cher ami, I mean to go to Simons Bay with my brother to see him on board & I shall then be able to say something of it –

August Wed: 16

– I dare not look at the 6 sheets already written, if I had time I woud transcribe them leaving out much *stuff* which I dare say has fallen in chit chat from my pen, but I absolutely have not half an hour to myself & have been so often interrupted while writing to you that I dare say you will find this a *vile* letter & full of repetitions. –

since I concluded the last page we have had a gallant whaler here who with 24 men (as I hear) has taken a Dutch ship from Batavia laden with arms and ammunition, it required finesse as well courage to effect this matter but I heartily rejoice we have got part & destroyd much of the powder, as the people of Graaf Renet (for which it was bound) are very ill affected* – Mr Barrow I fancy is there by this time, I fancy he will be able to give many Judicious accounts in various ways. – we have had a South Easter these ten days & a pretty strong one which has delayd the loading of the ships with victuals for the convoy in False Bay – I hope all will reach you safe when they do sail for great must be the riches of this fleet. – I have got a jar of pine apples from Batavia for Lady Jane & one for Lady Hardwick, but I fear much that I shall find it difficult to get them conveyd the captains are so fearfull of taking what they tell me will more than probably bring them to disgrace by being spoild or lost at the India house – Ill make another trial it vexes me to see my charming pines *here*, when I wish them on your table tho you have probably more of these things than you care about, but I *retract*, if it is difficult *now* to get such matters safely landed it must have been as difficult before – I wish I knew the best mode of sending this, whether by an India ship, letting it take its chance or by a man of war! – Ill try Mr Brice, Mrs Anstruthers brother, a modest pleasing young man who has lately been with us – *smuggled* I find they must be – Im afraid I Cant enclose to you my chart of our voyage, nor some little sketches of this place, I shall find leisure to get them ready I trust by the next opportunity –

*affected**
The District of Graaff-Reinet which had in 1795 established its independence from the Company's rule, was naturally loath to submit to the new government, though officially it did so in August 1796. It lay between the Gamtoos and the Great Fish Rivers.

you will see *Sir R: abercrombie* soon & col Abercrombie*– he is a gentle mannerd, & good man I believe – the gardeners as I mentioned, sail with Hugh – *remember* what I have mentioned respecting her is between ourselves – very soon she must be talkd of in *England*, because she cannot Help it – however if it is *possible* for her to reform I shoud wish not to have been the person to let past follys be known first – how I long for letters from England! not a line have I had since I left it – I have heard however from Genl Dundas that Lady Jane & you are well, or were, later than I heard from Yourself – God Bless you my dear friend – make my kindest love to her & your daughter & be assured upon the whole that I am as comfortable as I can be at a distance from those I love – yours affectionately & truly

Anne Barnard

I have had so little time to write to my sisters that may be they may *spunge* on you, for a few more particulars

August – 24 – We have been at false Bay since I concluded the above seeing Hugh on board – I find the place rather better *looking* than I expected the Houses on the *outside* being as is the dutch fashion all well white washd with their clean shirts on – but there is sadly little room for the poor sick fellows the honest Tars, multitudes of whom have been lost for want of air & wholesome accomodation they having been so close packd in their Hospital with scurvy – ulcers &c, that it was certain death going into it; of late the physician to the navy (Dr pattison) has got with *much* difficulty, leave to have the use of a stable made for those horses of some of the officers residing there, & since 60 men have been put into it many of them have recoverd – what a pity that more places are not erected for them, the price of 20 lives savd, even in bounty money, woud save hundreds – aye thousands of people in this Hot climate – what fools! or what dirty, nasty calculators some of the contractors for the publick must be, where is the Hospital for the navy *here* in cape Town placed? *above the publick ovens* where all the bread used in the place is baked & where the languishing creatures are baked into the next world along with it – but tis better to growl *here*, than to you across the Bay of Biscay. – I have been trying to persuade some of the wise people to give a great lump of the mountain behind the houses at false Bay to some old Honorable sea man to become Gardner & raise vegetables for the use of the navy – selling them at a small price yet getting a good livelyhood too – every pottatoe & cabbage at an immoderate price comes from Cape Town 20 miles over the bad roads, & at a rate that Government can hardly afford to purchase for the sick, how much cheaper the other way woud be, & what a benefit – there is a companys garden – Mr Trail askd it for the above purpose, but since he has had it the navy people are the only ones to whom he will *not* sell a pottatoe for fear of its being rememberd how he got it – I am told he is now worth 60,000 – he was a favorite of our friend L[d] Keiths, who certainly must have thought well of him *then* but he is sadly detested here for his extortionary practises – if he is turnd out which there is some talk of (I speak *merely* of common report) I wish

*Abercrombie**
Sir Robert Abercromby (1740-1827), c.-in-c. of the forces in India, 1793. Returned home April 1797 due to a disease of the eyes. His mildness of manner is spoken of elsewhere also. Regarding Col. Abercromby, the most obvious officer with this rank would seem to be Sir Robert's nephew Lt.-Col. John A., 53rd Foot, son of Maj.-Gen. Sir Relph Abercromby whose military secretary he was, but Sir Ralph was stationed in Britain.

the garden coud be turnd to the purpose I mention, Ill venture for *once* to launch a *womans* opinion about it – I have scratched the general look of the place* – the store house is the long building, above which there is some room for sea men & the small house is the stable I mention. –

the garden which Trail now has is round the mountain where the line is drawn – I did not see it – the house I have markd wt a star is a Mr Munichs [Munniks] he wishes to sell it & asks 4,000 for it & the ground round, it – dear enough I think – certainly it woud be very difficult for an enemy to land there & to get on to Cape Town as the road may be so easily deffended by a handfull of men, the sea coming close up on the right the road being bad & narrow & mountains rocky & almost perpendicular being to the left on which there are many little batterys raised & cannon pointed – there is a dangerous pass too to cross in one of the small bays, & a quick sand in another – the camp at Musenberg is a mere hut at present, but the officers are building a better. the situation must be Healthy for the men & easily deffended from the reasons I mention – I sketchd this with some pen & ink that stood on their table, they were all out a shooting but a soldier gave me a bit of broild beef & made us an apology that they had no beer or wine to give us, nothing *but* constantia – but when I tasted it, to be sure it was excellent – it is just behind that vineyard – that is to say a few miles distance the person who broild the beef had been Stewart [sic] to the Duke of Orleans!* I remember the man in paris, such are the chances of this mortal life! I dare say you think I have digested a democrative morsel when it was dressd by him – he kept afterwards a club in Dover st & is a bad subject in all senses of the word –

"False Bay", more exactly Simon's Bay

you woud have paused & fixed your eye wt a smile on our carriage had you seen us driving away in our dutch vehicle with one black wachman & 8 horses – but postilions are unnecessary here the horses being blessd wth a portion of good sense to pick their own steps, it woud have surprised you had you seen us at the narrowest passes, looking away & passing other carriages & waggons each with 8 horses & one driver, yet no harm ensuing – . adieu – adieu I know you must think I shall never finish – I shall not tell you of the allarm of an engagement w^c frightend many people but proved at last to be a species of varying clouds over the Horison w^c perfectly resembled smoke & vessels at a distance – we think that the admiral does not dislike the cape so much since he fell in love with a pretty little Miss – it threatend matrimony for some time, but like the engagement it has gone off in misty clouds of smoke & left the weaker vessel unmannd

– we have had some witty folks in the garrison here who I woud fain hope woud give it up soon viz caracature drawers, who I allways wish to hear have got a good licking – it is the bane of a small society – there has also been some publications in *manuscript* – one of which I have seen & there is a great deal of Local cheerness in it but I will not trouble you with it – Ill send it to Margaret, She will show you what a High place in the firmament Some of your friends occupy amongst the Heavenly bodys as our writer calls the government people from Europe –

*place**
See the sketch of 'False Bay' enclosed with this letter.

*Orleans**
Presumably the reference is to Louis Philippe Joseph duc d'Orléans (1747-93) who supported the revolutionary cause to a considerable degree as 'Citoyen Egalité', until arrested and guillotined in November 1793.

Letter 11a

W.S. van Ryneveld to Lady Anne Barnard (Translated from the French)

(?) 8 August 1797

A thousand thanks My Lady! for your charming letter which I greatly appreciate. It illustrates once more your kindness respecting my fellow countrymen. And as you do me the honour of addressing me I take the liberty of telling you that those who have told you that the custom of this place demands that foreigners call on the residents to make their acquaintance, have misinformed you. I believe indeed that there will be some of this opinion among those who have only the appearance of a civil education and they are to be found as much here as in all colonies, but I assure you that those who really know how to behave are not ignorant of the fact that it is for them to pay their respects to foreigners when they are desirous of keeping company with them; but permit me Madam, with regard to the ladies, to take their defence upon myself. I assure you that many are cautious in this duty, fearful of their inability to express themselves properly, knowing neither French nor English, and I do not doubt that you will again receive the compliments of several ladies who are now informed that you are quite willing to excuse their ignorance in this respect. It is for these reasons then that I advise you as a friend not to visit anyone who has not presented herself at your house, for those who find themselves in the position of being able to make your acquaintance will not fail to have themselves introduced.

As for the ladies that you met at my house, I must tell you that it was by chance they were at home with my wife, not knowing that we were to have the honour of your company. The one who received you is Miss van Lier, Dutch born, whom I have the pleasure of lodging in my house, and the other lady who also spoke French, is Madame D'Ozÿ who had at that very moment come to see my wife, she has already been intending for some time to pay you her respects together with Miss van Lier and my wife, and it is only my wife's indisposition which has prevented this and as soon as she is able to go out they will discharge their duty, being much disconcerted that you have anticipated them and I beg you to believe that the ladies in my house in particular will find it an especial pleasure to have your acquaintance. – As regards your very just remarks concerning the prejudices that exist, – the English being looked upon as the enemies of the Dutch – I admit that one should abandon these – at least in social intercourse – but what can one do, Madam? – No one has enough understanding to judge of the subject.

Willem Stephanus van Ryneveld, the Fiscal

I hope that the times as well as your agreeable conversation will cause this very much misplaced ambition [? attitude] to disappear – Meanwhile, I am delighted to have the honour of your friendship and I hope that the ladies of my household will share it as well. It only remains for me now to entrust you with my compliments to your sister [sic] and to Mr. Barnard and I beg you to believe that no one will be more sensible of your respect than

Thursday

Your faithful servant
W.S. van Ryneveld

Letter 11b

Mr. Andrew Barnard to Mr. Henry Dundas

Cape of Good Hope
August the 23rd 1797

My Dear Sir
As Lord Macartney tells me that he is writing to you in the fullest manner concerning the State of this Settlement and the Steps he is taking to form the Government and Trade of it, pursuant to the Plan laid down by you, and assisted by the information he has gained since his Arrival here . I will not trouble you with any thing on that subject, well knowing what able hands it is in: but as Lord Macartney cannot speak of himself, or sound his own Praises, I feel myself Particularly Happy to have it in my Power to do that for him, thanks to you Sir for having placed me in a situation so immediately connected with him, and which necessarily leads me to a thorough knowledge of a Man, who the more you know, the more you must Respect and Admire.

The Inhabitants here seem perfectly sensible of the Regard you have shewn to their Interests in choosing out for them a Governor who unites Good Sense with Experience and who by the Mildness and Affability of his manners to all Ranks Demonstrates plainly that altho they are a Conquered People they are no longer Slaves. Fortunately his health has been good since he has been here, consequently his labours have been more unremitting for the Public Welfare the good effects begin already to appear, as the People feel a Confidence now in Government and in its measures, that they did not before, and which I trust will be the means of their becoming more Dutyful, and Loyal Subjects, than they seemed inclined to be on our first arrival: the Inhabitants also of Graaffe Reynet have by our last accounts shewn the same Spirit, and I think the Fortunate Capture made by the Hope South Sea Whaler in Delagoa Bay of the Dutch Brig that was coming with a supply of Arms and ammunition for them,* will effectually confirm them in it, and we shall now have as little trouble with the Inhabitants of the Back settlements as with those of the Cape District.

I am truly sorry to hear Lord Macartney talk of a Promise you made him to allow him to return shortly to Europe and that he means as soon as his Business is completed to remind you of it, his leaving this place will be a Heavy loss to me, as I have experienced from him the Greatest Kindness, and Friendship. I am ignorant Sir whether I am indebted to your Goodness, or to his, for the Comfortable House my Family is now lodged in, without which we shou'd have been in a Miserable condition, as it is scarce possible to get a House here unless you buy one, and to have remained in Lodgings wou'd have been ruination complete. I trust and hope Sir that when you appoint another Governor to succeed Lord Macartney, that you will have the Goodness to recommend me to him in such a manner that he will suffer me to remain where I am at present it being so very convenient on account of my Office, but if he shou'd be a Military Man and prefers the noise of Drums, and Trumpets, to the quiet of living in a Garden, that he will allow me to occupy the Garden house, without which Indulgence, I give you my Honor Sir that I shall not be able to make both ends meet when the year is finished, as more is required of me than the Bare expenses of a Private Family. The size of our present House enables us to effect a purpose which you seemed to have much at heart, it was to conciliate as much as possible the Affections of the Inhabitants here, which cannot be accomplished by any other means but by mixing them as much as possible in our Society. Lady Anne is therefore athome once a Month to all who please to come and visit her, they have a Fiddle or two, and a bit of supper after, at first she found great difficulty in geting them to come to her, as the Dutch Ladies refused to visit her, as her Rank, or mine, was not Sufficiently Great to entitle her to a first visit, she therefore very wisely gave up that point of Etiquette and went to visit them, which had the Desired effect, and now we have our house full. The Dutch Gentlemen frequently dine with me, some of whom are Intelligent and Sensible Men, particularly the Fiscal who is a truly Worthy Man and a Good Subject.

I beg you will have the Goodness Sir to present my Respectful Compliments to Lady Jane, and tell her, that I have employed two Persons who have promised either to bring or send me Pieces of all the Different Sorts of Wood at Ceylon, which her Ladyship expressed a Desire of having, and that I will send them home as soon as I receive them. – I beg your Pardon Sir for having so long intruded upon your time, and have the Honor to Subscribe myself, your Truly Obliged and Obedient Serv[t]

R. Hon.[le] Henry Dundas A. Barnard.

&c &c &c –

*them**
The British whaler *Hope* of London (250 tons, 2 guns) captured the Dutch brig *Haasje* in Delagoa Bay on 20-4-1797. See declaration by the Mate of the *Hope* in Theal. *Records*, 2:149-51.

Letter 12

Castle
Cape Town –
Octr 15 – 1797

I hear there is a ship sails for England today and I seize the opportunity to tell you cher ami that we are all well – anxious for news from England as you will easily believe, when you know, that we first received the accounts of the Mutiny in the navy* by a foreign ship (as I think, danish) which was corroborated *first* by one East India man that put in on account of the Health of the captain & afterwards by the fleet bound for Bengal who were short of water – perhaps some idea of disposing of investments here benificialy, might co-operate – be that as it may, it was plain to all here that it was not intended that this fleet shd touch at the cape, as it brought letters to no one, exept one dated the 15 of may, to me from Lord St Helens sister,* recommending a relation to my attention in case of his touching at the cape, but the date shewd that it was wrote previous to those transactions which afterwards took place, and which thank God have terminated at last in quietness; tho I am sorry our navy has ever shewd a spirit so turbulent and Rebellious, as has been evinced. – French politics of course have taken the advantage of a disposition to call aloud for redress on matters where perhaps they were justified for *grumbling*, but which we suppose the french hoped to improve *beyond* the *point* they have affected. – newspapers reachd us in plenty tho nothing else – a peace talkd of as daily likely to take place, meets here with universal belief. – the cape to be ceded as one article, is allmost universally believd by the *dutch* – and terms so little to the Honor of England has been named, as necessary to be complied with by us in order to effect a peace, which is supposed to be called aloud for by the country, that a change of ministry is stated I see by the papers, & rather credited here, upon the *supposition* that the present ministers will not agree to be the makers of what they do not *approve* of, & also that the french wish rather to negociate with the *other party* – shoud the circumstances of the country be so low & the voice of the people so loud, and the disapprobation of the present ministry so great to the terms proposed that they will not compleat the peace which however upon the whole is settled to take place I suppose you will all walk out at one door of the stage while another sett of *better disposed* men walk in at the other who after finishing *their job*, will follow you out at the first door & you will come back at the second* – this, unless Some new man willing to do the business is incorporated with a part of the old body for that purpose, I suppose will be the case, because I hear others suppose it. – as to my poor little *impressions & expectations* – I can neither believe in a peace (at least not in the course of *this* year) nor in any change of ministry – and if there is a peace, I

*navy**
The mutinies at Spithead and the Nore in the spring and early summer of 1797 paralysed the Channel and North Sea Fleets. Moderation and the promise of better pay and living conditions – though severity was exercised in some cases – soon brought the revolts to an end. Pitt realised that there were legitimate grievances not French inspired.

*sister**
Alleyne Fitzherbert, baron St. Helens (1753-1839), diplomat, had two sisters: Selena, m. Henry Gally-Knight, and Catherine, m. Richard Bateman.

*second**
Pitt's cabinet did not resign till March 1801.

dont much believe that this place, will be made any great point of by the french – it will cost them money to keep it, and unless they wish to send a great many of their unnecessary troops out of the country to prevent disturbances at home, I dont much see why they shoud wish for it exept with a future view of taking India from us – but they have plenty of work to do *nearer home* before they come to that – there is plainly *a fashion* in every thing in this world – the English mutiny of course has *sett the fashion here* and we have had a swinging mutiny of our own at Simmons* viz Falsebay – delegates from the malcontents at home came out, it appears in the Arniston; and working on the minds of the seamen who only knew the *progress* but *not* the *event* of the mutiny at the *Nore*, it broke out on board the admirals ship this day fortnight – he dined with us the day before, and we saw something after dinner made him uneasy – but Lord Augustas Fitzroy* who came from the Bay knew of nothing amiss; he was also of the party, they both left Cape Town next day, Stevens* having come from thence on the business, who by the bye had been turned out of the Tremendous by the crew, who have a particular dislike to both captains of that name, we know not with what justice – the admiral & Ld each went on board their ships, but found that the orders of the *Delegates* only were to be attended to till such time as certain grievances were redressd – mean time all the commanders *but* the Stevens's were treated with the usual respect *exept* in allowing them *no command* – this disgusted of them, and from (probably natural) feelings of injured pride they quitted their ships and declared them severally in a state of Rebellion – not so *Tod,** lately appointed to the Trusty, a man who has risen from a very low class of life by undisputed merit in his profession – he saw the thing as I cant help thinking) in a better point of view, & remaind on board his ship, watching I believe the moment when the lassitude which follows an intemperate exertion shoud render it possible to make a few of his men *listen to reason* – mean time the other captains were all on shore – a signal from the admirals ship to attend him *there*, carried them on board. – when there, the crew *kept all their prisoners* they fed them well to be sure – denied them no mark of attention *But* the terms they offerd for reconciliation were, that the two Stevens shoud be sent home to England to be tried for misconduct, that their grievances, which chiefly consisted in their allowances being unfairly withheld by the pursers from them, shoud be redressd & that a *general pardon* to Delegates & seamen alike shoud be granted, on these terms & none others they offerd to lay down their arms. – and these terms the admiral woud not listen to. – the delegates *must* he said be given up – & the Stevens's reinstated – mean time All was Hurry here, but without much allarm for the event, at a critical moment a danish ship arrived that brought very Happy accounts of all being at last arranged in England & the execution of the delegates & others of the party – nothing coud be more furtunate than this news. – some people feard that it might have a contrary effect, and render the crews desperate, already possessd of power to do allmost what they chose, but the event proved it to be different, & that the seamen *really* had some grievances to complain of, which coud they hope to find righted made them willing to shake hands

*Simmons**
i.e. Simon's Bay. Nine ships mutinied on Oct. 2nd 1797, and three more which came in from sea on the 24th. Admiral Pringle wished to adopt lenient measures but was later induced to be more severe. Several of the ringleaders were ultimately executed. See Theal. *History*, 1795-1872, v.l. 4th ed. p. 42-45; Clowes, W.L. *The Royal Navy*, v. 4, p. 179-80.

*Fitzroy**
Captain of the *Impérieuse.*

*Stevens**
George Hopewell Stephens, who was charged with oppressive conduct but discharged with honour by a court martial on 21st Nov.

*Tod**
Capt. Andrew Todd, formerly commander of *Sphinx.*

& be friends with their commanders tho the delegates had certainly intended the matter to go much farther. – I must hear introduce in jest a little anecdote of Genl Dundas, he left this place for Simmons Bay as quickly as the occasion demanded him, but no one coud get him convinced that the crews coud be so head strong & intemperate as he was told they were, particularly in the Tremenduous, which he was determined to go on board of – "it is only *talking them round calmly* said he, not minding their *nonsense* but arguing the matter *coolly* & *reasonably* with them" – some of his military friends smiled at the idea of his supposing himself more particularly qualified than some others, to *talk the mutiny over coolly*, and they fortunately persuaded him against going on board, else both admiral & commander in chief woud have been prisoners – mean time all proper steps were taken by the ordinance – Engineers &c to entrench the troops who marchd on to Simmons Bay, it coud have had but little effect I suppose considering what a mouthfull the works there woud have been to the guns of the Tremendous – at last the ferment flattend, and the admiral found it Best in order to finish the dangerous business to compromise the matter, the Stevens's to have a court martial on them here – the pursers to be tried & all grievances to be redressd – A general pardon to be granted – . this we all were sorry for, as the delegates (even the best natured people wishd,) to be made examples of to the navy, but the admiral is pretty firm & we suppose he found he coud not work the point *farther* than he *did*. – women may say any thing without presumption, how well I remember saying to the admiral that if I were *him* I shoud be greatly tempted to tell the Navy that tho I had received no official intelligence from England yet I was apt to believe that there were certain benefits to be bestowed on the seamen & that whatever they were I believd I might confidently assure them that they woud share in all such – a few exhilirating words such as these I foolishly thought might have been said without taking too much responsibility on himself, or Incurring disapprobation at home, but he seemd to think nothing shoud in publick departments be taken for *granted*, or *risqued* – he had no right *officially* to know or say anything. – of course he must be right as he is a clever man & knows his business, but how often have I not seen, (to use a vulgar provcb) "a stich in time, save nine" – I believe there was a judicious speech issued in publick orders to the army within these few days, which will have a good effect, they all *expect* I presume what is not however promised in it –

The Cape hangman

something is needed here to the poor Military for things still remains sadly dear, and I fear the dutch heads will contrive to keep them so by their manouvres, tho there is the prospect of a Harvest *plentyfull beyond* what *has been known* – owing to the immense quantity of rain which has lately fallen & swelld out the heads of the corn in a manner that Madam Nature is not accustomed to esperience, for this is a dry season in general. –

what will you say when I tell you that I am writing to you in bed – I had very near met with the ugly accident of being killd a few days ago – the servant had somehow been out of the way – the coachman got off the box open the carriage, I am allways a coward of Horses standing at their own discretion without a governor, cape Horses are not to be trusted – I calld to him to go to their heads, but they did not wait – off they sett round the circle, or parade in the garrison, as I coud not guess *where* they might land me, or whether they might not overturn me at a sharp angle in running to their stable – and as the door was open – and step down I was tempted to jump out & thank god as I felt ground – but I felt no more for some time – the carriage came round safe to the door galloping – but no Lady Anne – I was found in the middle of the circle laying on my back, my head cut and insensible – I recoverd myself however in a quarter of an hour – my sholdder and ancle were both bruised & my head had a considerable contusion on it, but the docter who by the bye is a right good man – (pattison) – said there was no fracture, so for any thing else theres no great matter, I have lain in bed these two days and am now going to rise, bones whole, take this However as an apology for all errors, which this letter may contain, what can be expected from a woman with a plaister on her pericraneum. –

what a bold South Easter we have had these tow days! how the wind raged & how a tall tree which is in the court yard before my windows Bent & tossd its great brances in at the casement, where the wind blew out a pane every half hour! – I shall see more of these winds I hear – how I long my dear friend for letters now to tell me how you all are, if safe and prosperous, or invaded by a foreign foe – I long also to know what is to become of us little mortals at the extreme point of Africa – the last month has sent in from the country quantitys of waggons chiefly loaded with wine – butter – skins – oranges – feathers grain are sometimes added as the farmer Happens to have them, – the waggons are very narrow, about the size of a large pipe of wine & long enough to hold 3 in length – this is drawn by 16 oxen and drove by one man, a Hottentot besides generally walking at the head of the first pair. to govern these they have whips of immense length w^c they lay on to produce no small effect, one lash is quite enough to sett all the team into motion – these animals are much larger than our general breed of bullocks in England – I made a tallish man try the height of one of them he guessd the team at 16 hands & a half the men that drive these are in proportion to their cattle of a very large & Robust Stature – but their countenances gentle & nothing rude or boisterous in their manners. – I long most ardently now to get up the country a little, I shall try hard for it whenever I am quite well which I expect will be in a day or two – I have two offers – the offer of good living – lodging – carriages, & civil hospitality from the Land Rost of Stellinbosh,* the governor of the district you know – & the offer of an empty house two beds & five chairs from the Fiscal who has a house in that village inhabited only by mice – of course by no means uninhabited by *Fleas* – the empty houses here being always richly stockd with that sort of Ferae naturae; I love liberty & believe I shall prefer the mice – fleas – a conjurer for my Cook, and the power of doing what I like to the good things the Landrost proffers me with the Hospitable attentions of his Wife & Daughters w^c I shall gladly accept of now & then – but not all day long – the brig which was sent round to Graff Renet* to meet Barrow is returnd, the first Lieut sleeps here & tells all he saw to my Lord and master but I Have not been stout enough to see him myself yet – he describes that part of the country as extremely

*Stellinbosch**
The Landdrost, i.e. magistrate, of Stellenbosch was Ryno Johannes van der Riet (1758-1828). He held office from 1795-1812.

*Renet**
This would mean to Algoa Bay, the principal natural harbour for the Graaff Reinet district.

cheap and extremely plentifull – one of the Bays (Musslebay)* he mentions, does not know of, or drink wine – pitchers of milk are put on table after dinner by way of beverage – there ought to be beautifull shepherdesses & true shepherds at that board, as it surely pourtraits the golden Age. – I wont write more nonsense – but send off my present quantity – I shall not have time to write to my sisters So pray have the goodness to let them know you have heard from me – all y^{r} friends here are well – one of the last times I was in company with Lord Macartney he *danced a reel remarkably well* to the *Scots bag pipe* with Lady Anne Dashwood Mrs Campbell and a Brigade Major – . – perhaps you think this is a *cross reading* or a puzzle or conundrum – but no such thing – it is *true*, he was in excellent spirits and paid a compliment to "*the Laddies ain piper*" and the reel of Tulloch,* w^{c} neither the general, nor the transported piper will soon forget – I dare not add what I believe is true too that I fear the little twinge in the toe next day whisperd to his Excellency that he had been rash – he is vastly well now – & I fancy there are many in this country who will wish for him again shoud they find the difference of French Masters. – kind love to Lady Jane & your Daughter & niece – there is a chance that this may be taken I hear, if it goes with the English ship talkd of, that being the case I shall conclude with that which I esteem my *highest title* – Your affect Friend –

*(Musslebay)**
Mossel Bay, in the Swellendam district, not Graaff Reinet.

*Tulloch**
One of the most characteristic Scottish reels. See Grove's *Dictionary of music*, 5th ed. v.7, p. 87.

Table Mountain, from Lady Anne's window in the Castle

Letter 13

Cape –
Octr 30 –
Monday – 1797

I wrote you a long letter my dearest friend by a danish ship that calld from this the 13. or 14th of this month, & made you an apology for its stupidity by telling you that having Jumpd out of the carriage the night before when the horses were galloping away (the coachman having left his box for a moment) I had sprained my ancle, – hurt my shoulder, & cut my head, and was at the moment I wrote to you in bed with a fine patch on it behind of the size of a crown piece – tho stunnd for ten minutes – no bad effects however took place *or are* to be feard as there is no fracture tho a narrow escape from one – the *world* fractured my skull, & lamented over me, but I am happy to tell you that I am still an inhabitant of Africa & hope to remain in this world for a good many years longer, if the maker of it pleases to permit – *you* can tell me as far as *Africa* goes, whether I am to be an Inhabitant much longer of *this* division of it – we expect news from England with *eager anxiety* – Lord M: not less anxious than the inferiors – he is very unwell at present – he never complains but Mr B. is sure he feels himself extremely indisposed: – on his leaving him tother day, as he was going out of the door he said in a mournfull voice – Mr B – and paused a little, I am very ill, I feel a complication of ailments oppressing me, Mr B. said he was very very sorry for it, but remarked that it was the body only as he was rigorous & clear as usual in the mind, he said he was so, but that Business was allmost too much for him and made him an apology for asking him to write some dispatches which he had meant to do himself, "I can depend on their being right said he if *you* do them, & that shoud their be any call for me to act when I am unequal to it that you will supply the Exigence as I myself woud". – this shewd a pleasant confidence in B. but he was vexed to hear him express this as it betrayd a despondency about himself which he had never before expressd – of course this is between *ourselves* – I hope it is but a fit of the gout hanging over him which sometimes (I have heard) affects the spirits till it fixes itself – you may easily suppose he is not *very* ill as he dines today with General Dundas – a Turtle feast, to which we are all going – but *where*, is the point I must make haste to come to, as I have but *ten minutes* to write this letter in, which goes by a whaler, and will reach England probably if not taken [,] sooner even than my last letter – I have desired him to throw this in the sea if he *is* taken so under the confidence of this, I go on to say that you will hear from Better Hands than mine that the mutiny here in the fleet, *was* after a weeks daring resistance *compromised* – a general pardon granted by the admiral – and the promise of a court martial on the officers who were complaind of. – all other grievances

Groot Constantia

to be redressd, but mean time he stipulated that the Stephen's the two officers complaind of (excellent men I am told) shoud go on board their ships & command there as usual [.] these terms I fancy woud *not* have been granted to the mutinists Had not the admiral been *prisoner* on board his own ship, & with him most of the other officers, who had gone on shore, & had a signal from the admiral to go on board of him – to hold a conference (Todd exepted, he as I mentiond in my last, never quitted his ship & was not therefore of the prisoner party with the admiral) – it was generally regreted that the ad: was obliged to give a general pardon as even the mildest people here wishd the delegates to have been made an Example of – the consequences of their escaping punishment has been seen since, as the Blew Jacket, (the sign of mutiny) has been hung up in two of the vessels from St Helena, the Raisonable & the Sphynx – but are now taken down tho a strong disposition appeared in the fleet to sett off anew; Subordination is by no means established – the ferment is working secretly still, and with a degree of Intrigue & plan in it that seems to originate from clevrer heads than those of the mere John Bulls who are only the Tools – the sailors come on shore in Numbers, partys of 12 at a time, they pillage the markets, get drunk – riot – & endeavour by every means to corrupt the army, – their Influence begun to be felt, and Genl Dundas wisely orderd the army to be *encampd* – this was done at 24 hours warning, & near Rondebosh* which is 6 miles distant from Green point where the sailors often land & four from the cape, he & Lord M: saw it indispensably necessary to break the dangerous friendship forming between the army and navy by this move; now the troops have something to *do* & that is in favour of the continuation of their loyal principles – all the garrison has marchd out but a company or two, so we are solitary enough, but have no fears, and the sentinels have orders to permit no sailor to pass into the castle – there was a great wine House there, where the sailors constantly resorted, the man & woman were sent off, on board of the Man ship* & six other wine houses, or punch houses as they call them, [were closed] up by government the evening before last – men tell wom[en] little Truth when their is real or supposed *danger* in question therefore I cant well quote any thing that I hear from masculine reports. – but I *fancy* that the ferment here will cease in a few days more, without further Harm, it has produced only the bad effect of forcing a measure (the encampment of the army) which I suppose must cost money –

our turtle today is one of three that have arrived by the last fleet here – I am delighted that we have not had one too – i go on with my monthly ball, & have had all the respectable dutch familys round in Turn to dinner, I believe I may tell you very Honestly that in our different departments Mr B: & I are very great favorites of the natives. – we are both very civil, and never despise any thing which I can perceive has been one great error in some of the English – I was askd at a Ball given at a dutch house on account of a wedding the day before yesterday – the partys, a Lady d'une certain age with 8 or 10,000 w^{c} is here a *rarity* the women having little money – the man Mr Bianki an italian who came out with Sir G: Elphinston* – they were half married the day of the Ball that is to say, for I know you are beginning to laugh, they went to be examined by the

*Rondebosh**
The Camp Ground, now Rondebosch Common, used by troops even before the British occupation.

*Man ship**
The *Manship*, East Indiaman, arrived 16/10/1797.

*Elphinston**
Vice-Admiral George Keith Elphinstone (1747-1823), created Baron Keith in March 1797, and Viscount in 1814. He was the naval commander of the expedition against the Cape in 1795. Nothing further is known of Mr. Bianchi.

notary – two or three weeks hence the ceremony takes place – was an exellent Ball – & voluminous supper – to be sure the dutch women dont flirt with the English officers!! – I say nothing – Mr Bianki – says his future is very ugly and old, but she is rich, sensible & good humoured & he'll contrive to be Happy enough – I mention this in case L[d] K: shoud like to know particulars – she is not a *favorable* likeness to Lady Grantham* – but has a resemblance – adieu mon cher ami – I *must* conclude send this to my sisters when you have read it – I write to them by the China fleet – love to L[y] J: & yr daughter & niece – all yr friends here are well – Sir. J: Craig &cc is arrived well at Bombay – it is thought he is not a likely man to live long in Indian climates, he is very fat & lives very high – perhaps you know that there are 7 provinces in China in a state of mutiny – the china ships bring this news – Barrow writes in raptures of Caffre Land & of the King a young man of 20 who is pleased with the visit & glad to treat on terms of friendship with us – God Bless you –

*Grantham**
"Lord K:" was presumably Lord Keith, just mentioned, whose first wife had died in 1789. Lady Grantham was Mary Jemima Grey Yorke, widow of the 2nd Baron Grantham (d. 1786). She was the second daughter and co-heir of the 2nd Earl of Hardwicke and hence sister-in-law to Lady Anne's youngest daughter Elizabeth. (See Letter 2 note 4.) Whatever the gossips may have had to say however, Keith did not marry her but Hester Maria, the daughter of the celebrated Mrs Hester Thrale, friend of Dr. Samuel Johnson, in 1808.

Dragoon stables at Rondebosch

Letter 14

Cape
Novr 29 – 1797 –

The last ships my dear friend has sailed without any letter from me to you. I had made myself sure of finding them *still here* on my return from the country where we have lately had the pleasure of spending a very interesting fortnight – it is the first time since we arrived, now seven months ago, that Mr B: has taken the indulgence of a little country air: I shoud hardly mention this as an indulgence granted to himself, he being *sent* to Stillingbosh by Lord Macartney to enforce the oath of allegiance* which has been constantly evaded by certain Mauvais Sujects who live there, in number about a dozen – Friday the 10th of this month being the last day granted as I believe by the 2^{d} proclamation, it was necessary for Mr B: to leave this the ninth, the very morning when the admiral gave his Ultimatum to those in mutiny on board his, and the other ships. – two hours was the time he allowed, for or by pulling down his flag to declare open rebellion on them. – this circumstance had been concealed from the *ladies* till we were a couple of miles out of town when Mr B. told us of it, and that the two hours were within ten minutes of being expired: I need not say how anxiously some of us stretched our throats out of the dutch cabriole we were in to look back on the Bay, where still – still as we lookd the admirals flag remaind, and a few minutes before the time was finally over, we heard a gun which led us to send back one of our servants to bring us the news, well authenticated in the evening. – we hope the Best, nor were we disappointed in the end, each ship coming to the resolution of sacrifising its ring leader, rather than being blown into the air by the artillery placed against it. 21 mistaken Fellows, blind agents of Blind agents of french miscreants were brought on shore all of them daring and fearless of the event, which is not as yet brought to its final issue* – as the little tour which this absence from the cape permitted us to make, is the first good opportunity I have as yet had of seeing the country and being able in any degree to form a Judgement of the *Real natives*, the people at the cape being scarcely to be named as such, I will in a short Journal of this period give my dear friend the account of things as they presented themselves to me, allways trusting that you will forgive ten thousand Inaccuracys & *Frivolitys* while I repeat matters that even at a distance you have a more just idea of I daresay from your better informations than any I can give you. –

our road from the cape to Stellingbosh was not distinguishd by much variety, we went by the Koyle*, a long sandy hill, having first passd the Salt riviere and that long tract of sandy common (if I may call it so) that bears many traces of having one or two hundred years ago been coverd by the sea,* but which is now only coverd scantily by Heaths, and such

*allegiance**
Lord Macartney's first proclamation requiring all heads of families to take the oath of allegiance to the King, was issued on 28/5/1797. This gave those living within 4 hours distance of the Castle until 16/6/1797, and those more distant, until 15/9/1797 to comply. His second proclamation, dated 28/6/1797, gave no extension of time but announced that those who had declined or neglected to take the oath would be deported to Batavia or other Dutch territory.

*issue**
Two mutineers were hanged on 23/11/1797 and another two on 24/12/1797. Three others were severely punished.

*Koyle**
The farm "De Kuylen" (the Pools) was the halfway house to Stellenbosch, now Kuilsrivier.

*sea,**
The Cape Flats.

The Drostdy, Stellenbosch

plants & brushwoods as partake a little of both Sea & Land, but as every plant, bush and tree in this country has its flower and fruit, at some season of the year, even in the barrenest soils there is novelty & entertainment to the eye which has never seen the thing before. – we passd a considerable number of waggons loaded with wine as is the case at this time of the year, each of them had 16 oxen to draw it, but were then without any, the cattle been turned to graze amidst the bushes, where it was lucky if they coud pick up any thing as these poor animals never taste food or drink from the time they enter the cape till they leave it which is often two days if the wine they have brought hapens not to be immediately disposed of. – certainly there must be somthing rich in the dry herbs of the soil here for the oxen are now as fat as they can be and yet I have no where seen the appearance of verdure, exept the verdure of green Barley or other corns, for there is no *grass* any-where – what they have to draw seems quite ludicrous behind 16 great beasts, simple one or two Leagars of wine, which I fancy does not amount to above three pipes, and which I shoud reckon four oxen quite equal to. – I have often wonderd why they dont sell a dozen of the 16 when they come to the cape and return with four but their Honor and respectability amongst each other (& this exists in a still greater degree amongst the Caffres) is to have an immense number of cattle. – the drivers are a race of men as large in proportion as their oxen, which is much above the size of the European breed, one man drives the whole, another taking care of the casks and being ready to assist in case of accident – I belive I have mentiond part of this before. – no matter – as we drove along, our only English dog who has survived the ailment which attacks all who arrive here, and who is a stout vulgar pointer called *Chops*, we saw pointing at something, running back to the carriage, returning and pointing again – Mr. B: said he had not his *usual manner* but a mixture of fear with his alacrity, he went with his gun, and found *Chops* pointing at a Serpent of between five and six feet long. – Mr B: killd it with his whip, and I have kept his skin. –

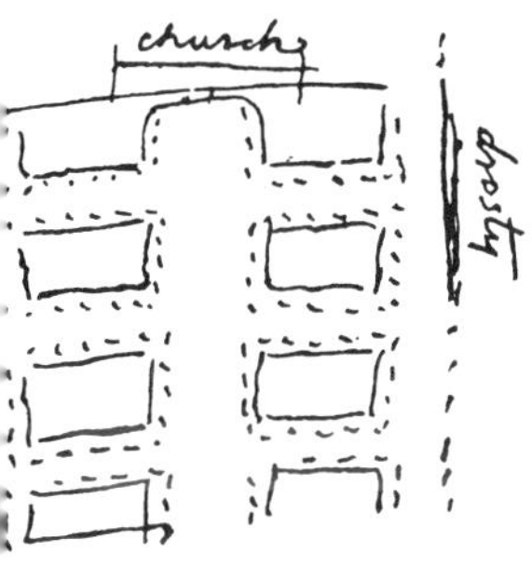

The Landrost of Stillingbosh had pressd us to come to his house, he has two pretty daughters and a good humoured wife, but as the Ladys coud neither Spraken English nor french, and as we have never before found any necessity of speaking dutch consequently are too ignorant of it, I preferrd accepting of the empty house of the Fiscals in the same village where I thought we shoud be more at liberty, and give less trouble; consenting however to dine with them every day and to accept of their carriage and Horses together with the most illustrious Coach-man of the old governor Zluiskin* now theirs, to drive us to all curious sights near or at a distance. – we arrived in time to dinner, and had a plantyfull one, really good, tho in the dutch stile; the Drosty or Land-rosts house* is more spacious than any other I have been in here, having a sort of second row of rooms behind the first, but the division of every dutch house in the Colony *is the same*. – A Hall – a square room on each hand & another family eating room behind, with two bed chambers – before his door there is the only two fine oaks I have seen exept the others in the village they measure 18 feet round each but the perfection of this place consists in its extreme coolness in the midst of

**Zluiskin*
Abraham Josias Sluysken, governor 2/9/1793-16/9/1795, when he capitulated to the British.

**house*
The Stellenbosch Drostdy, completed in 1687, stood in Dorp St. at the end of Drostdy St. The foundations and walls are incorporated in the present Theological Seminary. (Fransen & Cook. *The old houses of the Cape*, p.45.)

Ryno Johannes van der Riet, Landdrost of Stellenbosch

the most sultry weather, it is built in this form – perfectly regular, each street having on each side a row of large oaks which shadow the tops of the Houses keeping them cool and forming a shady avenue between thro which the sun cannot pierce, whichever way one walks one finds an avenue, right or left, each house has a good garden, Stillingbosh therefore tho there may not be above 100 familys in it covers a good deal of ground, and is so perfectly clean & well built that it appears to be inhabited only by people of small fortunes, but I am told there are many very poor people in it, without means of having become richer, during the dutch government no manufacture was permitted there and any person endeavoring to gain a livelyhood by such means woud have been severely punishd – from this cause the place has few young people in it, it seems rather an Asylum for Old age than anything else, and I am told, people live longer in it than in any other part of the colony. – at the Fiscals we found a small clean house on the same little plan with the rest, kept by a black woman wife to the Landrosts wachman, she keeping in her turn a slave, who was mother of 8 little naked mice that run about the garden and offices as they came into the world "without being ashamed" –

we had a very good bed, partaking however of the error of the country that to be cool a bed shoud be made of the finest feathers, instead of which a matress of hair pretty Hard and coverd with leather is the real Luxury. – next morning being friday I thought I woud take a peep at the Drosty and at the ill affected faces that were to come to take the oath, as I walkd thro one of the avenues I was pleasd with the singular appearance of innumerable quantitys of birds nests hanging suspended from every bough, built thus with a hole at the bottom for the birds to enter by, instinct instructs them to form them so to avoid weasels, monkeys & serpents who woud otherwise devour the young, the Husband bird, builds the nest, and it often Happens if he is awkward that the wife is so much displeasd with it that she tears it in pieces and he has to begin again – *

out of 12 gentlemen who meant to evade swearing allegiance, 8 had now taken the oath and were gone, the others had made various *excuses* and had *not* appeard at all – this being the *case* it only remaind for Mr B: to give orders for them to be laid hold of, but he thought the more moderate way better, of giving them still two days more, and going back to the cape to receive Lord M[s]: further orders, he concluded however that he shoud find it necessary to appoint a party of soldiers to be in the neighbourhood on Saturday evening, and to have very express orders sent to the partys to enforce their attendance on Sunday morning. – I amused myself this Day by taking a view of the Drosty and of the village from one of the hills, it is only done in lead pencil, but is exactly the place, the valley there, tho not extensive is rich, fertile was it well cultivated, but the farmers are bad ones – I cannot help thinking that wherever a soil is stony as it often is here, that dibbling as they do in Norfolk woud be a good plan: – wine is the chief produce of the lands thereabouts, and a small piece of ground only being necessary to make a great deal of wine the rest of Mother Earth lays barren & neglected – 1000 vines make a Leagar of wine, and it con-

*again**
Probably the Cape weaver, *Ploceus capensis*.

Kerkstraat, Stellenbosch

tains 8 times 80 gallons – the vines are planted in rows and there seems to me to be about 4 feet between vine & vine – but to what an extent the cultivation of vine might be brought here if the farmers were sure of a good market! at present there is one thing greatly against the improvement of the vine by any better modes than what are used, viz that wine from the country is bought by the merchant in town at the market price without any reference to superiority or inferiority of quality, they dont give themselves the trouble to taste it & sell it off in the same careless way they buy it. – I never saw the force of prejudice more apparent than in the way our countrymen turn up their foolish noses at the Cape wines, because they are Cape vines. – they will drink nothing here but port, claret or madeira, pretending that the wines of the country give them *bowel akes*. – it may be so if they drink two or three bottles at a time and that very frequently, but it will not do so if used in moderation – Mr B; drinks nothing else himself, tho we have every other good wine at table champaign and Burgundy excepted – I must tell you (an episode) of what happend yesterday after dinner – we had a little hock on board of ship two bottles of which remained, and we keep them for Lord Macartney when he is ill and wishes for a bon bouche as they happen to be very fine. – after dinner I found myself drinking up one of the bottles of hock and said to Mr B, "O Fye why do you give us this today, it is some of our fine hock" a certain Lieut Col who shall be nameless, on this filled his glass, "Lord Bless me what fine wine this is, said he, I have not tasted a glass such as this since I came here" – I found on asking that it was Stejne wine which Mr B. had not liked and orderd for common use in the family – in a moment the Col found out 50 faults with it –

on Saturday evening Mr B, returnd with powers from Lord M: to do as he saw best on the spot, and next morning our Jacobins arrived; stout, sulky, democratic fellows, who with wives and children prefered refusing the oath of allegiance and going to Batavia of course, to swearing to be honest & quiet members of the community, taking up no arms against us. – there was now nothing further to be done, the Landrost and Mr B: had argued with them till both were worn out with vexation and fatigue – the dragoons then appeard, and the five men escorted by them were carried prisoners to the cape, fully expecting, as a dutch servant of ours told me who stood by them, to be sett at Liberty on arriving there, and the matter to blow over – the villagers in general disapproved of their conduct & the Lady Landrost with tears in her eyes, said "How can you justify yourselves to your wives and children for this" – but their reason was plain, fully persuaded that the government of this place will not remain in the hands of the English, they are taking grounds to be *great men* when the french get possession of it, but they may reckon without their host if they think the french are bound by any tye exept what they suppose for their own Interest, – we went to church here, tho we understood not a word of the language; – what amazing people for fat some of those good people are! a tendency to dropsy at the same time perhaps increases it, but after 30 it is rare to see a woman in the 2[d] Class of life particularly weighing less than from 12 to 15 stone. – the clergymans wife, talking

"Sketch of the Hottentot mountains as they appear from the camp at Meusenberg" i.e. the Hottentots-Holland Mountains. (Enclosure in Letter 14)

of the numbers of children christend in the parish told me that the Sunday before this, there had been 12 children and only five mothers to those 12 – two of the mothers had 3 each, and three others 2 each. – I thought Madam said I, that twins even, had been rare in this country – "O no Madam, I had two myself but four months ago" – these prolific mothers came from Overbergh*, behind those mountains all sorts of good things are, as I hear to be found. – I wonder the dutch allowed such a race to live, they being equally against population and Cultivation. – I believe it is a bit of a reflection on people here to have no family, one or two dutchmen on hearing us say we had none, replied Oh Miserable! Miserable! in such a dolefull tone that I believe I shall give myself credit for half a dozen left at school for the future; –

on monday Mr B. returned to the Cape for a day and Anne Barnard and I took the opportunity of going into Hotentot Holland to see a famous pass in the mountains called Hotentots Cloof which one of our English magazines pencil tremendous.* – the day was cold (indeed as yet we have had no heat to complain of) but it was better so than if it had scorchd us, but still – still the same want of cultivation appeard, with a soil, which as far as my poor share of farming knowledge goes woud be equal to any fair crop that coud be required from it, but why raise grain unless there is a market for it? – I was sorry to find the season of flowers over, the spring here is a short one and the flowers are soon dried up and witherd by the summers sun. – I dug up a few bulbs which I send Lady Jane, I know not if they are curious, but the color was bright and handsome, and have accompanied them with a few seeds

which I cannot vouch for, exept that the seed is good, for tho the flowers do not change their classes, they change their colors, and what was scarlet last year may be yellow blue or white this. – the *green* flower struck me as being singularly genteel. I shall endeavor to get the finest plants of the sort for her but mean time she shall have part of what I have procured with my love and must be godmother to the flower which I have called the Lady Jane – my unlucky sprained ancle prevented me from getting out myself during the best season for taking up the roots. – I have also got a rose tree which bears seven different kinds of roses, and blows every day at 4 oclock – the cook ought to have it instead of a watch to regulate his dinner, but as we are now folks who dine at *two* it coud not be of the proper use. – N:B. this is a young plant, and as I have not *seen* its *scavoir faire*, I do not vouch for this. – but I have got something for you which I *do* vouch for because I have seen them used, Mr B. proposed writing to you and sending them himself, but for fear he shoud not think them worthy of your notice I will. – it is a specimen of the vegetable wax made into a candle *chez moi*, extracted from the berry of a plant I mean to procure, and a specimen of sirrup made from the blossoms of the sugar tree, the seeds of which I shall also send you whenever I get good ones; this last (woud it grow in sufficient quantity in England) – might render Jamaica* allmost unnecessary. – but to return to my little tour – Hotentot Holland we found totally uninhabited by *Hotentots*, they poor things having been driven up the country by their avaricious masters – and nothing can better prove the grasping Hope of each Individual to possess him-

*Overbergh**
The district lying beyond the Hottentots Holland Mts.

*tremendous**
Hottentots Holland Kloof was the old name for Sir Lowry's Pass which crosses the Mountains east of False Bay. Lady A. was probably referring to the engraving which appeared in the *European magazine*, v. 29, facing p.82, Feb. 1798, entitled "A west view of the famous Pass near the Cape of Good Hope, called Hottentot Hollands Kloffe"'

*Jamaica**
i.e. rum.

self of large domains, than the distance at which the settlers have placed themselves from each other; instead of placing their houses within the vicinity of rational society, the farmer has only thought of keeping himself as little circumscribed as possible and as far away as he coud from the Landrosts eye – the consequence of this has been, that whenever familys have settled wide from each other, there has been but a poor increase of them, whereas, in places where they have been more confined there is ten times the increase, as in Graffe Renett. – 25 years ago there was 100 familys in that district, they were not permitted to emigrate beyond a certain distance and are now 800 – . I think in Hotentot Holland there seemd to be a house and farm every mile, or mile and half – but no Hamlet – no village – as the land is cultivated by slaves, and as they are the property of the master, his house has generally a slave house belonging to it, which is in place of that Happier cottage where each European man, has his wife, his child, his pig, and his cat or dog, as great within its four walls as any Emperor within his pallace; – and till we see Hamlets raising up their Humble heads, and the artificer receiving his shilling or two a day for his work, and spending it as he pleases, unlashd by any ratan* or any chastisement but his wifes tongue if he has spent too much of it in porter, we will not see this a flourishing country, at present, unwilling Drudgery, toils unthankd, for Indolent apathy! – the 2[d] house in Hottentot Holland was purchased lately by a Mr Thibaud a french man, one of Morons people* I believe he is supposed to have a hankering after the doctrines of that nation, it is situated near a lake, and that lake is within a mile of Modergat Bay*, I mention it particularly as the lake is famous for a fish called *the Springer,** the very best fish I ever tasted in all my life, any where, the most delicate and the fattest, we are in negociation to procure its breed, and its spawn, I shoud be delighted were the great events of his Majesty's reign to have added to the list of occurences the acquisition of "that charming fish the Springer introduced into this country by the wife of secretary Barnard" – it weighs about 3 or 4 pounds but *fancy* cannot paint how good it is, it is *the Fish* only that coud convince you. – I found the horrors of the cloof like most other things repeated by those who love to astonish others very much exagerated. – it is to be sure a very narrow steep road cut from the side of a mountain, but I do not think it *more* terrible than penman Mewre* in Wales, this last is rather the more frightfull of the two in my opinion as the sea rolls below the rock, but the other may be the more dangerous on account of the badness of the road in ascending, and there is no wall or guard to prevent one from tumbling down the precipice shoud an accident Happen – as I saw this object of fear grow less and less the nearer I approachd to it, I stopd to take my sketch of it at some little distance, in this I hear I was wrong as it appears the most terrible when on it.

– on t'other side of the mountain there grows a profusion ~~of~~ what is calld *everlasting flowers,** some of which I shall send to Lady Jane, the white remain for ever the same, the red ones are the most curious, being as bright as if made of red foils, but the foolish flowers after being pluck'd instead of remaining as they were or withering, spread from bud to flower, shed bad seed and fall to pieces, I must try to *Kill* them by

*ratan**
Ratan or rattan – a climbing palm growing chiefly in the E. Indies but also at the Cape. It is used as a switch.

*people**
The Regiment de Meuron, raised for the Dutch E.I. Co. by the Swiss Comte Charles de Meuron in 1781, is clearly referred to. It landed at the Cape in Jan. 1783 and remained until 1788. The Regiment transferred its allegiance to the British in 1795 in Ceylon. (Theal. *History* v. 3 p.207, 238). Louis Michel Thibault, the Cape architect, came out as a lieutenant in this regiment, but the Thibaud here named can scarcely have been he as he was fully occupied in town and furthermore Lady A. always spelt his name correctly.

*Bay**
In the neighbourhood of the present Firgrove, east of Eerste Rivier.

*Springer**
Mullet or Harder (family *Mugilidae*), often seen in estuaries. The lake referred to was probably a lagoon in the Gordon's Bay neighbourhood.

*Mewre**
Penmaenmawr, the northern end of the Snowdon Range, Carnarvonshire.

*flowers,**
Certain species of Helichrysum and Helipterum. Their brittle petals retain their colour up to seven years.

some preparation *after* they are *Kilt.* – next day Mr B: returnd from the cape. – our dutch friends safe lodged in the castle till a ship is ready to take them to Batavia, silly, bold, foolish people! No African was ever known to live there, Europeans sometimes do, tho rarely, what a pity that so fine a town and country shoud have so shocking a climate!

we now arranged another party which promised to be still pleasenter, viz to the Paarls a village at the bottom of mountains so called from two*enormous stones being at the top of them of a size so immense that it took a friend of mine half an hour to walk round one of them, they are however each entire stones, somewhat shaped like imperfect pearls, and awefull from gigantic an[d] unique singularity, they are of granite & one of them is Hollow, it is supposed it coud contain 20,000 men, but this must be nonsense, let us call it *one* thousand and then I shall have a better chance of being believed . the valley beneath is rich, fertile and pretty, being tolerably wooded, waterd by the Bergh-river and coud produce any thing & every thing was it tryed – almonds – walnuts and oranges grow in plenty but wine is also the chief article here. – the paint stone* is found in this neighbourhood in quantitys, viz an impalpable powder which mixed with oil serves the country people with color to paint their waggons, houses &c, this powder is contained within stones of different sizes, and on breaking them the powder comes forth ground as fine as, if it had been done in bond street. – it is found of all colors but green. – we dined with a civil, hospitable Dutch man of the name of Alling*, the clergyman of the place and the largest man of height and breath I ever saw in my life, and went on to Waggon makers Valley* which is reckoned one of the finest countrys of the cape – but here, or rather on the road here, I still found the same want of trees. – still noble mountains – fine soil – but the Human face wanting – we passd a river by a rope & kind of Ferry boat which two men contrived to be the means of towing us over at twice, the contents of the Landrosts waggon going first, viz himself, his wife 3 daughters, a slave Anne and me, the coachman waggon and eight horses following, which eight horses in hand he drove with as much facility as he woud have drove two. – we meant to sleep at the house of Myn Heer Wygg,* which is here pronounced *Veh*, we were received at the door of a very respectable looking English farm house by the good people themselves, He was an old soldier with the great King of prussia and has therefore a little more of the world about him than most of the other peasants have, his wife is a Hale oldish woman full of Hospitable frankness, but as to size and appearance, suppose John Byng my friend near six feet high and married to Sir Horace Mann* seven feet high and rather more masculine and then you have both husband and wife – what a Happy man Lord Monboddo* woud be in this country! how it woud corroborate all his Doctrines that were we as nature meant us to be, no Luxury to ennervate, that we shoud be seven feet at least, or more. – certainly Myfrow Veh fell nothing short in her way of Mynheer Alling, and several dutch neighbours who came there partly from curiosity and partly to pay their respects to their Landrost were equal to the others – we found here what is universal in this country – a constant drinking of coffee going forwards – it is to be found boiling on

*two**
There are actually three rocks at Paarl, the Paarl Rock itself (1783 ft.), and 100 yds away, the Bretagneklip and Gordon's Rock (2, 146 ft).

*stone**
Yellow and red ochre are found in the Southern Cape.

*Alling**
Ds. Robert Nicolaus Aling (1751-1800), at Paarl from 1784 till his death.

*Valley**
Now Wellington.

*Wygg**
Benjamin Gottlieb Weigt, arrived 1772 and died 1814. (Hoge. *Personalia of Germans at the Cape*, p. 452.)

*Mann**
The Hon. John Byng (1740-1813), briefly 5th Viscount Torrington (See Letter 31). Sir Horace Mann, 1st Bart. (1701-86) who was British envoy to Florence.

*Monboddo**
James Burnett, Lord Monboddo (1714-1799), Scottish judge, but chiefly famed for his then advanced ideas on anthropology. He studied man as one of the animals and savage tribes for the light they might throw on the history and problems of civilisation.

the table over charcoal all day long – wine handed about half a dozen times in the course of the evening, pipes filled and smoaked by the gentlemen, and the room filld with slaves – a dozen at least. – here they were particularly clean and neat, Myfrow sat like charity tormented by a Legion of devils, with a black babie in her arms, one on each knee and three or four larger ones round her, smiling Benign on the little mortals who seemd very sweet creatures and develish only in their Hue – she and her husband having (for a wonder) no children of their own, they mean to leave their slaves free and to give amongst them all their fortune, of course, these people are likely to be well served for life –

we walkd in an orange grove he had planted himself about 18 years ago & which is now extremely beneficial being loaded with fruit, the trees are above 30 feet high and some of them are nearly as thick of oranges as of leaves – he had sent 27 waggons to the cape loaded with oranges, in each waggon six thousand & he had as many more to send, when the market is little stockd these are sold for two and *even three* rix dollars a hundred, formerly they were but one rix dollar the average price now, is about two, which is nearly 8sh: pr hundred – not very cheap you will say – Mr B. pointed out to the master several articles he might cultivate with great advantage on the warm side of these shelterd mountains, cotton particularly – coffee rice &cc he meant it he said and knew that it woud answer, as to rice they gave us some to supper much better than any of the Indian rice I have seen as it was free from the musty taste the last has. – we had for supper, a cape Ham, fat enough but it was fat hurried on a lean pig; – a bucks hind quarters served up as you woud serve a child going to be whipd – it was well larded and good – two fat ducks, a fowl done with currie – rice well boiled – fine pease – stewed beans – cabbage, pottatoes, sallad with two dozen of hard eggs for garnish, and a dish of egg puddings which seemd rather too greasy for me to attack them. – we had pastry and fruit after as is the custom here – plenty of strawberrys of the wood sort, but I do not think a strawberry is a strawberry without sugar and cream – we here found the misfortune of the very scanty accomodation the cape people have for friends at their houses, as with every possible exertion there was only *one* room for the Landrost, his wife and 3 daughters, and another for Mr B. and me and anne. – N B. I must here sett your mind at rest tho we had but one room, we really had two beds, matters were not so bad as to one only for all *three*. – above annes in the corner, there was a large opening in the roof I begun to congratulate her on its being a trap door and that we shoud see half a dozen dutchmen swinging her up to the regions above before morning, but we were mistaken, the only Harvest drawn up by this trou in the roof is grain, or stores, the upper part of the House being used only as a loft or store room, the dutch having no idea of converting it (a few people in the cape exepted) into any accomodation for their family use – indeed they woud not believe it was *possible* to do so in waggon makers valley; –

next morning we were up betimes, and the first thing we were offerd, was coffee again – a second time also – I feared there was to be no other breakfast but I soon saw a plentyfull one of more coffee, tea butter hard eggs and meat, this over we went to pay a visit to Myfrows brother Mynheer Latigaa,* this was by much the best planted and romantic situation I had seen, I only regreted that I coud not ask the Landrost to stop his Waggon for me to take some views of it, but we had much to do that day without the stop I shoud have produced. – I never saw so fine or so thick an *Oak hedge* as there, I am told that an oak is almost at its growth in this country in 25 or thirty years & that its wood is inferior to the European oak in consequence, I dont believe it is – many things are taken *for granted*, few people give themselves the trouble to make experiments, the firr was reckoned unfit to repair the wharf till necessity forced its use and it has proved superiorly good in its quality – as for an orange grove, that at Mynheer Latigaas exceeded, or at least came up to anything my Imagination had formed as Luxuriant. – Mr B. and I measured some of the trees, and found them nine feet round, and were told they were between 50 and 60 feet high, some of the branches were loaded with fruit in clusters as our plumb trees sometimes are, with 40 or 50 great oranges that were as sweet and good as they looked Handsome; little vandeRiet the Landrosts youngest daughter seemed rather too busy amongst them, I feard she woud do herself harm, "o no, she said, she had only eat eleven" – of course you will easily believe there were a few *gripes* the day after – we went thro this gentlemans wine house, and bespoke some excellent wine, some of which I hope we shall drink together in London if we can make them leave out their Sulpher this year we will, to me it is not a great fault as it gives a clean sharpness to the taste, which I dont dislike but it makes Traitors of the wines – it makes them Betray their *Country* which is against themselves from the reason I have before mentioned, prejudice

– we found Mynheer Latigaa still taller than his sister Sir Horace, but lean, and his wife broad enough to have made half a dozen wives. – he was making an experiment from which I have good hopes of getting a Liqueur nice and new for you, extracting brandy from the sweetest ripe oranges. – I think it will answer. – nous verrons. – after strolling about an hour we returned to *Vehs* where we dined and proceeded back to the Paarl, where Mr B. and I remained all night with the Allings that I might early next morning go up the mountain and take a view from it, and another of the great stones which as yet I had only seen at a distance, the rest of the party returned to Stillingbosh, and next morning we appointed the landrosts lightest equipage (a second hand carriage from England) to Clapmutch,* a military post half way back to meet us, intending to ride there – the evening woud have been a long one had not this dutch conversation with Mynheer Alling been worth many lessons to Mr B. who I was charmed to find coud make himself so well understood by the Honest Clergyman that it was 12 oclock before they separated about 3 hours later than their family hour, however it was his own choice, for the benefit of having a little conversation with a well bred, well informed civil Englishman which I fancy is a being the dutch do not very often meet with, the military quarterd amongst them having much too contemptuous a way of treating them, indeed I often hear things said of themselves, before themselves, which nothing coud prevent a gentlemans taking notice of, but a supposed ignorance of the

*Latigaa**
Lategan or Lategaan.

*Clapmutch**
Klapmuts, about 25 m. from Cape Town.

English Language which however they often understand enough of to *resent deeply* tho they say nothing. – this man Alling is a singular compound of learning and ignorance in my opinion, curiosity and Incredulity – he has a good deal of science such as books without the intercourse of conversation upon them can give, but some of the simplest things in life are new to him if he has not read of them. – he askd Mr B. many questions respecting the dutch and supposing there was a general peace what woud be ceded to us *by* them, what ceded by us *to* them and the french, he particularised a variety of dutch and french possessions as far as I coud understand him, to which Mr B. constantly replied, "we have *that*, at present – we took that, at such a time" – he seemd astonishd and coud scarce believe we had all, Mr B. advanced – at last, "St domingo said he – Sellon* – ". we took both of these places & have them now replied Mr B: "what! Sellon cried the other half angry – you are certainly mistaken – Non non cest un peu fort! – in dutch – . I wonder how he coud be ignorant of this! on the other hand he is full of intelligence on naturall productions of the country – minerals, Fossils, has a good museum of value stockd with many curious things, in particular a fine collection of the Horns of African animals some of which he made me take drawings of – I took a sketch of himself too which he sat for – as like as possible, but I dare not shew them at the same time time to any of my English friends here, they sett up such a *Halloo* and make such game of it. – Mr Barrow was with him some months ago and he gave him a considerable collection of minerals and much usefull information of the country. – I often wish when I hear any thing new, curious, or usefull, that I coud divest myself of that portion of false shame which prevents me from taking out a memorandum book and marking it down while I remember the particulars which afterwards escape my memory and the thing sinks into oblivion – but for a woman, being ill informed on most subjects, I might have said *All* subjects, to give herself the *air* of wisdom, while she knows how superficial she is, by marking down any thing that passes in company, I cannot endure it! it is wilfully drawing on a pair of blew stockings she has no right to wear – in this I often put myself in mind of what an old friend used to say to us when children at her feasts "My dears, eat as much as you *can*, but pocket nothing" – was I a *man* I woud pocket without shame, it becomes at sometime or another usefull to him, and teaches the mind the good habit of reflecting on what it hears. – unfortunately for us, next morning was so very – very bad a day, raining so Heavily, that it was impossible to stir out, which was a sad disappointment to me, the only good this rain produced, for every thing has its fair, as well as foul side, was self congratulation to the farmers, who now ventured to calculate on the richest Harvest, this only, being necessary to ensure one, it had another good effect, it swelld a cascade of 100 feet high which we had meant to have gone to see, with such a volume of water, that at the distance of some miles it was so evident as to render no nearer inspection necessary –

it did not clear up till the middle of the day and then, I durst not spend two or three hours in Drawing as the carriage & Horses were waiting for us, I deferrd taking these views therefore till we coud

*Sellon**
Ceylon was captured by the British in 1795-96.

Ds. Robert Nicolaus Aling of Paarl

Benjamin Gottlieb Weigt of Waggonmakers' Valley

Stellenbosch from the west

pay another visit to Mr Alling who we were informed woud accept of no money for his hospitality, which we therefore coud only repay by six dozen of English porter since gone to him – we left him and his wife promising to return and proceeded on horseback sending on our servant before to have the carriage ready – in this situation cantering along Mr B. fell in love with a horse which a slave rode without shoes or stockings – he described his master to live across the fields at a certain farm; – to it we scamperd with the confidence of honest people who suppose no harm is to happen to them tho in Africa and under the guidance of a black man and a stranger – nor did any harm happen; we reachd the farm house where I found a bundle of Hearty Hospitable Yonge frows who seemd delighted with my visit and begd us to stay all night with them. – but the horse was too dear, £60 – the carriage now reachd us and into it we stepd, not without being considerably amused to find that it was an ancient Vis a vis of Old Q^s:,* which I well knew again and which has still his coronet upon it. – it served our turn however very well while we skirted the lowring mountains which rose above our heads in all sorts of extraordinary shapes which constitutes their beauty to me. – but how out of all calculation it seemd to us, that we shoud be driving together amongst the hills in Africa in Old Q^s: vis a vis with 6 horses *in hand*, for the landrosts carriage being light had *only* that number for which *he* made us an *apology* – woud the St James Street people believe that a Hotentot driver shoud be able to guide 6 or 8 horses better than they do two? – no – we reachd home safely, Mr B. off again to the cape next day and returning the day after to accompany us to the valley of Drakenstein which is reckond one of the richest in the whole country – we went by that mountain calld Simons bergh with its high forked top, where an adventurer some years ago pretended he had found a mine – melting down a quantity of spanish dollars into a mass mixed with a certain quantity of rubbish, to take in the dutch East india company who paid him Down a large sum of money to furnish him with the means of returning them a larger, in the mean time they converted the mass of silver into a chain to suspend the keys of the Castle gates as a proof of their riches where it *still* remains, tho now a proof of their folly, as the man never found the mine nor they the money they had lent him to search for more – we found the road thro the valley of Drakenstein in many places so very bad that we trembled for the Fiscals Cabriole in which we were on that occasion with the Landrost – but we got thro it safe – the finest mountain that fancy can form is to the left of this road; Had poor Burke,* who I fear is no more, seen it, he woud have said, that when found, the Almighty had *Riven* it in two, to divide between his countrys, but had stoped in the intention when half executed – I do not think it is the simons berg which I allude to but another mountain whose name I have not yet obtaind* – this valley is without doubt the richest land and the best in the country – some bulbs that I have pulld up came with a fat soil round them which coud have raised better things had it been put to good account – it is plentyfully waterd by streams that are never dry – it was extraordinary to us however, that in all our progress we had neither seen buck Hare or partridge – there is plenty of game I am told 100

*Qs**
A vis-à-vis was a light carriage for two persons sitting face to face. 'Old Q' was the nickname given to the dissolute 4th Duke of Queensberry (1724-1810) in his later years.

*Burke**
Edmund Burke, the great statesman, died on 9-7-1797.

*obtained**
Lady A. would appear to have been right after all and the Simonsberg the mountain she described.

miles or more up the country but as far as *we* have seen of it nothing to be compared to England – game however there must be, from the quantity we receive from our friends – we dined at Herolds farm,* a plain peasant with a large family of children as they all have, I liked to see the ducks and chickens walk about in the room as if part of the company and with pleasure observed two or three swallows nests in the corners of the room which I imagine it woud be deemed unlucky to pull down else their love of proprieté woud make them do so – there were two pretty daughters who will be so for a year or two more, but then, one of the chief features of beauty allmost invariably begins to go – the front teeth which are rarely possessd by the women after 30 – smoaking saves the mens, but it leaves them black – I am quite delighted to find that their pipes are no longer offensive to me, I even begin to like the smell of the Tobacco and to wish that when I sent away all the little furniture from this to the government house to his Excellency who, poor man had none, that I had received a few of the *Jars* which they use on these occasions

– Jesting apart, we have not yet had any smoaking in this house, but I see it must be such a want to a dutchman when he has not his pipe after dinner that we are going to provide ourselves with some for them – I was pleased with the reception of the Herolds, indeed I have met with in all the people I have seen on this little tour an open frankness that gave one a share of what they had, apart as I believe from any views beyond the pleasure of bestowing. – I think the peasantry of the country as far as I have seen or heard of them a better characterd race than the people of the cape – viz Cape Town – the first are plain unletterd folks, without emulation and without ambition, the others are greedy and jealous of each other but along with this they are equally void of emulation, or of any ambition beyond that of gaining a livelyhood out of the chances that arrive, no man having any fixed calling, but living by his wits and by the purchase of such articles as can be kept up and sold out or bartered to advantage at a future time – their plans therefore and turn of mind is on a very contracted scale, the first men remind me of the 2[d] or 3[d] class of mercantile life in England, this accompanied with a degree of pride above acknowledging what necessity forces the individual to do, forms an awkward and inconsistent manner – . I have not seen in any man or woman of this country one sparkle of what I coud suppose genius, or of any ability towards any thing which shoud make one regret that improvement from education shoud have been wanting – the Fiscal is the pleasantest, and I fancy the best informd and laborious man in the place. – his size is immense for his age which is only 32, but he is not Lazy, & has a more gentlemanlike turn of mind and a better fund of conversation than the others – I like the Landrost of Stillingbosh his brother in law, very well too, because he has been kind to us, (N:B. they all come to pay us a family visit soon) but he is dull, he does not, to quote some lines on Wolfe* "put so much of the heart into his acts, that all must follow that which all approves" – I believe we have been of some use to him on shewing him more of his district than he ever saw before, as civility to us, has carried him farther than curiosity ever did before, but as he has been Landrost only two years, he has probably had as yet, but little time to go about, it is a situation of

*farm**
Probably Rust-en-Vrede, Simondium, acquired by Willem Herold, former sick-comforter at the Cape and builder of Grosvenor House, Stellenbosch, in 1796. (Fransen & Cook. *The old houses of the Cape*, p. 127.)

*Wolfe**
Presumably Maj.-Gen. James Wolfe (1727-59), victor over the French in Canada, 1759.

considerable business, one day with another bringing him on an average not fewer than 50 people, or 50 differences of some sort to settle – but when the landrost is a sensible honest man how much better is not this than to have a breed of lawyers in the country! – tho the partys shoud come at the most inconvenient times, as they often have to come far, he does not keep any one a moment waiting but leaves his dinner scarce touchd to discuss the affair. – an instance of this I shall particularize because it will make you smile. –

he was called away the beginning of dinner to talk to an old man and old woman who had come together, they detaind him long. – at last when he returnd he told us it was an affair of jealousy, founded on what often takes place in this country the partiality of the master to one of his black slaves, that all was amically settled as he had consented to *sell* the *object* of contention. – he had not had two mouth fulls when another message came from the Husband, that there being a sale in Hottentot Holland *next day*, he begd leave to sell her then. – the Landrost gave permission, thinking his hurry a proof that he knew his own weakness and was resolved to put future error out of his power. – two more mouth fulls were not swallowed, when the wife came back. – "come, said I, Ill lay a Rupee on old Sarahs head, that she means to be generous, and since her husband is ready to sell the Bond woman to satisfy her, that she is now willing to let her and Ishmael remain – the gentlemen shook their heads, but no one took my bett as the appearance was in my favour; – at last the Landrost returnd and we eagerly inquired the old ladys business – "only to persuade me to give her leave to *Whip* Hagar said he before she is sold. –" "Oh D-n her cried Mr B: "Amen,' said I – but I hope you did not consent? " "no no said he, I thought the concession of selling her quite enough and refused her revengefull request," – I since hear, that instead of having sold her, she has brought her to town here, and put her into the Fiscals prison, in hopes of obtaining from his ignorance of the matter, the general permission to whip her ill-behaved slave, but the Fiscal does not condemn so slightly, he inquired into the merits of the case and poor Hagar has once more escaped her licking but is to be sold *Incontinently*. – on Sunday evening we had an impromptu ball at the Landrosts, the young dutchmen of the neighbourhood attended, awkward enough youths indeed, and a dozen of young ladys amongst whom was a lately married Jacobin beauty of the name of Rousseau, of 6 feet high & two inches, broad in proportion, a Glumdalclutch* likeness of the Dutchess of Devonshire. – her age is only sixteen so we may prophecy much from her future greatness! – the young women are often good looking at that age, but they all want softness. – when they are, what is supposed here *well* educated, they have great ideas of *keeping up* their dignity and not being *put upon*, which dignity being rather coarsly supported, becomes a Haughty pride, or saucy gayety as the fair one happens to be grave or merry. – I can only quote by way of instance of the last, the reply of a young lady to an officer who was lamenting that he had not seen her for a long time – "well, you see me now dont you? " – there was no harm to be sure in the speech, but I felt that if I had been him, I shoud not have cared whether I saw her ever again or not –

*Glumdalclutch**
Glumdalclitch, a 9-year-old girl, 40ft. high, in Swift's Brobdingnag.

we had some droll menuets at this Ball, but I am one of those never known to smile at any body, or any thing, so I was a simple spectatress. – aft the dance we had an excellent supper, the thing which ammused me most at it, was the entrance of two sucking babies, the mothers being of the party and suckling the children themselves – Here we might have venerated the simplicity of the golden age, no false delicacys created by Luxury stepping in between the cup and the lip to prevent the little ones from having their repast as well as we, for while the partners eat and drank heartily, the *Clynies*, viz, the Moye Kinders* – (pretty little children to translate for you, you European great man) were busy in their way to the great discomposure of my Liege Lord, who drew up his eye brows and lookd at me in despair having no other place where he coud throw his eyes without meeting with, what seemd very unfit company for a Ball – however I look on this as of little consequence – tis nonsense to expect the polish of countrys that have been refining themselves for ages till they refine themselves away altogether, which is the lot of all worldly things in one that has not been discoverd or inhabited by christians above 150 years. – I am in no hurry to send off the *Kinders* from the balls. – the more the mothers attend to them, and the less they flirt with the English officers so much the better for Mynheer – I believe I told you the speech of Goetz the late secretary to Lord Macartney when talking of Mad: Goetz his wife. – "Grace a dieu ma femme est bien laide" –

after having made a very pleasent expedition we returned to the cape I should gladly have gone farther up the country but Mr B. coud no longer remain absent, Lord M: himself means to make a tour of the same sort but waits the arrival of the next accounts from England, very anxiously indeed do we all long for them from various motives – . we have seen old England (well governed) rub thro so many Hazardous moments, that we hope alone as she now stands allmost, to hear of her doing the same again, but certainly the last accounts of the french successes and the plans against England which were supposed to be ripe for carrying into execution a few months ago, must make us very eager to hear of a satisfactory result. – invasion *somewhere* I suppose we must expect to hear of, Well! – let the worst Come! I suppose the worst that can Happen will be a bad peace; – to make one such, or to see one such made, woud vex you all as ministers while as men perhaps you might be contented with a sacrifice of a Lump of national Glory to private repose & cessation of Hostility – commissary pringle* told me just now that he had been advertising for a contractor to build chaff houses, or some sort of publick store for such matters as fall within his department, this has thrown the dutch into great astonishment! "Mon dieu the English then believe they *still* are to keep the cape" not one of them, believes it, and even amongst those of the English who treat every thing serious lightly, Betts are laid of 5 to 1 that the place is ceded on a peace; all the world believe in one before Christmass but me, and I hear I am a fool for not believing in one, nous verrons – I can't think that *we* will consent to all the french require to make one. – if there is one, and there is still longer use for us here, Well – we shall pass our time the more softly that we are on terms

*Kinders**
i.e. Kleintjes (little ones); Mooi kinders (pretty children).

*pringle**
John Pringle, commissary-general and agent for the H.E.I.C. He became British agent at the Cape in Feb. 1803.

of the very best sort with the natives. – if there is no more for us to do, we shall see you all again the sooner. – come what will, I shall never regret having visited Africa, I have seen new scenes, and the able master B. has had to initiate him in a life of business has given him that *Method* which will probably on many future occasions render him usefull. – certainly it has been of use to himself already by developing powers which have never before been calld into action. – I shall not give you in this letter any particulr account of your friends here exept by saying that all are well, our soldiers at their camps, our ladys, I hear Gay – and I have been living with country folks picking up flower roots and opening our eyes wide on the face of nature instead of opening them on the Human face divine adorned with scarlet coats, so I cannot give you more than this general information. – by the bye I shoud tell you that I hear Mrs Capt: Campbell is in a way of increasing her family – it is so. –

When I look to the top of my page I am really frightend to think that it is the 23d and that I have not yet done, it is much too great presumption in me to suppose you will read above the 3d part of it but yet I write on, for living as I at the present do in a part of the world that is interesting to you I feel reluctance to conclude while there remains anything untold that I may think you coud like to know: – this ship sails tomorrow to take the convoy of the Dort home from St Helena,* by Lieut Bryce, brother in Law to John Anstruther.* Lady Jane will receive two Jars of Batavian pineapples, one of them is for Ly Hardwicke and the Margaret in partnership – the flower roots I am advised since I begun this letter not to send for six weeks yet, that they may arrive in England at the proper season for planting – I long to send you, indeed it is now on board a great curiosity, a *Rump of Cape Beef – salted by the Fiscal* "oui mi Ledi, par mes propres *mains*" "Monsieur, Les grands Hommes sont egal a tous"! this with a mutton Ham by Madame the Landrost, will give you a proper idea of our fare, if they are not good when they arrive it is no fault of mine, I am *sure* they were good when They sett off – I also send you a box of ostrich eggs, the freshest I coud obtain, I am told by oiling them well & packing them with bran, they often keep to reach Holland good if so they may reach Wimbledon – there are 6 eggs, one of them being emptied by me to make some cakes & to try if it was good – nothing coud be more capital than my cakes, make your cook open one in the same manner and if what it contains is sweet which I hope it will be, then Boil another to be quite hard which is the way they are here reckond most delicious, taken *whole* out of the shell and ate with oil and vinegar, but be sure to have it served up entire and not cut into pieces – if you will give one of the eggs to my sisters & one to the Douglas's or a share of one of them I shall be much obliged to you – in the same box you will find a candle of my own making of the vegetable wax, I have not burnt any yet but I believe it burns dim as its color gives one a right to expect – & a small speciment of the sirup of the sugar tree, I could not make the box contain a quart, wc I was sorry for – I forgot to put in a specimen of lead ore rough from one of the mountains, Ill enclose a scrap of it only to shew you how pure it is found, in large pieces as great as your Hand. –

I am sure there must be many wonderfull things hid in these stupendous

*Helena**
H.M.S. *Dordrecht* (sometimes abbreviated to *Dort*), a Dutch prize (taken 17-8-1796) commissioned for service on the Cape Station, had been appointed to convoy the E.I. Co's fleet to St. Helena in Aug. 1797.

*Anstruther**
Lieut. Gilbert Brice, R.N. The Rt. Hon. Sir John Anstruther, Bt., chief justice of Bengal, married Maria Brice. He had played an important part in the impeachment of Warren Hastings, 1786-88.

hills – I have not told you by the bye that on our return home we dined with Genl Vandeleur* at Stickland* and saw for the first time this very barren & cheerless station for the cavalry, there is but a scanty portion of water and that not good, no pasture or shade for the horses so there is not any visible motive for having fixed them there in preference to other & better situations, however this was before our time – I think my dear friend I ought here to make you a common sense apology, for the many vague [things] I say & repeat; I never mean to be unjust or erroneous, but ignorance may often make me so, for which reason I confine myself more to the subject of *things* than of people as the first cannot be equally injured by any misapprehension of mine – wise and worldly people are allways conchious of committing to paper opinions respecting any thing beyond the merest trifles, unless they foresee events – I for instance was I to treat you like a minister instead of a man and a friend woud not send you off my details of this place, nor say what I think of it till I knew whether it was to be kept or not, in the last case it woud be flattering to speak highly in its praise, in the first to hold it light, but this is not a way of dealing fit between you & me; I must therefore conclude by saying that I hope it will be found possible to keep the place, that barren & ill cultivated as it now is, it strikes both Mr B. and me to have great powers in itself to become one of the finest countrys in the world, how far it will be the wisdom of England to encourage it to become so is for England['s] Sovereign & his ministers to determine or whether it will be more for her advantage & for that of our possessions in India to keep it subordinate So that it may never interfere, while it aids and assists the to and fro constantly going on between the countrys is for you to determine and you only – the choice climate here and fertile soil might certainly make it a 2^{d} India but whether in that point of view Sellon might not be a better pis aller supposing any thing to go wrong with us in the East is a point, And was I a monarch I shoud like to portion a younger son with this country, supposing him little, for a ten years *Minority* woud produce such a difference on this country if it was as much encouraged as it has been represed! – yet it is possible (if we keep it) that you may *all* be obliged to adhere to the same selfish considerations from policy which governed the dutch & of which the most enlightend of the natives complain, who felt their hands tyed up from being [dis] possessed thro their own industry of the riches they might so easily have had, they tell me there is nothing this place is not equal to particularly if we can suppose the intercourse between the inner part of the country & the cape town renderd more easy – it is certainly a healthy spot, we have lost but one officer here poor Col. Grey,* till Capt Ormsby* died of a distemper he brought with him & a gentleman from India lately did who came to recover a broken constitution – I have been enquiring if Mr B. wrote to you, he says "my dear Anne what between Lord Macartney & you, upon my soul I pity poor Mr Dundas too much for all he has to read to plague him with more – Lord M. very properly takes the business part, and the accounts of every thing upon himself & you write all the lighter parts, so what is left for me?" he bids me however add his kindest and best wishes to you to Lady Jane & your young Ladys, in which I beg

*Vanderleur**
Brig.-Gen. Thomas Pakenham Vandeleur, 8th Light Dragoons. His must have been a local rank as his rank in the Army was only that of Colonel.

*Stickland**
Stikland is on the Cape Flats about 13 m. from Cape Town on the Paarl road.

*Grey**
Most probably Lt.-Col. Thomas Grey, 12th (E. Suffolk) Foot, though his death is not recorded by C. Graham Botha in his *Extracts from the register of deaths at the Cape, 1795-1815.*

*Ormsby**
Lieut. Philip Ormsby, 8th Light Dragoons. (*See* Botha, op. cit.)

leave to join – I will not write to Lady Jane at present as I feel tired of my pen, nor will add more than a cordial –

God Bless you all –

Anne Barnard

this will be deliverd to you by capt Stevens*,& a *mild good man* by character, tho tried lately by court martial in consequence of the mutiny on board his ship, he was of course *Honorably acquitted* but I believe he has *felt* the circumstance very severely, indeed too much – I hope he will recover his spirits before he reaches you –

*George H. Stephens. (See Letter 12, note 6.)

Mevrou Jacob van Reenen at Church

Letter 15

After the foregoing lengthy epistle it was two months before Lady Anne again addressed Dundas. She complains of the lack of letters from him but doubtless the presence of distinguished visitors made letter-writing more difficult.

Feb 3 – 1798
cape of good Hope

this letter was too late for the ship

– I cannot let the Buccleugh sail my dearest friend without a cordial line, expressive of the happiness I feel on this great and gallant victory of admiral Duncans;* – added to many other powerfull motives for rejoycing, the exultation with which you woud feel the manner in which your favorite has distinguishd himself and the transport of his wife & family come in for their share – she is my old acquaintance tho it is a thousand years since we saw each other* tell him that the ballad wrote on his victory & conduct on that day, & repeated to me by Lord Mornington* had the same effect on me Lord Landsdown had on the present Lady Campden* "made me all over *goose skin*" – but it went farther it made me *greet the Triumph* with a few salt yet sweet tears such as the geese called women sometimes shed on such occasions – I wish we had oftener cause. – I do not mean to encroach much on your time at present as you will hear everything worth knowing from a quarter so much superior, Lord Mornington. – he and his brother,* with Sir Hugh Christian* arrived here the 28th of January, both well and greatly enjoying dry Land after their voyage. – I mentioned in a former letter that we had got ready a comfortable suite of apartments for Lord Mor: & pressd him to accept of it, till we perceived that our *own Lord* rather wishd him to reside in one of the houses that admit of lodgers here, from a unwillingness I think to see him accommodated in any *other* House connected with the government than in his *own*, yet in his own Lord Mornington coud *not* have been, as Lord M: has only furnishd what is necessary for his family. – fortunately for us, and for Lord Mornington too I think, he was attackd by Bugs in the abode he went to, which settled the matter and put it fully in his power to say to us "pray, pray as you offerd to take me, do" – here he came and is, the pleasantest companion and easiest guest, as is his brother too who tho sick at sea is now perfectly well – as to Lord Mornington he is as well or better than I ever saw him, eats heartily of any thing & every thing & says he takes many libertys with the governor general he never

*Duncans**
Admiral Adam Duncan, Viscount Duncan of Camperdown (1731-1804), defeated the Dutch fleet under de Winter off Camperdown on Oct. 11 1797.

*other**
Duncan married Henrietta, daughter of Robert Dundas, and hence Henry Dundas's niece.

*Mornington**
Richard Colley Wellesley, 2nd Earl of Mornington and later Marquess Wellesley (1760-1842), governor-general of India, 1797-1805. It may be remarked that his younger brother, then Lieut.-Col. Arthur Wellesley (or Wesley), afterwards Duke of Wellington, was at the Cape from June 1796 until early in 1797, en route for India. He had left by the time Lady A. arrived.

*Campden**
Presumably Frances, countess Camden, wife of the 2nd Earl who was Lord Lieutenant of Ireland and Secretary for War and the Colonies 1804-5.

*brother**
Hon. Henry Wellesley, youngest brother and private secretary to Mornington, and afterwards 1st Baron Cowley. He had a distinguished diplomatic career.

*Christian**
Rear-Admiral Sir Hugh Cloberry Christian (1747-1798). Appointed to the Cape station fresh from his success at St. Lucia, Windward Is. He died the following November however.

before dared to take with Lord Mornington and that he finds no bad effects from them – he is much charmd with Lord Macartneys manners, he finds them more pleasing in some respects than he looked for, abilitys and knowledge he expected, but there is a mildness and consideration of every body, with a sort of parental affection to those immediately attachd to him which he did not expect in the degree he finds it – wines of strong body and high flavour are sometimes meliorated by time to be more gracious to the taste than when new. – we have dined twice with him, and today he dines with us, generals – cols – admirals & 22 of the *great men of the Cape*, so I being a little in the Martha way, *thinking of many* things, tho not *troubled* about any will bid you adieu for the present: – in a few days we shall give a ball when every body will have the opportunity of paying their Respects to the Governor general, he once thought of giving one, but there was no means, the Fair Scold of the great Ball room having lost her husband ten days ago, and being now wedded to a dutch officer who thinks it beneath his dignity to permit any more. – this day the Belvidere arrived & I have seen Mr Hollande* who has been anxiously expected for some time past to Judge on prizes in their nature doubtfull – he seemd surprized that any one shoud [have] lookd for him with anxiety as he had supposed he shoud be quite an idle man, the more he has to do the better – Lord Mornington expects to be able to proceed on his voyage in a week, & while necessary repairs are putting the ship in order he is having some accomodations put up for himself which however he swears he will sail *without*, if the other business of the ship can be finishd sooner than this can, he little knows how unlikely it is for any ship that touches here to get off in ten days, if there is but a nail to put in or a cask of water! – if he is off in three weeks I shall say his captain has made more haste than any other my twelve months experience of them has ever shewn me – however as his ship will in many respects be improved & lightend she will sail the faster for the present delay & certainly the more securely as she was dangerously overmasted before they were cut lower. – by the time of his departure we expect the Anstruthers will arrive – that is a very bad ship, when they leave us we shall endeavour to get to our cottage in the country for a couple of months, february & march being Hot months in town. – as yet we have felt no inconveniencys in the castle from the heat of the weather, flys, or muskatos, but indeed all has been comfortable to us, and we have been as happy as people can be at a distance from some of those they love best – the object of our being here is fully answered & that to me is the great point, I trust that Mr Barnard has filld the situation well that you placed him in, & acquired under his skillfull and kind master that method in the transaction of business which will render him on future occasions usefull. – my kind love to Lady Jane, tell her that Lord Mornington expresses himself often of her in terms so high & at the same time so affectionate that I have wished her more than once behind the curtain – I might safely wish her this in *our* drawing room which has french ones, but in any of the dutch drawing rooms she woud be discoverd as all the curtains are highlanders, their kilts reaching only half way down to the ground –

*Hollande**
John Holland, appointed judge of the vice-admiralty court, arriving in Feb. 1798. Later he became post master.

my letter was too late for the Buccleugh, and I find it very likely that by the present conveyance it may reach you sooner than by the other – my prophecys have been right – we have still our friends with us, and I declare that we shall see them depart with great sorrow, they expect however to go on board the day *after* tomorrow, and I believe them when they tell me that they shall be equally sorry to bid adieu to us, as they have both amused themselves in a quiet way extremely picking up a little Fun out of every thing yet laughing at some of our *Grandees*. – as to Lord Mornington if ever I saw a man the purity of whose conduct under any temptation I mean of the oriental sort I coud count on I think it is him, his whole soul seems turned to do his duty well – his pride, his pleasure the anticipation of approbation from you all at home and of his own conscience – added to this there is the certainty that from the savings of his large income he must make a handsome provision for his *elder younger* children which composes a duty in his situation which I do believe he will fulfill in its fair and honorable extent.

– having talked over such views lately in the confidence of mutual good opinion you may judge how I was intertained last night when I saw offerd to him what I called his *first bribe* – his *Excellency* the governor of Mosambique* a stately well-stuffd portuguese full of dignity and grave folly suppd here last night with our two Excellencys – N:B. he has to attend him a black dwarf of about 34 inshes high dressd in uniform, he is a fool, but the governor says he has beaucoup D'esprit, which gave us no high idea of *his*. – while at cards he was in a great fuss when supper was announced least all the first places shoud be taken before his rubber was over, not having at all supposed it possible that the other two Governors & the Mistress of the House shoud wander about sans facon while the company seated themselves, fortunately a place at the very upper end remaind vacant in which (after being assured they did not mean to sit down) he placed himself, and did great honor to the provisions before him – when the company, all but a few rose Lord Mor. and I sat down next him – Lord Mor: for conversation praised a cane which he carried, or very fine workmanship in gold – gold ribbond – head – tassles &cc quite a representation thing – it was immediately offerd to him by the gallant portuguese – and declined with a very disconcerted air by Lord M. who was not aware what his compliment was to produce – again it *was* offerd – pressd [,] insisted on – he had *plusieurs des autres* – milor seignor must do him the honor to accept of the bagatelle – at last Lord Mornington vexed & allmost angry assured him that Les Anglois were *si gauche* that they did not know the use of a cane & *never carried* any – we laughed a good deal at Lord Mornington for having been so publickly attackd by a golden fee,* and it all passd over mighty well, till next day when happening to mention to somebody the politeness of the Governor to him, a person *more* gauche than the Anglois in general said he had been told that his Lordship had *accepted of it* – this led on to the persons repeating the conversation which one of the people at table during the transaction had held with him – a man who might have known better, – never saw

Mosambique *
Captain of Infantry João da Costa Soares was appointed governor of Moçambique in 1796 but was driven out by French corsairs in Oct. of that year. A new governor was not sent out until 1799.

fee *
'Fee' used in the obsolete sense of 'bribe'.

I any body so angry – so vexed – so provockd as Lord Mor: – "he may be an excellent *Judge* said he, but he is a d – d bad evidence when he can so grosly mistake the fact his eyes witnessd" – inspite of his being out of all patience however he coud not help laughing with Anne Barnard & me, at the Hopefull paragraph this might make in the newspapers for his friends at home to read in a private letter from the cape, that the new governor of Bengal had not even postponed to his arrival in India his taste for his *Douceurs* having accepted of a cane sett with jewels value *5,000 £* from the governor of Mosambique, – trifle as this appeared to be to us who had seen it all, it has been deemd worthy of a few words to the narrator to put him right as to the fact – N.B. dont suppose from my having mentioned the word Judge that it was our friend Sir John Ans[t]* or Sir Henry Russel* – but look amongst our Cape department & the head of a certain board for the Malentendue – it fidgeted Lord Mor. for a day & a Half more than you can well imagine – within these two or three days various ships are come in, in particular one from Bengal loaded with *generals* – Duff – Jones – *Morgan** – the last is plainly made of the Teak wood, which is so Hard & firm you know as to endure time & be insensible to decay – Many other Indian men of some ability are residing here, so we have a Bengal levy every morning at breakfast the individuals of which are closetted & pour the riches of their knowledge & experience on Lord Mor: who seems anxious to gain all he can from them – . Sir Hugh Christian I like much he appears to be a mild, firm Intelligent man and a pleasing companion I expect satisfaction from his society – ad. Pringle is certainly very clever & entertaining, Lord Mor: is delighted with him in the midst of all his singularity but he is too great a growler – well & how do *you* like the Cape my Lord said he to Lord M: – upon my word Sir I like it very much – "Aye – aye – that you woud say after such a voyage as *yours* if you had landed in Hell" – he says Lord Macartney understands a table no more than *a whale* – which is a good seafaring simily for a great man – with all this I do *not* think that he likes to go and shrewdly suspect he woud not have been displeased had a little douce Violence been used to make him stay Malgré lui – at present tis an awkward situation for sweet Sir Hugh to be in but he says nothing, tho I can see he feels himself out of his place, I hear about a fortnight hence, ad. Pringle will be going home, but I cannot help thinking it may be longer, if he waits the return of a cruising expedition which some time ago took away some of our ships – added to other motives w[c] may detain him a little Almighty love may have its share perhaps, tho it is said that that god has already engaged him to a Lady in England now laying at anchor to wait his return – he & Sir Hugh dined here yesterday – L[d] M: & brother – the Anstruthers & a couple of navy Captains, a snug – small party – it quite delights me now to hear a little pleasant *talk* – things run rather more than was quite agreeable in the flirting line at one time here, but the minority viz Anne Barnard & me, have received great additions by the arrival of Mrs Hollande – the Morningtons – Sir Hugh Ch. &c, and hope to be able to make time amble away agreeably without drinking – gaming, or making love – *more than reason*, I own these three auxiliarys give the strongest *Zest* of any to society but all *three*

*Anst.**
Sir John Anstruther, see Letter 14, p.95.

*Russel**
Sir Henry Russell (1751-1830), judge of the Supreme Court, Bengal. Succeeded Anstruther as chief justice, 1807-13.

*Morgan**
These were probably the following officers holding the local rank of Major-General in the East Indies: Patrick Duff, Thomas or William Jones, Charles Morgan.

are *intoxications*, which produce mischief to heads & hearts. –

– this has become a longer letter than I meant, I do not think I judge it well by the bye, in giving you so many – vessels have succeeded to vessels and I have not yet received any letter from you – I will not answer for it that this may not soon mortify me into silence and save you a world of Idle reading – for the present however I will throw aside all foolish distrusts and continue to expect as before, with a better chance I hope of success – God bless you –

Mevrou Goetz's coach and eight

(*Extracted from* Lives of the Lindsays; or a memoir of the Houses of Crawford and Balcarres, [*ed. by Alexander, 25th Earl of Crawford and 8th Earl of Balcarres*] *London, 1849, v. 3, p. 411-476*).

On the 5th May 1798 the Barnards left the Castle at the Cape of Good Hope on an extensive tour of the interior extending beyond Swellendam to the east and on the return journey going round by Saldanha Bay. The original letter describing this tour and dated June 6th 1798, according to W.H. Wilkins, has unfortunately been lost. Its especial interest and value was realised sufficiently for it to be removed from the collection of letters bought from Melville Castle in 1926, either before or after the transaction, though it was known and published by Wilkins. Fortunately however Lady Anne's impressions were also recorded – more fully in fact – in her Journal of a residence at the Cape of Good Hope and of a short tour into the interior, addressed to her sisters in England, *extracts from which were printed in* Lives of the Lindsays, *vol. 3, p.369-476, in 1849, under the editorship of Alexander Lindsay, 25th earl of Crawford. We have reprinted this account of the journey here.*

The present of an idle month, and that the month of May, to a poor Secretary who had been screwed to his desk for one whole twelvemonth, was an offer much too welcome not to be accepted with joy. Do not however suppose that it contained all the pleasure it sounds to do. The month of May here is not "bella madre de' fiori," as it is in Europe, – it is on the contrary our Cape November, and the commencement of the rainy season, when the roads become impassable, and when a man and his family with their waggon may be stopped on the wrong side of a river for three or four weeks, so deep are their beds (in general), and so steep their banks. But in spite of this, Mr. Barnard and I determined to catch the golden opportunity of piercing a little into the interior of a country we might never find as good a moment to see again. We felt very grateful to Lord Macartney for this holiday, but no one is more disposed to suggest and propose what he thinks will conduce to the pleasure or advantage of those around him than he is.

Our young friend Miss M—— * preferred accompanying us to remaining at the Castle, though with a pleasant party which I proposed to invite to keep her company; but she assured me that upon the whole she would so much rather go than be left behind that it was so settled,

*M—**
i.e. Ann Barnard, the younger, elsewhere referred to in this journal as 'Jane'. No reason is known for this.

Little
Koud Bokkeveld or Freezland
Warm Bokkeveld
Roode Sand
Waaveren
Little Drakensteen
Great Drakensteen
Bosjes veld
Groene Kloof
Zwart
the 24 Rivers
Plains
Hex River
Zwart be
Hyle Kraal
Soetendals valley
Cape of Good Hope
False Bay
Table Bay
Campe Bay
Chapmans Bay
Saldanha Bay
Robben Island
Dassen Island
Berg Riv.
Breede Riv.
Zwellendam
Hot wells
Tower of Babylon
Produce grain fruit Wine and Tobacco
Pasture and grain Country
Corn Wine and fruit
Corn wine and fruit
Blue Antilope once in this part of the Country
Hontebok Reeboks Steenboks Duykers and small Game
Steenboks Duykers & Greisboks
Good pasture Country
Witteberg or white Mountain
Smiths Winkel or Smiths shop
St. Catharin's Bay

[Cornet John Dalrymple]

much to my satisfaction. As a young lady, however, like a great general, is nothing without a proper staff on such an occasion, Mr Barnard kindly invited my cousin, John Dalrymple, to be her *aide-de-camp.** Johnnie is somewhere from five to seven feet high, for, as he grows an inch or two every fortnight, there is no knowing where to fix him, – about seventeen years of age, good-humoured and very obliging, fond of his gun, fonder of his horse. When we add to this that he was to be jolted in a waggon for some hundred miles with the beauty of the garrison, to the exclusion of all generals, colonels, and field officers, I can paint no happier cornet.

The first thing to be procured was our conveyance. Any carriage *but* a waggon it was impossible to think of; those of the country, long and narrow, are the best calculated for the business they have to perform. An ox-waggon would have suited our pockets best, as it is exactly half the price of a horse one, but it takes double the time to travel over the same space of ground, and we wished to see as much as our month could possibly afford. For the horses therefore we determined, though on many occasions we learnt that we must hire oxen also, to take us over the *kloofs*, or steep passes amongst the mountains, which no number of horses are equal to accomplish. Our friend the Fiscal arranged the bargain for us for twelve dollars per day, all expenses besides to be paid by us, which added three or four more, and brought the price to somewhat above three guineas per day for our waggon, coachman, and eight horses.

Thus furnished with a wooden case to pack ourselves into (over which by the bye there was a stout sail-cloth cover), each one provided what was necessary to render the month as comfortable as possible. The first comfort I wished Mr. Barnard to procure (I introduce him here as if he were stock) was an interpreter – some Dutchman to be of the party who could talk a little French or English, who would not grudge leaving his house for such an excursion, but would be patient in replying to all my questions and intelligent in answering them. This person was not easily found – to quit the Cape in winter and go into the country without having any business there! Mynheer did not comprehend it. At last however the Fiscal recommended to us a Mr. Prince,* a sort of clerk in the Orphan Chamber and auctioneer, who, from having to sell at all parts of the country (there being constantly a sale and division of effects on the death of every head of a house), was well instructed in the best roads, and, from knowing all the farmers – or *boors*, as they are called here – could best tell us the places it would be wise for us to stop at.

But unfortunately this comfortable Mr. Prince at the first setting off we could not have, – business detained him in town for ten days or a fortnight; but he settled it with Mr. Barnard to meet him at Swellendam, about two hundred miles' distance from the Cape, the 19th of the month. Though bad, this was far better than no prospect; I therefore made up my mind to travel on for two hundred miles ignorant of everything but appearances, and to return by his means wise and good for something.

Mr. Barnard took his own servant, Pawell, the Brabanter, master of French, English, and Dutch – a little Latin too, if necessary, – active,

*camp.**
Cornet in the 28th Light Dragoons, aged 17. See Letter 18, p.176.

*Prince**
Presumably his name was Prins. He has not been traced elsewhere.

young, and fond of excursions, he heard with delight that he was to be of the party. We only regretted that we could not make our *knecht* sit down at table with us, and pass him off for a cousin, – but a trick of this sort would never have been forgiven in this place, had we lived for two thousand years. And now let us see what the careful *haus-vrow*, Anne Barnard, put up for resources upon the journey.

In the first place, I had a couple of strong sail-cloth bags made to hold a pair of mattresses, two pair of blankets, sheets, pillows, &c., in case we should find a want of beds at any of our nightly quarters, or in case the beds should be very dirty. I carried some dozens of coarse handkerchiefs to give to slaves, farmers' servants, &c., ribbands, gold lace, needles, thread, scissors, a bag of good tea, coffee, sugar, rice, for the higher classes, where people would not take money, – a good many common beads for Hottentots, of different colours, and a quantity of white pearl beads such as we all wear, which I put in without supposing they would be of much use, – some dozens of common knives about sixpence value each – a large bale of tobacco – a bag of raisins – a bundle of candles – some oil – a lamp – two or three pine-apple cheeses – the conjurer* – plenty of cold meat – and in the corner of the waggon a jar of Batavian ginger – with a little bag of *schellings*, or bank-notes of sixpence each, in my pocket, from which I expected much satisfaction.

Mr. Barnard furnished on his part two good hams and a half, a large piece of Hamburgh beef, and two tongues. He added a small cask of good Madeira, a box of gin, rum, and liqueurs, and plenty of powder and shot; which baggage, with some other things in great coats which lined the sides of the waggon (and which I did not attend to), he stowed up himself. Each of us possessed a box of our own containing our goods, over which the seats were hung, and the coachman, Gaspar (lent to us by a friend for the journey), sat enthroned, lord of his own, which was filled with nails and all sorts of tools for reparation should it be wanted. So provided, at nine o'clock in the morning of

Saturday the 5th of May, 1798, we set out in our waggon and eight, – on the front seat of which sat the illustrious Gaspar on his box – behind him Lady Anne Barnard, on her knee an old drawing-book stoutly bound, which had descended from mitre to mitre in the Barnard family, and which little thought in its old age, as Sarah says, that it should be caught turning over a new leaf and producing hasty sketches in the wilds of Africa. By her was Mynheer the "Secretarius," for the express purpose of popping out at the partridges in half a minute when they

*conjuror**
"Apparently a small portable machine for making stews, fricassees &c." (*Original ed.'s footnote*).

The start of the tour

The construction of the travelling waggon

appeared. Behind them, seated on the wool-sacks, viz. mattresses, Cousin Johnnie and Jane, – a situation, she said, she preferred to the front seat, where she could have *only* seen the country, and which Johnnie highly approved of her for preferring, as the country was not fit to be looked at. The care of Jane's knitting-case, containing some pins, pen and ink, and a half-finished purse, was divided between her and her *aide-de-camp*. Behind these good children was Charles, my little black boy, a West Indian, lolling on his own mattress, – he was appointed Inspector of the baggage, to be ready to holla out when anything dropped, and what with great coats and a few baskets, powder-bags, &c., we foresaw his department would not be a sinecure. By him was Hector – a stupid old slave belonging to the coachman, somewhat younger than myself I believe, but rather harder worked, whose business it was to walk through all questionable places, see if fords were passable, run before to observe if the drag was necessary, and put to rights the harness on any of the refractory leaders. Behind our waggon followed Pawell and another Charles, a slave of Mr. Barnard's, who rode his horse and led Jane's stud, viz. a couple of riding-horses, and a Hottentot riding Johnnie Dalrymple's "best of all possible horses, Hobgoblin," – he led up the rear. And now, having brought us to this point, I transcribe my waggon memorandums.

We left the Cape by the same road we went to Stellenbosch, – indeed there is but one egress from Cape Town, which, being at the extremity of the peninsula, has no variety of roads from it leading into the country, – after we pass Rondebosch, they branch out. The road was sandy and heavy. As we proceeded, a few branches of the wax-tree appeared, and some low brushwood – white sandy hillocks – a few partridges – two bucks – "Give me my gun, Anne – my gun, my gun!" – "Gun! have we any guns near us?" A smile – he reached across and took down one of the lurking villains out of its great coat, charged for murder – out jumped Johnnie, seizing another; but the bucks escaped scot-free, and the gentlemen returned. – "You must not mind a gun or two, for that is the beauty of the thing, to have all ready at a moment's warning." I now saw there were five, charged, in the waggon with us, and believed it was best to give up all fear at once and trust to Providence. All that Jane and I stipulated for was to have them placed where

The tutor at Onverwacht

we had the best chance of escaping being shot. – Two pheasants – some wild turkeys – one house seen at a distance – what savage sounds they use to their horses! an English horse would say it was not language fit for a gentleman. – Mr. Barnard had laughed at me, after we were all packed up and ready to depart, for taking a good quantity of small cord – "useless," he called it, "as there was plenty in one of the boxes." I put up my cord, however. Down came one thing at the end of a few miles – tumble went another – I repaired all out of my disdained store – at last, pop there came Mr. Barnard's powder-bag, which was imperfectly slung. – "Anne! do hand me THE cord." 'Tis I who place the emphasis – he did not; the triumph was too great for me to use it, but he used the cord. Traveller! constantly have little resources by you of small value, and never be laughed out of anything.

I saw no tillage till we arrived near Mynheer Meybourgh's,* a wealthy man, where we hoped to bait and dine, having come about twenty miles in five hours. We found he had expected us some days before, and was now gone to the Cape; his vrow was at home – a perfect Dutchwoman. I was afraid at first by her air that she was angry at a *malentendu* which had probably been the death of some of the poultry, but I found it was only manner; she gave us an excellent dinner. After it was over, a child of eighteen months was brought in, which no one could lift from the ground, it was so heavy. I gazed with a wonder, which being translated into admiration, her daughter ran for hers, – it was still sucking and eleven months old, but I could not contain it in my arms, it was such a porpoise. – "Ah! what would *mi vrow* give to have

*Meybourgh's** Myburgh of Meerlust near Faure.

such an one!" said one of the party, looking to me. I thought, if I had, that like Solomon I should be tempted to make two of it. This is one of the great points of vanity with the Dutch – the size and number of their children. Mr. Barnard has given me leave, as I before mentioned, to take the credit of three or four whenever I find the tide of pity and self-complacency running too strong in the other party. I shall use it with moderation, for fear of detection, but they must all be in England, and all boys, – I will not enact the careless mother and leave my girls behind.

While we dined, the horses refreshed themselves, as they call it, that is to say, had liberty to roll in the sand with all their hoofs in the air, except one which is tied to the bridle to prevent them from escaping; and even to this restraint a Cape horse gets so accustomed by habit, that I see them often in the fields cantering off on three legs as nimbly as a dog.

We left these good people at four o'clock, and proceeded to Mynheer William Morkel's,* where we heard we could be accommodated for the night. We arrived there about eight o'clock, and to our sorrow for the point of good cheer, and gladness for the point of liberty, we found Mynheer and his wife were then on a visit at some distance. Of course all the children and most of the slaves were of the party, the Dutchmen never leaving any of them behind, which I do not think proceeds so much from affection (of which they have not any in the anxious and tender degree of European parents) as from its being their custom. The children's tutor, viz. the schoolmaster, received us during their absence.

Sunday, May 6th, 1798. – After making a tolerable breakfast from our own tea-chest, with the addition of fresh eggs, we started. The tutor lent us a team of oxen to carry us to the foot of the Hottentot Kloof* – we reached it in about an hour, having passed but one farm-house by the way – little game – no tree or bush – and simply a field or two attached to the house in tillage.

A farmer at the bottom of the ascent stood ready with twelve fine, stout, beautiful oxen, with horns which spread from pole to pole, ready to be put to the waggon. Sensible creatures they seemed to be, for much did they dislike the business they were going on, and lowed piteously when they found themselves in the yoke. – We were advised to let them draw us up as far as we chose to sit. – the ascent is about a mile and a half or two miles long; but we soon preferred leaving the waggon, the sight of their exertions being painful to me; besides, I wished to take a flying sketch from the Kloof itself of Gordon's Bay, the wide prospect we were leaving, where bay succeeded to bay and hill to hill, carrying on the eye with an infinity of bare beauty; but there was unfortunately a distant fog, which was a little untoward, considering that it was not every day I could find myself here.

From this spot, half-way up the mountain, wherever the eye turned there was heath, sand, sea, mountain – scarce a house to be seen, no cultivation, and of course no population. I therefore hoarded up my little portion of hope, which had been given me by the Dutch I had conversed with, who assured me that round Cape Town it was nothing, but that, when I got to the other side of the Hottentot Kloof, a new country would open on me, so fertile, so many houses! the face of

*Morkels**
Willem Morkel of Onverwacht, now De Bos, Strand.

*Kloof**
The pass then used over the Hottentots Holland Mts., about 1 mile north of the present Sir Lowry's Pass.

nature so bespangled with flowers that I should be delighted with it.

As we ascended the path was so perpendicular, and the jutting rocks, over which the waggon was to be pulled, so large in the middle of the road, that we were astonished how it could be accomplished at all, particularly at one pass, called the Porch. At length we reached the summit, and the new Canaan opened on my view – hillock on hillock, mountain behind mountain, far as the sight could reach – a slight thread of rivulet here and there, like a silver eel, winding through the valleys, but scarcely perceptible, and the only objects on which the eye found anything to pause were sometimes a few pointed stones, on the summit of rising grounds, under which fancy would fain have laid the bones of Hottentot heroes slain in battle, had not observation pointed out that this was only the natural form of the country.

The descent was not much better, though less fatiguing than the other side; in about half an hour we reached the bottom, where we found the waggon safe and the horses put to it. Mr. Barnard stood by the team of oxen, and called, "Anne, don't look this way!" but, at the sound of his voice, I naturally and involuntarily turned my head, and saw what made my heart sore, how much the poor animals had suffered in our service, their sides streaming down with the blood which the knives of their savage drivers had brought. They are very cruel here to their cattle; the whip itself, which carries away with it the hide, is not thought enough on some occasions; with their sharp knives they cut the poor creatures, till, bellowing and kicking, they perform their almost impossible task, and they are sufficiently good anatomists to know exactly the vital parts to be avoided.

Travelled on – fields still innocent of the plough – a long range of grey barren mountains – in a few miles a quantity of greenish knolls looking verdant at a distance, but it was only young vegetation on the tops of brownish evergreens; the cattle eat this, and grow fat on it. Passed by Grietsgate farmhouse and riviére,* (as the rivers are pronounced here,) then by the Steinbrass Riviere*, and some miles further by the Palmite,* the broadest we had passed. To these succeeded a very dangerous pass along the sloping side of a hill with a precipice beneath. – this, with a high-loaded waggon and eight horses in hand, was not pleasant; but Gaspar seemed to know so thoroughly well what he was equal to perform that we soon began to place unlimited confidence in him.

After travelling about four hours with no other variety than I have mentioned, except three or four partridges killed by our gentlemen, we saw at a distance the farmhouse where we were to stop for the night. The name of the proprietor was Jacob Toubert* – a mere boor; Mr. Barnard had seen him at the Cape in his blue jacket, driving his waggon, and there he had given him a hearty invitation to his house. His wife received us at the door, not out of size, about thirty-five, plain, stupid, but civil. I expected to have seen a dozen of children, and was primed with my four boys; but to my surprise I found she had none, so I thought it kinder to give her a companion in misfortune than to lord it falsely over her. Being extremely hungry, we ate up part of their dinner with them, to which they had added some boiled fowls, which, with plenty of potatoes and good butter, was a repast for an Emperor.

*riviére**
Grietsgat or Grietjesgat, just to the north of the present village of Grabouw. The river has now disappeared.

*Riviere**
Steenbras R. See Letter 11, note 8. Barrow set out for Namaqualand on 10 May 1798, returning on 2 June. See note to original text.

*Palmite**
Palmiet R.

*Toubert**
Arie Jacob Joubert of 'De Rust'.

Monday, May 7th, 1798. – We set off from this place at seven in the morning – the weather glorious, all our animals well – with a fresh team of twelve oxen, which we had provided to carry us over the Howe-Hook, another tremendous hill, and for the use of which oxen for two days we paid twelve dollars. These cattle were so strong that they pulled us with ease up ascents which made me almost think they could pull us up to heaven like Elijah. The vegetation of tender green on olive and brown was still fresher than the day before, and not ugly. We ascended the Howe-Hook,* and found it a tolerable road, but tedious. As one gains the summit, a fine rock presents itself, and on descending there is another, resembling a giant shooting at the passenger. Here we were obliged to get out, the road became so bad, – it was hardly exceeded by the Hottentot Kloof. The ascent was two miles long, the descent the same; the rocks appeared to me chiefly of a bastard white marble, but Mr. Barnard said it was only limestone. Quantities of the most brilliant everlasting flowers, pink with black hearts, grew amongst the heath. Jane and I loaded ourselves with them, we were so intoxicated with their beauty, glittering as they did in the sun like the brightest foils, although we knew the impossibility there was for them to make the journey and return with us in any tolerable state to the Cape.

I remarked, on looking at the oxen as they picked their way down this steep descent, how ingenious they are in avoiding to hurt each other with their horns, which it sometimes appears wholly out of their power to avoid, yet they never do. We met four waggons at the bottom of the hill, the oxen all lowing at the prospect before them.

Before us opened a wide desert – pathless, untenanted – one little bit of smoke only ascended to heaven – it looked like the burnt offering of Cain – probably it was the fire of some poor Hottentot, cooking his humble mess. We now turned off at the foot of the mountain, and quitted what is called the Great Road (it being tolerably beat by waggons) to pursue the path which leads to Mr. Brandt's, – there we intended to pass the night, though he was not at home.

We stopped about half way at a farmhouse of Mynheer Cloete's, to rest our wearied horses, – he spends three months every summer there – two small rooms is the whole of it, and a nasty little kitchen, inhabited by a very old man slave and a woman, into which we did not much wish to creep; but the day was fine, and the *stoop* which hung over the sea was the pleasantest of all seats. At the mouth of the river,* about half a mile distant, we saw a fishing-boat that had been successful; the old man put up a signal to bring us the fish, which he contrived to inform us was excellent, but the fishers made him understand that they were to carry it to Mynheer Brandt's on the other side of the river, where we were to pass the night, so, as that which is deferred is not lost, we contented ourselves with examining our present resources.

I had fortunately when I inspected the hamper put in a piece of bouilli, had one of our tongues boiled, and I thought a couple of fowls would make pretty company for the tongue; the poor people of the house could only afford us a little dry fish and a few hard eggs, – I was mistress of a jar of butter, and by signs got the old slave to dig me up a few potatoes which I saw in his little garden. Table we had none, but we

*Howe-Hook** Houw Hoek.

*river** Hendrik Cloete had a farm near the mouth of the Klein R., on the west bank.

had the top of an old barrel, and by no means any want of company. – cocks, hens, and every living thing assembling round to partake, and they had their share. One of the horses was much fatigued, and Gaspar, while he shook his head at the distance he had still to go, said he must take another half-hour to rest poor Osberg.

As the day began to decline, I pressed Mr. Barnard to let us remain there all night, – that we could sleep in the waggon, or take our beds into one of the out-houses; but on consulting Gaspar, our chief and governor, he said it could just do still to go on, that we should reach the river we were to ford before it was quite dark, that he had put up a signal for a guide to meet us on this side of it, – and, as the house we were going to belonged to his master, I saw he wished to push on, and to get his horses put in his own stables.

At last, all being ready, we set off, leaving the slaves happy with knives, handkerchiefs, and a sprinkling of Danaes, or, if you please, you may call it Anne's paper-shower, the schellings.

A Hottentot

In this country the sun sets at once; there is hardly any twilight, and the difference of a quarter of an hour is the difference between light and total darkness. There happened to be no moon, and very shortly we began to have serious apprehensions, from our having to travel still an hour and a half, that we might find the fording of the river a dangerous thing. The road too – Gaspar was ignorant of it on the side of the river we were then on; on t'other side he was at home. I requested him to make Hector walk at the heads of the horses, that we might lessen the chance of an accident. For about half an hour matters went on pretty well, though the shades of night fell fast about us; at last – "Hey!" cried Mr. Barnard – the waggon rocked – "Sit close!" – I felt its wheel sinking on the side I was, and in a moment down we came like a mountain! The waggon was overturned – my head lower than my heels; and everything in the world I felt was above me. Mr. Barnard rushed out to see where we were – Cousin Jane, Johnnie and I, were laid low.

"Anne, are you hurt? " – "No – are you?" – "I can't tell, I believe not, but – your hand, your hand, Anne!" cried Mr. Barnard, "and immediately get out." I felt suffocated with the luggage – the left I could have given, but my right arm was wedged in between two of the bars of the waggon, and I felt that if the other was pulled violently, it must be broke. Thank God! I got myself disengaged, and crawled out safe on the heath, – Mr. Barnard returned for Jane, and brought her out, bruised, but no bones broken.

How we all blessed Providence for an escape which seemed almost miraculous, for, added to other dangers, there was one which I said nothing of, but which I thought by no means trifling; had any of our guns gone off, some of us would have stood a pretty chance of being shot. But how did this happen with so many servants and a person at the head of the horses? The foolish old Hector had led us too near the edge of a sloping bank, under which ran a little brook, and, while he walked on before, the wheel of the waggon had tipped over the bank. But what was to be done? Dark as pitch now, Gaspar pronounced that the waggon was not broken, though shattered; and if the gentlemen could lend their assistance to help on with the head of it, we could proceed in half an hour; but to do it things were to be moved so very heavy, that, except on a strong emergency such as this, they did not conceive they could have been equal to it, – now, each seemed to have been endowed with strength for the purpose, and all was replaced, nor did there seem to be much damage done except among some liquids, the extent of which ruin we were ignorant of.

While this was going on, I walked about to discover if I could what sort of road was before us, level or hilly; while Jane sat on a stone, the statue of patience, condoling with herself over the bruises of her white marble arm, the rest of the figure in a state of perfect preservation in the saddest, sweetest sense of the word, as the cask of ginger had had its top knocked off in the fall, and had poured its contents in at Jane's neck, and out at her toe, by which means she was a complete confection. I should have ventured to laugh however at this misfortune, and to have counted my bruises with her, had not my attention been called to a voice in the dark saying, "Well, to be sure, this is the devil's own circumstance!"

I found it Cousin Johnnie's, who had embarked the whole of his fortune, amounting to thirty dollars, in Jane's netting-case, which happened to be the only thing lost in our tumble; and he had groped on the bank, and felt in the brook, and nowhere was this unlucky netting-case to be found. Nor had we a tinder-box to strike a light. At last – "Well!" says he, "I don't care – a light heart and a thin pair of breeches," – as he accompanied this with the swagger of a cornet's philosophy, he kicked his foot against something that jingled: – I leave it to you all to judge of Johnnie's transports when *here* was the box, the fortune of thirty dollars, and, what was better still, all the ivory pins safe, and Jane's half-finished purse.

In about an hour, everything being replaced, Mr. Barnard wished us to get into the waggon again, but cowardice was now much too strong to listen to argument; side-saddles were put on both the horses, and, attended by the gentlemen, we rode to the ford, which was at half an hour's distance, the only house that was near on this side the river finding it impossible to accommodate us, the man and his wife being from home, and the *yonge vrow* was afraid of us. At last we reached the water and followed the guide; the ford was marked out only by a stick or two to the right, and even at this time, when no rain had fallen, it was so deep that it took us pains to avoid being wet. Safe on the other side, we once more got into the waggon, and after three-quarters of an hour drove up to the door of Gaspar's master, whom we had left at the Cape.

We entered through a kitchen filled with slaves, many of them blessed with a very scanty portion of covering indeed. We had not been long here before we found that the talents of our coachman were by no means confined to driving; he had no sooner given his horses their feed, rubbing down being out of the question here, than he set all hands to work; the sleeping chickens were called up to be broiled, the sheep to be stewed, while the admirable fish which we had wished for in the morning now blessed our eyes in a hamper, and put into the pan, cut in pieces, with a good lump of mutton-tail, came forth delicious. A little hot wine and water crowned our repast, and decent beds rendered no trouble in unpacking necessary.

"This will all be very pleasant ten years hence," said I, "dear Jane!" – "Ye – s," said she, "but I am so tired I must go to bed." – Johnnie, also being very sleepy, and having vowed vengeance against the whole feathered race in the morning, did so too, and my lord and I, shaking hands, took a cordial glass of wine and water "to the health of all those we love and who love us!"

Tuesday, May 8th, 1798. – Had an excellent sleep in one of the tallest beds I ever saw, and a good breakfast – our own tea and sugar, but fine butter, eggs, and milk – all the bruises tolerable – white marble arms today become verd antique, which I tried to convince Jane was the more valuable article.

Having heard of a curious cave for petrifactions called the Drup Kelder,* at five or six hours' distance, although we had little expectation of finding it equal in beauty to some of our own in Derbyshire and elsewhere, yet, as it is always well to see everything in a country where nothing has been looked at, we determined to go, and Gaspar lent us one team of his master's oxen, and sent another on before, that were still more powerful, as a relay – the road being heavy beyond all description, particularly the latter part of it. We set off at eight o'clock, going for some time along the edge of the river, opposite to that where we had met our disaster.

A quantity of game here bolted out on us, of various sorts, partridges and hares chiefly; several of the last appearing and standing still; the gentlemen were after them in a moment, requesting us not to stop for them. Gaspar and Hector, however, being both keen sportsmen in their hearts, were off to assist the gentlemen, giving a good lash at parting to the oxen, to keep them up full speed. To be sure, Jane and I, in spite of fear, could not help laughing at the mode in which we now seemed to put all our hopes in destiny – alone in a waggon, no driver near, and at the discretion of twelve galloping oxen to go where they pleased; but the oxen and horses here are so little accustomed to made road, and so much used to pick their own, that we soon found ourselves as safe when under the guidance of a good team, and much safer, than if we had had a London coachman on the box.

On these banks there grows in little bunches the Cokima-cranki,* or what I call Hottentot pine-apple; it has the same colour, the same flavour, and is filled with an aromatic juice and seeds – which I do not recommend to be bruised with the teeth, as they leave a taste of garlick in the mouth. The Dutch are so fond of this root, which by the bye is not a root but a fruit, that they give twopence apiece for them to the black children who pick them up in the country and bring them to the town – no small price for a luxury here – I mean for them to give for one, which is a different thing.

We passed through a low brushwood afterwards, the trees so close that they met over the backs of the oxen, who butted their way through it, – to the left there was a good deal of the same; this is a harbour for wild boars, of which there are a quantity here, and some tigers.

When we had pierced through this, and travelled a few miles further, we met with our fresh oxen, and soon plunged into a pathless world, sandy, but covered high all over with evergreens of various descriptions,

*Kelder**
De Kelders, 23 m. east of the present Hermanus, where there are mineral springs in a cave.

*cranki**
Kukumakranka (*Gethyllis afra L.*)

breaking down our way as we went by the mere weight of the waggon, which was driven by Gaspar's brother, who was employed on the farm, and more conversant than he was with this part of the country. The brushwood seemed to me to be of a more brittle nature than what I was accustomed to see in England, which would not have given way so easily.

How many various plants might not a botanist have discovered here! I have eyes, but I see not, from ignorance. – Sometimes we went over bushy mountains, sometimes dipped into sandy holes – every here and there a buck skipping out of a corner, and Mr. Barnard after it, or Johnnie. At last, at a distance appeared the stupendous hills of white sand which I had before observed no mortal surely could have courage to pass, but cross over them we must, or no Drup Kelder. It was a beautiful thing to see the quantity of bucks which now begn to run all over the snow-white mountains; the figures of the gentlemen too at a distance were picturesque – all appeared to be in deep snow, while the air had the charms of summer in it without its oppressive heat. The first remarkalbe thing I saw was a range of rocks, in one of which there was a natural porch, the sea having beat through an opening in one of them for its foaming surge.

Many tremendous mounds of sand did we ascend and descend, our wheels above the axle-tree, before we reached the top of the cliff where was the cavern, – and when we did, our oxen were quite spent. It was now rather later than could be wished, and Gaspar's brother told us we must not think of halting here above an hour, else we should be benighted; we therefore sought for the path to the cave immediately, to lose no time – no one could find any, each took his own – I found some large shells of bad mother-of-pearl; but while looking for better, Mr. Barnard called to me that he had discovered the way, but was afraid I could not follow him, – he bid me try, however, and not be afraid.

I did, cautiously grasping by the bushes, much inconvenienced by my great-coat. In this way I descended the precipice which hangs over the sea, under which is the cavern, till Mr. Barnard called to me there was no going any further, and, in a calm, indifferent tone of voice which I perfectly understood, said, "Follow me up this road, and don't look at anything below."

I vigilantly followed his advice, – I felt all my danger; it was even greater than he knew of, as the soft, woolly-cloth of my great-coat adhered to the bushes, and sadly retarded my progress. Had my head turned round, or had I not exerted in myself all the philosophic calmness I was mistress of, I must have tumbled, my knees trembling as they did.

"Don't be afraid," said he, "follow me – I cannot assist you; but turn your face to the rock as I do, and hold fast by the shrubs; the road is narrow – take care to lay hold of the bushes that are firm in the rock."

These bushes were small twigs which grew about shoulder high in the stony wall to the left. I did, while a glance of my eye shewed me I was passing along a two feet broad path, which must have dashed me to atoms had I fallen. When safely at the top, I thanked God with a trembling but a grateful heart. No part of the ascent of the Table Mountain was equal to the dangers or horrors of this. The first was merely fatiguing – this was hazardous.

We afterwards found the right path, though not a good one, and got down to the cave. In a cavity of the rock, far far out of the reach of man, we saw an immense hive of bees, which have as good a chance of eating their own honey as any bees of my acquaintance, – and a noble porch is to be seen in a contiguous rock, through which the sea appears. At the cave's mouth there lay scattered bones, but we could not judge what animal they had belonged to. Tigers often infest it, and feast on what they drag within it; it is therefore necessary to fire a gun before the cavern is entered, and to have plenty of light, to intimidate the creatures from appearing who may be there concealed. Unless in the greatest want, no savage animal will attack a man. The guides remarked by the trembling of the horses, as they approached the cavern, that they smelt the tigers near; but they did not appear. We had fortunately brought a tinder-box, and the gloom of the recess was soon illuminated with a set of wax candles, which had been packed up after my last party in Berkeley Square; they little thought, when their tops had the honour of shining upon some of their Royal Highnesses and all your right honourable faces, that their bottoms would next illuminate the Drup Kelder at the Cape of Good Hope.

They, however, did not refuse to shew us the curiosities of the place. The pointed *drup-stones* descended from the roof in great numbers, and sometimes met with others which had risen from the ground to meet them. The largest piece of petrifaction that has ever come out of the cavern is in the possession of Mr. Cloete at Constantia. One day in the cave he said to some people that were there along with him, "That is so fine a specimen that I would give a thousand dollars to have it at Constantia." A boor asked him if he was serious, – he replied, he was – he did not believe any one could bring it safe over the Kloof – the boor effected it, and landed it entire at Mynheer's door, much to his sorrow. Had there been the least flaw found in it, he would not have paid the money, but as there was none, and witnesses present when his offer was made, he was obliged to pay the sum.

We stayed too short a time in the cave for me to draw it, but I have endeavoured from recollection to give you an idea of it. We now remounted our waggon, but found great difficulty in getting to the end of our journey, as the cattle sometimes lay down quite exhausted on the sand-hills; in particular poor Tea-water (all the oxen have their names, and this was his) – Tea-water was so weak, that they were obliged to put him in the place of Landsman, and make him a leader.

We changed our team where we had before changed in the morning, – it was not easy to find it; it is by cracking of the whip the drivers let each other know where they are, and, as there is no trace of a road, they cannot in a dark night guess within a quarter of a mile, or perhaps more, of each other's situation. At one time I observed our driver lashed his oxen into a gallop; I apprehended some wild beasts were near, but he explained to Mr. Barnard that we were passing by one of the spots where the cattle usually assemble together at night, and, had our oxen smelt the others, off they would have been over bush and briar, and we should have spent the night with Tea-water's friends.

We did not reach home till eleven. Mr. Barnard was not well, and went to bed. I made a fricassee in the conjurer, much to my own satisfaction and that of the others. The aide-de-camp once more vowed to be up betimes to pop at the partridges; but waking vows are sometimes lost in sleepy infidelity.

Wednesday, May 9th, 1798. – An admirable breakfast of a mutton-chop of a particular kind, being the side of the sheep after the shoulder and leg are cut off; it is salted, peppered, with crumbs of bread and parsley, – nothing can be more savoury. We had also very fine wild honey.

One of the slaves here, seeing me take notice of one of her children, pleased and flattered, brought me seven more. One of the little ones she made me understand was dumb. I looked into its mouth, and saw evidently that the tongue was tacked down by a ligament I have often seen cut. How I wished that I durst have set it a-going with my scissors; but while I looked the child began to roar; and as it was a girl, I thought it possible I might do more harm than good by giving liberty to an unruly member. Jesting apart, I feared the locked-jaw, which I have sometimes heard was the consequence of any injudicious step of this kind; and, like a coward, I did nothing from the terror of doing ill.

Wherever we turned as we left this place the bontebocks bounded away before us, and set Johnnie's heart a-beating. No tillage – no trees – and but one human being appeared as we travelled on. We passed the Clyne Riviére Kloof* – not steep, but stony and dangerous from the frequent slopings of the road – some very marshy passes – to the right, a range of hills and a cascade – to the left, a long row of mountains, which on turning the angle we found was succeeded by another. We passed the Hartebeast Riviére – a good farm belonging to one Tesler* – the Steinbrass Riviére – and arrived about six at M. Wolfram's,* who rents the Government baths, where people go for a variety of complaints – and slept there.

Thursday, May 10th, 1798. – While breakfast was preparing, I made acquaintance with two very distinguished personages, a pair of young ostriches of about eight months old. There was something in their appearance so unlike anything I had seen before, that, when I perceived a couple of creatures whose long throats reached about four feet higher than the horses' backs that they stood by, I rubbed my eyes, thinking my head was giddy. Mrs. Wolfram called them to her, and they ran directly at the sight of two oranges, one of which they swallowed at a gulp, – the second orange, being rather large, stuck in the throat of one of the immense creatures, who instantly picked up a stone of nearly the same size, which he swallowed to put it down. I never saw so fine a drawing as might have been made of a battle between an ostrich and a man; it would have been worthy of Herculaneum, – the ostrich, baulked of his orange, getting at last so wildly, madly, and beautifully angry, that it was a charming sight; but then he becomes dangerous, for, if he puts his foot on the man's, he treads it flat. He is an astonishing creature, not without a resemblance to a horse and to a camel; he makes a wonder-

*Kloof**
Kleinrivier Kloof, now Akkedisberg Pass.

*Tesler**
Teslaarsdal, one of several farms owned by J.J. Tesselaar, lies on the northern slopes of the Kleinriviersberge, 12 m. S.W. of Caledon. The Steenbras R. is here named by mistake for the Steenboks.

*Wolfram's**
Marthinus Wolfferum appears to have been the owner rather than the lessee of the Baths. (*Duminy Dagboek*, V.R.S., 1938, p. 71 n.)

ful link between the bird and beast, partaking of both, as the penguin does of fish and fowl in his low class, where he is, however, as perfect a link as the ostrich.

Having expressed a wish to see the baths, Mr. Wolfram took us in the waggon. The Government House consists of three or four rooms, which could be divided so as to contain a dozen or two of invalids, but there are bare walls only at present. The water is introduced in its own stream into a small house where there is the bathing-place; I put my hand in it, and could just hold it there.* In the kitchen I admired a very picturesque group – a Hottentot woman in her ornaments, a boor, little Charles, and slaves of different countries, all collected together; but the boor's figure, supinely smoking his pipe, first looking at the Hottentot he was accustomed to see, and then at the Englishwoman he had never seen before, would have been in itself a picture.

When we returned to the house, Mr. Barnard settled the expense of the horses, as Wolfram would not hear of accepting of money for our eating. He of course overpaid the other bill, which was the same thing. – As to the slaves, they ask for nothing, but they gaze one out of scissors, needles, ribands, and whatever else, poor things, they covet – and they accept with transport; a Dutchwoman, on the contrary, pockets your gift, how much soever she may like it, almost without thanks, and rather with an air of offence, being too proud to praise.

But now all was ready. We ascended, and packed ourselves again into our waggon, and, with another charming day, the gift of the Kind Power who blessed the journey, we set off to see those humble missionaries under Him, who, sent by the Moravian Church about seven years ago, have made so great a progress in civilising and converting the Hottentots to Christianity.* Of these men, of their worthy undertaking, of their primitive manners, I had heard much, and this it was I desired with my own eyes to judge of, and to see what sort of people the Hottentots are when collected together in such an extensive *craal* as that which surrounds the mansion of the Fathers.

In the houses I had as yet stopped in I had seen only the servants of the farmers, kept to hard work and under humiliating subjection. I had reason to guess the Fathers, or Herrn-hüters, as they are called in this country, were no favourites of theirs, – and ere long we shall see the reason. Their abode we were told was at the foot of the Baviaan and Boscheman's Kloof, at about four hours' distance, viz. sixteen miles, and we hoped to get there by two o'clock.

The river which runs from the Bath accompanied us part of our journey – we had two ugly steps to drag through, of boggy brooks – saw one farm-house at a distance amongst the mountains – then lengthy hills and hills succeeding to each other, but with some little appearance of verdure, from the same cause I have before mentioned – the vegetation of heaths and evergreens. Baron Kilderness* has a house here, a comfortable-looking farm, the first appearance of ground in tillage since we left the Baths. Here we met a specimen of Hottentot cavalry, an ox saddled and bridled, which seemed to be carrying his bare rider just as well as if he had been an Arabian and the rider dressed in the best buckskin. Sweet Milk Fly, or Valley,* was seen at a distance, or rather its

*there**
Burchell states that the temperature of the water was 118°F.

*Christianity**
Genadendal, Baviaanskloof, founded in 1737 by the Moravian Georg Schmidt, abandoned in 1744 and re-established in 1792.

*Kilderness**
A remarkable mishearing by Lady A. Clearly this should be Barend Geldenhuys! 'Geldenhuisens' is marked on Burchell's map 5 m. north of Caledon over the Swartberg.

*Valley**
Zoetenmelksvlei, Company's Post. (See sketch).

mountains rising over knotty hillocks – more mountains when we left these, and another range beyond,

> "Never ending, still beginning –
> Was this country worth the winning?
> Yes! here's climate, soil, beside thee;
> Cultivate – the gods provide thee!"

"Good morrow, moeder!" said Gaspar to an old Hottentot woman with a dog running by her side; "Goeden morgend!" – "She is coming from school," said he. She smiled to us with much benignity, and pointed to the country she had left, saying "Herrn-hüters?" – "Yaw, yaw!" said I. She clasped her hands and looked at the place as much as to say "God bless them!" and passed on.

To the right we passed another farmhouse of tolerable appearance – we passed over another hill, and then at a distance we saw the humble mansion of the Fathers. Each step we took we now found a bit of grass or a few cattle, a craal or hut, a corn-field, a little garden interrupted by heath – then more cattle, a larger field, cows and calves – these cows and calves, the look of peace and prosperity, I need not tell any one of you what sort of sensations it conveyed – it was the tacit manna of the Almighty showered down on his children.

A waggon now appeared at a small distance before us, and Gaspar had not so little of the *esprit du métier* as to be without the desire of getting to the house before it. There was not much accommodation for the horses to be expected, and the "Secretarius" himself, he seemed to think, would have no chance of having his horses put into stable if the others arrived first. He therefore whipped on through a marshy ground, by which he meant to jockey the other party, – our cunning had almost lodged us in a bog, but two or three Hottentot women, seeing our distress, ran before us to put us in the right path, which we gained with some difficulty. The other wagon however won the day, and the horses were in the stable when we arrived – but Gaspar's were also provided for.

The Fathers, of whom there were three, came out to meet us in their working jackets, each man being employed in following the business of his original profession – a miller, a smith – a carpenter and tailor in one. They welcomed us simply and frankly, without artificial gladness or more than hospitable civility, and led us into their sitting-room, a small but neat apartment, in which there was a chimney and a grate. 'T was here I began to regret more than ever the absence of Mr. Prince, whom I should have pinned to my sleeve and found such use in! However they made us comprehend that the house we were then in was built with their own hands five years ago; that they were sent by the Moravian Church in Germany; that their object was to convert the Hottentots, to render them industrious, religious, and happy; that they had spent some time in looking out for a proper situation, sheltered, of a good soil, near water – and that they had fixed here, – that they had been furnished with money by their Church to collect materials, and to assist them till they could earn something for themselves, – that they had procured some Hottentots to assist them in the beginning of the work, and by their treatment of them more had been encouraged to creep

Baviaans Kloof (Genadendal)

The Moravian Church, Genadendal

round them. "This grate," said he, "and all the iron-work, is my broeder's making; he got the bars, and fashioned it himself." The other two had raised the walls, which were of clay mixed with stone, and had done the wood-work and glazed the whole, – the tailor had taught the Hottentot women to make rush mats of a sort of reed, with which the floor of the church was covered over the clay, and which also lined it all round, shoulder high. They bid us step in to see it, which we did, – we entered from the small room we were in, and found it about forty feet long and twenty broad; the pulpit was only a few steps raised above the ground and matted with the same rushes, on which three chairs were placed, and a small table and desk, on which was the Bible. The church had benches on each hand, the right side for the men, the left for the women, and to these they entered by separate doors at the end.

I regretted much that it was Thursday and not Sunday, when I should have found the whole community, about three hundred Hottentots, assembled to divine worship; but I found I should have only seen them more dressed, and such as had acquired any clothes by their industry would have worn them, – I should also have seen a greater number; but that I should still see plenty, as at sunsetting every day, when business was supposed to be over, there were prayers. We retired to our parlour, and, the church-bell now ringing to bring them all together, when the church was full and all was ready, we begged leave to make part of the congregation.

I doubt much whether I should have entered St. Peter's at Rome, with the triple crown itself present in all its ancient splendour, with a more awed impression of the Deity and his presence than I did this little church, of a few feet square, where the simple disciples of Christianity, dressed in the skins of animals, knew no purple or fine linen, no pride, no hypocrisy. I felt as if I was creeping back seventeen hundred years, to hear from the rude but inspired lips of evangelists the simple sacred words of wisdom and purity.

The service began after the Presbyterian form with a psalm. Then indeed the note that raised itself to heaven was an affecting one; about one hundred and fifty Hottentots joined in the twenty-third psalm in a tone so sweet, so loud, but so just and true that it was impossible to hear it without being surprised. The Fathers, who were the sole music-masters, sang their deep-toned bass along with them, and the harmony was excellent. One fault only I found, – the key on which they took the psalm was too high, by which means the shrill pipes of the women rang upon the ear too sharply, and made one apprehensive of their own voices being injured by it. This over, the miller took a portion of the Scripture, and expounded as he went along, – how I wished to have understood him! but by the chapter he spoke from (St. Matth. viii.11), and a word now and then, I knew the subject he dwelt on, – that the goodness of God knew no distinction of persons, and that the Dutchman who was great and rich, with abundance of slaves and cattle, was not more sure of a place in a better world than the Hottentot was who was good, and who would find a seat in heaven kept for him to eternal happiness.

Mild and tender by nature, oppressed by the Dutch and often sinking under it, the poor creatures blessed God as they listened, while the artless tears of gratitude and hope fell down on their sheepskins. The Father's discourse was short, and seemed to be whatever came first without study, – the tone of his voice had no puritanism in it, it was even and natural; but when he used the words, which he often did, *myne lieve vriende*, "my beloved friends," I thought he felt to them all as his children. Not a Hottentot did I see in this congregation that had a bad passion in the countenance; I watched them closely – all was sweetness and attention; I was even surprised to observe so few vacant eyes, and so little curiosity directed to ourselves; I own our dresses, the great coats I have mentioned, well pounded in the waggon, were not very attracting.

Dinner was now ready, and we were well disposed to do it ample justice, but that dinner – bread, eggs, and vegetables excepted – was drawn from our own stores; we had one fowl by the bye, but that was all, – the Fathers never eat meat, unless the Hottentots bring them game, or an animal meets with an accident, in which case he is cut up and divided into numberless portions, and all fare gladly on what they are too economical to kill. They live on the produce of their garden chiefly, on milk, eggs, rice, coffee, but by no means object to meat when it comes their way. I helped the sweet old men to great lumps of cold meat again and again, particularly to ham, the half of one of which we had boiled, and never saw I finer appetites – "Broeder, eat this!" – "Broeder, take another slice." – "Ledi, ask him, he likes it! – at the same time telling us they had not tasted ham since they left Germany, – of course the piece was put aside for them, and thankfully accepted. Our cask of Madeira and our gin were next produced. They had no affectation about it, but gladly took, as a day of fete, all we offered them, and said they should often like to have wine, but that, their pride being to cost their Church as little as possible, they had accustomed themselves to do without it.

They professed themselves to be perfectly happy in their situation, though it was by no means free from danger, not from the Hottentots, who loved them, but from the boors, who were angry at their having come amongst them to teach the others how to be industrious and independent, – that, as to religion, they did not care whether they were enlightened or not, provided they were kept poor, lazy, and subordinate, – that the farmers had found the Hottentots more patient, tractable, and laborious than the slaves of the other countries that they bought – they also came infinitely cheaper to them. They had been in the habit of hiring them at three or four shillings a-month, – at first they used them well, but kept their wages in their hands; by degrees, as the debt grew longer, the Hottentot had more and more required of him without any means of redress; he felt himself compelled to stay on to move his master to do him justice, which was seldom or never done. "You see, therefore," said the Fathers, "that they have an interest in getting exclusively into their power the people who cultivate their grounds and do everything for them. – We, on the other hand, have taught them to do many things by which they daily become more and more independent of the Dutch; we have taught them gardening, made them attend to the seasons of sowing and reaping, got them to make butter and a kind of cheese, to work mats, to make flour; we have prevailed on each family to have a spot of ground round its craal to rear things on, – tomorrow you shall see them; and every morning at sunrising and sunsetting we meet in prayers, which keeps them regular and cleanly, – they are a mild, honest, but very inactive people; our religious tenets they understand enough to be charmed by them, and the more so that through us they find peace, ease, and no necessity for laborious servitude, – the farmers of course find it more difficult to get them for servants than they used to do, for when once a Hottentot gets to Baviaan's Kloof, and under this hill is taught religion, industry, and good order, he is frightened at the idea of service.

"At first they came but scantily to join us – by degrees more arrived; those who came first live the nearest to us – the new settlers are more distant, and begin to extend wide. You observed all those little patches as you came along, – they are the property of the craals; one man raises one thing, another another; they barter them or sell them at the Cape, and get clothes for them, pots, or what they may want, – but in the mean time we are here but to-day; we know not how soon the revenge of the farmers may take us off. Again and again there have been plans laid to murder us, – the last, when we erected the church-bell that you see there, which we put up to assemble the people together, as they could not always in bad weather guess at the hour, we were to have been shot with poisoned arrows when the congregation was assembled near it, for the church was not then finished; but it was the will of God that the plot should be discovered. Those who laid it live near us, and there is no security against the skill with which some of the African tribes shoot their poisoned darts, – a button or a bit of tobacco may be the price of a life."

You may easily suppose that this was a point to engage Mr. Barnard's warmest attention. We knew the thing before to be the simple fact, and a narrow escape they had; but as some of the Fathers, as they told us, meant to be shortly at the Cape to receive a new brother whom they expected from Fatherland, he thought there would be an opportunity then of laying the matter before the Governor, and settling what was best to be done for their security.

Jane and I had intended, with the assistance of Johnnie, to spend the small portion that remained of the evening in threading up our beads for the Hottentots, and drawing from our stores such little trappings as we thought would please them; but there was something in these worthy men that made me pause over this, – I had a presentiment that their good sense might object to the measure, and was determined to do nothing without consulting them.

They smiled when I shewed them my hoard, disapproved of nothing, but, thanking me for giving them leave to speak their minds freely, said, they would be glad if I kept back the beads and all other ornaments; they wished their minds to be turned to industry and not to ostentation, which is their natural turn; but if I had any garden-seeds, common knives, coarse scissors, or thread, they would be grateful for them, but reminded me that there were three hundred of them, and that, unless

Soetmelksvlei

some little civility from some of them justified particular gifts, it might introduce jealousy amongst the others.

Guided by his opinions, I put up my beads, and employed myself in new packing all the trunks, – like Esop's baskets, ours had been eaten lighter, and misfortunes (the effects of Pawell's bad packing) had made us still more so, the bottle of lamp-oil having been broken by the jolting of the waggon, and a bag of raisins finely soaked with it. My next object was to collect for the Fathers all the things we could spare, amongst which there was an English cheese, some tea, sugar, a piece of beef, a small lantern, a crockery lamp, a little rice, coffee, and brown paper.

But the present of all I put most value on, and which they seemed to value most, was the third part of the fleshy Margaret strawberry. Fond of their garden, and extremely neat in the divisions of it, I painted how delicious this fruit would prove if well taken care of, and that it was sent me by my sister Margaret, the most beautiful woman in Europe, who desired it might be called by her own name, – and you, Fathers," said I, "are the only people in Africa who have this." – The circumstance pleased them, – even under the Baviaan Kloof a pretty woman is not without her influence in creating the glow of vanity in a holy heart – they eagerly seized the paper.

In the small sitting-room a couple of cane sofas were put, and we contrived to spend the night very comfortably.

Friday, May 11th, 1798. – This morning I rose betimes. Mr. Barnard had told me that I had but three hours to make the best of, as we must get to Sweet-Milk Valley that evening – a military quarter for the cavalry, and reckoned the most beautiful situation in the country.

The first thing I did was to visit the garden, with which I was greatly pleased, but there were many things wanting in it which I hoped to be able to supply them with from seeds with good effect. Indeed I see no reason why these people may not be as rich as they please, having hands and soil. I mentioned the cotton-tree and indigo, both of which grow wild in this country,* – the marshy ground where we had almost been bogged I thought would do well, if drained, for rice – they believed it; and I recommended a very extensive plantation of potatoes as a capital good granary against starvation either in man or beast, – hemp and flax, I thought, might grow well, and there was a noble spot for a vineyard and for orange-trees. On these points we agreed and comprehended each other, which I was vain of, as I doubt much if my whole stock of Dutch amounts to two dozen of words. The miller attended me, the others prepared the breakfast and waited on the contents of the other waggon, in which there was a handsome, very fat young woman, whom Rubens would have married for a fourth wife if he had seen her and been a widower – an old woman, a bunch of children, and slaves.

We returned to breakfast, and sallied forth the moment it was over. My first object was to take a view of the place from a distance, where I could not only bring in the church, but have a view of a part of the craals which surrounded it; many of them reached far beyond what my drawing could take in.

The Father and I climbed the mountain to the right; the sun was warm, and shone inconveniently bright on my paper, – I put him be-

*country**
Wild cotton – katoenbos (*Asclepias* L.) and Indigofera, widespread in Southern Africa.

tween it and me till such time as little Charles should reach me with my umbrella. I then gave the old man his liberty, but he was pleased to see me work, and would not go. I did not succeed to my wish – the sun was too vertical to give me the proper shadows, and I do not understand drawing from a height. He was transported when I traced the church-bell; the erecting of it, I saw, had been a flattering epocha in the calm tenor of time. – I then descended with him, and hastily went through a dozen of the little gardens of the Hottentots; they were not very neat, but each one had something growing in it. The huts were of clay, thatched with rushes, some square as in Ireland, others round in the original Hottentot fashion, and brought up to the top without rushes, a hole only being left in the middle to serve as a vent, and another for the door. I entered one or two of the round ones, – the Hottentots were out, working in the field, furniture there was none, a few sticks were in the centre to boil their kettle, and tied to the sticks of the roof were a few skins, some calabashes, an iron pot, a couple of spoons made of bits of wood, to the end of which a deep shell was spliced and tied on, some calabash ladles and bowls. I saw nothing further to remark among the craals but the bakehouse, a nice round oven, where a Hottentot was baking the loaves of the others, – they nodded to us without awe as we passed.

The brothers who remained in the house were delighted with my drawing. The smith begged me to walk into his workshop; there I saw rough tools for hammering out iron into common shapes, and two or three Hottentots at work, making knives. He shewed me one that he said would soon be able to make knives without any more directions from him, an ingenious-looking lad of fifteen. "Here is what he does already," said he; "all my penknives are gone, but I have these remaining." I bought a couple – I suppose it is the means of livelihood to them; they generally sell something to the strangers who go to see them. This done, I sat me down by the door of the workshop, and took a view of the church and house nearer; it pleased them still more than the other, but the smith, in a woeful tone, asked *where* his workshop was, for *there* was the church and *there* the house, but his workshop was not there, though it was *here*, – he was not aware that I could not introduce the place I was drawing from. But I wrote under the sketch, "This was taken from the door of Mynheer Küpnel's workshop," which seemed at once to content him.

All at last being ready for departure, Mr. Barnard paid for the barley the horses had had, or rather the *bear*, as there is no barley here. We loaded the Hottentots who particularly belonged to the house with little gifts, – money would have been of no use to them. To the Fathers we gave presents, not forgetting the relics of the ham, – they gladly took all, with thanks, and we departed – pleased with the twenty-four hours we had spent, and only sorry we could not have doubled them.

We arrived at Sweet-Milk Valley early in the evening. Mynheer Tunis* gave us an excellent supper, dressed by Gaspar, who, I find, is head cook wherever he goes.

*Tunis**
'Bass Teunis', i.e. Marthinus Aegidius Theunissen, field-cornet.

Saturday, May 12th, 1798. – This same Sweet-Milk Valley does not at all answer my expectations. I was told of charming woods where the greatest variety of choice timber was to be found – stink-wood, ebony or black-wood, satin-wood, the wild olive, which resembles tortoiseshell when polished, and many others; but I saw not a tree. I learnt afterwards that there is a deep glen between the rising ground and the mountains, which is wooded all over, – this may be very useful, but does not beautify the country much. I had no time to go to see it, which I was sorry for.

Proceeded this day to the Landrost's of Swellendam,* but found to our dismay that they had been detained a day or two longer at the Cape than they expected, and were not yet returned. But here was another civil schoolmaster, the tutor of the *yonge vrow*, who is an only child, and whom he reports as quite clever enough, if she would mind her book. Like the other, he bewailed that all was locked up – even the apartments were – beds, bedding, wine, everything but such eatables as did very well for us; we therefore made a good supper on what we could get. The good *meister* gave us some of his private bottle of punch, and we got out our mattresses, sheets, blankets – and, after a good deal of laughing, went to sleep just as well as if we had satin canopies over our heads.

Sunday, May 13th, 1798. – Woke very early after a good nap, but could not help laughing very heartily, we resembled so much a set of strolling players in a barn. Got up, and prepared a very excellent breakfast for my fellow-actors. Thieved a few feathers out of the wing of a flamingo for my sisters – it was used as a fan to brush away the flies. – Departed with a guide – saw no house for five miles, and then another of the Landrost's, with craals around it of Hottentots belonging to the farm, all naked.

A good deal of game had got up on our way, but here a couple of immense birds appeared, larger than geese. Off went Hobgoblin with his rider at full speed – he dismounted – fired: – "I have killed him, by Jove!" said the transported Johnnie, as he brought me the bird – "see how fat he is – look how handsome he is! Not an officer of the mess will believe me when I tell him this – give me off one of his feet, I pray, to put in my pocket, that I may shew my voucher." – I begged him to defer that till we reached our journey's end, and tied the *pow*, or wild peacock,* to the waggon – a very fine bird indeed, of grave colours, but rich brown. – Passed through a stony river, the road worse for the waggon than the kloof – a quantity of wild thorns now grew everywhere, sometimes they met so close as to endanger our eyes. Three ostriches appeared at a distance, and a secretary-bird – Mr. Barnard on horseback endeavoured to shoot his colleague – Gaspar shook his head, and cried, *Neit goed, neit goed*! It is in the first place reckoned very unlucky to kill one, and is, in the second, contrary, I believe, to law, as they are supposed to be necessary to destroy certain enormous snakes, &c. – Johnnie Dalrymple's happy star shone bright to-day, for two core-hens and certain partridges and curlews also fell victims to his gun.

After passing a small brook, where the water appeared thick and brackish, Gaspar told us we must alight and dine, as the horses must have an hour and a half to rest. At liberty from their harness, up went

*Swellendam**
Anthony Alexander Faure (1758-1824). He had married Catharina Hardens and their daughter was Petronella Sophia.

*peacock**
Dutch, Pauw; *Afrikaans*, Pou; *English*, Bustard.

all the two-and-thirty hoofs in the air – hoofs, I may say, for the horses in Africa have no shoes, and they go so well without them, that even Mr. Barnard begins to doubt if the practice of shoeing is a good one, or whether there is not more harm than advantage in it to a sound horse.

Our cold meat, our Hamburgh beef, our tongue, our excellent butter given us by Mynheer Tunis, all with the sauce of hunger, tasted exquisite. A Dutch party would have eat away, and left the slaves to throw up their hoofs and refresh themselves with the horses, or have given them scraps afterwards, but we divided with our crew, and, with a very small *sopie* of gin to each, made them as happy as ourselves.

I plucked from the great thorn-trees some of their prickles, of which I send you a few; they exactly resemble the horns of the cattle. I hear the plant has found its way to Kew Gardens, and is there called the cuckold-tree; it is certainly no scndal to give it that name, for richly does it deserve it from the quantity of horns it bears, and, all being white, at a distance it looks as if the tree was covered with snow.

The Pottenberg hills here appeared at a distance, under which runs the Braid Riviére.*

We now remounted our waggon, and without seeing anything else to remark – house, river, corn-field, or human creature – in the course of the ensuing twenty miles, reached (rather late) the abode of Jacob van Rhenin,* where Mr. Barnard had so much wished to find himself, on account of the excellent sport he was told he should find there. As it was dark, I could only judge that we descended a hill to go to it, and I observed Gaspar was cautious of his footsteps, – in the shade I thought I could espy some giants on each side of us – they were aloes, which grow here in great abundance, and with their long bodies and bushy heads make very good ghosts. We were met at the door by Jacob van Rhenin and his vrow, a whole clutch of fair children, and many clutches of black. We saw at once that we were both welcome and expected.

When we entered the house, we found it rather different from the common style of Dutch architecture – better in some respects, but not so well as it might have been. We came at once into the hall or family-room, which was a good one of thirty-five by twenty-five, without any intermediate passage, – on the one side was our apartment, viz. the best one; on the other a smaller, where Johnnie, Pawell, and the baggage were to sleep, – the third apartment was that which the good people occupied themselves, and where, I suspect, all the children slept also. The kitchen was the fourth, and there was a trap-staircase to the roof of the house, which was used as a store-room, like all the rest of the farm-houses, – in which roof many convenient pigeon-holes might have been used if the proprietors had ever been introduced to the knowledge of what it was to be comfortable.

The vrow was of the same size and age with all the rest of the married women in the colony, – the moment half a dozen children are born, five-and-thirty and fifteen stone seem to be acquired of course. They have no idea, I see, of continuing to look handsome to please their husbands, – I believe the husbands would even think it odd if their wives were to dress neat and smart like the girls. A blue stuff petticoat, or a brown, a cotton bedgown with long sleeves, a double mock shawl hand-

*Riviere**
Potteberg, on the west bank of the Breede R. mouth, near Cape Infanta.

*Rhenin**
Jacob van Reenen, third of the name (1755-1806). His grandfather, Jacob v.R. I, emigrated from Prussia in 1721 and died 1760. His father J. v.R. II, was born 1727 and died 1794. His farm was the loan-place 'Slang-rivier', 5 m. west of Heidelberg and 24 m. from Swellendam, now known locally as 'Onder-Slang-rivier'. The house still stands but is much changed. He married Maria Catharina Persoon in 1781. (Information supplied by Dr. Mary Cook).

kerchief, and a Scots mutch, or round plaited morning cap, is the dress of every woman in the Cape when at home.

The vrow here had one perfection, which to me is a great one, an open and sweet countenance, no solicitude about anything, and tolerable good teeth – a very rare thing to be seen, as the women here lose the front ones entirely when they pass thirty, and they have no idea of supplying them. She pointed to the table, where tea and coffee boil over charcoal all day long, and milk ditto, saying, "Mak – self – know best vat like" – which was sensible – and gave us a good white loaf and choice fresh butter, which we made great havock on.

Johnnie now began to whisper something about the foot of the *pow*, and, as this seemed to be a house without ceremony, I told them I should strip it myself of its feathers in my own room, which I did, saving the best for you all, and those of the core-hen.* The children assisted me, and we were all very jolly.

At nine supper appeared, and was the best supper I ever ate in my life. There was at one end of the table a large shapeless piece of fine juicy roast veal; at the other a round of something black, like beef, larded – it was bontebock stewed in its own gravy, and admirable – no fat, I own, but the flesh a mixture between venison and beef – Mr. Barnard, though no supper-man, did it ample justice – potatoes also, rice and curry – a sort of soup – a quantity of our own partridges spliced and done on the gridiron with salt and pepper – bad Cape wine only, which we cared little about, having a store of our own, and some very tolerable apples, dried buck, and butter for dessert. *Her* father, a very old and beautiful figure, supped in his nightcap with us, as did Jacob himself – a Dutchman is never happy till he gets on his cap and night-gown. I expected to have seen him with his pipe also, like the others; but he never smokes, having lived elsewhere at the time first habits are formed. The schoolmaster was also of the party, and all the children, who were attended by an equal number of slaves, chiefly girls.

Van Rhenin proposed that next morning, if the day was fine, Mr. Barnard should go a hunting in his waggon, – he concluded the ladies would not like to go; but as he told us we should probably fall in with troops of zebras and other wild animals we had never seen before and might never have an opportunity of seeing again, both Jane and I resolved to be of the chase, though he bid us prepare to be as well jolted as ever we were in our lives. – At a reasonable hour we separated, and slept "like the sons of Kings" – perhaps better.

Monday, May 14th, 1798. – Up at a tolerable hour – we breakfasted – the waggon was ready, to which there was no top – the vrow declined making one; she had to get us a good dinner against our return, and she hinted another reason which the jolting of the waggon would not have suited. Off we set – Mr. Barnard, Johnnie, Jane and myself, Adonis, the gamekeeper or rather gamekiller, little Charles – and Gaspar driving – with a forest of guns in the waggon, all charged – fear being the only thing that had been dis-charged.

I perceived the house was placed in a small valley, somewhat like the bottom of a bason, the ground rising all round it, which kept it sheltered; but there was not a tree to be seen, a few thorns and aloes excepted. He

*hen**
Korhaan, most likely the Black Korhaan.

had built it about two years before, – part of the offices were not yet finished. When we got out of our bason and to the top of the ascent, a boundless plain opened before us, boundless except to the left, where some mountains rose at a great distance, and by the sea, as I was told, at another point, but these did not interrupt the wide range which the eye took in. "And now lend me the whip," said Van Rhenin, "and do you, Gaspar, hold the reins."

The whip he applied to his eight horses, who, knowing their master's taste, set off at full gallop, leaving the winds behind them. Game bolted out on all sides – I took my pencil to mark them down as they passed – six ostriches – six pows – one ditto – one buck – twelve wild geese – one hare – nineteen ostriches – one young steinbuck – four bontebocks – nine bontebocks – four steinbucks – four roebucks. The bucks always run against the wind; we therefore knew where they must pass, and galloped our waggon at full speed to stop their course by a shot. Van Rhenin took one of Mr. Barnard's guns, – he liked to shoot from the waggon, being rather lazy, and as Jane and I had no right to object to anything, having shoved ourselves into the party, off went the guns round us; but Van Rhenin was always too high or too low – I believe Adonis would have succeeded better. Mr. Barnard and the aide-de-camp, unaccustomed to this sort of hunting, preferred mounting their horses and taking their guns. Four or five hours we spent in galloping in this manner over the face of this immense heath, where half a dozen dry ponds or pools are the only varieties of feature.

The soil, like all the rest of the country, seemed good, waiting only to be tried to prove itself so. The heath fattens the cattle well, and, as the horses know no better, they are contented with it. The hills which appeared at a distance are the habitations of the zebras, who come down to the plain in certain winds, but they were at that time contrary. Van Rhenin offered to get me a couple of young ones tamed, but he bid me take care what they drank; they will eat most things and drink whatever they can find; he had had one killed with lime-water. When they grow old they become fierce and bite.

Much as we saw of game, we returned without killing anything. Mr. Barnard said he had shot and (he was certain) wounded a bontebock, but, as he had no voucher so strong as the foot of Johnnie's *pow*, we would not believe him. We returned before three, and found our good-humoured hostess and dinner ready for us – the table clean laid – game in plenty – but no meat except the continuation of the calf, the head of which was served up, as is the custom here, entire, with the horns and its own fine set of teeth. All was good however, and not so much undone with grease as in other houses. After dinner the conversation turned on the melancholy fate of the "Governor" a great many years ago, which, you may remember, was wrecked on one of the most barbarous shores in Africa.

This Jacob van Rhenin was the man who proposed to the Dutch government to send a party from the Cape to explore the interior part of the country, and to travel along the sea-shore to ascertain whether any of that unfortunate crew still lived.* Some were supposed to exist, – in particular it was believed that several of the ladies had been carried

*lived**
See Kirby (P.R.) *Jacob van Reenen and the Grosvenor expedition. 1790-91.* Johannesburg, 1958, p. 43-49. Van Reenen was not the leader of the expedition despite what Lady A. wrote, but only the journalist. The leader was probably Jan Andries Holtshausen.

off and forced to remain among the Caffres, – six years had elapsed since the ship was lost, but still there was a chance that some might be alive, and Van Rhenin, joined by eleven other gentlemen, his particular friends, (one of whom died of illness on the journey and another was killed by an elephant,) traversed a country which no civilized person before had ever dared to visit.

At first they ran a considerable risk from the Boschemen and Caffres, but, when they found what was the object of their journey, they did them no harm. Upon the best enquiry, they found that the crew which was saved consisted of two hundred persons, and that they had been able to collect a good many useful things from the wreck, but, being without a leader, the men would not bend to any authority, which was the chief cause of their misfortunes afterwards. They divided themselves into three parties instead of keeping together. The first went into a peopled country where the natives were fierce and poor, and would give nothing without a return, – those, alas! were starved to death. Another division, amongst whom were the women and children, remained in the middle part of the country, but they ultimately shared the same fate. A third party travelled by the banks of rivers and by the sea-coast, taking their chance of what they could pick up for subsistence, and were also lost in the end, all but five, who reached the Cape. Traces of many of these unfortunate people Van Rhenin saw five or six years afterwards – their skeletons, part of their clothes, two pieces of spermaceti candle which remained undamaged by the elements, and a silver coat-button, on which the unfortunate proprietor, "Colonel Johnstone,"* had engraved his name, leaving it, the last legacy of misery and affection, on the barren sand, though with but little hope that any pitying chance should ever send over that trackless desert a person who should find and convey it to his family. Van Rhenin gave the button to Colonel Gordon,* who commanded at the Cape, to find out by the spelling of the name and number of the regiment who had had such a relation. What a melancholy pledge it would be to receive of a son or brother!

The five people I before mentioned (probably sailors) surmounted ten thousand difficulties, and by following the tracks of the rivers, living on muscles and shell-fish, reached Cape Town. One of them, an Italian, carried all the way in his arms an infant belonging, he said, to the Governor of Bengal; but, on enquiring more closely, we found it must have been the child of Sir Robert Chambers.* He had nourished it on plantains and water, – at last he came to a spot of safety – he made a fire to warm it, and left it for a moment to see what he could gather for its support; the infant being cold crept to the fire, where it lost its balance and fell in; he found it alive on his return, but it died next day. Its parents never knew the manner of its death, and so much the better.

He told us, however, that, although no person remained of the crew, there was an old woman, near sixty years of age, an European, who had been found when a child by the Caffres under similar circumstances. She did not know from what country she came, but remembered to have sailed a great way in a ship. He proposed to her to come down and visit the Europeans at the Cape; she seemed intoxicated with pleasure at the idea, but said she could not till her harvest was got.* She had been married

*Johnstone**
Col. Edward James Johnstone of the Madras Artillery.

*Gordon**
Col. Robert Jacob Gordon (1743-1795) who surrendered the Cape to the British in 1795 and afterwards committed suicide.

*Chambers**
Thomas Fitzmaurice Chambers (aged 6) son of a judge of the Supreme Court of Bengal. There were at least two Italians in the crew of the *Grosvenor*.

*got**
According to Kirby this woman was never proved to be a *Grosvenor* survivor.

in the Caffre fashion to the richest man of the tribe, – that is to say, he had more cattle than anybody; and her sons by him were all Captains – a preeminence given to them voluntarily by the rest in compliment to her as a white woman. She still lives, and still proposes coming to the Cape, – I wish she would make her words good while I am here; I should be very glad to give old Caffraria an apartment in the Castle.

To-night we had what was a treat to Mr. Barnard, a large dish of oysters, and some very fine fish. Johnnie said the oysters were good, but they did not look so well as ours. Their shells are singular – I send two; every oyster has a room and a dressing-room, so, when she is "crossed in love" and unhappy, she may retire to her "boudoir." There are pearls frequently found in them. I wanted Van Rhenin to make an oyster-pit, and try to fatten up some jewels, – I must look into the 'Encyclopedia' for this – a book which, if thrown upon a desert island with one, would shove one forwards about a hundred years.

He proposed next day, if we liked it, to go on a fishing party to the mouth of the Breede Riviére, which is joined on its way by four others, and here falls into the sea. He dined there generally twice a-week, he said, in fine weather, "and my fat woman," said he, kindly taking his wife by the hand, "will have no objection to accompany you." She nodded assent – she has but little English, though she understands all that is said. This settled, we separated.

Tuesday, May 15th, 1798. – The charming weather still continuing, we mounted our waggon – not the light hunting machine, but one to hold all the family, and set off, partly the same road as before. Bucks, pows, and ostriches again appeared. At a distance a flock of birds still larger than pows were seen; they were so busy about something as not to perceive that we were approaching them, till, scared by guns, they mounted and hovered, half unwilling to depart. We found it was a company of eagles feasting magnificently on the identical bontebock we had faced Mr. Barnard out of the day before, – the spot was nearly where he had shot. But little more of the buck remained than the head. Van Rhenin took possession of it as a perquisite to the Lord of the Manor, and departing we gave the eagles liberty to renew their meal.

I met with a very aromatic grass here, which I took some of, but the smell has gone off. I wished to have had another plant, a miniature aloe, which is used as a kind of birdlime, but I felt shy of proposing it to others to stop for my fancy.

I got some curious bulbs of an odd plant, the leaves of which spread like a fan, thin and flat; and longed to have picked up some stones, so like French rolls, that it would have been impossible to know the difference. On falling down to the river, there was much fragrance from the bushes, a thousand agreeable but old-fashioned smells, such as the noses of nieces and nephews have been regaled with on the opening of old India cabinets of their grandmothers or aunts. On the shore there are flat black rocks to which square bits of iron are fixed, and are sometimes found detached; Van Rhenin supposes there is volcanic matter below – I send a specimen. I had not time to proceed on to where the sea-beans are found, but they gave me some, – they are highly esteemed by the Dutch, I know not why; they mount and hang them to their watches,

– I think they would make curious earrings. After taking a slight sketch of the shore, I saw the boat return, loaded with fish. Gaspar had lighted a fire amongst the bushes; the Vrow van Rhenin tucked up her sleeves, and, by the time my drawing was ready, dinner was.

On the grass we arranged ourselves – a sail-cloth for our damask; each one had his plate, each his appetite; mustard, salt, pepper were in calabashes. Adonis arrived, not loaded with game to the expecting Venuses, but with the tridents of Neptune, viz. four three-pronged pitchforks, on which were spitted fish, salted, peppered, buttered, roasted, before a clear fire on these forks, which were stuck in the ground, and a pan accompanied them of a hot sauce of butter, lemon-juice, soy, and cayenne. Nothing could be better – how I wished you all to have had a share with us, on Fortunatus's carpet! A fish-soup also came, which the others eat with rice; and a great variety of other fish, cut in pieces, and fried, made up the entertainment. Never did I see Mr. Barnard make so hearty a dinner, – he said the same of me with equal justice.

The nets were now hauled again, – they produced a huge skate, as large as a house, which sighed bitterly and died with difficulty; it was ordered into oil. There were a great many little fish like eels with it; they have bills like woodcocks, and are called bécasse-fish.* – We returned to our station, and there, reclining on the grass, while the gentlemen took a moderate sip of our Madeira, we looked round us pleased and praising the entertainment of the day.

Van Rhenin seemed to enjoy our satisfaction, and, conversation stealing on with ease and confidence, it insensibly turned on his first setting off in life, and what had led him to fix on a spot two hundred miles distant from the general residence of his family.

"My father," said he, "left Holland for the Cape when I and my three brothers were infants;* as they grew up, they married and settled; I remained with him as a sort of clerk, and he particularly loved me. On a certain occasion French troops were obliged to put in at the Cape; they were in distress for money and for necessaries, having neither credit nor bills; my father at his own risk ventured to let them have what was necessary, for which they gave him bills on the French Government, at the same time stating their obligations to him, – for which he was thanked by the great men in power, and by the bankers of the Court, but – not reimbursed.

"Years after years passed, and the want of the money became so inconvenient, my father having had other losses, that he raised the little he could, and, taking me with him, determined to go to Paris and seek redress there himself.* We were possessed of three hundred pounds in all. We went – we spent near three years in useless solicitation. In vain I called on the minister – he acknowledged the justice of my demand, but evaded the payment. Madame de Pompadour sent us a private message, that, if we would give her a third of our claim, my father should have the rest directly, – my father did not like to accept this offer. In this situation he was taken ill; vexation preyed on him, and we were at the bottom of our purse. He seemed resigned, and rather to wish for death, had he known what would become of me. I looked at my store – three guineas was all that remained. In vain I had of late pressed for admittance

*Bécasse**
Probably *Hemiramphidae* – 'halfbeaks', sometimes incorrectly called 'needle fish', (*See* Smith, J.L.B. & M.M. *Fishes of the Tsitsikama Coastal National Park*, p.85. Information kindly given by Mrs. M.M. Smith.)

*infants**
Incorrect. See note p.128.

*himself**
There has been some doubt about the accuracy of this narrative (see Kirby op. cit. p. 47), though it is understood that family tradition holds the story to be true. It is on record that J. v. R. II went to Europe in 1779 with the deputation from the Free Burghers to the Heeren XVII, but it is also a family tradition that he went earlier in 1772 when Louis XV (d. 1774) and the Abbé Joseph Marie Terray (1715-1778) were both still alive. Mme de Pompadour died in 1764 however and it must have been Mme du Barry that was intended. J. v. R. III would have been 17 years of age in 1772. A fundamental question however that is unanswered is, what were the French troops at the Cape which incurred the debt? There were many there in the years 1781-83, but not before 1772.

– the minister's door was shut. I now took a guinea and gave it to his Swiss – 'Friend,' said I, "I must see your master.' I was ushered in directly – I saw him look angry at the Swiss. – 'Sir!" said I – and I told my tale – 'my father lies perishing for want – there is three guineas; it is all that remains after three years that we have asked for justice – I have just given one to your servant.' – I remember," said he, smiling, "the figure of that man, as if I had seen him yesterday – he was galled by my misery, and writhing on his chair – wherever he turned, I saw him covered with orders and stars. – 'Well, well, well! there is a bill for five thousand livres, and the rest shall be paid by and by.' – I took the bill; saw it was all I had to expect. I went to the house of a friend, a man in trade, and, unhappy, opened my heart to him. He bid me come back to dinner and fear nothing. I did – a little old Abbé was there. After dinner my friend turned the conversation on what passed in the morning. I told my story with the eagerness of youth. The Abbé said, 'And is this so?' asking me some more questions. My papers happened to be in my pocket – 'Come to me tomorrow at twelve,' said he, 'and you shall find your business done' – I thought he was an angel, and asked my friend if I could depend on him. He said it was the Abbé Terrai who told me I might. I seized my hat and ran to my father, to tell him all would be settled; he shook his head and would not believe me. Next day proved that the Abbé had not deceived me. He carried me to the Court banker's and waited in the carriage till I carried in the order the minister had given me and received the money. The tone of the banker was changed in a moment, – he asked me to dinner the first time in the course of the three years since I had kissed his threshold. My father recovered, and we returned to the Cape.

"I had some genius for speculation, and I struck out a plan which, had it been permitted to go on unchecked, would have enriched me; but the great men in power here grew jealous of me; they wished to share the advantages with me, and I saw no reason why I was to give them away. They entangled me with lawsuits – I grew sick of my plan – I was not certain that my life was not in danger. I offered to the Dutch Government to go on the expedition I mentioned to you after the crew of the Governor, if they would pay my expenses. They were glad to get me out of the way. I left *her* at the Cape – for in the mean time I had fallen in love and married. I wished to see the country and to calculate my resources, for my father was dead.

"I returned – I spent six months in the Cape. I observed that qualities were wanting amongst the individuals – that a man appeared one thing and was another. I was disgusted with what I saw, and asked my wife if she could be contented to live with me at a distance from the Cape and from the haunts of her youth. She said it was all the same to her where she lived if I and her children were with her. We looked about for a spot to fix on – we placed ourselves at the foot of those hills I shewed you. I improved a little place, and three years ago I sold it well. I then looked out for another, and soon determined on this. I am fond of sports, and yet of an indolent habit – I dislike the labour and anxiety of farming, nor have I slaves who understand it. I have therefore chosen a place where by breeding horses, instead of raising grain or making wine, I am always supplied with the best for my own use, and make a gain while I amuse myself. By hunting and fishing I keep my table well provided and feed my children, while I am also pursuing my pleasures. I am perfectly contented and happy – she is so too:" – (she looked at him – it was the first sparkle of mind that I have seen in a Dutchwoman's eye since I came here): – "I was feared and hated while I was poor and supposed to be clever; I am now independent, and, away from rivalship, I am beloved and respected, – the first did not mortify me; the last does not flatter me, – but we are forgetting to put to the horses."

"This is the first *soupçon* of philosophy," said Mr. Barnard, "I have heard since I left Berkeley Square." We both united in liking this man, his wife, his children, his horses, his fish – all his ways, all his tenets; but we did not pay him any compliments – he saw we did not; many words are not necessary amongst honest people.

We returned home the way we came, only stopping at a house belonging to his brother, another Van Rhenin* – a great stable to it – two hundred horses, which Mr. Barnard looked over, but found none worth his purchasing. A little more size in the breed would render the Cape horses very good; they have already got a cross of the Arabian fire, and are hardy to the greatest degree, and as easily contented as to fare as mules, never having been pampered in their youth. At his place we found a garden in no order – good offices falling out of repair – a house dirty and inconvenient. How these people have everything, but possess things so unneatly, so indiligently, that there is the appearance of misery where there might be all the charms of comfort!

When we got home, we found a boor and his wife come to stay all night, – she the same age, the same size, the same petticoat and handkerchief, cap, bedgown; he in his blue cloth jacket, trousers, and white nightcap. I hope old England furnishes all this blue cloth. – Made the girls so happy with necklaces of the white beads I had by good luck put up – I see they are excessively admired.

Wednesday, May 16th, 1798. – A strong tendency to rain, which went off in the course of a few hours; but we thought it best to take an early dinner, and go out afterwards in the waggon. Van Rhenin said he was almost sure if we drove towards the hills we should see the troops of zebras. We dined therefore at one o'clock, and had for the top dish Johnnie's *pow*, stewed and then baked in the pan, with coals above and below. I never tasted any sort of game equal to it for delicacy and flavour. Its size was larger than the largest goose; its legs and back were white, like those of the finest woodcock; the breast was dark brown, and tasted of venison and pheasant. It was dressed with a *sauce piquante*, and was such a dish that I said I would give twenty guineas had it been at his Majesty's table that day instead of ours, – to which Van Rhenin assented, and drank his health like a loyal subject, contented with a good master, though not the old one.

Before I went out, Dunira, a pretty black slave, wife to Adonis, came into my room, and in a bashful way pointed to one of the white bead necklaces which lay on the table, and then to her own neck, seeming to beg for a row. This threw me into a sad quandary – to give a slave a necklace the same that I have given to the young ladies of the family! it

*Rhenin**
Dirk Gysbert van Reenen who also owned 'The Brewery', Newlands, Cape Town. His farm was Rhenosterfontein, one of the large circular horse-breeding farms, on the north bank of the Breede R. about 3 m. from its mouth and about 20 m. south-west of Slangrivier.

The Drostdy, Swellendam

would have been nearly as much as my life was worth in some houses, and to have displeased my hospitable landlord and landlady after all their civility to me – No, no! – I therefore shook my head, and made Dunira suppose I had no more – "All done!" – but I promised she should have something better. She left me, mortified. I thought, if I could manage the matter, that it was worth the trying, so I bid Mr. Barnard tell the story to Van Rhenin before his wife, and at the same time mention my objections to her request, that I had given of them before to the young ladies.

They both laughed, and cried out aloud, "Not to think anything of that, – that she had been born in the house, and was a sort of child of the family, – and that, if I had the beads, to give her them," – which I did, making her happier than a young beauty would be with a diamond necklace. I gave some of a common kind to a wonderfully clever little boy of the name of Fortune, a son of Adonis's by a Hottentot wife, who has since abandoned her colours, and left the field to Dunira.

We now set off after the zebras, and saw them at a distance, but they were wild, and scampered off. We saw the round hole where they come down from the mountains to roll themselves and spend the night. The gentlemen shot some game. We returned to the house, and I spent the evening in making memorandums of these simple matters, and in packing up anew our baggage, as we meant to depart early next morning, that we might reach the Landrost's of Swellendam by a tolerable hour.

Van Rhenin declared his intention of accompanying us for a day or two. He seemed to hook himself on to Mr. Barnard with a cordial feeling in which the "Secretarius" had no share, as he wanted nothing of him or of anybody, – and which Mr. Barnard returned as it deserved. – How to repay them for all their kindness we knew not – money they would not have accepted of. To defray the mere expense of the horses we always found practicable, as whatever the farmers buy they are never unwilling to receive back the price for – but for our living we saw it would be unfit to offer anything. M. Barnard therefore made him a present of a gun which he had praised, value in England fifteen guineas, and here, I suppose, double; while I gave his wife a share of all the articles I could spare from future calls, and a smelling-bottle with a double gold top. I tied up the heads and waists of all the children with scarlet and white checked riband, and gave to every slave a handkerchief, scissors, thread and needles, knife, and two schellings.

Dunira now stole into my room, and in her bashful way said, "You – you!" slipping into my hand a pair of cliches, or grey sea-beans,* which I send to the Queen of Dunira, Lady Susan, for a pair of earrings.

Thursday, May 17th, 1798. – Left the Van Rhenins at eight, bidding her adieu with the most cordial feeling of thankfulness for her kind reception of us that I had felt to anybody here. She had made us happy after the right fashion, given us liberty and the best she had to bestow, without ceremony and without requiring exertion of me – the most oppressive of all bills which can be drawn on my gratitude, and one I pay to be sure, but pay it fatigued and annoyed. Had I a fortnight at my command, to spend pleasantly where I should be sure to be welcome, I should not make a scruple of going to Jacob van Rhenin's, to partake of

*beans**
'Cliches' have not been identified, but 'sea beans' are seeboontjies or *Entadagigas*.

his fish from his pond, the ocean, and of his bontebock from his park of two hundred miles in circumference. She promised to come to the castle when she visited the Cape, but she had a bit of business to perform first, and then she must bring the *clyne kint* to get its name.

We proceeded to Swellendam by a different road from that we came by, driven by Van Rhenin and Gaspar in company – if one can call that a road which is pathless amongst the mountains, where no trace of human creature or blade of corn is to be seen. Gaspar seemed resolved to lay in a stock of talk to last him for some time; he never stopped chatting to Van Rhenin, – indeed, he had been sadly stinted in that way with us, so this was to him the feast of tongues. – On this hilly and heathy pasturage game seemed to abound still more than at Van Rhenin's; in one troop of bontebocks I counted seventy-two, and at a distance twenty-six zebras.

We reached the Landrost's at seven o'clock, after again crossing the abominable Stony River,* so rude a river, with so rough a bottom, and that so far extended, never did I see. They were now returned home, and we hoped to get a good supper and good beds, no longer comedians in a barn, but great people received by a great man, the prince of the place, or rather the Viceroy.

Friday, May 18th, 1798. – All slept well, but not the better for our rise in life – Johnnie thinks our barometer stood higher at Van Rhenin's than here. After breakfast I tried to find a good place to draw from, but could not, so fixed myself where I could find a stone for my seat. The sun shone bright and hot; a couple of African slave-girls, sisters, stood between me and it, unconscious of anything but how much pleasure they had in being of the party. I drew them, and they did not know it.

The mountains rise nobly at a couple of miles' distance or so; their bases were lost in a bluish vapour; greenish hillocks rose between us and them, – 'tis between them and the mountains, in a glen, much the same as at Sweet-Milk Valley, the woods are to be found which have been reckoned so luxuriant, but they are of no use to beautify the country, as their highest branch does not rise above the surface of the earth. Mr. Barnard and the gentlemen had gone out a hunting, or rather shooting; he had passed through those woods, and saw much fertile and well-watered country; he said it was the finest situation for settlers of any he had seen. They had killed a good quantity of game.

Our dinner was eatable though greasy – the evening was long. I must not, however, omit mentioning a present from the good Landrost which delighted me – the old great-coat which the serpent drops when he gets his new suit, which he does annually. It is rare that one is found in such preservation. When he has reason from his *feels* to think his new skin is stout enough to bear the air, he fixes the tip of his tail upon a thorn-tree, generally in a wood where he is not likely to be disturbed; he then cracks the skin under his jaw, and, like Joseph of old, glides off, leaving his garment behind him. I was so pleased with the skin, when shewn me, that my looks begged it, and the Landrost replied to their language; it is as fine as Cyprus gauze, with a beautiful net all over it. I shall send it to Lord Hardwicke.

Saturday, May 19th, 1798. – Detained here, waiting for Mr. Prince,

*River**
Not the Kliprivier to the west of the town but Buffelsjagt R. which is even stonier.

without whom we could not proceed on our journey, he knowing the roads, and Gaspar not.

Sunday, May 20th, 1798. – Attended divine service here. The audience was reverent and attentive, but in natural elegance the Hottentot assembly beat this hollow. Never did I behold so large or so fat a collection of human beings! Opposite to me there were eight women on the first row, who could not weigh less each than from fifteen to twenty stone – and the men the same, for, though they were not in general so fat, they were taller. Some of the young boors, however, had fine countenances, and two or three of the young women had much Flemish beauty, which one saw would swell within a couple of years into immoderate perfection. We had a good many *kinder* baptized, the boys in their little man's nightcaps; they had three names apiece.

But what did I see the moment after service was over? – a thin wizened man in black arrive, round whom everybody crowded – it was Mr. Prince, and with him a whole packet of letters to me from Europe! – How I passed the rest of the day I need not tell you – in my own room feasting; much good reading I had – everything to please, nothing to pain me – and only regretting the want of one or two letters to make me completely happy. I leave conscience to sting the guilty.

Monday, May 21st, 1798. – All being ready, I had only to dispense my presents – no disagreeable moment, for nothing being necessary to give, as in English houses or inns, to servants, everything is gratefully received. We breakfasted, and at eight o'clock, the weather still brilliant, cool, but comfortable, we remounted our waggon, with the addition of Mr. Prince sometimes along with us, when he was not mounted on his horse, Van Tromp, in pursuit of game.

As we drove off from the door a flag was hoisted, and the sound of cannon surprised me. Jane told me it was a compliment paid to the Secretarius, whose horse seemed to carry his tail rather higher upon the seven discharges. I should have preferred some cold beef or veal to this ostentatious respect, but the veal would have been to us only – the cannon was to be seen and heard of men, that they, bearing our good report, might glorify King George who is in England.

We dined as usual to-day at a farmhouse about half way to Jacob Corradi's,* where we were to halt for the night. We were received by the vrow, the mistress of the house – O house, unworthy such a mistress! as she was larger than her mansion. She seemed to me to be about forty, nor could she weigh less than twenty stone, – if she weighed twenty-four I should not have been surprised. We have seen Mrs. M——, she is a mere nothing to this woman, for Mrs. ——, though large, has not an equal portion below; on the contrary, the Dutchwomen, like respectable piles, have a balance beneath the surface of petticoat, which steadies what is above. Her eldest daughter was very handsome, and must have weighed about eighteen stone; she was the picture of the goddess Ceres, a goddess more of the earth than the heavens. Her child of fourteen months walked and talked, and was so heavy I could not pretend to lift it from the ground. Their dinner was over, which I was sorry for, as I like to take part of what is going, without putting any one out of the way, – they regretted it, because we should have a hurried and

*Corradi's**
Probably Jacobus Conradie, born 1752, who married Else Sophia van Rensburg.

bad one; but I believe we gained by our loss, as we had it cooked by Gaspar, to the great saving of the contents of the grease-pot.

Johnnie soon provided entertainment for us, by shooting two or three fowls who had baffled the attempts of the slaves to catch them. Meantime the Hottentots got round me, and I drew one little girl, not arrived at woman's estate, who had a sweet countenance, and whom I should have liked to have taken with me; but she would have been too dear a purchase, being the property of the farmer, unless I had known her qualities to have been good. Every Hottentot child born in the family when the mother is receiving wages is the property of the master of it for twenty-five years, which is supposed a proper length of time to compensate for the charge of maintaining the child in infancy. It is in reality about twelve years too much. A Hottentot child is at seven years of age employed to tend fowls, sheep, cows, and its work fully repays the expense of its miserable board. The six following years are certainly sufficient to liquidate the past and pay the present; at thirteen, fourteen, or fifteen at most, I should think the child ought to be free; and I have some reason to hope the Governor will shorten the term of slavery to those poor oppressed creatures. I am sure he will, if he thinks it just.

While taking the picture of the Hottentot girl in her own attitude, I spied a poor *clyne* Hottentot in a chair which had lost the matting, by way of a go-cart, to keep it from harm. Its mother, they told me, was a Boschewoman and in the fields with the goats. I had never seen a right Boschewoman, and begged them to send for her, which they did. Meantime I took the child out of its chair, set it on the floor, gave it an apple, and bid it sit still.

It looked like an Indian god, but it sat well – very well – better and better. I drew on, and soon found the little god had fallen asleep in its attitude. In this situation it remained till the Boschewoman arrived from the goats and entered the room. She was not a *figure ragoûtante*, but instinct rendered her dear; and there was something beautiful in seeing the little god wakened from his sleep (probably by her smell), and crawling on all fours directly to the place where stood its miserable parent, who, pleased and proud, gave it something for its reward that no one would have robbed it of.

Her countenance was sweet to a degree – extremely like Lady —'s; her size about four feet, and her shape singular enough behind, as far as one could judge by the rotundity which her sheepskin seemed to conceal, though a slender woman. I cannot think this was a real Boschewoman, her countenance had so much of the Hottentot mildness in it.

After dinner I begged Mynheer Prince to invite the vrow and her husband to visit me at the Castle, when they came to the Cape, and desired him once for all to ask every boor and his wife who shewed us any civility. Mr. Prince stared at me – "Are you serious?" said he. "Certainly," said I; "I feel obliged to them; they give me what they have, and will hardly accept of payment – I wish to be civil to them in return" – "Nay," said he, "you are perfectly right, I believe; but I never heard any one talk of returning a civility in all my life." – "The more shame to them," said I, "Mr. Prince." – He spoke to the vrow, and she nodded assent, as is the Dutch fasion, very few words being used on such occasions.

141

Ds. J.H. von Manger, predikant of Swellendam, and a little girl, possibly the Landdrost's daughter Petronella Faure. The decorated floor was recently rediscovered in the Drostdy and restored.

Mynheer Hoffman of Swellendam

This settled, we shook hands and left them – but not them only; their *stoop* was covered with a set of large idle boors in their blue jackets, sons of the family – men who do hardly anything beside eating and smoking, scarcely superintending the work of the farm, which is carried on by the slaves, but certainly never digging, threshing, or holding the plough. All looked at us with great curiosity, but none had disaffection or hostility in his countenance. I believe the farmers are far better contented with the English government than the people of the town, yet all benefit by it, a few excepted, who have lost good places and whose wings are clipped respecting monopolies, and who cannot, when the fancy strikes them, encroach on the rights of the weak in their farms distant from Cape Town.

Can there be a greater proof of the flourishing situation of this country, compared to what it was formerly, and the increasing riches of its inhabitants, than the complaints the president of the court of justice makes, that there is now not above one bankruptcy in a hundred to what there used to be, and that he is an undone man for want of customary fees – great part of his salary being paid in that way? The hangman too complains that people are either growing honest or rich, for that he has no longer anything to do. All this is very flattering testimony in favour of our Governor's jurisdiction.

We left these good people, and passed nothing worth marking down, heath and hill being all, enlivened by a few partridges, till we arrived at the house of Jacob Corradi, where we slept.

Tuesday, May 22nd, 1798. – The family were all dressed, and had drunk the dish of coffee with which they begin the day, before we appeared. They rise by candlelight here all the year round, stinting themselves much, as we should imagine, in sleep, did not the two hours' nap they take in bed after dinner make amends for their early rising. They certainly make the most of life by contriving to have two days and nights out of every twenty-four hours, and their plurality of meals, two dinners in one day, being equal to their plurality of sleeps, – but I do not like their division of time, nor the effects it produced either on the mind or body, sloth and constant eating being certainly the cause of the unwieldy fat, which they have not an idea of preventing or regretting, looking upon it entirely as a matter of course; nor am I sure that they are not a little vain of it, as it testifies of good fare, and enough of it.

When we dressed ourselves and got into the next room, we found Mr. Barnard making his toilette in the corner, and busily talking Dutch with the young vrows, who had attended him through all the manoeuvrings of a tidy man's morning ablutions. A toothbrush they had never seen before, nor indeed anything else almost, combs excepted. I went into the kitchen – the roof was hung as full of dried meat of different kinds as the Drup Kelder was of petrifactions, but chiefly of mutton and buck, – it was filled with servants belonging to the farm, Hottentots, &c; but such good fare as the dried meat comes not to their lot. I believe I have before mentioned that they have rarely anything given them but bread; at some of the farmhouses they are even worse off, getting the fourth part of a raw pampoon, a sort of pumpkin or bad melon, which they carry into the fields with them when they have cattle to tend, – it must last them for the day.

Amongst others, there was a Hottentot woman in the kitchen so near her time that she could not have had many days to depend on. I made Pawell ask her if she had anything to put on the little one. He did. She shook her head. Did she expect to lie in soon? She shook her head again. "Is her husband belonging to the farm?" "I need not ask her that," said Pawell, "they have no husbands, my lady!" – "So much the worse for them, Pawell – but tell her, then, that here is some check to make clothes for the *clyne kint*, when it comes." – The poor creature now "bloshed" (as Pawell said) with pleasure and surprise – a present for the child she was to have! she did not quite understand it – but it was very entertaining, and she laughed heartily.

Whatever I looked at or mentioned, the two good-natured strange girls brought me with unaffected generosity. I had given them some of my stores – they could not in return heap enough on me. I even saw they had secreted dried buck and sausages in the waggon, because I had praised them. On departing, they permitted Mr. Prince to pay them for our horses and fare, but they added, or rather would have added, honest people! gifts of their simple sort worth more than their bill came to. This was very unlike the inhabitants of Cape Town.

We now got into our waggon, after giving them a cordial invitation to the Castle, and proceeded on our journey, falling down first into a valley, rendered almost green by a variety of such plants as our greenhouses in Europe are stocked with, and from which we fell down into another valley of the same description. Of these valleys or basons there were four. The country is called the Noray.*

I plucked from one of the high bushes some black round berries like small shot; they made a beautiful purple dye, which in an hour became a bright Prussian blue, and might I think be converted to some use, – but how many useful things lurk in Nature all around one, which the eye of ignorance sees not, and which the eye of the skilful botanist and chemist has not yet discovered! Wherever I go, whether in Africa or in Europe, I cannot help being often possessed with the idea of being hoodwinked to things around, – but we shall all see more clearly when we have no mortal eyes to look with.

After travelling about three hours, I saw a little brook that wandered at a distance through some low bushes. I had just been regretting to Jane that I had not seen any of the Hottentot ladies in their natural but also ornamental state, the servants of the farmers being kept to too much drudgery to be vain, and the disciples of the Herrnhüters have the disposition in them checked as much as possible by the Fathers. I had hardly expressed the regret when my good genius presented to me Pharaoh's daughter in the very brook before me, washing her royal robes, and perhaps one of the most picturesque creatures it was possible to see.

From afar I saw my copper-coloured princess seated on a stone, and all over ornaments, and hinted to Gaspar that his horses, I was sure, would be glad of a sip of water, but found him inflexible, – to give any gratification to a horse to make him go on the better was Greek and Hebrew to him. I was therefore obliged to tell the truth, that I wanted to draw the vrow. He shook his head. Mr. Barnard said he would not witness such doings, and scampered off. I dropped two minutes of the

*Noray**
Probably Nuy, 9 m. east of Worcester.

five I had prayed for, and I trust no one will expect much from a sketch done in that time. I bid her stand up – she saw what I was about, and was delighted with it. From whence can a Hottentot girl have acquired the idea of having a picture done for her? She stood as if it was familiar to her, yet I dare say it never happened to her before.

When I had marked the form a little and the dress, I offered her four schellings or a *dook*, viz. a handkerchief; she preferred the last. I recollected having some old silver lace in my workbag which had been on a court-dress, – I thought it a royal present, as it had seen their Majesties, and fit for her Highness. Her transport on seeing it passed all bounds; she clasped her hands to adore it, tied it round her head, then took it off, and spread it out on the bushes. I fancy the washing was over for that day, so fully had the finery taken hold of her heart. She was the best-made woman of her sort that I had seen – extremely tall; her countenance, though less sweet than that of many other Hottentots, was frank and ingenuous to a great degree, and she had much the air as if she had been told she was handsome, and had nothing to reproach herself with in want of tenderness of heart. She was really a gallant-looking girl of eighteen, and resembled extremely my old and kind friend Mrs. L —— when she was about that age.

We reached our destination, the Brandt Fly Baths,* between seven and eight at night, our bones complaining much of an eight hours' journey, and flattering ourselves, from the title of "The Baths," we could not fail to have good fare and good beds, the season for the sick people being over. The look of the place, however, soon shewed me what was to be expected.

The master was a fat boor, decent enough in appearance, though dirty – his wife a peevish-faced Madonna, *passée*, with a child rather needlessly large for its situation in her arms. A very old grandmother, of whom I shall say nothing, an infirm man on crutches, two men with bad legs, one with a much worse, five or six children baffling description, and a dozen of slaves and their children, were contained in the eating-room. They apologized for supper, which was ready to put on the table – they had some cause. There was a dead chicken, which had paid the last debt to nature by some malady, and was half-boiled; it was swimming in rice and water – some pieces of boiled dried mutton – ditto of beef, putrid – a dish of terrible spinach – a stewpan with a dog's mess in it of yellow pumpkin – and brown bread, which, though bad, was the only thing which could be tasted. I forgot to mention a pot of sheep's-tail grease for butter, – and all this amidst stinks of every description. I durst not look, but tried to float my eyes lightly over everything, fixing them on nothing. Johnnie tugged away at boiled mutton, – Jane put on her plate a bit of the fowl, which there remained. Mr. Barnard knew not well where to apply, – and I declared that, as I never ate supper, I would beg permission of the vrow to have some tea and bread and butter, – that I had everything with me, and only requested boiling water. I perceived the countenances of two of my friends rise on this proposal, which I carried into effect, and certainly there never was a heartier meal made in the nursery than Mr. Barnard, Johnnie, and I made of what my stores produced. Jane would not join us, but retired to bed in silent despair.

*Baths**
Brand Vlei near Worcester.

Pieter du Toit's homestead, Breede River valley

We soon followed, and found her laid along for the night in her powdering-gown. I had got some little arrangement made for her bed and Johnnie's, but nothing good; he therefore laid himself along in his clothes, as did Mr. Barnard and I, foreseeing that, if there were any fleas in the colony, here they would be at home.

Wednesday, May 23rd, 1798. – The event justified my apprehensions, – we were all bit to death; and before it was light our room was invaded by men, women, and children searching beneath our beds for shoes, stockings, shirts – everything which had been stuffed there out of the way on our arrival. Mr. Barnard attempted to scold them off the field, but, as he was not understood, they returned to the attack. – At daybreak we got up – no bason, no bottle of water to be found in a house where washing anything seemed to be unknown. We sallied forth therefore to the spring, where hot water being in plenty, we availed ourselves of it to wash the hands at least.

When we returned to the house, we found all that we had required, boiling water and a very dirty leaden teapot, which I soon made a clean one. Jane arrived after us, and, finding no clean cup, called for one. The Madonna had not another, but she gave her one of the child's nightcaps to wipe the one Mynheer Prince had used. I hoped this would have made Jane laugh, but she was more ready to cry. We have all our different ways of taking small misfortunes. I feel all those sort of ridiculous inconveniences which I cannot help (provided they do not happen at home) as jests – Jane as injuries – Johnnie as nothing at all, or, if as anything, as "the devil's own circumstance," – and Mr. Barnard remembers how it was at St. Lucie,* and how much worse that was than the present ill, be it what it may.

As soon as the horses could be got ready, off we bowled, rejoicing to have escaped from this abode of needless nastiness – for I have not told one half of the horrors that hemmed us round.

The farther we proceeded through the valley, the more bold and picturesque became the mountains, their form more varied and striking than any I had seen before. These as usual were succeeded by others and others. We were to dine, Mr. Prince told us, at the house of one Peter de Joy,* where we should be tolerably well off, and where it would be advisable for us to spend the night, as we had a long journey to make next day to reach the house of Mynheer Du Val,* – we had but little expectation of good from so faint a recommendation; but there was still another farmhouse some miles further on, where we could halt if we found this one too bad, though at some risk of being too late. We determined however to try Mynheer de Joy's first, and after a dreadful deal of jolting we drove up to the door.

What a noble near mountain – what a nobler distant one, spiral like a cathedral – and what a capital rock as a foreground! Trees were wanting, but, as Margaret would say, the "bones of the country" were charming. The farmer, his wife, and two daughters came out to receive us. The farmer had an unformed fit of the gout hanging over his spirits, which sometimes attacked his stomach, but had not yet reached his toe, – I never saw a poor man more evidently under its influence. His wife was a clean woman of forty, with a cap well washed and nicely pinched, and two pretty daughters.

*Lucie**
St. Lucia, Windward Is., W.I. Andrew Barnard was there during his army career.

*Joy**
Du Toit.

*Val**
De Waal.

When we entered the house we were agreeably surprised with a cleanliness as singular as the contrast we had only quitted; the Staffordshire plates in the inside of their glass cupboard shone bright, having been well wiped with a clean cloth – no greasy nightcap, – the brass spoons and ditto tea and coffee urns were polished as looking-glasses. – "Mynheer Prince," said I, "this house is delightful, it is so tidy." – "Ay, ay," said he, "well enoof." – but he did not seem to be struck with the difference. We resolved to rest here for the night, – further on we might fare worse; so we declared our intentions and found no difficulty.

Dinner was soon ready – a milk-white napkin spread on the board – all was good, clean, savoury – and as we were all not a little hungry, having had nothing for twenty-four hours almost but bread and butter, we did it justice. The master of the house sat melancholy in a corner – Mr. Barnard called for his Madeira, and, very much against his inclination, made him drink some glasses of it, – he had an idea that any strong liquor would kill him; whether it do so or no we shall see to-morrow.

Amongst other dried things they gave us excellent dried peaches, done without sugar, and cured in the sun; the dried fruits of this country are much liked, particularly in India, – at first they are not particularly palatable, as they fully as much resemble leather as fruit; but on chewing, the taste of the fresh fruit is found to be more preserved than in the fruits that are done with sugar. Mr. Barnard is so fond of these dried peaches that he became purchaser of Mynheer's whole stock. – "You will bring these to me," said he, "when you come to the Cape, Mynheer." – Mynheer shook his head, and bid Prince tell the Secretarius he should not live to be there again. We hoped better things from the Madeira. This man was the picture of good health – rosy, and scarcely forty years of age.

[Cape Coloured girl with monkey]

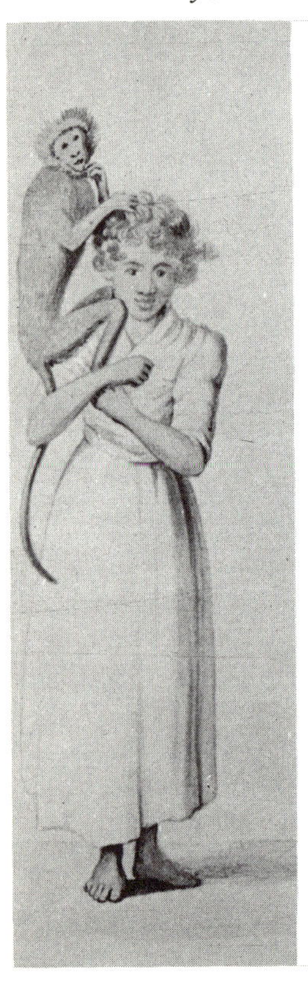

While standing at the door, an old Hottentot, who might from her appearance have been two hundred, came up, dressed in all her finery; her business was to tend the goats, – she wore beads in profusion, and, as I expressed a desire to have some of hers, which from their equality were such as are most valued, Mr. Barnard gave her a couple of dollars for a part of her necklace. It appeared to me that they do not know distinctly the value of money, for Jane gave her two schellings for her bracelets, and she seemed full as happy.

These good people were very civil to us – gave me calabashes, Job's-tears – a pretty sort of grey seed which the Hottentots string into necklaces – and everything else they could think of, – in particular, a milk-basket which I looked at with a covetous eye, in which the Caffres carry their milk – which they weave so close with certain rushes that, after once using, the milk cannot get through.

We retired to roost betimes – we had but one sheet to each bed, but it was clean, as everything was in our apartment.

Thursday, May 24th, 1798. – We were scarcely out of bed when all the vrows and all the slaves invaded our room. I saw from the anxious eyes which darted into my boxes that, if they liked to give, they also wished to receive; so I gave the young ones all the ribands and beads I could spare, tea and sugar to the mother, and handkerchiefs to the slaves.

On entering the public room, which in all houses is the same, that which one walks into from the outer door, I saw Mynheer with a new countenance – the enemy was no longer triumphant – the Madeira had done its duty, and, after battling it bravely and keeping him roaring half the night, the disease had retreated to his toe; of course he thought himself in heaven, and talked as if he expected and wished for no other these fifty years. Mr. Barnard left him a legacy of some bottles of the physician.

After travelling about four hours, we crossed a pretty deep though narrow river, and stopped at a farmhouse of good size, where Mynheer Prince told us we should dine. No invitation on such occasions is necessary from the farmer, – when a waggon stops at the door, he concludes of course that the passengers want to *scoff* (to eat), and the horses the same after they have rolled themselves. Here we fell in exactly with the dinner-hour, twelve o'clock, and got to be sure a very greasy one, dressed after the right Dutch fashion.

The farmer was a complete boor, in his white shirt and a slouched hat of an enormous size, such as is to be seen in old Dutch pictures, but not more enormous than the figure it had to shade. The board was filled with sons and daughters, the sons equal in size almost to himself, the daughters promising to follow the example of their mother. In this house I saw the first trait of female industry, the vrows being employed in making clothes for their "men." I found the mistress of the house was mother-in-law to the children, so I presume she had not encouraged the same indolence in the ladies that would have been permitted had they been her own.

Since working was the fashion here, I gave needles and thread to all. On endeavouring to pay the charge, the boor would not listen to receiving money, but talked in a high but liberal style of the pleasure of giving a share of what he had to a stranger. To say the truth, I find the whole of this class of people very hospitable; and I hear they are equally so to others whom they may be supposed to have less interest in obliging.

We left this boor's house, whose name was De Foset,* and proceeded to the Roysand Kloof,* a very long pass, which we were obliged to walk, the waggon slowly dragging on before – the road very bad, but romantic. As we reached the summit, the sun was beginning to set with a glowing orange ray to the left, behind the hills, but where he still permitted us light to see and start at the image which presented itself – a jet-black castle, turreted all round, with a strange oddity of a rock or building at a small distance, on the top of which was placed an enormous urn, which seemed to be the sarcophagus of some giant who had been slain by the prince of the castle, who of course must have been the King of the Caffres, by its sullen, dark appearance. I was grieved to hear that it had no history, but was simply a production of Madam Nature's in one of her freaks. I drew it, but have done it no justice – I'll do it more if I find leisure and get into the humour; for I'll give it a history, write an original Hottentot song, translate it myself, put it to Hottentot music, and celebrate the fair maid confined by the cruel giant in the dungeon of the Black Rock till rescued by her lover, the Prince of the Caffres!

Nature had even gone so far as to make some windows in this tower,

*De Foset**
i.e. de Vos. According to Fransen and Cook (p.192) this was the farm Aan de Brederivier (now Olifantsberg) of Jacob de Vos.

*Kloof**
Roodezand, i.e. Tulbagh.

The duckpond at Mynheer Leiste's farm, Gelukwaard

through which the rays of light darted. I liked it much – it was the finest object I had met with in a country where objects are thinly scattered, unless we count in the mountains, which are generally splendid ones. In the more interior part of the country I believe Nature is more various and less barren. King James used to call the county of Fife a worsted petticoat with a gold fringe on it; I fancy the Cape reverses his simile, and is rather a gold petticoat with a worsted fringe – the skirting of the sea being far inferior, as I am told, in fertility to what Africa is in those parts through which Mr. Barrow* is now travelling, and is probably still more so in those remoter quarters to which he cannot pierce.

It now began to grow very dark, but Mynheer Prince knew the road, and went before us till we descended into the more civilised part of the country, and after travelling some miles more, and passing the Lion's Rocks, so called from a fierce one having been killed there about fifty years ago, we reached the house of Mynheer Du Val, a wealthy man of rather higher class than the other boors, and one of the tallest men I had seen. He and his wife welcomed us with cordiality.

Friday, May 25th, 1798. – Pawell having sprained his back, we gave up the plan of proceeding to Saldanha Bay till we saw if he was better to-morrow. Mynheer Du Val drove us in his waggon to a farmer's of the name of Leester,* where we dined. We were received by a lady *d'un certain age*, with a black patch on each side of a bright black eye, a pretty daughter, and an old lady, very infirm, who I afterwards found was the mistress of the house, and about twenty years older than her husband, who, I was told, was a "smart young man," then at the Cape; he had married her for money, she him for love.

This was a most comfortable-looking place – plenty of trees – a good garden, from which I took two samples of indigo – a nice pigeon-house, well stocked with tame pigeons, which are the only ones used here, unless wild ones are accidentally shot, like other game, – a pond for ducks, geese, &c., over which birds' nests hung in hundreds from the branches of the trees, made of the stalks of grass, with a hole at the under end by which the bird enters. Where the nests are exposed to danger from serpents or other noxious creatures (which they could not be here, hanging over water), the entry to it is made like a long narrow tube.

All looked wealthy and flourishing here; even an honest barn-door hen I admired, chuckling about, with forty-six chickens behind her; probably she had had several clutches consigned over to her care more than her own; the slaves told me she was *goed hunder*, a good fowl.

In a corner of the room, stuck up with a pin through him, I saw what was to me a great curiosity – the king bee, – for here bees do not submit, as in Europe, to a female government, but have a king of no small size and power.* His body is as large as a large moth, his face marked exactly as a death's-head, and his sting is mortal. They gave us an instance of the rapidity of the poison, by mentioning that a Hottentot had been found dead with his hand in the nest, robbing it of the honey, – the king must have inflicted speedy justice on him. I longed to ask the dead body of this monarch, but they did not offer it and I was modest. When I like anything much, I suppose it is equally valued by the possessor, and that seals my lips, – I have generally found myself wrong,

Barrow* undertook three journeys at the Governor's request to improve knowledge of the Colony. This one was the second – April-May 1798 – when he visited Saldanha Bay and Florisfontein and returned via the Roggeveld and Kardouw Pass.

*Leester**
Christoffel Hieronymus Leiste, a German and former land-surveyor. His farm was Gelukwaard. (See Forbes, V.S. *Pioneer travellers*, p.84.)

*power**
No justification for this assertion can be found.

and that the possessor, from having had it long, is so tired of it that it had not been offered to me from the idea of its being unworthy of my acceptance; but in spite of knowing this, I go on playing the fool.

They gave us a very eatable dinner, – it was scarcely over when our waggon was ready for departure, and another with eight horses drove up to the door, out of which alighted a short, round, quizzical man of fifty, dressed in dark blue, bound with gold – it was Mynheer Leester, the master of the house, returned from the Cape. "Ha, Mynheer Prince!" – shake hands, – "Ha, the Secretarius!" – shake hands again – talking away to the coachman all the way as he walked into the house – smacked the old lady – still talking – smacked the vrow with the patches, and then the daughter; 'twas all in the day's work, – these businesses over, he set himself down, put on his nightcap, and was ready for a pipe, or a *sopie*, or whatever the Mynheers pleased. But it was too late – we were obliged to return to Du Val's; so, getting into the waggon, we bid them good evening. I had kindly invited the old woman to visit me at the Cape, – I saw it was the fashion of the house to neglect her, by the gratitude of her manner to me.

Saturday, May 26th, 1798. – Left Du Val's – St. Helens Bay* at a great distance to the left, the Sandenberg and other mountains to the right – before us, but far distant, Elephant's River, with the mountains where is the source of the twenty-four rivers.* – Nothing struck me remarkably on the road except the strong resemblance there is in the first part of the country we passed to part of Fife – the lands carrying good corn, but there is little plantation.

We dined at a farmhouse, situated on a rising ground which commanded the view of an extensive sporting country, – the master, whose name was Losper, had a degree of civil, serious polish about him, that was genteel in a boor.

After dinner we travelled on; it grew late, and, the further we went, the heavier grew the road – at last it became a deep sand, up to the axle-trees, which lasted till we reached Mynheer Slaber's, where we slept. * Mynheer was at the Cape, but we were received by the old moeder, by his daughter-in-law, two daughters, and a granddaughter of her own, of whom we shall say something to-morrow, – at present, as we all are a little fatigued, let us bid each other good night.

Sunday, May 27th, 1798. – Long, long before I thought of rising, I heard a little gentle wandering through the house, and found it was the old lady, who, though seventy-seven years of age, gets up before five every morning, and gives out the barley for the horses and necessary directions for the farm. She is reckoned a prodigy at her time of life; her person is erect, but her face more wrinkled than anything I ever saw, though not without remains of beauty. Her family, which are numerous, are reckoned the tallest people at the Cape, running on between six and seven feet high – I have seen others quite as tall, but the curiosity is, that there is none, man or woman, amongst them that is shorter.

She and the rest of the good folks had had their dish of coffee three hours before I appeared, and when I did, I found a respectable company assembled, whom I had not seen the night before, – from twelve to eighteen favourite cats, who breakfast with her every morning, and do

*Bay**
St. Helena Bay.

*rivers**
While the general direction of Lady A.'s progress is fairly clear, the mention of various mountains and rivers is sometimes rather surprising. There is a small range of hills named the Sandberg 2½ m. south of the Heuningberg and 15 m. SSW of Porterville. The Olifants R. Mts. begin some 15 m. beyond Porterville and the Twenty-four Rivers have their sources in them and the Gt. Winterhoek.

*slept**
Johannes Slabber of Theefontein.

Mevrou Slabber of Theefontein

Christoffel Leiste of Gelukwaard

not reappear till next day, but hunt for themselves amongst the low bushes. They were very beautiful ones indeed. I thought of the Hermitage, my dear Annie Keith! – of the old Commodore – and wished Auntie Babie had had the pleasure of seeing them, though she would not have allowed them to be as handsome as her own.

The eldest daughter is rather what may be called a fine woman, not unpleasing, and she alloys her masculine size with a little tender affectation of manner, which did very well. Perhaps gratitude made me think so, as she took much to me, calling me a *lieve vrow*, a dear lady, – and in return I did for her a resemblance of her old mother, which she told the poor old lady she should look at many a day when she "was gone." The struggle between two different ideas here reached my ears in a sigh, which it was easy to explain.

Miss Slaber gave me some calabashes, and a slave taught me how to clean and prepare them. I plan having a parterre in my garden at Paradise full of them, and I think it very possible to make them grow into Etruscan forms, and also the forms of elephants and other animals of the country, by covering the young fruit with cases into which they will grow and take the form they are compelled to. Nothing keeps water, wine, fruit, butter, so cool in summer as these receptacles, which are sometimes very large, and cannot receive injury as glass or stoneware would by being tossed about. I have a thousand little plans of travelling cases for my friends made of these matters, but whether they will ever be carried into execution depends on too many accidents for me to insure them. I often wish, while others have their secretaries and their clerks, that I had a plan-realiser, to bring into effect the many little inventions which daily start into my thoughts, and which I am convinced would answer if followed up – but I want continuation in my industry; I am ardent and active when employed in anything, and do not quit if I can possibly help it, but if I am obliged to leave it, and a different train of thoughts intervene, it is a chance if I return to my work.

The journey from Slaber's to Mynheer Stockberg's, the postholder at Saldanha Bay, being a long one, not less than forty miles, we found it necessary to secure three relays of oxen, – one set, of fourteen, we were to have from this place; at Longue Fountaine,* a spot where we were to halt and dine on the grass, another set were to meet us from a farmer in the district; and at another house further on Mynheer Stockberg's were appointed to carry us to his house. We set out at eight, and arrived there about seven, and had a very kind and hospitable reception.

Monday, May 28th, 1798. – The day being a fine one, we proposed going to the Out Keek,* or look-out post, about four miles distant, to see the bay and adjacent country from the highest ground. Mynheer Stockberg took us with his oxen, and we had to ascend some hearty pulls by their means. I saw great quantities of oval pebbles of a blackish colour, but so uniformly alike in shape and size that I requested to have a few picked up. I suppose other collectors of curiosities are at moments of their researches not without their knowledge of similar disgrace – though perhaps they don't tell. I found my oval pebbles when cracked neither more nor less than sheep's dung – and was laughed at by my friends accordingly.

*Fountaine**
Langefontein. Here the road divided. To the right it lead the traveller to the present Langebaan and to the left to the south arm of the Bay. (See Barrow's map facing p.280 of *Travels into the interior of S.A.*, 2nd ed. v. 2.)

*Keek**
Uitkyk = lookout. The highest point on the south arm – and on the Bay – is Vlaeberg (633 ft.) clearly the eminence referred to. The Post House was close to its foot and the Old Post about 2 miles further south. Lady A.'s description however suggests that the Post Holder (Jacobus Stoffberg, d. 1831) lived even further away.

We mounted the eminence after a considerable tract of bushy and rocky ground, rendered fragrant by the aromatic scent of the wild shrubs which grow here in profusion. We got out and walked to the Out Keek, which is on the top of a rock, and where the signal post is placed and the flag hoisted when ships appear. I sat down on a stone and endeavoured to take a sort of panorama of the place, while the gentlemen went in search of game – the young ladies sat down on another and fell to their reveries, while I went on with mine. My first was to look round the wide-extended prospect with wonder at my being here at all, – the second was to wonder whether, if we had kept the Cape when first discovered, we should have found it an advantage to us to-day.

After I had spent a couple of hours in this way, our gentlemen returned, and I found it was time to depart. We stopped at the old post-house where M. Stockberg used to live. At the door there stood a Belisarius – one of the finest-looking grey-headed men I had ever seen – an old soldier, who, he said, was teacher to his children. His manner was so dignified and so polished, his bow so genteel, and his French so good, that he struck me much. On inquiry, I found he also was a Prussian. I had my hand in my pocket to bring forth three dollars, which was all my stock at the time, to give him in some way or another if I could contrive it without indelicacy; but the smallness of the sum, and his manner so much above his situation, awed me. Mr. Barnard read the whole of this in my face and attitude. "Don't," said he – "What?" said I. – "Don't," he replied again. I saw that he advised me under the same impulse that I hesitated, as he feared to give offence. With a sigh I was obliged to depart, and my old Prussian lost his three dollars because they were not a dozen, or he less like a man of birth.

When we reached M. Stockberg's, dinner was ready, and I had the pleasure of finding the son had shot me two flamingoes; one was dead, the other had lost only the tip of his wing, and I am in hopes of his living to be the wonder and delight of all my friends in England.

Tuesday, May 29th, 1798. – At half-past eight the waggon and oxen were ready for our departure. I had found Mrs. Stockberg a very civil, honest creature, obliging and good-humoured. She undertook to get me flamingo feathers, to nurse my bird and send it, to get me a barrel of good salt fish, a large one of which was to be purchased here for a guinea, and, dressed with potatoes, I foresaw it would be no bad mess during the continuance of a South-Easter, which does not permit any fishing-boat to venture out from shore. In return I liberally dealt away my stores to the poor good people, Mr. Barnard adding afterwards a still more useful present in ale and porter.

We reached Mr. Slaber's at a proper hour, and found Mynheer had returned from the Cape. I must not forget to mention a curious anecdote which transpired at supper, – it shews the value of a Frenchman's journal. Le Vaillant, it seems, narrates a story of his own prowess in having killed a tiger while at their house.* Barnard asked if this was true, on which the young Vrow Slaber, and even the old vrow, burst into invectives against him. "He was the greatest liar it was possible to imagine, though very civil and well bred – but the tiger was killed by one of their Hottentots, nor had Le Vaillant seen it till the fellow brought it

*house** François Le Vaillant, the French traveller, took refuge with the Slabbers in July 1781 when his ship the *Middelburg* blew up in Saldanha Bay when attacked by the British fleet. He called there again at the end of his eastern journey in March 1783 and also after his journey northward. For the tiger episode see his *Voyage.*

dead into the back-yard. When Le Vaillant looked at it, I well remember what he did," said the old woman; "he thrust his spear through the skin, though it spoiled it for sale – (but he did not care for that) – saying, 'Now I have it to boast that this spear has been imbrued in the blood of one of the most savage animals in Africa!' " – On points, however, where his own vanity was not concerned, I imagine his representations are tolerably correct.

Wednesday, May 30th, 1798. – While getting ready for departure, the old lady gave me a kind and even tender farewell, which from extreme old age is always rather affecting, but she promised to visit me at the Cape in a manner that did not bespeak any doubt of her seeing it again. I collected the remains of my finery for the three ladies, who, though higher than most other vrows at the farmhouses, I saw, were not above accepting of all I could produce.

I had some neat shoes, though large, which I meant for Miss Slaber, – they were too small, but her sister-in-law said she was "sure they would fit her," so on she forced them, and I saw the shoes were "lost muttons." The others I found ribands for – needles, thread, a gold bandeau, and sash for my friend. I was now almost at the end of my stock, but they had all been well bestowed, for I plainly found that we had left no house where kindness had not been felt to us from our civil manners – at least as much as it is in human nature to feel for those of the conquering nation, who now are by compulsion the masters. They accepted at this house of payment for everything, which I was glad of, though the fare had not been so good as it was in many other places where nothing would be taken.

We departed at ten, the gentlemen having mounted their horses in order to shoot on their way to Groenekloof,* where we proposed to dine and stay all night. It is a government post, where dragoons are quartered, – a very excellent house, stabling, offices, and farm, but we found all much out of repair.

While dinner was getting ready, I walked out to see the view of the Cape from the rising ground at the back of the house. After taking a slight sketch, I came back to the yard in time to see about five hundred ewes returning from their pasture at a distance to the fold, where as many lambs were anxiously waiting their return. The door being opened, it was pretty to see the little creatures running out to meet their dams, no one mistaking her own, and each in haste to have its little long-delayed supper.

I regretted that the master of this mansion was dead. He had been kind to me, and had given me the two secretary-birds I mentioned as such charming creatures, and my little buck. How I grieved that I could not bring it with me. I never was so fond of an animal before, – it is so fond of me and so careless of every one else that it is impossible not to love it. – It licked my hand the morning of my departure, and seemed to beg hard to go too, but the cook promised faithfully he would take as much care of it as if it were his child – he is fond of birds and beasts. My little buck would have been in danger too from every dog he met with whom he was not acquainted with, as they have no respect for wild animals which are become tame. Had he been in the waggon with

*Groenekloof**
Mamre, later a Moravian mission station. A military post was established there as early as 1697.

me when we were overturned, his slender legs must have been broken. If I could say however that an animal had a presentiment that he should not see his friend and mistress again, I should say it of my buck from his complaining note when I bade him farewell. I believe I should not accept of any favourites, – I never ask for one and generally refuse them; but when a little creature is left an orphan without fortune or guardian, it is impossible to say no.

Thursday, May 31st, 1798. – None of us had slept so well as to render the sacrifice of rising a great one. By ten we remounted our waggon, and set off for a farmhouse called Blueberg, where we were to dine, and from that proceed to the Cape.

The road was much the same as usual, heathy sand, scarce any cultivation or grass. We passed about four houses in the space of fifteen or twenty miles, and about one o'clock arrived at our farm, where a clean, civil old vrow gave us some dinner, – we then proceeded homewards. It would have been a foolish enough matter, after a tour not without its occasional dangers, to lose one's life the last day, and within a few miles of our journey's end, but Gaspar, to save some heavy road, drove down upon the sea-beach before we came to the Salt River – a pass sometimes dangerous from the quicksands, which, if passed unskillfully, are hazardous.

Gaspar had mistaken the hour, and imagined the tide was retreating, instead of which it was coming in; and every five minutes he was obliged to whip up his horses to their full speed to avoid sinking in sands almost alive from the approach of the sea which foamed under our wheels. We were all not a little afraid, – Mynheer Prince afterwards confessed to me that we had had great reason; however the event justified Gaspar, for we got through safe, and by eight o'clock at night, accompanied by a heavy South-Easter and rain, we reached the Castle, where I hoped to find all clean, peaceable, and comfortable, from a comparison which after the last month was likely to be in its favour.

The first person I saw was Revel, the cook – who, instead of welcoming me back, seemed to avoid me. This I felt as a sad omen – I need not say why. He burst into tears – or pretended to do so, and told me my little buck was dead – that it had never been well from the morning of my departure, constantly bleating and running about, looking for something – would not taste food, and died in ten days!

Though I knew the half of this to be untrue, it affected and worried me more than common sense can justify, and indeed gave the moment of return a shock which I leave those to pardon me for feeling who have had a favourite and lost it in some measure by their own want of judicious arrangement. I should not have trusted Revel – I knew he drank, and I should have risked it with Madame Goetz in spite of her children and dogs, or with any other friend in my absence, rather than with him. But he had talked me over, with so much specious fondness for my animal! What a pain did I not suffer when I heard from the other servants, who now crowded upon me with their grievances, that, from the day I left the Castle, no one had seen my buck, and that he had it locked up, but had been constantly drunk himself, – that he had sent a slave with it into the country to have it buried in my garden of Paradise, but with strict orders to let no one see it. – But let me leave this subject.

Whoever leaves home without a very steady person in rule will be apt to find that all has gone topsy-turvy in his absence. The coachman and the cook had quarrelled; the cook had cited him before the Fiscal – two men in the stable had been fighting; both were black and blue – Margaret, a soldier's wife, whom I have to keep the apartments when we are out of town, complained that Revel would not permit her to enter, but had sent for the two black slaves, whom I had returned to the slave-lodge while absent, as they are all thieves – he and they had finished a cask of wine in three days, which was to have lasted the family till our return – Jane's dog had been stolen by a Dutchman, who, finding it in vain to bribe the coachman, had enticed Tartar away; but we hoped to find him out – Martinus, a black boy, whom I had desired to water some plants, had never given them a drop, and had permitted regimental goats to walk in and eat up a box of fine young nutmeg-trees – the cats had established a temple for Cloacina under the sofas of my drawing-room – my penguin, who had lived with me a month, and with his long ruffle wings and solemn gravity as respectably filled the link between fish and fowl as I hope my little ostrich will do that between bird and beast, had been choked by a bone – and, to sum up all the misfortunes and ill-humour of the component parts of our family, the cow, hitherto mild, had become insolent, and had offended the laws by walking on the parade, the consequence of which was, like other caitiffs, she was put in the *Tronck*, where she then was.

If anything could have made me laugh, it was this last misfortune. It reminded me of the mice which fell into a certain great personage's mess, when he was in prison, – hungry and oppressed, he thought, as things were at the worst, they would surely mend – his prison-gates were thrown open, and he was proclaimed Emperor! But no change for the better could give me back my little buck.

Our tour finished and all well, the 1st of June, Mr. Barnard thanked our kind Governor for the pleasure he had afforded us, and we were all glad to have made the journey. Though small the portion of ground we had gone over, it shewed me at least the face of seven hundred miles of Africa, and enabled me to judge a little of the peasantry, whom upon the whole we found hospitable and good-humoured, at least to travellers, but without industry, emulation, or capacity, attached to habits and careless of improvement – in their persons and houses slovenly and dirty, a few excepted; but, while improved minds are happy from religious contentment, from philosophy, or from a combination of blessings, these good folks seem to me to be equally so from their want of care, thought, or feeling, from a good deal of self-conceit, and from the charms of power, experienced by every master, mistress, and child, of every house.

The slaves and Hottentots, on the other hand, seem happy too upon the whole, from knowing no other state than that which they are in, – the idea of drawing a comparison between themselves and their masters is one belonging to the first step of civilization, and they have not reached to it, as far as I could judge. Their pleasures consist in eating what is given them, and in sleeping whenever they can; and all their pains are bounded by the lash of the whip, which is occasionally applied if they are disobedient, or what the master may call insolent. Could we weigh happiness in a scale, I do not believe, on the average, they are less happy than ourselves, though they have much less reason to be so, and meet death with an apathy which one would be apt to imagine proceeded from the dislike to life, were it not that it certainly arises from the want of strong or precise feelings about anything.

Whether we shall ever, in a family party, venture farther into the country, I cannot tell; I think it probable we shall not. I shall therefore confine my little migrations henceforward to the quarters where I'm likely to pick up flowers, which may be done within a hundred miles of the Cape, and shall endeavour to stock myself with such things previous to that return which will put it in my power to embrace you all, my dear friends, with affection unabated on my part, and undivided by any new ties which the head or heart can form here.

Anne Barnard.

Ganse Kraal, a van Reenen family farm

cape of Good Hope
June 11th – 1798

it seems to me an age since I wrote to you my good friend, but
your silence to me so long continued begun to make me very
much doubt whether my letters were not rather plagues than
pleasures, and as I was withholding them from several very dear
friends that I might heap the more on you (ungratefull
as you appeard to be) I begun to think a little pause
at last and do no harm; ~~[illegible]~~ of late however
tho I am still without any thing under your own hand
I have recived thro Lord Macartney & Margaret so many
kind & flattering messages, apologys for your silence &
requests that I would continue to write to you that I will
give doubts to the winds & as the winds at the cape
Blow very fiercely off shore my distrusts will be half
way across the ocean before the sentence is finished allmost
at the present I cannot add more however, this much-
I hurry off with my blessing to you & Lady Jane but the
ships are to sail sooner than I expected And I wish to send
you a long & comfortable account of our tour into the
Interior of the country the particulars of which I kept
memorandums of, but have no time now to finish it
it shall arrive by the china ships expected shortly & which
may possibly arrive in England as soon as this and till
then god Bless you All —

Anne Barnard

All are well here — every body that you wish well to &c —
Lord Teignmouth will carry this, he and his family were
on board the Britania when it was struck with lightning
there is a doubt of his being too late for the convoy at
this moment, the admiral is in a Hurry to get
all the ships off — adieu — adieu —

Lady Anne to Henry Dundas, June 11, 1798

Letter 16

A few days after the Barnards' return to the Cape Lady Anne was writing to Dundas, bemoaning his long silence – a theme expressed even more strongly in the letter with which she followed it two months later. As will be seen, Lady Anne had not yet had time to send her friend a full account of their journey inland.

cape of Good Hope
June 11th – 1798

it seems to me an age since I wrote to you my good friend, but your silence to me so long continued begun to make me very much doubt whether my letters were not rather plagues than pleasures, and as I was withholding them from several very dear friends that I might heap the more on you (ungratefull as you appeard to be) I begun to think a little pause at least coud do no harm; – of late however, tho I am still without anything under your own hand I have received thro Lord Macartney & Margaret so many kind & flattering messages, apologys for your silence & requests that I woud continue to write to you that I will give doubts to the winds & as the winds at the cape Blow very *fiercely off shore* my distrusts will be half way across the ocean before the sentence is finishd allmost [.] at the present I cannot add more however, this much I hurry off with my blessing to you & Lady Jane but the ships are to sail sooner than I expected And I wish to send you a long & comfortable account of *our tour into the interior of the country* the particulars of which I kept memorandums of, but have no time now to finish it it shall arrive by the China ships expected shortly & which may *possibly* arrive in England as soon as this and till then God Bless you All –

Anne Barnard

*Teignmouth**
Sir John Shore Bt. (1751-1834), created 1st Baron Teignmouth in Oct. 1797. He succeeded Cornwallis as governor-general of India in 1792 and was replaced in March 1798.

all are well here – every body that you wish well to &c – Lord Teignmouth* will carry this, he and his family were on board the Britania when it was struck with lightening there is a doubt of his being too late for the convoy at this moment, the admiral is in a Hurry to get all the ships off – adieu – adieu –

this is of a very old date – but my next shall be *fresher*

Cape of Good Hope – August 13 – 1798

"A soft word, saith the proverbs turneth aside wrath" and the repetition of a kind expression from the mouth of a friend who one fears is forgetting one entirely, is so conciliatory and so satisfactory that it is impossible to do any thing else than to fly to pen and Ink to hold a little mental communication – Why – why do you express yourself kindly of me and of my husband and say you have pleasure in my letters & even honour me so *unexpectedly* far, as to say Information from them, yet never tell me so yourself by one line? remember that (inspite of *Doctor Da Mainaducs* doctrines)* one cannot be *quite* sure at the far end of the globe, without the intervention of a little pen & ink, what ones well beloved *Antipode* is feeling for one! – but you have to more than one said obliging things of me for which I thank you, less because they were flattering than because they sweep away a sett of little vile painfull suggestions which begun to Haunt me and which have renderd me silent for the last three or four months when I had plenty to say to you, and when "old love and kindness" woud have been glad, if pride woud not have laid on its heavy *Embargo* on all scribblings, till you shoud say "go on and prosper, and tell me *All*, without fancying yourself tiresome or being Ashamed" – all you shall have, and that directly for there is a signal for three ships from the N. W: and if any more arrives from England without my hearing from you I will not answer that I may'nt *relapse* & then I shall not be able to get over the ground with any comfort to you or myself – at present I have a fair field for Hope, and even If I shoud be disappointed, the letters of my too good natured friends about you, and a message or two from yourself thro Lord Macartney will last me a little while longer – where did I leave off? – I believe I sent off the Governor of India in my last, to his Government in good Health, resolved like Sancho panca to be an upright governor, and went out ourselves to paradise* – there we remained for about six weeks, rising with the sun and exhaling in the fresh morning air at the back of the table mountain, the greatest fault of this situation is, that we have about two hours less of his majesty, Sol, than if we were on the other side of the hill as he is sett to us when he shines on the rest of the world. – the only Experience this short residence in the country gave us was, that whoever means to build any thing in Africa (Mr B. was building a kitchen) must do it in the height of summer when the heat may dry the clay and lime quickly – it approachd the rainy season when ours was roofing in, with rushes, the consequence was, that a Heavy shower swelld the raw mortar and "down dropd Dido" – which was the loss of the conveniency it woud have been of, the discomfiture of his projects & the expence of the materials – as to the labour, the walls had been

*doctrines)**
Dr. J.B. De Mainauduc or Demainauduc, an 18th century exponent of animal magnetism and hypnotism.

*paradise**
Paradise, originally Paradijs, a farm granted to W. ten Damme in 1706. It was on the slopes of Table Mt. above the junction of the present Paradise Rd., Newlands Ave. and Union Ave. The ruins of the Barnard's cottage on the estate remain. (See p.55). According to a letter from Andrew B. to Macartney, March 1800, the cottage became uninhabitable and he built a new one at the Vineyard.

Stoep and chair

Mode of building with clay and water

The garden of the Brewery, Newlands, the home of Dirk van Reenen

run up by a couple of Dragoons, from a military quarter at the bottom of the Hill, & a very great advantage it is to have a few days of one or two of his Majestys scarlet coats occasionally, in a country where artificers are not to be had, or if obtaind with difficulty, are to be paid with *still greater difficulty* – a soldier to whom we give 1-6 pr. day, his fare, and wine will do more in one day than a duch [sic] man, or slave in three, for a dollar a day. – the largest chestnuts I ever saw by many many degrees were here, I collected a bag for you, but on cracking one, two months after, I found it quite witherd and gone, unworthy therefore to be sent – I must plant a few to convey them safe – at this place I had hoped to have had all sorts of good things – poultry – pigs – garden stuff – fruit – but the first I coud not keep, as they wanderd & were lost amongst the Heaths, sugar trees & silver trees with which the hill is coverd half way up – pigs had the same reason against them, they woud have certainly prefered a state of freedom, and acorns, to my chains – Garden Stuff can hardly be raised the soil is so cold on that side of the mountain & exept pears the fruit trees are all gone – troops of monkeys from the Hills considerably annoyd the gardener – he shot – and shot but no lives were lost, and as the pears are of a kind to ripen & decay all at once I mean this year to stipulate that the monkeys may have their fill, they are the old proprietors – we cut two or three beautiful walks on a sort of Terrace which looks to the sea & the Hottentot mountains, the bushes on each side gave it shade, I must make a sketch of this & the noble rock, as it rises above, for you, but how many things I propose to do! – how few execute from want of time!

we had meant to have remaind here quietly for a month or two more, & had requested the Anstruthers to come to us, but the gout prevented him, and a considerable taste for the pleasures of the cape seemd to prevent her, when Lord Macartney told Mr B. that if he wishd to see a little of the country and did not think it too late in the season that he might go for a month, as there was then no business which coud not be transacted in his absence, that it was possible that at the end of that time he might be receiving dispatches from England that might give him leave to depart in two or three months, when he coud not do without him, and still less coud any successor spare him, who might be new to the business of the Colony – on these considerations & even the *possibity* of a peace, and of the place being given up (unlikely enough perhaps but within the chapter of chances) we thought it best, late as it was & approaching to winter viz the months of May & June when the roads begin to be impassable, we thought it best to 'catch time by the forelock' and to sett off – from little memorandums I put down as I drove along in the Waggon I shall give you each days Journey & you will then be compleatly one of the party & will Judge of it better than by a more Hasty account – but this I shall put on a separate sheet or two – I was sorry that we saw no more of Lord Hobart by this departure of ours, he is a pleasant man, but seemed to me to feel rather mortified at having his face turned to England instead of *Bengal*, I coud not get him to enter on the subject of Lord Mornington atall, which corroborated this, on the contrary Lord Mor: was constantly talking of Lord Hobart & presupposing the pleasure of their meeting. – as to the Anstruthers I have loved him as a good friend all my life, but she is a sad fool!* – if there coud be two opinions about this I woud not say so to *you*, but she allways has been reckond ill temperd & this new greatness which you have bestowd on her, thro Sir John, has turnd her poor head quite round; she woud not allow Sir Mor: to know any thing – Sir *Jann* as she calld him was the fountain head of all political intelligence and after she had disgusted the other with her foolish vanity, she bewailed to Lord Hobart afterwards (who she very much courted) that he was not to be Governor of Bengal instead of the other* – what a Blessing to Lord Mornington who is a domestic man & fond of womens company* if he had had the pleasant Judicious, good mortal Lady Strange* for his first *Lady in command* instead of the Begum, who goes with powerfull intentions of changing all old customs that are disagreeable to her – "and if she trys to change one of them, says General Baird,* she will live alone" –

we were scarcely returnd from our months absence when the Stranges & Clives* arrived, we certainly shoud have askd Lord and Lady Clive to take part of our "pot luck" at the castle as old friends which both were, she of mine, Lord Clive of Mr Barnard at Naples, but the near connection with Lady Strange, she being also L[y] Hardwicks particular friend & their having less money to spare for cape expenses which are not light, determind us to invite *them* & their ward Miss Roberts, to *reside* with us rather than the *greatest personages*, & they did so during their stay here which was two or three weeks – he bears a high character amongst all who know him & I am convinced a deserved one – she is a Happy creature at getting away from the East Nook of fife to be the Lady Recorder at Madrass – she & Lady Clive will go on like lambs – what a sensible, pleasant, & happy woman Lady Clive is, she has a mind open to receive pleasure from every thing, to please as far as she can, is incapable of offending, and will not tire I am sure of any situation she is placed in – but How comes it that they are going at all! people so wealthy, a man apparently so little ambitious! by implication tho not by direct words I had reason to think the matter was offerd to him, and I did not think administration – any administration I mean, was so rich in great appointments as to give without the boon being sollicited. – perhaps his *Name* is held to be a lucky one to go to India – he seems in good spirits – but says little, and when he visits wise men, has Mr Petrie allways with him – to me he used to come alone & we talkd of every thing *but* Madrass or governments. – while they were here, we had also a Mrs Hart for Madrass, and a Mrs Floyer – the first is a daughter of the chief Baron [?] in Scotland I find – she is rather Handsome – to them succeeded Lord & Lady Tienmouth* who has reachd you ere now, never saw I such a succession of governors, the sea has been quite coverd with them for the last six months, happy shall I be if it sees nothing of the departure of our *own* dear governor for some time yet, I have ever thought he woud stay till the begining of the year 1799 and I believe I shall be proved a witch – I wish I coud give him a right fit of the gout and lodge it in his toe, it flys about his stomach & Head and sometimes a little affects his spirits but never the force & firmness of his mind which when called upon can rally, and rise above pain – it is wonderfull to hear how he can jest and talk away with memory & fancy at a

*fool**
Sir John and Lady Anstruther stayed several months at the Cape. Lady Anstruther, formerly Maria Isabella Brice, eldest daughter of Edward Brice Esq. of Berners St., London, was nicknamed 'The Begum'. She made herself most unpopular wherever she went. Writing to Lord Mornington in India on 3-6-1798, Lady Anne described her as "That haughtiest and fattest of fools . . . Indeed she was at least one strong reason why we set off in the beginning of winter to make a tour into the country that we might avoid the vexations she produced to us . . . All pity Calcutta which is to contain her."

*other**
Lord Hobart, governor of Madras, was returning home having been recalled as the result of a dispute with the Governor-General, Lord Teignmouth. He had had expectations of becoming governor-general himself.

*company**
Lord Mornington had married his mistress, Hyacinthe Gabrielle Roland in 1794, but they separated soon afterwards. He had thought of sending for her to join him in India but abandoned the idea.

*Strange**
Sir Thomas Strange, recorder of Madras, married twice, 1stly Jean, daughter of Sir Robert Anstruther, bt. (no near

Notes continued on p.169

Acheson Maxwell, comptroller of customs

Lt-Col James Catlin Craufurd

Miss Ann Barnard, afterwards Mrs James Craufurd.

Country house, possibly Protea, now Bishopscourt

relation of Sir John's), and 2ndly Louisa, daughter of Sir W. Burroughs, bt. It is not certain which of them Lady A. was commending here.

*Baird**
Major-Gen. David Baird (1757-1829), afterwards General Sir David, was a colonel on his way home from India when asked by Macartney to stay at the Cape with the local rank of Brig.-General, because of the unpopularity of Gen. Francis Dundas with the troops. He was promoted Major-General in June 1798 and sent to India with the Scotch Brigade. He returned to the Cape in 1806 as commander of the force which captured the Colony and became acting governor for a year.

*Clives**
Edward Clive (1754-1830), eldest son of the great Lord Clive, was created Baron Clive of Walcott in 1794 and Earl Powis in 1804 after the inheritance by his wife, Henrietta Herbert, of the estates of the last Earl Powis. He was Governor of Madras, 1798-1803, but Lord Mornington said of him that he was worthy and zealous but lacked the talents needed by a governor.

*Tienmouth**
i.e. Teignmouth. (See Letter 16.)

Notes continued p.170

time when (his company gone) he can hardly support himself – we anxiously long to hear what is become of Col Crawford* we are told the Zephyr is taken, if so there will be much delay in the replys to his dispatches – I wrote to you by him, but I suppose when a stone was tyed round the neck of all his Excellencys secrets & they were drownd mine woud accompany them to the bottom. – I know not how it comes into my head *now*, what is an old story by this time; (by the bye some of my letters *Yesterday* by Mr Bulkley* mention it a very silly & ill natured account of the Races here wrote & sent home by some dull wits with which this place was a good deal infested at one time – there certainly *were* races here but Lord Macartney whose servant is stated to have broke his leg in *Running* not only had no Horse but privately disapproved of there being races *atall* & did not subscribe – Mr Barnard the *same*, he declined being a member of what they call the Turf club & out of a little picque they call him in the paper the "life & soul of the Turf" he *went into* the country to avoid them – I gave my ten pagodas* the Ladys purse as two other Ladys of my own rank in society had subscribed their names to it without consulting me, and I did not like to thro a tacit stricture on *them* by refusing mine or run the risque of being calld shabby, tho privately I liked no *part of the business* thinking the place too much in its infancy for a sort of amusement which woud be likely to introduce with it many other foolish things, but where there is a great body of idle young men, with a few ladys not ill disposed to cooperate in any plan of amusement one cannot be too cautious of appearing to sett up as reformer – too delicate of blaming if one wishes as I do to possess universal good will – with respect to Faro* Tables, to my great sorrow I found that the great good nature of col Hope* (who is to be sure one of the best conditiond good creatures in the world) had been overpersuaded by a Mr Bird deputy quarter master I believe under Genl Frazer,* a young man who seems to love play, to hold a bank with him during these races; – Mr B. I have reason to think hinted this privately to the governor who send a message to desire it might be the first and last time he heard of such a thing in this Colony – in Lord Macartneys house there are no cards – at my assemblys and balls, half crown whist or casino, but no game of chance is allowed here, if people dont like the rules of our house they will not come to it. – as to the ostentatious splendour of my appearance on the race ground, tho possessd of the neatest chariot and four in the Colony, the only day I appeard there I was in the Carriage of a dutchman with his wife and family Not in my own, very much quizd indeed by my country men and women for being so, but very well pleasd to give this publick Testimony that the secretarys wife wishd to connect herself as much with the people of the country as they chose. – in the course of the morning how angry I was often made by the folly and bad breeding of the thoughtless John Bulls who were constantly galloping up to the carriage I was in, *evidently* a dutch one, to bid me remark the figures that were to run the *Dutch race*, "Lord what a saddle" – "Christ what a Bridle!" "I woud give twenty guineas to see that one thrown – "ay, & his neck broke" – 'how he woud kick in his Demi picque! * &c – &c – holding them all in such contempt and forgetting that the company I was with were not all

*Crawford**
Lt.-Col. James Catlin Craufurd, 98th Foot. His ship was taken by the French privateer *La Vengeance* and his dispatches thrown into the sea. The prisoners however managed to obtain passports for England from the Spanish government. Later he married the Barnard's cousin Ann. (See Fairbridge, (D.) *Lady Anne Barnard at the Cape of G.H.*, p.93.)

*Bulkley**
Presumably Edward Buckley, civil paymaster.

*pagodas**
A gold or silver coin from South India.

*Faro**
Faro, a gambling game in which bets are made on the order in which certain cards will appear when taken singly from the top of the pack.

*Hope**
Lt.-Col. John Hope, 28th Light Dragoons.

*Frazer**
Brig.-Gen. John Henry Fraser, deputy quartermaster-general.

*picque!**
Demi-pique – a saddle with a peak about half the height of older war saddles.

*Grenville**
William Wyndham Grenville, Baron Grenville (1759-1834), foreign secretary 1791-1801; First lord of the Treasury Feb. 1806-March 1807.

Notes continued opposite

deaf, & that some of them might understand English enough to comprehend an Insult – I believe I remarked in a former letter that it is the supercilious mode in which the Dutch find themselves treated by the English which makes them partly prefer French Insincerity & french politesse – but to return – Lord Macartney is as much displeased with this same news paper wit as a *great Man* can be with a *little matter*, and I a *little great* woman am displeasd enough with it to make it a *great Matter* by having thus taken up *your* time with the exposition of the truth.] –

talking of Clever and of great men, I fear the plants I sent to Lord Grenville* have not reachd him safe I procured them immediately after Lord Morningtons departure & sent them off by Young Elphinston* with the strict charge to take good care of them, but I was not then possessd as I am now of the knowledge how to make a proper botanical box for the sea conveyance, I have since commenced a very *usefull flirtation* with Doctor Roxburg* the great botanist at Bengal who is here for the purpose of making a thorough good collection, If I can get any thing curious for Lady Jane that I think She has not already, I will build my box, & associate with her plants some others for friends who woud have less chance of getting theirs safe than YOUR wife – by the bye – I hear the jar of Batavian pines I sent her were seizd – also one of d[o] ginger to my sisters, thus it is when a commission is handed over from one person to another – Mr Bryce* had the care of them, but I am told he has been broke lately for Turbulent conduct to his capt, – he seemd mild when he was with us, but I have since heard he has a little of his sisters fire, I remember Capt Brisbain* told me he was the best officer he had, and therefore he coud ill spare him on shore, but personal altercation since has made them at variance & Mr Bryce has, as I dare say he ought [,] fallen the sacrifice, I hear it was about an invitation to some Ladys house at St Helena –

septr 22[d] – so far I had got my dear friend when I was seized with a sore throat which confined me for a fortnight to bed and a week more in my own room, nothing did me any good till a charming packet of letters arrived from England & one from you amongst the rest – "My dear Lady Anne" at the top in your great *Collossal* hand delighted my eyes, but the hand of another succeeded to it, it was not Lady Janes as I thought, and I was sadly afraid that your eyes must have been very weak to have forced you to apply to an Emanuensis [sic] – you say many very kind, very flattering things to me, *too* flattering was it not that I know where you feel kindness you are a most *partial* judge you cannot be too much so to please me, may I never be judged impartially of by those I love, nothing alloyed the pleasure these very agreeable complements gave me exept there being wrote in another Mans hands, but as I found "Adieu my dear friend" in your own, with Henry Dundas to the bottom in pledge of your sincerity I was perfectly contented and now I shall go on as before, scribbling away from such funds as this place gives me without a fear of Your [being] tired or annoyed. – was it not that here is Mr Maxwell* come to tell me that he must have my letters in ten minutes as the government box is to be seald up I woud give you a couple of pages of Gazette – I mean a set of such Cape Anecdotes as have taken place since I wrote to you last some of them curious enough – but I will reserve that for my next letter, it is possible I may have still two or three days more to write in – I will however shove in here the agreeable intelligence of Capt Linzees* arrival in the Bay two days ago with 5 prizes behind him – a spirited little fellow – for the present then adieu my dearest friend & *You My Sweet Lady Jane* I thank you for your kind message & shall write to yourself very soon – Shortly I shall have A gallant opportunity by the going home of the East India Ships now here – at present all are under Embargo – I have had letters from Lord Mornington within these three days, & rejoyce to see that he is likely to enjoy good Health & speaks in raptures of the Magnificence of all around Him –

I am called – and Hurryd to conclude
God Bless you both – My dear friends –

Anne Barnard

*Elphinston**
This was most likely the young Mountstuart Elphinstone (1779-1859), 3rd son of the 11th Baron Elphinstone and nephew of Viscount Keith. He held an appointment in the Bengal Civil Service and in May 1798 had narrowly escaped a massacre at Banares. He rose to be Governor of Bombay, 1819-1827.

*Roxburg**
William Roxburgh (1751-1815), F.L.S., F.R.S.A., F.R.S.E., the Hon. East India Co.'s botanist in the Carnatic and superintendant of Calcutta Botanic Gardens. Invalided home in 1797 but returned to Calcutta in 1799.

*Bryce**
See Letter 14, note p.95.

*Brisbain**
Capt. Charles Brisbane, afterwards Rear-Admiral Sir Charles. He was placed in command of the prize *Dordrecht.*

*Maxwell**
Acheson Maxwell, controller of customs.

*Linzees**
Capt. Samuel Hood Linzee.

Letter 18

There follows as light a letter on purely social matters as Lady Anne ever wrote to Dundas.

Cape of Good Hope –
Sep^{tr} 1798

this is very charming – I find I am likely to have still another day or two before the little Hasty vessel is permitted to sail which carrys this to St Helena, the Government box is made up I believe, and why the ship does not sail Immediately I know not, but I am glad of it as it gives me a few hours to add another letter to the stupid one already put up for you which contains little exepting growling at yourself & forgiving – this shall be the Gazette I promised of all the Cape occurences since I last wrote to you – small as the place is, there is a wonderfull number of little Bizarre incidents half European half African which makes as good Gossip for those who like it as if the actors were Dukes & Ladyships. – what happens to be talkd of before me I *hear*, because I have a pair of ears, but no one brings me a *secret* or a *wonder* because it is known that I am not fond of *tittle tattle*, at the same time *observe* that I am going to write a perfect *tittle tattle letter to you* in the midst of all my descretion & rigidity, tis the way with All *prudes* to frown publickly at what they privately smile at. – I shall not confine myself however to *any thing*, but bring out *every thing* as it comes into my mind having no time for arrangement. – we have had Elopements, Marriages – half marriages – marriages to be – we have been taking prizes – had ships in distress – beautys that went to Bengal last year to be married – married & return-ing for their Health – the oldest occurence that presents itself is the wedding of a mad capt Barklay, who insisted on having a license to marry a woman whose Character was so very bad that Lord M. sent Mr B: to advise him against it – "tell your Lord said he that I am 45 years of age & shoud know what I like" – as that woud not do, Mr B. next hinted that Report actually circulated it that he Mr Barklay was married already, & of course a license coud not be given – this he denied, pro-fessd himself ready to take his oath before the Fiscal that he was single – he did so – and was married next day – he now says that he is perfectly certain he is justified for taking that oath as his wife by the last letters was so ill that he is *Sure* she must be dead now – the present one will suffer no loss if he separates from her as it is supposed they will do

A slave woman and her children.

soon – he has a brother, a man of Honor & credit in England, I fear he will get a poor account of some bills he sent for the purchasing him up in the Regt. – soon after this a fair Lady Eloped with the purser of an India man – Mr B. was also sent to prevail on her to return to her Colors, but she woud not & is with the purser still. – we had next the Elopement of the Young Frow Vandenberg with Capt Hamilton Ross,* a young man of very good character who had made fair & Honorable proposals which the father objected to, having a right to keep her fortune till she was 18, if she married without his consent, mean time his own wife died & he informd his daughter he meant to give her for a mother in law a person who had been in the Habit of whiping her, & who had a son who was intended for her husband – she told him if he did, she woud marry Mr Ross – the father married – the Young frow chuckd the Dutch lover under the chin for a few days to lull suspicion & went off – he has been roaring like a mad man to catch her but she is where no one can get at her – his Rage is so loud that it has even reached the Tars on board of their ships, one of the Jacks lately came to him & told him if he woud swear to keep the secret & give him the reward of 100 dollars, he woud shew him the House where she was secreted, – the father agreed & paid him the money forgetting his caution in his eagerness for revenge – John Bull led him in the dark thro street – after street, at last breaking suddenly from him he bid him good night & turning down a bye corner was out of sight in a moment – . he is an officer in the Scots Brigade & she sails with him to India & will be married *there* when she is 18, but she has a year to wait, it makes no difference, her lover is a man of perfect Integrity & she may depend on him, he has offerd so fair & behaved so well as to conciliate everybodys esteem & whenever she is married the English ladys of the place & I for one will support her thro, her father only is to blame & avarice is at the bottom – the dutch ladys will not visit her I dare say, she has a dash of *the Blew*, her mothers mother having been a slave, & as we are as proud as *Lucifer* on point of birth there is no quality or virtue not even the *virtue of being rich* which is not spunged out by the word slave born, or half cast – this is a very pretty girl – much genteeler than the generality of the women here but I have much offended two of *the quality* by asking if they were Acquainted with her. – there is a Miss Du Wal* who sails for England with the first ships *after* a Capt Manning – he proposed to her but she coud not make up her mind about leaving her friends & what was of *still more consequence* she coud not *make up* her wedding cloaths in time to sail on a certain day, I shoud not have thought that was of much importance, but I have heard they esteem it so here – well – the lover embarkd & the lady begun to repent that she had not accompanied him – she now means to follow him to England against the advice of all the English men here, who think she had better remain where she is, it is a bold undertaking & justifys the old proverb, "A stitch in time saves nine" – a stitch in her wedding cloaths more hastily put in woud have certainly saved her a most precarious *sailing match*. – within these two days *another* fair one has eloped with *another* officer. – she too being under age, is taken up by the Fiscal and in prison, but as the lover says she never *proposed* or even *hinted marriage* to him I suppose this will

*Ross**
Hamilton Ross (1774-1853) of the Scotch Brigade, had the distinction of raising the Union Jack at the capture of the Cape in 1795. His regiment went to India in January 1799 but in 1803 he left the army to open a mercantile business at the Cape. He married Catharina Elizabeth van den Berg (b. 1781) daughter of J.J. van den Berg, merchant, at Fort St. George, Madras, in Jan. 1799.

*Wal**
Arend de Waal was receiver-general at this time.

blow bye without any Hymen in the case – the young ladys seem to have no dislike to our English officers but I think they *risque* a little *too much*, to secure them, they are not all Mr Ross's there was a dutch wedding that took place lately, which intertaind me a good deal – the master of the family has been supposed rather of the Jacobin sort, & Lord Macartney was not a little displeased to find he had sent out his invitations to his friends for the Wedding & Ball to Citizen *this* – citizen *that* – a *title* not permitted in this colony of course. – no notice was taken of this, – till – "They were in the midst of all their *Din*, Fa fa limanididle and lamanideedledilly – In came the cat, and her Kit – tin* – the cat appeard in the shape of the Town Major & the Kitten as *twenty dragoons* who arrived in time for the Ball & put the party into a glorious fright – Mynheer instantly begun stroaking down the whiskers of the Town Major, & noble ones has that pussie, (frizled out on each side of his face) – he was invited to dance – the whole treated as a jest & Mynheer professing himself ready to make the Governor *every apology* he coud desire for his foolish method of naming his friends w^{c} he professd to be a *Jeu d'esprit only* – the town major was just begining to dance with the daughter of the family when he saw standing above him General Dundass *cook* just ready to *lead off* – he had askd the generals leave in the morning to go to a neighbour pour *faire de patties*, he is a french man – . & *all* other things which *that* class of french men are, he did not tell the general that he was pour faire *Douce yeux aussi*

– we are glad to have got back the navy again to the Bay. the Blew coats make the place cheerfull – I like Sir Hugh Christian much as an agreeable man in society – I liked the last Admiral too – Pringle – he was a growler with his tongue, but I believe as Honest & liberal a man in his conduct as possible – with many oppertunitys here I have heard of benefiting his fortune I fancy no conduct coud be purer – I say the more on this, poor fellow, as I dare say he is not on good terms with any body at home because he cannot be prudent with that unruly little member of his, the tongue, and I coud almost think he repented his having waggd it so freely before he went, for I thought he had got reconciled to the place & woud have liked to stay. – I think Sir Hugh has rather better Hopes of the nautical possibility of navigating round the coast than Ad: Pringle or others before him have had, whether this is founded in sound sense, or the pride of superior genius *Time* will shew, one thing I can see, who am *no witch*, that as vessels *this year* have been cruising about, at *a season* & round *points* which they formerly *durst not have lookd at*, there is certainly less fear now of the shore round us than there was, or *Danger* has *become more familiar* – a ship was lately drove in distress to a Bay I think they call it Aligoa Bay* where some of the passengers left it & came by Land – the captain & others have dined often with us & the Gentlemen who came by land arrived & dined with us yesterday – they describe the country (as it has also appeard to us on our tour) as bare – but soil good & people Hospitable & Hearty – there is another ship the Ganges which contains some English Captains on their way Home – one of the name of Lambert, another Broughton – the last a thin little fellow who I believe You sent on a voyage of discovery – his vessel has been lost – he mentions an Island near Japan where he

*tin**
Presumably an early version of "A frog he would a wooing go." (See Opie *The Oxford dictionary of nursery rhymes*, p.177-81.) The well-known refrain is a 19th century addition.

*Bay**
Algoa Bay, 500 m. east of the Cape of Good Hope.

was kindly treated by a Gentle race of people intirely Coverd with Hair* their manners Mild & Humane — no Tails — so I fancy they will class in finely, at a point in Hunters gradations* from Mr Pitt down, to the Least little monkey of the forest — there being a link or two wanting I have heard say between negro & ourangoutang which this sweet Island will afford a means of supplying — observe I am writing you all sorts of stuff & nonsense without remorse, it is your own fault & your wifes. — I suppose we shall have more tricks soon above these prizes of Capt Linzees & the only words sounding thro the castle yard where the admiralty court is Held will be the *CAPTORS*. — N.B/ we all like Mr Holland very much — I believe he is reckond by *impartial people* (which of course the *partys* seldom are) an upright Judge — he has bad health, but I think is a good humoured, agreeable man & I mention this with the more pleasure that just at the first setting off I remember there was a trifling circumstance which empressd some friends of mine here with an idea of his being silly & rash — but *he* was not to blame — another *was* who attempted as the wits of the garrison call it to *Shave*, Lord Mornington, & was so frightend on seing him angry, that he playd false by Mr Holland — apropos — I wonder if the races here now going forwards will produce any more lying paragraphs — remember I take the earliest opportunity to tell you *not* to believe any about me as I have not been there *at all* — nor Lord M. nor Mr B: — my former letter has told you all about that matter — but when people dont stick to truth perhaps I shall be put in as drawn by *Elephants* this time. — I must write a letter to my cousin Lady Dalrymple, she will be frightend when she sees her Son Johnnie has won a purse,* and yet it happend so naturally that there was no harm in it — a great many East India gentlemen being here, they literally proposed making a purse & I believe all horses of all sorts were permitted to run, Johnnies horse was a tolerable one with some bottom — A friend offerd to ride it for him which he did — 17 horses started for 50 guineas and Johnie to his astonishment won the purse & is I believe the Happiest creature now in africa — but I must not have his mother suppose him a *Jockey* for that — he has volunteerd going on with his Regt to India & then returns Home — our Bay is full of ships at present, & the place as I am told by a skilfull merchant here is stockd with European Goods enough to last for 3 years, but all is lockd up out of sight & the prices remain as high as ever — inspite of this we make our ends meet, & to say the truth they encompass a good deal, but it all goes in giving good fare to others [,] no drinking or parade God knows but the solid enjoyment of making others as Happy as we can — Mr. B. is greatly flatterd by your kindness for he thinks he derives it from you the increase of his Sallary by 500 pr an: tho the mony is convenient the testymony of *your* & Lord Macartneys being pleased with him goes nearer his heart — sorry we are that he talks of leaving us in two or three months, but perhaps he may stil lengthen it out a little more. — Mr Barnard is fully made up to do any thing that possibility can put in his power, to give satisfaction to General Dundas, & friendly (as well as official) assistance. — but shall I tell you in the *perfect confidence* of friendship that he is a *little* afraid from the generals manner, that he is not disposed to like him. — it is I am convinced *but* manner, how can it

*gradations**
Presumably a reference to the researches of the great anatomist John Hunter (1728-1793).

*Hair**
The "Hairy" Ainu, the aboriginal inhabitants of Japan, driven into the northern islands.

*purse**
This was probably Janet Lady Dalrymple, daughter of William Duff of Crombie, wife of Sir Hew Dalrymple-Hamilton, 3rd bart. of North Berwick, her cousin. Sir Hew was Lady Anne's cousin also, being the great-grandson of the Hon. Sir Hew Dalrymple, 1st bart, her maternal grandfather. "Johnny" would be Lady Dalrymple's 2nd son, b. c. 1780, who became the 5th bart. of North Berwick on his brother's death in 1834 and died himself in 1835. He became a major-general in 1819 and should not be confused with General Sir John Hamilton-Dalrymple, 5th bart. of Cranstoun, who succeeded to the viscountcy of Stair. At this time Johnny was a cornet in the 28th (Light) Dragoons.

be otherwise where unremitting attention is paid. — the Genl: is Hasty & he has not learnt that charming page in Lord Macartneys book, to Respect, and mark respect to *others* in their departments, in order to have it from them, but Hurriedly & hastily does as he feels at the moment & I suppose privately repents at leisure. — but Mr Barnard tho a high minded man is so uncommonly Mild in temper that I have *no fears*, as I believe what he suspects is *mere* manner & have not a doubt that they will go on perfectly well, with caution on the one part to counteract any little impetuosity on the other; — is not this talking with the relying confidence of friendship when I am venturing to speak of your nephew & my Husband, but you know the one party, & will not think it unnatural for me to have let my private thoughts escape to *you*, on a subject so intimately connected with all that is interesting to me — Mr Barnard woud not be pleased with me if he knew I Had said thus much, *therefore I shall not tell him I have* — but I do not think I am wrong. —

on looking over the former sheet I see I have expressd myself of this new Island as if it was a jest, but it is not so, & I fancy will be found rather a curious matter — I askd the captain to shew me the drawings he had had taken of the people & their Coustume but I perceived from the distress of his countinance that he wishd to evade letting any one see them & have since heard he means with the approbation of his superiors to publish the account with the plates.

I have been told that I shall *not* have the power of sending this off to England before the fleet sails — but inspite of this I shall send it to Sir Hugh & let it take its chance — he is very — very secret in his intentions — no one knows what is to be done till it is performd, & vessels with their captains are on the seas before the commander guesses where he is bound for, which often puts them in a puff, it may now & then be needlessly secret but upon the whole it is surely right & a man must be *needlessly* secret in order to prevent his being suspected when *needfully* secret — Lord Macartney is very unwell today — I wish he woud let himself have a good fit of the gout but he enfeebles his constitution to ward it off, instead of soaring it out heartily once or twice a year & enjoying himself the intermediate time — . we have had most wonderfull bad weather this winter, four months have elapsed or nearly that, with very few days escaping without rain — sometimes it falls in deluges, — the winds have been also extremely high this winter. Hale stones of considerable size — lightening or thunder three or four times, & on the seas I believe very severe tempests, last winter one week exepted was as mild as this has been the contrary — I am really tired of the rain & of the cold which has forced us to have fires very often inspite of our having what is very uncommon here, our rooms well carpeted over — . by the bye I have not mentiond yet in my Gazette what you no doubt already know, that we have found coal here* — I fancy it is not of a very good quality else I shoud see people more elated about it, we have tried it, but it lights with difficulty & we have generally mixed it with English coals some chaldrons of which we got out before the coal was found — they stood us between nine & ten pounds a chaldron at the castle — but at that price whatever we coud spare was gladly taken from us — However, whether good or bad, *any* coal, or any thing to burn so near the cape as 15 miles is a great *pis*

*here**
This cannot have been any considerable strike as it is generally stated that no coal is to be found in the W. Cape. Coal was still scarce and imported according to official reports of Feb. 1800.

aller, as wood must become more & more scarce the more inhabited the place is, all being cut down for fence & no one replacing a bush with an acorn – we have some hopes that we have also found the *coarse silk worm* which makes the Bengal common silk, Doctor Roxburg apprehends it is the same, but Mynheer will not be at the pains to cultivate it – that will fall to the lot of some industrious English man if you keep the place – we have also found water at Hutches* bay, which will be a good thing *if* the quantity is sufficient – it is *said* it is – but I do *not believe it* – the *doubt* is against it – it is of no very great consequence as there is plenty at a short distance which coud perhaps be brought by pipes for less money than digging & making a reservoir woud come to. – remember I throw out what I hear like a mere newspaper person & like a parrot talk away without having either sense of knowledge of my subject to form any reasonable opinion. – when on our little tour I took a sort of *slight panorama* from the *OUT Keek** – (the place they look out from, with their glasses) of Saldana & Hutches Bay which Ill send you that while you have the regular & fine plans of Engeneers & chartsmen, you may laugh & joke over the female one. – are you tired of me yet? – I think I see you shake your head & say upon my word I have some reason – indeed you Have, but allways look at *Meanings* & *motives* to find apology for *frivolity*, dullness or *prolixity* – Ill add no more, exept kindest love to your Ladys & to renew my promise of writing to Lady Jane, by the next ships – there is a little something I want her to do for me, but I knew not whether it will be worthy of passing thro her hands –

*Hutches**
Hoetjies Bay at the northern extremity of Saldanha Bay.

*Keek**
Uitkyk = lookout.

God Bless you my Dr friend, keep your Health well for the sake of All at home & all abroad –

your most affectly
Anne Barnard

["Natives"]

Letter 19

The light touch of the previous letter has been banished by the shadow of Lord Macartney's imminent departure for home for health reasons.

Cape of Good Hope –
Nov[r] 1 1798

I hoped to have sent you a long letter my dear friend – many foolish little trifles pickd up on our tour up the country, and to have referd you to my sisters for the sight of a few poor Sketches of Different places & an account of them taken in the waggon, but I now find to my sorrow that Lord Macartney is going home so soon that I will prefer sending what I can, by that opportunity – He comes to stay with us about a week hence for a little time previous to his departure, when I shall do my best to put him into good sailing order, and to coddle him up with good chear and idleness – I never touch on any of my letters to you on the situation of affairs at home, 8 or 10 months spent on the sea or at St Helena makes a *conjecture* or a *fear* so old, & out of date, that it woud be folly to trouble you with them. – I long to see some English papers to find by them that Mr Pitt is better – how I pitied you when all his arduous business was added to your own. –

I must add no more at present it is very late & the ships sail early in the morning – I told you in my last that matrimony flourishd – Elopement has since been the fashion & the embarkation of the Scotch Brigade & 24th Regt has disembarked four Yong frows out of their one pair of stairs window with their bundles –* . did I tell you in my last of Young Sturts* marriage – the connection is not a very Honorable one – but there was no disuading him from it – Mr B. was employd by Lrd M. to entreat him to think it over cooly – I fear he has not listend – there are several others who only wait the sailing off of their friends to marry without being laughd at. –

Kind love to L[y] Jane & your daughters
God Bless you –

Yours - Anne Barnard

*bundles**
Lady A. wrote to Lord Mornington on 23-10-1798 as follows: "The Embarkation of the Scots Brigade & 84th Regt. might make a good caracature print if we were to add the disembarking of Yonge Vrows from their windows with their band boxes and bundles eloping with the officers & the black slaves with the men – there is an order to search the ships in case of any of the last being secreted there, but it does not I believe extend to young ladys – one girl was caught by her mother and stopd by being undressed & put to bed without any cloaths Mama locking up her means of future escape – She is on her way to Bangal – a Miss Robinson but her *name* is *entre nous.* – the other is gone – a Miss Bocett – very pretty indeed, with a Lieut. Blakeney of the Kingdome of Ireland – more were expected to be off last night & the Fiscal was charged to be on the Watch – he has two or three eloping ladys in the Tronck – My good husband wanted to convince the Father of the young lady that he ought to force Mr. Blakeney to marry his daughter by sword & pistol, but that does not seem to be the way in which those things are taken here."

*Sturts**
There were two Sturts in the garrison: Capt. John Ashley Sturt, 80th Foot, and Cornet William Sturt, 28th Dragoons. The latter would seem more likely to answer the description.

Letter 20

Cape of Good Hope –
Nov[r] 10 1798

Sorry am I my dear friend at the *opportunity* by which I can now write with safety to you, the departure of our own dear Governor who this day leaves the garden house & takes up his residence with us during the short time which will be necessary to get all arranged for his leaving the colony – if he felt he *coud* have staid longer with safety to himself I am *convinced he woud*, but the Gout Hangs constantly over him never fixing itself properly, and often making him feel himself hardly more than the Tennant of the Hour, I wish I had not to add that the poor admiral, Sir Hugh Christian seems to be still worse than Lord M:, he has never enjoyd his Health since his arrival & lately had when at Saldana Bay an attack so violent as to lay for dead for a short time, I have my fears that he will not find it possible to remain here long, & I shall be sorry for it, as I take him to be an excellent officer & zealously eager to fill his part in his profession to his own Honor & the good of his country, but his mind is too ardent & anxious for the strength of his poor constitution, a little more indifferent & I believe it coud be better for him. – last night he had a relapse and I think his physician doctor pattison is considerably allarmed about him. – I find that the Stately is to be convoy to the ships now laying at St Helena, I wrote by them, and meant to have followed them by another letter, but as all woud reach you at *once*, I will not trouble you with more of my nonsense at present, you will have in our Governors conversation the cream of all that can be said or told, I had hoped to have presented him with a panoramo of the cape before his departure but I must send it after him as the South Easters have been so violent that I coud not pretend to draw on the top of my Citadel else I shoud have been blown into the air like a skittle cock.

in my foolish Journal sent to my sisters* there is a Hasty sketch of Saldana bay & the Hern Huters church,* which is all that I coud accomplish at the present, shoud you like to look into it dont let it fall I pray into the hands of any one who will laugh at your poor friend for many things which need the eye of lenity – I am safe with sweet Lady Jane – I wish I coud find any thing pretty or curious to send her, but here we have no collectors of curiositys & much pains has it taken me to get the *miserable trifles* which accompany this. – I have put up a specimen to you & to Mr Pitt of what my friends the Hottentots do, I believe I mentioned this in my last letter – a couple of knives made at the Hern Huters church – * a couple of walking sticks, made of *wood* I *own*, but with some little notion of drawing – I believe they are the first that ever crossd the Line – pray present these humble offerings to Mr Pitt with the *Frow Barnards* very best wishes that God-almighty may long continue him and you to take care of us both at Home and abroad. – I will

*sister's**
See p.120.

*church**
Herrnhuters, i.e. Moravian missionaries or United Brethren. Hurried writing suggests here that the Moravian church was at Saldanha Bay. Lady A. is of course referring to the one at Genadendal.

not trouble you by adding more at present you have greater things to mind and I have today to make some preparations for a bunch of wedding people in the evening who I have invited to introduce to our governor before his departure, our officers have of late been marrying the dutch Frows at a great rate; and it is civil to shew them every civility possible when so married without minding their pedigree which is not sometimes very correct; Mr Sturt is one of the new married men —. the evenings is the time when they like best to visit me, not so the Boors from the country who generally come to pay their respects at the castle at Seven oclock in the morning & allways have their Sopi* of Gin with me while I am at breakfast, I am glad to see the country people who were civil to us when amongst them coming to see us in return. here, it marks a confidence in the assurances I made them of their being welcome, in the Dutch time none of the peasants durst presume to enter the gates of the castle with their Hats on, now they come in freely & some of the Frows bestow their Kisses both on me & my better half very liberally, however their Heartyness pleases & flatters us — but I am running on —

God Bless you —and believe me ever affectionately yours

Anne Barnard

Mr B. tells me he has put it into Lord M[S] Hands to request from you a discretionary power of returning home to pay you a visit by and bye shoud Health, affairs, or the Maladie du pay make us wish it, both man & wife being well & comfortable we are unlikely to use it Hastely or needlessly, but it woud be a *great satisfaction* to think we had the *power* of going to England with your full *approbation*.

*Sopi**
Afrikaans (sopie) = a tot

Making candles

Lord Macartney left the Cape in H.M.S. Stately *on November 21, 1798. The following night a terrible fire broke out in the cavalry stables near the Castle and many buildings on the sea front, including the East India Co.'s warehouses, were destroyed (see illustration below). Major-General Francis Dundas, (1759-1824), Henry's nephew and commander of the forces, became Acting Governor until the arrival of the new Governor, Sir George Yonge, in the following December. With Macartney's departure the Barnards' happiest days at the Cape were over, firstly due to the wrangle over the right to the best apartments in the Castle and secondly to General Dundas's business relationship with Andrew Barnard whom he tended to ignore.*

View of the store houses burnt down, November 1798. From left to right: The Tronk and court of justice; the admiral's; the (?) and some stores; Maxwell and Queen's Offices; D. du Wals; a Dutch officer's house; storehouses burnt; corn magazine behind the stables . . .: storehouses standing.

*Col**
The young Ann Barnard had recently (14-2-1799) married Lt.-Col. James Catlin Craufurd of the 91st Regt.

*victorys**
Doubtless a reference to the destruction of the French fleet by Nelson at the Battle of the Nile, Aug. 1798, and the abortive attempt by Napoleon to land an invasion force in Ireland.

*peer**
Nelson was created Baron Nelson of the Nile on 6 Nov. 1798.

*fortune.**
H.D.'s widowed second daughter Anne (see Letter 3, note 1) married James Strange, an Indian government official, 18-12-1798. According to Cyril Matheson (*Life of Henry Dundas*), her father disapproved.

paradise
April 4th – 1799
Cape of good Hope

My last letter to Lady Jane took grounds for another to follow it shortly to yourself, I hear of a ship to sail the day after tomorrow and let my Husband – my cousin and her new Col* go off to pay visits at the cape while I stay here for the pleasure of spending an hour with you. – First let me in three cheers express my Joy in all the late glorious events which I dare say will form as bright a moment in History as England ever saw, as light gains double by shadow, and dark was the shadow which preluded these victorys* – I see Lord Nile or Lord something of the Nile is the new peer,* I hope his eldest son wont be baron crocodile, I shoud like to see a dozen more such creations – but do not let us forget private congratulations in publick – I see the marriage of Mrs Drummond in the papers and find it has taken place, he has an excellent character an easy fortune.* – I trust it has your approbation, it woud have had still more of mine if he had been a *wie bit bonnyer* – perhaps you call me very impertinent, but she is such a Handsome creature herself & I am told is so clever that I do not think a moderate thing good enough for her, but I must own myself unreasonable for no one coud speack more Highly of another than his brother and sister here did of him when they were with us – . Bless my heart! it is not *impossible* that we may see him and her here! to see Mrs Strange at the Cape! when do *you* come? when does *Lady Jane*! wen does *his Majesty* mean to honor us? – I despair of nothing; every Day sends me somebody un-

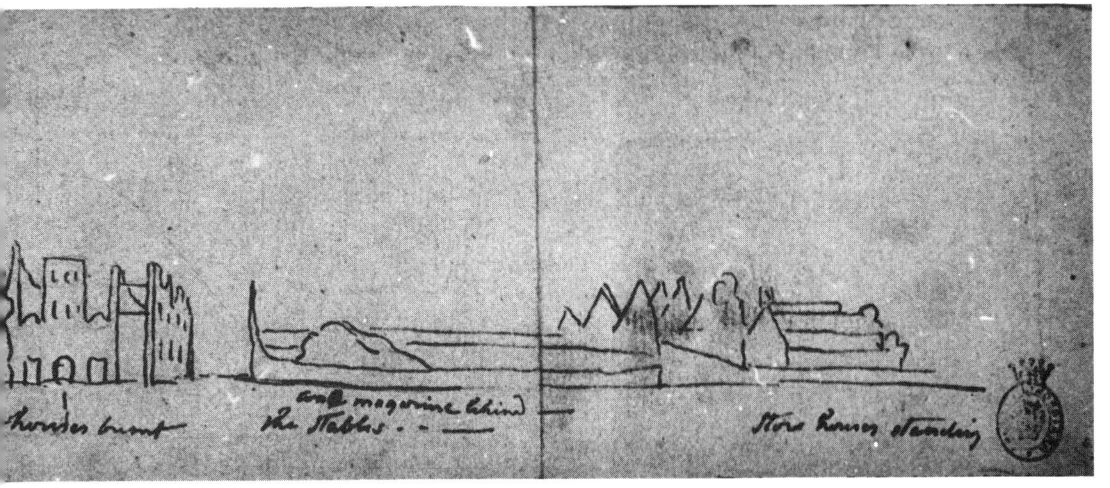

lookd for, and that makes me think I shall see *her*. – I find a considerable difference in the climate this last season to what It was the first I arrivd, this summer has been much warmer, and the South Easters more violent, the weather more various – inspite of that I still think the climate a very pleasant one, and prodigious as the vississitudes of heat, Hot, Calm, Storm – in one day are, it is surprising to me to observe how few colds are caught – one Singular effect of Atmosphere I observe in myself, when in the castle close by the sea shore at the cape, I am constantly Hoarse, cannot sing a note, when at paradise which is reckond the dampest situation & most dangerous for that reason in the colony my voice is as clear as it was when I was sixteen – I do not look quite so *young* However, there is no Help for that "one cannot eat ones cake and have it too," if my friend will pardon a few wrinkles in my face I will pardon as many as they please in theirs, and reckon them only reasons for loving them the more, as it proves I have known them long. – while all goes fair & well with you in England we have got our little bit of insurrection here, at a distant part of the country Graaf Reynet the old bad news I suppose (& none of the modern good yet) has travelld there and inspired them with the desire of kicking up a dust & trying if they cant be masters still; it is nonsense for me to pretend to give you any account of matters which the General of course must convey to you at length, and yet there is a possibility this ship may sail without his dispatches as I hear he is at Stellenbosh & am told this moment that the vessel is absolutely to go tomorrow morning instead of the day after as I had before mentiond – . these Graaf Reynet people have always been Turbulent & unwilling to bend to any laws, or to the Landrost, they particularly dislike theirs, a very good sort of man I hear, and affect to think themselves ill used now that they are British Subjects in not having an English Landrost, but I believe this is a mere pretext to get rid of the present one* – the ground of the present quarrel is their having forced him (and the soldiers who had the charge of a prisoner) to give up to them the said prisoner* who is one of the most seditious amongst them & was for wrong practises of some kind sent to the Cape by the landrost –. they threatend his life & from that time have kept him in constant fear, by a sort of guard being placed on him that he may not run away – general Dundas sent General Vandeleur there with a party of Horse – also Major Abercrombie* & one or two small vessels with troops, it was the general Idea that the seditious people woud instantly be reduced to order by the sight of the scarlet coats & woud surrender their arms but I hear they have retreated as it is thought into the Caffre country & more men has been requested by Genl. V:* – I cannot say however that I feel atall allarmd at this, it will cost a few lives & that is a pity, but I fancy some examples must be made to preserve peace in the country – one of the party having remaind behind & being desirous of Joining the others by a short cut almost lost his life, being pursued by a troop of Buffaloes who fairly huntd him like a Hare, and the speed of his horse only, saved him, – what a Blessing that while troops are called away to that purpose, & others sent on to India,* that the people of the Cape have that spirited *OLD Corps* the *CAPE association* to trust to – A corps almost two months old, & commanded by *Col Barnard* – who of course is command-

*one**
H.C.D. Maynier, Secretary of Graaff Reinet since 1789.

*prisoner**
Adriaan van Jaarsveld, arrested for forgery, released as here described but re-arrested. He later died in prison.

*Abercombie**
Presumably Capt.-Lieut. Peter Abercromby, or Abercrombie, 8th Dragoons.

*V:**
Brig.-General T.P. Vandeleur. See Letter 14, note 38. 16 men of a party under Lieut. Chumney of the 81st were ambushed and killed on the Bushman R. in Feb. 1799.

*India**
The following regiments left the Cape between Nov. 1798 and Feb. 1799: 84th Foot, 28th Dragoons, 86th Foot and the Scotch Brigade. The 61st Foot arrived in Jan. 1799 to reinforce the 8th Dragoons and 98th Foot, the only units remaining. The formation of this volunteer force is understandable.

ed by Lady Anne, that old and Experienced officer! her Ladyship I hear is soon to present the Regiment with their colors, in which the Whittebomb* (native of this country) is Happily blended and united with the Royal oak of old England, a compliment her Ladyship means for Mynheer – if he has *NOWS** to understand it) – the gentlemen volunteers who compose the corps had in the original plan professd themselves in readyness shoud occasion require, to stand forwards with any aid in their power, but general Dundas very naturally thinking that, *that* aid coud not be properly administerd unless they are drilld into the knowledge of what was to be done on emergency, mentiond the associations in England, and their conduct as the model for this which hint was of course adopted – the officers were chose by Ballot & Mr Barnard chosen Col; he being an old soldier the business went on so much the better, All were eager in the cause a very few gentlemen exepted who shy of being smiled at by the military & disliking the sacrifise of time to the necessary field days, are no longer of the corps, much to Mr Barnards regret, as they are good men, tho bad officers. –

so far had I wrote last night this moment Mr B. asks for my letters to carry to Town, I wish I had another hour allowd me as I have a thousand things more to say of various sorts; however this shall go as it is for fear of delay, and you may depend on hearing from me again by the next opportunity. – Lady Jane made me feel so happy by the assurance both from herself & you that accounts of our goings on here were prized from me, that I shall certainly continue to converse with you both in the confidence of friendship & kindness –

God Bless you – in haste

AB

*Whittebomb**
Witteboom or silver tree (*Leucadendron argenteum*). Lady A. presented colours on 27-4-1799, and "gave a public break upon the occasion." (S.E. Hudson's journal.)

*Nows**
Nous (Greek).

[Three-legged pot]

Letter 22

Just a month later Lady Anne writes from "Paradise" the country cottage they had resorted to in the winter of 1798. (See Letter 17, note 2). The problems resulting from the new regime – albeit only an interregnum – were clearly causing concern, though so far the Barnards were clearly hoping that everything would turn out for the best.

paradise
Cape of Good Hope
May 4 – 1799

I am quite ashamed my dear friend to begin writing on such bad paper* to you, but I am a farmers wife in the country and forgot to tell the farmer who goes into town to market, viz the business of the office every day at nine oclock that mine was done, you will pardon it however, not being a man of much minutia of ceremony when a friend a womans letter is in the case. –

I wrote to you a short letter the 21th of last month, and Lady Jane had a long one some time before that; I now go on chearfully writing to your both, with my little doze of kindness & flattery mixed, which has done me a world of good, but which at this Immense distance from you is necessary to invigorate & enliven one who must like the spider spin chiefly from her own materials. – by the bye (for you know it is my way to bring out things as they pass across my mind) are Cape Spiders reckond curiositys in England? Doctor Roxburgh tells me they are, but I hate spiders of all sorts handsome or ugly so much that I shoud not thank any body for giving me a Bushell – think then what I sufferd lately when after having found in the bushes as I supposed a very large mausoleum of a silk worm, like a gooses egg, I put it into my writing drawer, & some days after on opening it a whole legion of young spider broke forth on me – it was a spiders nest & I had innoculated every room in the House at once for off they run to every Hole they coud find. – I assure you it is needless in this country to propagate gentry of the unpleasant kind, for there is one breed of little animals of a dark complexion which are in summer the plagues of society, the only comfort is, that the more a house is inhabited there are the fewer of them. – Since I wrote last the disturbances at Graaf Renet are happily terminated thro the exertions of the general and of the Clyene* General, who went; Vandeleur; All have submitted I hear & two or three only remain un-

*paper**
The writing paper referred to is laid foolscap with Britannia watermark dated 1797, made by A. Blackwell of Apsley Mill. It does not take ink as well as most of the paper Lady A. uses and it is the type of paper used for official business.

*Clyene**
Lady A. meant "klein", i.e. lesser, with reference to Brigadier-General Vandeleur.

taken amongst the disturbers of peace & good order. – the Caffres have expressd the strongest disposition to be on friendly terms with us, as has the Boshie men, who possessd of nothing were robbers rather from necessity than choice, and who by the presents of cattle &c conveyd to them by Lord Macartney from the English government are won to the love of peace and good fellowship by having something to lose. – I went with Mr B. to the Cape yesterday to see the Captain of one of the tribes; what is called here the *Right* Boshies men – what a courageous fine fellow that young man must be, who after having gone on plundering a neighbours nation (the Hottentots) for such a length of time, trusts himself with a band of them to come down: for the first time. A Boshie man ever voluntarily so far, to see the English Governor at the Cape. – his brother only accompanied him – the Captain whose name was Philan I am willing to Hope a contraction of *Philander*, was coverd with old military ornaments of different Regiments some of which we had brought with us from England, having stored ourselves at an old shop for such things with all the ornamental brass we coud pick up. – different people had given him some *very* old cloaths before he came to pay me a visit at the Castle so I did not see him quite in his unadornd State of lovelyness but over these cloaths he wore his own, the skin cloak & all his decorations – gorgets – belts and pouches – his countenance was good-humourd to the greatest degree, with more character in it than the Hottentot face, which has rarely more than gentleness to boast of. – his hair was perfectly different from the hair of any other Human creature I have seen, as it was like fringes of fine knotted black worsted, such Knotting as old ladys do for beds. – in the front of his forehead he wore a little button hanging down somewhat like a pagoda – & behind he had a Queu* (I dont think I have spelld this word right, but Im not sure) viz – pig tail, which hung down an insh with two shells to it – I was quite delighted with the dress of the tail it shewd he was no *democrate*. – but it is not *exactly* such as is worn by our Captains in St James Street – as they *speak* no dutch, and as the interpreter (a Hottentot) was obliged to leave them to fetch the rest, I coud not get so much of their minds as of their faces – but they seemd much pleased with the English, & are to bring their Vrows to visit me this winter. – the Gonaqua man took great pains to tell Mynheer Barnard, what pretty girls there are in that country, theirs is the country described by Valliante so perhaps there may have been some truth in his representation of Narina.* – they have some ideas of marriage, the captain & his brother had two wives each, but one or two of the Hottentots who accompanied them only one a piece. – we gave all coarse Handkerchiefs, knives, scissors, needles, thread, beads, to the Captain I gave a very fine *Button* which he instantly tyed round his neck & Mr B. a coat and wastecoat which he also put on, throwing off his cloaths to do so, fortunately Mr B. at *that* time gave these two articles *only*, else I know not to what lengths the captain woud have carried his Toylette in my presence – there is something singularly delicate in the make of the Boshie men, their arms so finely turnd – hands so small on[e] of the fingers of which was witherd off by the bite of a serpent. the wrist was as delicate as that of a ladys, yet when he bent his bow, it seemd to be strong, and the wildness of his figure was striking – but

*Queu**
Correctly "queue".

*Narina**
The reference is to François Le Vaillant's description of a 16 year-old Gonaqua girl living on the banks of the Great Fish R. as given in his *Voyage dans l'intérieur de l'Afrique . . .* 1780-85. (1st ed., 1790), v.I. p. 186-192 and plate IV. It was agreed by travellers that the Gonaqua were the best looking of the Hottentot people. (cf. Swellengrebel, Cape Archives, Accessions 447, as quoted by Forbes, *Pioneer travellers in S.A.*, p. 72.)

their Tones! oh how strangely savage! they have all the clicking noise of the Hottentots, each word being so divided, but accompanied by sounds, or rather *groans* quite uncouth. – we gave them some brandy which they greedily took and previous to their departure some gimlets, an old sword & to each some Tobacco & a new pipe – they were quite happy! and bidding us farewell made each a sort of bow with his hat or Handkerchief in Hand, the captain rapid in his motions made a low one, a table was near and the Tobacco pipe (stuck in his hat) knocking against it was shiverd to pieces – Never – No never did painting convey such an Attitude, or the feelings of nature speak so plain – he did not gaze at it, or pick it up – he coverd his face at once with his hand, Desolation was in his heart, & stood there, till ready to burst into tears he coud just turn aside to prevent them from dropping – mean time we had sent for another pipe. – the Hottentots *cluckd* to him that here was another, he took his hand from his face – saw the pipe – received it – but the remedy to his sorrow was too sudden for the transition of Joy to follow it, the pain of the broken pipe stuck, tho the new pipe was in his hand. – he then pickd up the fragments & placed all once more in the Hat, of which he seemd very proud – & with a deep sigh & a consoled *Tankee* wint off. – by the bye I askd him if he had no objection to giving me a little of his queer hair & his queu – giving him a fine large shell to tye on in its place which enchanted him, he was greatly flatterd by my request & held down his head to have it cut off which the brother seeing, came forwards with his fringed top also – I had meant this modern relick for Lady Jane, & had wrote her a note, but it looks so odd and *uncouth* that I think it woud rather frighten than please her, perhaps as you are a bold man & not easily scared I may send you it, or a little of his hair –

I have lately had many letters from Bengal & Madrass, from Lord Morng:[n*] – the Clives and Stranges – the gentlemen seem all well & comfortable but the ladys by no means like the heat of the climate. – Lord Mor: writes in the highest spirits, full of hopes of a glorious & speedy termination to the *young* war, for it will then die but an Infant – his measures seem to have been prompt and vigourous, I fancy they are the best to ensure success. – we have had two ships come into Simons bay within the last week in great distress the one an old shatterd vessel containing, besides the crew 600 french prisoners, those who have been for some years in the prisons at Madrass & those who were lately seized at pondcherry on suspicion Justly founded of their carrying on machinations against our interests with their country men & with Tippoo, of these there are some oppulent & creditable men of good manners – they, in number about 50 have the half of the captains cabin – the other 550 are stowd below; I suppose the ship came off in a Hurry, but it appears as if the agent employd to provide for them had not done his employers Justice as they were more than half famishd, in want of every thing, disease had begun to sweep them off & it was daily gaining ground, the General has permitted the sick to be put on shore & they are now at Muisenberg, I wish there was the means here of affording some vessel to take away the half of them but I hear there is at present not one *carriage* of that sort on this coast all being cruising out, thank

*Morng** Lord Mornington. See Letters 15 and 17.

Heaven however for the success of your British Navy over our Enemys, we have little now to fear from Invasion – the other ship contains convicts, it was in still greater distress for food, & in great want of medical aid, the ship surgeon is a Humane good man who exerts himself night & day to do his duty, but is so ignorant of his profession that he did not know there was a putrid fever on board, tho 8 and 10, died of it a day. I have not learnt (being in the country) if they are got better but I suppose they are, as they are under the care I presume of Doctor Pattison a very Humane excellent man – Mr Barnard & his corps dined with the General a few days after the colours were presented, he took the invitation extremely kind & I fancy *all* were flatterd by it, I have said nothing since Lord Macartney went of a fear of Mr B. that I expressd in one of my confidential letters to you, that the General was not partial to him, I said at the time I was sure he woud find the apprehension groundless – I did not however like to be rash in pronouncing, but now I have the pleasure of assuring you that all has gone on & I think will continue to do so as I coud wish, the genleness & candor of Mr Barnards nature making allowances sometimes for a little thoughtless hastyness in the other which I had hoped was gone, but which [,] was it greater than it is, his Attachment & gratitude to *You* woud lead him to mannage, rather than to establish perhaps into coldness by *silent* offence by no means so good a way amongst friends as speaking out the grievance – certainly on some points where Mr B has found it indispensably necessary to speak, for his own dignity in the Colony, he has done it properly & in a manner to hit the Generals temperate Key, as they have parted better friends even than before the remonstrance had been made. – you have now Lord Macartney with you [and] from him will receive such accounts of Mr B^{S} conduct in the department he owes to your goodness as you will naturally place more store by than any representations I can make, I have always said that I think he has one of the most judicious sound Heads for following up in the best manner the wishes of his Masters at Home that I know, without the inventive genius for striking our bold Ideas in politics which belong to an early insight in the *Metier*, which sometimes agreeably surprize the Employer & sometimes *Annoy* – but of his official abilitys Lord Macartney only, can be the Judge, as to say the truth I have had wondrous little opportunity of forming opinions about them, Mr B. has the idea (not a bad one you will say) that women have nothing to do with the Knowledge of politics or measures, by which means, the "Shoemakers wife" is generally very ill shod.* – all I learn is by accident, however that does not mortify me, as I have no pleasure of *knowing any thing* merely from the *Vanity of the thing*, or care I about publick matters here, exept in as much as conected with those I esteem & love – In writing to you I skim the surface of appearances very *accurately* right on no point I dare say, but as I do not *affect* to be so, no harm is done – wise matters as I ought, I left to Lord Macartney in the first instance & to the general, now in the second. – by the bye Mr Barnard has often said to me that it was very hard on him while he longd very much to write to you that there was no pretext for him to do it all the subjects been engrossed – Lord Macartney so ably & so copiously giving you publick accounts & private also of every thing

shod*
"Who is worse shod than the shoemaker's wife?" (John Heywood. *Proverbs*, 1546, Pt.I, ch.xi.)

worthy of observation in the place, I, taking the Gossiping department wholly on myself, but he threatens me that he will not take things as he has done, I have no right to expect he will shew me his letters to you as I do not shew him mine to you, I believe if I did, he woud *Clip* out a bit very often. –

May 14th – I shall simply seal my letter for I feel in too low spirits to add more – my poor cousin Mrs Crauford is very ill & I am stepping into the carriage to go to her –

God Bless you all – Yours truly

Anne Barnard

my dear Lady Jane – I am putting up for you an immense number of Cape seeds – Heaths, proteas, &, [th..................] very small quantity which I have with much courting got [out of] Doctor Roxburgh Bengal botanist who is here for the purpose of co[llecting] cape plants & seeds – make your gardner look them over, & take what you have not already in your green house – this done be so good as send the remainder to Lady Hadwicke who I have not yet sent any to of this sort

evr yours truly
AB

Eksteen's Farm, Kirstenbosch

The next letter was long delayed, due to a ban on ships leaving the Cape while the naval squadron was occupied further east. No proclamation to this effect has been found, either issued by General Dundas or by the Admiral, but Lady Anne's excuse seems justifiable. It was known that the Graaff Reinet rebels had requested French aid from Mauritius and in February 1799 the Prudente *with volunteers on board had been captured en route for Algoa Bay and in the September following the* Preneuse *was chased off by the sloop* Rattlesnake *after an action in that bay. With such hostile threats and the need to transport troops to meet the rebels and the Xosas in the 3rd Kaffir War, it was not surprising that the Cape itself should feel denuded of naval protection.*

Meanwhile relations with the Acting Governor had not improved. An exchange of correspondence between Andrew Barnard and General Dundas, directing operations in the Graaff Reinet district in August, was thought by Lady Anne sufficiently significant to warrant transcribing by herself and enclosing with this letter for the information of the General's uncle. The exchange may seem innocuous to us but it must be viewed in its context of increasingly strained relations.

Cape of good Hope
Castle
Sep^{tr} 12 – 1799

I am told my dear Friend that the Embargo laid on any thing sailing from our coast, is to be taken off, now that we are Strengthend by the return of our Squadron, and that a Vessel for England will sail in two days, the time is short for me to write to you as I coud wish, but after a pause so very long, during which time we have heard nothing from England & sent nothing to it; I cannot permit any opportunity to escape without giving you a letter, hurried as it may be – I have had the mortification of hearing that several of mine to you have been lost, some destroyd; too humble about their value to send you *duplicates*, you have of course missd a good deal of my chitchat; I believe I shall act differently in *future* and trust less to chance I have however regreted some of them the less, as we have not for a considerable time had those peaceable and safe times which produced nothing but "*rosecolor*" in our minds or corrospondence. – Glad I am that before you receive any news from the Cape to give you uneasiness (temporary uneasiness only I hope) that such a fund of triumphant Joy will be laid from your brilliant Indian Successes as to render our Caffre and Hottentot war a less important feature.* – the fall of Tippoo, and the victorious six weeks campaign of the *Gallant* Mornington I fancy has about this time sett your great guns a singing,* the pleasantest music in times of publick danger is the music of the *Tower*. – we have had a feu de Joye on the occasion and glad we were to spend a little of our powder, wanted as they say it has been at Graaf Renet, to awe our fellow country men the dutch here, and what is of more importance, their *slaves*, into some opinion of our force, by our Successes –

The last very long letter you have probably receivd from me, was followd shortly by others, containing accounts of *more fires* at different parts of the town, fortunately prevented from doing material harm, which if all *accidental* at least was liable to a different interpretation. – to those succeeded a new species of Calamity which lasted but for a short time but threatend us all in the *castle* with a watry grave. – you will not suppose me to be painting *only* thro a womans fears when I tell you that we were obliged to fire *guns of distress*. – A couple of days rain, almost amounting to the deluge of old, begun the ill; – towards night (the 2[d] day) water rose so many feet suddenly in the castle as to fill up all the ditches, go near to drown the officers of Artillery in their Mess room & all the Banditts in the lower court yard, *four* of which only *did* suffer, but as it rose a foot or two every moment, the encreasing danger appeard considerable, and while we paused, the moment for flight was over! the uncertainty of the cause of this, doubled the allarm, by some the sea was supposed to have broke in, others imagined it to be like the Earth quake at Lisbon which was so fatal to thousands,* – this Phoenomeno however proved only to have been some Water Spouts, or clouds loaded with rain which broke over the Table Mountain, falling down the gullys there, where joined by other waters from the ajacent hills they had become a torrent impetuous enough to break down all before it, but not such as to have been dangerous had it not taken the *direction* of the *castle* the outer gate of which it enterd, in a volume of ten or twelve feet high & the natural consequences followd from the general dismay in the dark. – having had fire – water – and allready somewhat of an Insurrection in the Graaf Renet district, we needed only Mutiny in the Army to render the measure of our vexations compleat, and this we had a taste of the 6th day of last month when a plot was reveald by a soldier of the 91st Regt, who had been solicited to join it by one M[c] Gie, a soldier of the 61st, who had told the other that the 81, and 61 Regts were ready at a minutes warning to assist each other to murder or otherwise secure their commanding officers who slept in the Castle, to seize the powder Magazine, take possession of the Castle and become the new masters of the Cape. – The Rogue M[c]gie who was at the head of this scheme, finding it defeated by discovery, turnd *Kings evidence* under promise of pardon from the general, and by accusing a couple of Innocent Men, whose excellent characters bore them thro, Screend his *real* associates, and it remains still in the dark who they were; but tho thereproved to be much *less* the matter than was at first imagined, there still was in the opinion of many, *Something* – but this

*feature**
This refers to the attempts of the British commanders to settle the frontier question with the Xosa and to combat the menace of raiding Hottentots and Bushmen nearer home. It was the 3rd Kaffir War.

*singing**
The fall of Seringapatam to General Baird took place on 4 May 1799. Tippoo was slain in the stampede which followed.

*thousands**
Nov. 1755. 40,000 persons were reported killed. Regarding the water in the Castle, S.E. Hudson records in his diary that it rose 16 – 20 ft. in half an hour. (Diary, 27-6-1799).

is an unpleasant Idea to their very worthy commanders Caruthers and Barlow* who are excellent officers & good men. – they wish to think this the mad scheme of one foolish Boy, it however put the whole garrison in allarm and reared the gallows for instant execution. – none were condemnd however for the above reasons –

This circumstance took place the day before General Dundas left this place to co-operate with and effect a junction with General Vandeleur, against the Caffres and Hottentots. – So far I have narrated common events on which every one is entitled to think, it becomes a more delicate and difficult task to add our subsequent history, as in the course of it I fear I may be led to place myself in a presumptuous and improper point of view to my dear friend, by throwing out opinions on the wisdom of some things going forwards here which I have no business to touch on, yet I love you too well to be *cautious*, and I know this place to be so favourite a child of yours, that if I as a bye stander imagine that *whipping* is a worse measure than *coaxing* it, I think I shoud fail in my *duty to You* if I did not privately say so. probably you will not have many letters at *present*, where there is a little good to be told, people are more shy of writing to a minister than on prosperous occasions, but it is the very time when a friends narrative, however poorly stated, may chance to be of some little use. – I mentiond in one of my last letters, that General Vandeleur still remaind in the northern district,* after having reduced the *Boors* viz farmers, to obedience, a measure easy to be effected from the known dastardly spirit of the dutch here who run from a musquet or scarlet coat, and I fancy were only refractory from imagining themselves at too great a distance from the cape to have any military force sent against them. – I believe I also mentiond his having sent as prisoners here about 24 persons, supposed to be the ringleaders of the Turbulent tribe who were immediately confined to the castle till the pleasure of government at home shoud be known respecting them: this produces a *Tedious* delay to such as are innocent, comparatively speaking – I have heard it said that if they had been tried by the laws of the Colony and by the Judges here, those who deservd it woud have been *fairly condemnd, Now* that there is an English Government, to support the court of Justice, otherwise No dutch man woud venture to condemn a Dutch man. – no sooner were those men sent off & the remaining farmers reduced to submission, than general Dundas recalld the greatest part of the troops, had they been permitted to have remaind some time longer perhaps it might have been more *Judicious*, as they were at *that* time become *eminently* necessary to deffend the property of the prisoners, & of the Boors that remaind from the Caffres their neighbours, who finding from the Hottentots in the service of the farmers (& now left by their wives & familys with the care of the farms) that the *usual Amunition* which government allows them as a *necessary* deffence against wild beasts and plunderers was at this time *withheld*, for fear of its being applied to bad purposes, saw nothing to oppose their natural taste for Rapine. – the two dutch men, the original cause of all,* who had been rescued from the Landrosts Authority by the boors, had shelterd themselves with the Caffres. – not amongst the subjects of King gayka,* the friend of the English, but with this *Vagrant tribe*,* in

*Barlow**
Lt.-Col. Francis Carruthers and Major John James Barlow of the 61st (South Gloucestershire) Foot. Hudson states (4-8-99) that the ringleader of the mutiny was sentenced to receive 1000 lashes and be disgraced.

*district**
The revolt in Graaff Reinet. (See Letter 21).

*all,**
Adriaan van Jaarsveld and Marthinus Prinsloo, "protector of the voice of the people".

*gayka,**
Gaika (c. 1780-1829), chief of the Rarabe clan of the Xosa.

*tribe,**
The Gunukwebe tribe under Kungwe and the Ndhlambis occupying the Zuurveld area.

number it is supposed about 3.000, who driven from *His* country for misdemeanours some years ago have establishd themselves amongst a range of wooded mountains, extending about two or three hundred miles, bounded by the dominions of King Gayka & by the Fish River behind, and on this side by the Dutch Settlements. – this boundery of the *Fish River*, (which had been the *accustomd* one I hear for the Caffres in general) General Dundas it seems thought it expedient that general Vandeleur shoud insist on their retreating behind, and to force them to do so General V: drove away their cattle to its banks knowing they must follow, for subsistence, How far it was well to enforce the old – old policy on *this occasion* you will best Judge, it seems natural however to expect they woud *resist*, for had they been compelld to cross that River they must have found *Death* from their country men on the other side who are numerous – they of course refused, & Hostilitys begun. – on the other hand the Hottentots I have mentiond, long habituated to oppression & unjustly dealt by on all occasions by the farmers, seeing no disposition (at least that they knew of) in the English to redress them, begun to think this was a fair moment for them to *redress themselves* they took possession of the Arms and horses of their *absent masters*, mounted themselves & along with the other Hottentots the servants of the remaining farmers Joind the Caffres, assisted them in resisting the attempts of the English and in making depradations on the dutch settlements which they plunderd and destroyd, this met with opposition from our small force, and in dividing it for different purposes, an officer & 20 men were cut off. – General Vandeleur wrote for more Support. – our Garrison was weak – our Squadron absent – our troops were hardly returnd when they were sent 800 miles back again to effect the purposes I have mentiond, & at the same time to awe the rising spirit of rapine & *cruelty* which *once* awakind in the people becomes soon desperate & dangerous [,] field pieces & more amunition was sent. – the Dutch saw our danger from the experience of 150 years, *Nor were they silent.* – "My Lady said the old president of the court of justice (even to me) "I can Judge of the Caffres *now* by what I found them five years ago when I was sent to *negociate* on a quarrel between them & us nothing will ever be made of them by force of arms, Hostilitys rouse their natural taste for plunder, they have every thing to gain by it nothing to lose & from their knowledge of the country fight with every advantage against us; indeed they rather *Annoy* than *fight* lurking by two & three amongst the bushes but avoiding action by day light, we have allways found that to keep well with them is our only safety and if a quarrel takes place to make it up *quickly*. – if peace is wanted 1.000 dollars well laid out will do more in tempting their chiefs to amity by copper Hatchets – gew gaws &c – than the expense to Government of a hundred thousand pounds laid out in men & amunition" – Lord Macartney was so much of the opinion also that it was dangerous to rouse the Hornets nest; that he never woud allow any one to Mollest them, or even permit trafick with them for fear of any difference. – his known Maxims on this Head, together with such councils as the experience of old dutch men such as I have mentiond coud have afforded, one might have supposed not wholly free from *Use*, but I fear our friend too sanguine of success his own way, has the unlucky pride of calling in no ones Judgement in partnership with his own, which cannot be very experienced, on such points, while his Temper is so eager for Action that he does not even give his *Own* Judgement *fair play* by a little consideration. –

day after day bringing worse and worse accounts of familys murderd, women carried off, and the quantity of men General Vandeleur was possessd of becoming equally inadequate to An offensive and Deffensive war, he being also at one time cut off from his main body, General Dundas declared he woud "go himself and finish the business one way or another", but in what manner, I fancy he is not thoroughly made up, from the orders which followed his departure for more troops to be sent (300) countermanded the day after, & this day reorderd another field piece & 150 men being this morning sent! – Mr Barnard most Anxiously ventured to recommend to him to take with him some respectable persons understanding the languages of the country & likely to be Clever at *Negociation*, but the General said Abercrombie and McNab* were sufficient; I hope he will find them so – I have heard he has since been Joind by some other person better calculated for such measures & I hope it is so. –

I presume Mr Barnard will transmit to you the Generals own accounts of what has passd since his departure, collected from his letters to Mr Ross,* the only letter Mr B: has had, was to desire him to communicate to *you* the situation of things, A painfull enough task, & one that Mr Barnard regrets he must perform in a manner so very Inadequate to what you must naturally expect from the situation he fills here. – but he cannot help it. – the General I am grieved to say, neither consults with him, nor permits any of his opinions to be advanced without that silencing manner which renders a man fearfull of subjecting himself to what it woud be difficult to bear –

In one of my letters I gladly mentiond to you that I trusted & hopd things woud go on well, as Mr Barnard had on an occasion (I might have said occasions) where his respectability in the Colony was much compromised, remonstrated with him in a manner so dispationate and Judicious as to hit the Generals temperate Key & from what then passd Mr B: had good Hopes that he woud rectify the unlucky Habit of making him A Cypher; indeed to such a point that the Landrost of Stellingbosh &c askd Mr Barnard if he was any longer, exept nominally, the Secretary of the Colony; but unfortunately his hopes were soon vanishd, dispatches were receivd, answerd – all sorts of business done without the Generals even mentioning the facts to Mr Barnard; when orderd by him to write to you, he took the opportunity of expressing his mind on that point, *by the few lines a copy of which I have stolen together with the Generals answer*, that you may be enabled to Judge *How little* Mr Barnard has had to do with measures which are so generally reckond here to have been *incautious*, that I shoud grieve if you coud suppose *Mr Barnards councils had any share in them*, which you might be led to suppose from knowing the earnest manner in which Lord Macartney recommended it to the general, and even left it in his instructions to take no step without consulting it well over with *him* . –

In *this*, read my *Apology* for having *presumed* to take up *your* Atten-

*McNab**
Capt.-Lieut. Peter Abercromby, 8th Dragoons, and Lt. Robert McNab, 91st Foot, afterwards Town Major.

*Ross**
Hercules Ross, Deputy Secretary.

tion by my poor details on what is so *much out of my walk* as the war, its commencement, or duration but I wish you to know privately from me, what I think Mr Barnards delicacy will spare you the knowledge of from himself, that he has all along in the most respectfull manner as far as he *Durst* markd his disapprobation when any of the generals methods of going on appeard to him too hasty, or wanting in *discretion*, and perhaps it may be owing to this that the General corresponds with another person who will still less venture to speak out. – I take this opportunity to mention that the conduct of that Young Man (Mr Ross) is perfectly prudent, Mr B. has in many points a very excellent opinion of him, nor have they ever had a difference as Mr B. is above all Jealousys where none is due. – but I do assure you my best friend that nothing but the solid gratitude Mr B. feels for your kindness to him & patronage coud have made him bear, as a Man, the Degraded situation in which the Generals thoughtless want of *All reference* to him places him in. – but he lookd upon his situation as Governor to be one which woud not last long, he thought he coud best mark his Gratitude to *You* by avoiding the smallest dispute or quarrel with so near a relation of yours, & I often preachd to him that if he thought the General did not treat him exactly as he shoud, he was at least on *better* terms with him than *others were*, of the same rank in society, most of whom have in their turn had words of such a nature as I presume have reachd home, unless the respect they pay to his very high connections have on reflection seald their lips. –

with all this, to feel any further resentment at the General than that of *the Moment* is impossible, he is *as God made him* an honest man, with many disinterested, manly, good points, I had once hoped he was improved from what he was originally made by having Lived longer in the world, but I see he is better calculated to do well under a good master, than as the head; – I suspect You think as we do here, by your sending out a new governor at present, *Your* nephew, great as the employment is, might doubtless have filled it till the peace if you had seen it proper, unless that is likely to be a very distant period. – Sir George Yonges appointment was one that at first surprized people here, A successor to Lord Macartney was lookd for in the more brilliant Class of Ability than the world is apt to class Sir George, but this apart, I am sure he will be receivd in such a manner as to please him. – tho I am not pleased with some of the English, who have been at pains to communicate his embarrassd situation to the Dutch, this with no other view I believe but that of being witty, and *sneering*, that Bane of all conversation. – it is with every attention we shall welcome him to this shore and with Joy I shall welcome Lady Yonge if She comes to every civility in my power to offer till she becomes the Patroness of the place to shew them to me. – all the little aid my experience of it can give she shall have. –

it is with *not a little satisfaction* I can say at the end of the generals administration that it will close without he and Mr B, *ever having had a rupture* & it is with much satisfaction we mean to invite a young Lady who we are told comes out to become Mrs General Dundas, who shall remain with us if she will accept of the invitation till he returns which is not expected to be by any means a near prospect. – I know not how you approve of this invited wife who braves the dangers of the seas to

Join him but if she is a sensible, reasonable woman, whether possessd of a penny or not I shall think he will be the better for her. – with respect to Sir George & L^{y} Yonge if they do me the Honor of consulting me atall on their modes of life, as applicable to the place, I shall give them such hints as I think will conduce most to their own & the general Happiness as well as to the respectability of his Station as Governor – . this place is not wholly to be governd by wisdom – abilitys – or elevation of mind, there are a sett of ways of thinking & prejudices amongst the natives which it is worth the while of a man & his wife who are placed at the head of affairs & likely to remain here some time, to study. – the dutch in particular *respect parade*, and all sorts of high Etiquette so far from lowring the person who expects it in their eyes is only reckond a proof of his being *A great man*. – Sir George Yonge must wear a double row of gold lace on his coat to what Lord Macartney did, to sweep away the impressions given of his poverty, and as to Lady Yonge I shall endeavour to sett her up a gracious Queen, *but a queen*, and shall be the first to bow down to her. – there is *no call* for any extravagant expence to sustain the *representation*. I mean they may easily save five thousand a year of their income, but *representation* will be well, and if I do not forget the sort of woman I recollect to have heard she was, she will not dislike my advice; – I have not taken *my own advice* – I never gave into parade but my line was different from hers, the wife of the Secretary to the Colony has no call on her, what she does, is her free choice no Devoir, & I do not like nonsensical constraints or formalitys, tho I pay every attention to the dutys of Hospitality. –

A word more respecting Caffre Land, or rather the present scene of the war before I finish – I hear the General begins to suspect that matters might have been better conducted at first & is anxious to make peace with the Hottentots & Caffres foreseeing no end to the war; that General Vandeleur thinks it also the best scheme, but that both have an idea of *Licking them first*, and a very good idea it might be if they woud stand still to be lickd, but as pitchd battles are totally opposite to their modes of fighting I hope they wont count on one. – I shoud imagine it is by verbal explanations by presents to their leaders, by the promise of protection & future justice to their Hottentots, that they will be more likely to succeed, & if the two dutch men who have shelterd themselves amongst them & are partly at the bottom of this were to have promise of pardon & a douceur privately I shoud think it might be usefull. – this is not a very *Noble plan* you will say, but people must fight with such weapons as are in their hands if they are not indifferent about the event or if the danger is great –

it is supposed if the Caffres condescend to negociate atall now, that they will stipulate to keep the part of the country they have lately pillaged, it is the richest to be sure and along with part of their own and Gaykas territory affords most of the Cattle sent to the Cape – any proposal of this sort on their part woud probably be rejected in Toto. – perhaps I am about to Launch a very foolish Idea – I have launchd it by way of question in common conversation and always found it *Hooted at*, I think it fair to tell you this, but Ill launch it to *You* because I have often heard you say "Speak out all your nonsense Anne, I like to hear every bodys ideas" – were we to give up to the Caffres that part of the country I mention, supposing they stipulate for it & supposing that we *can* according to our treaty with the dutch where woud be the Harm? – the farms are already plunderd & destroyd the implements of Husbandry burnt – the Cattle *lifted* as they say in Scotland – the farmers fled – nor will they dare to return unless their thinly scatterd houses (for thinly scatterd they are inspite of its being the richest part of the colony in our possession) are protected by *one Regiment* merely, quarterd so as to render each individual farm secure, and they are at a distance of about six miles I believe from each other – it has generally been allowed here, that the dutch settlements reach inconveniently far from the cape, 800 or 1000 miles is a long way to send our troops to guard a few farm houses. – their motive originally in going so far I have heard was not because the lands nearer the Cape are not fit to raise grain, rear cattle &c, but because each man wishd to have a large range for his beasts & the power of turning up new ground every year for his grain, one crop of which comes up well without manure & with little trouble. – if we gave up that country to the Caffres, which by the bye they must keep *if they please* whether we give it up or not, & make the farmers a compensation by giving them portions of the unapproperiate lands *nearer the Cape*, we shoud save future quarrelling, expence of men & money, *have our grain & cattle much cheaper* as the heavy charge & much difficulty of Land carriage woud be savd, and be more collected together in case of future wars. – the lands woud be better cultivated the cattle soon raised in quantitys, if we eat *mutton* in the mean time of which there is plenty at an easy distance from the Cape, instead of *Beef* it will do us no harm, but if we make peace with the Caffres they will gladly furnish us as usual with cattle in return for such articles as they want, & if they from time to time pillage our farmers, at 200 or 300 miles distance the matter will be easier ajusted than if it was at 1000. – if we cannot effect peace with them now, I sincerely hope we may withdraw our handfull of men without thinking it necessary to fight longer – a better chance than our fighting is that the Hottentots and they may quarrel about the booty, or that Gayka may become Jealous of them and attack them behind – to retain *his* friendship at any price I fancy woud be wise, was he to join the others, then indeed it woud be time to think of departure – as to the Hottentots my poor friends who from having seen a good deal of I am always disposed to say a word for, some military men have proudly said if they lay down their arms & make peace unconditionally then it will be time enough to see justice done them, this may be very good doctrine in the Army or Navy not to appear to be forced into any thing, but the Hottentots are the free natives of the woods and may stipulate for fair laws between them & the dutch & ourselves & for justice in case of breach – if we had protected them sooner & forced the farmers to be *just* & kind to them I do not believe they woud now have turnd against them "A stitch in time" it is said, they are of a timid gratefull nature, slowly roused to resent but when they find the sweets of liberty I dare say they will value it. – the original complaint the Boors made against Mr Faure the Landrost of graaf Renet* was that he was a favourer of *Infidels* & had been

*Renet**
A slip by Lady A. Anthony Alexander Faure was landdrost of Swellendam when the "Nationals" of that district followed the Graaff Reinet example in seeking independence in 1795.

LETTER 23

*Sayb**
Capt. D. Richardson of the Bengal Army and Mirza Abu Taleb Khan. The latter was born in Lucknow but his father was Persian by birth having fled to India for political reasons. Mirza held various high offices under Indian princes but was temporarily unemployed and in somewhat straitened circumstances when invited by his friend Richardson to accompany him to Europe. (See *Mirza Abu Taleb Khan in Asia, Africa and Europe, during the years 1799-1803*, trans. by Chas. Stewart. 2 vols. London, 1810. In v.1, p.73-74, of this account of his travels he describes his visits to Lady A. as follows:

"Were I to relate all the civilities I received from General Dundas and the other British officers, they would fill a volume. I cannot however refrain mentioning the many delightful evenings I passed at the house of Lady Ann B – t, who every week gave an entertainment to all her acquaintances, and who constantly did me the honour to invite me. Lady Ann is the daughter of an English nobleman, and has all the dignified manners of a person of quality. At her house I frequently met with a Mrs. C – d, a young Irishwoman, who was exceedingly beautiful, but spoke little, and was rather reserved: in short she had quite the elegant behaviour of our Indian princesses, and completely won my heart."

"Mrs. C – d" was of course the younger Ann Barnard who married Col. James Craufurd.

known to sustain the Hottentots cause against the dutch master – *pardon* I dare say might get those Hottentots back still and new regulations bind them to us. See the Hottentot corps carrying the Kings Uniform. they are steady to us (because we use them well) tho brought against their country men – that Sir George Yonge may be a Governor of Peace, treading in all Lord Macartneys old footsteps is the wish & hope of all here, this sounds like the ending of a sermon, I fear you will think it a very tiresome bit of reading equally presumptuous and foolish, but all my aim is to give you what I know you like, *Truth* as far as I hear or know, altho it may be at my own risk, yet I do not think (*repeating as I must do* the strong motive I have for writing) that you will condemn me for being ingenuously open with you – if you do I can only beg your pardon, and feel very sorry. – if I have misapprehended or stated any thing incorrectly impute it to my ignorance only. I do not choose to ask any questions of Mr Barnard who coud put one right as it is so little my practice to enquire after political matters that he woud ask me why I do so now – we expect Sir George every day, our accounts are divided as to her coming, when they arrive you shall have a *short* account of how they find us & how they like us, I will hope that the Ladys may have a bad-ish passage in order to make them *prize* the pleasures of Dry land the more – all new marriages & the Cape follys of the day in my next –

God Bless you – & love to Lady Jane

Your ever affect friend
Anne Barnard

I have sent a few lines of Introduction with Capt Richardson & Khan Sayb* the first is a man of learning and Intelligence who returns for health chiefly after 20 years spent in India he is much esteemd, & is of the party with Khan Saijb a persian chief, a clever, agreeable & good man, a man of letters also, and far superior to most of the grandees of Indostan – he has the Honor to be a particular friend of Lord Cornwallis & travels chiefly to see the world, possibly he may combine some other motive which he will communicate to Lord Cornwallis but both are worthy of *your* notice I believe – Capt Richardson has translated many things from the persian & in particular part of the asiatic researches – The figurative style of the East breaks forth from the Khan whenever his Imagination is struck – a person remarked to him tother evening at our House, that he was supported by a pretty woman on each side, he smiled and pointing to himself, said in English – "one night – two days – ." alluding to his dark complexion of course –

Letter 23a

ANDREW BARNARD TO MAJOR-GENERAL FRANCIS DUNDAS

Cape Town –
18 August 1799

Dear Sir –

I yesterday had the honor of your letter desiring me to write an account to Mr Dundas of the situation of affairs, as your distance from Cape Town might prevent your having it in your power. – at the same time that I execute your orders I cannot avoid suggesting to you what upon reflection you will be well aware of, that I am very unequal to perform this task in the manner Mr Dundas woud naturally expect from the secretary to the colony, as I have not from the begining of the disturbances at Graaf Reinet been made acquainted with or ever consulted upon any of the measures of Government, or informed except casually of the facts which woud enable me to draw up any accurate account of the proceedings. – I shall however collect such circumstances as have come within my knowledge previous to your departure, and also such materials as your letters to General Fraser and Mr Ross afford to give Mr Dundas all the information I can; – The present crisis is one which requires all the attention of your mind, without your thoughts being drawn aside to any consideration of less moment I shall not therefore add an unnecessary word but beg you to remain assured that you have only to express your wishes to find me Zealous in the performance of whatever duty you require from me and that I remain with the greatest respect Dr Sir

Your most faithful
& obt ser^{t}
A Barnard

It will be a satisfaction for you to hear that the most perfect tranquility prevails here both in the garrison & out of it, General Fraser has paid the most unremitting attention to the execution of all your commands –

Letter 23b

MAJOR-GENERAL DUNDAS TO ANDREW BARNARD

Dear Sir –

The contents of your letter of the 18th have a good deal surprised me, and as every communication relative to the affairs of Graaff Reinet not of a private nature is in your office I cannot conceive that you are ignorant upon that subject, having the same means of information as Any one else. –

I must confess I have not made it a practise to consult any person whatever on matters of publick consideration, though many are better qualified than I am to conduct them, but in transactions respecting which I am solely responsible, it woud I imagine be not very agreeable to you to share a burthen from which you coud neither derive Honor nor reward. –

I am your faithfull H Sert
Fra^{s} Dundas

Widow Souten^{s}
24 August 1799

A. Barnard Esqr

Cape of good Hope
Nov[r] 8 1799

Mr Barnard tells me my dearest friend that a vessel sails almost this moment for England – I thought it had been already gone, he says he has wrote to you at length on the melancholy event that took place the night of the 5th of Nov[r] of the loss of the Sceptre* and grieved to me that his correspondence with you at present shoud be of so sad a nature, but we will hope for better times & the power of conveying pleasanter news by & bye. – the Gale which has lost this poor old ship was one from the N:West which rarely blows at this season of the year here, the wind was high to be sure but it was the Heavy sea rolling in from the Ocean on the Beach which it was impossible for the ships to resist – the Sceptre broke four cables, & five other ships which were lost were equally unfortunate but their crews were saved, the Sceptre we always understood to be a very Crazy old ship & one that woud be broken up on coming home. the spectacle her wreck exhibited was melancholy to a degree the pieces she was in, being by the Gale broken into such atoms as reckond fit only for fire wood – Capt Edwards was a mild mannerd & well esteemd man, he made it a constant rule which he did not even depart from after he had the command here of never sleeping on shore, & to this excellent rule he fell a worthy sacrifize. his son was with him a fine Boy of 12 years of age – his body has been found & in his bosom a prayer book – many – many more might have been saved than what were saved had they not been bruised in the water by the small pieces of the wreck – the beach was coverd with people – fires were kept burning all night & every assistance afforded that coud be given – Mr B was there, but nothing coud surpass the Zealous Humanity of Col Crauford, who loves a good sleep in a good bed as well as most people but was up the greatest part of the night encouraging his old fellows of the 91st to do their best in saving the floating creatures – nearly 100 were saved – that is an honest good Regt the men all infirm almost but trusty – another mutiny has been Hatching in the 81st Regt. – again found out by privates in the 91st & their officers put on their guard – what can be expected from Vinegar Hill boys* – I suppose when Genl Dundas returns some of the people concernd in it will be likely to suffer – our Bay has of late been crowded with danish Vessels, their purpose seems rather equivocal – Genl D. being absent no one has stepd forwards to shew them much civility, I exept ourselves, as Mr B has frequently invited them here, they seem well bred plain men – on this late sad event when the ship of the danish commodore was lost (tho the crew was saved)* Mr B. pressd him & one or two of his first officers to make this house his Home while he remaind at the Cape a variety of reasons made him wish him to accept of this civility which he pre-

*Sceptre**
H.M.S. *Sceptre*, 64 guns, was, as Lady A. says, in a bad state of repair. Apart from Capt. Valentine Edwards, commander of the Cape squadron, and his son William, a cadet, 9 officers and about 280 men perished. (See letter from Cmdre G. Losack to Admiralty, 7-11-1799, in Theal's *Records*.) She was wrecked off Fort Knokke which stood on the shore below the present Victoria Park, Woodstock.

*boys**
The 81st Regiment of Foot bore the apparantly misleading name of the Loyal Lincoln Volunteers. It was raised in 1793 and after service in Ireland and San Domingo returned to England in skeleton form. With its ranks filled up with boys, it was sent to the Cape to acclimatise for service in India. The connection with Vinegar Hill is uncertain. The latter was an Irish Rebel camp and the scene of the defeat of the Rebel Army on 21-6-1798 in Co. Wexford, when the 81st was not present. The conclusion must be that there were Irishmen in the Regiment.

*saved)**
Oldenburg, 64 guns, Cmdre Fischer.

sumed is politic as well as Humane to offer, but he said the Danish Consul had given them beds at his House & they were too much occupied & agitated to be comfortable Guests at present – the Collector of the Customs* offerd them place for the accommodation of their things if the commodore woud pledge himself & his word of Honor that he had no goods on board but such as were not illicit (perhaps I dont express myself properly) he *did*, he gave him his Honor he had not, the question was a necessary one to put, & the firmness & boldness of the assurance to the contrary rather surprized – . I write to you Hurriedly all the little particulars that I think can interest you had I time I might repeat them more accurately – Nothing Final yet from Graaf Renet – Col Craufurd has a letter to tell him his Grenadiers are embarkd & coming to the Cape, & that a peace with the Caffres is negociating – I am a little surprized at the men[']s coming away before it is concluded – I *hope* it will prove a lasting one, but in truth we have no expectation of it as plunder is a better thing to a Caffre or Hottentot than a peace he is to gain nothing by & which he is only forced into by fear – I hope if the General makes peace with them he will settle something of the nature of Annual presents to ensure its continuance [,] unless their [sic] is a prospect of gain, by behaving well now, they certainly wont but will begin pillaging again whenever they conceive our force to be inferior to theirs – What a pity they were ever annoyd by forcing them out of a Territory where they were doing no Harm – but I am told I must conclude instantly

God Bless you All Dear friends –

Yrs affect
Anne Barnard

no governor yet –
Abercrombie is married –
Barrow – is married –
Erskine – to be married –*

*Customs**
John Hooke Green.

*married**
According to D. Fairbridge, Major (i.e. Capt.-Lieut. Peter) Abercrombie married a Miss Laubscher. Writing to Lord Mornington Lady A says Losper. The name may have been Loubser. John Barrow married Anna Maria dt of Petrus Johannes Truter (see de Villiers *Geslagsregister*). Major Henry Erskine of the Scotch Brigade married a dt. of Arend de Waal, by elimination Jacoba (b. 1783), though de Villiers does not record this.

[Head of a Dutch woman]

Sir George Yonge, 5th Bart., K.B. (1731-1812) arrived at the Cape on 9th December 1799, to assume the governorship to which he had been appointed the previous February, already at an age when he would in those times have been regarded as an elderly man. He had held various state appointments including Lord of the Admiralty (April-July 1782), Secretary for War (July 1782-April 1783 and December 1783-July 1784), and Master of the Mint (July 1794-February 1799). His wife, Elizabeth, daughter of Boucher Cleeve, Esq. of Foots Cray, did not deign to accompany him.

Although it was not until page 3 of her next letter that Lady Anne mentioned the new Governor, it had clearly not taken long for the latter to display his character and for Lady Anne to form her opinion of him. The house controversy moreover was reaching its climax and a great deal of unpleasantness was being experienced.

Castle –
Cape of good Hope
Decr 14th 1799 –

A ship sails tomorrow for St Helena I hear, by which I may have an opportunity of writing to you my dearest Friend, and here are two thirds of this day gone already in nursing the sick, but I have something for my pains as I have assisted in introducing into the world *a little girl* which Mrs Craufurd was safely deliverd of two hours ago who as the old nurse in Romeo & Juliet says, will "be the mother of boys here after" – I have therefore but a minutes time to say a thousand things! my heart is filld with a mixture of sensations which it is perhaps well for your patience that I have not leisure to develope, but upon the whole the pleasure of seeing your hand writing again adressd to myself, of reading that you are well, happy, tho busy, that every thing is "prospering" in your hands, the pleasure of receiving long letters from the dear Margaret & the dear Lord Macartney which tho they suspend a favourite *Hope*, yet convey the disappointment in by no means an unflattering or unkind form, all, all, fill, agitate, expand, contract, yet on the ballance *content* my heart. – the wish has then been fully expressd by him of our obtaining leave of absence to return home *for a time*, but you did not then choose to comply with it, because you did not think you *ought* as the face of affairs stood & considering the period of our stay to have been then only two years; – you say nothing on the subject *yourself*, I believe you grievd to hurt me by a denial but you need not have feard it at *this moment* my best friend, for had you given us the permission, we shoud not at the present time have made use of it;

– the arrival of the new Governor gives Mr B: a Hope that his stay may really be of *some use* to the Colony, during General D[s]: administration his place has been a Synacure owing to his neither having been trusted nor employed, but this I hope will cease, be well assured my best friend that your approbation of his conduct hitherto & the dependance you place on him for assisting in *future councils* are such motives as woud keep him (& me along with him) chearfully for any length of time almost while his assistance appeard necessary – nothing certainly can be sweeter than the approbation of those we respect and love, to Mr B: it is *all in all*, contented therefore shall we go on for some time longer, fulfilling to the best of our abilitys what we conceive to be *your* wishes, but while we do *I pray you* grant Mr Barnard the discretionary power as soon as you think you *can*, for tho we have not at *present* even the *desire* of leaving this place, *foreseeing solid objects* to render our stay of use to government for some time, yet, things once put into a train, it woud be an infinite satisfaction had we the *power* unknown to any one of returning to England with *Your* sanction for a *time*, supposing that Health, Affairs, or any very pressing, unforeseen reason shoud render it desirable to us. – you may judge how little we have thought of returning *directly*, ever since the appointment of a new governor when I tell you that at *this moment*, and for the *last month* we have been eagerly pressing Mr Ross the under Secretary to go home he being at present under the pressure of a malady which requires the best advice else I think immine[n]t danger may attend it, and the physicians here happen to be so divided in their opinions that his constitution is sinking under their different medicines & making him aged at 24 – from time to time you must give me liberty (in the Hope of being forgiven) to reiterate my wishes however for this discretionary Liberty to Mr B:, which woud carry us home by & bye to pay a visit to our old parents all of them past 70, who fear they are never to see us again – without Mr Barnard I cannot go. – contented & Happy in my domestick life, under circumstances, rather singular & not *fairly assorted*, shoud I risk the future comfort of my advancing years for any other duty, or gratification to myself by letting him find out that he can be happy without me which at present he does not believe? – no, no my dear friend, the risk of breaking up such Harmony woud be too great an one to run – give us therefore this leave I pray to come *together* & trust to our limited circumstances and to our being much liked in this country for our returning. – you said to my sister, as an advice for her to transmit to us that she shoud council us not to think of returning to England till we had made enough to render us a little more at ease in point of finance, but my dear friend recollect that tho whatever we can save out of our Salary, or lay up from our funds at Home is money to be counted on, beyond this there is not the possibility of advantage with either *Honesty* or *propriety* from the wise rules that you yourself made, abolishing all perquisites to those in office, which I rejoyce in every day

Rustenburg House, Rondebosch

of my life from the knowledge I have of Mr B^{S} character who never *coud* have accepted of a *questionable* emolument & who I am certain is glad that from the *impossibility* of the case no one can alledge it against him. – a little matter I think may be *saved* at Home & here, in the course of our stay, after paying the expenses of living & a few small old scores of Mr Barnards to no great amount but it cannot be much, I shall tell you truly the sum & as I am really an *Honest* woman you may trust me. – I shall add no more on this subject exept one word, You said to my sister that you shoud have been ashamd to have askd his majesty, so soon for leave for Mr B: to go home, a twelve month from the time you said this I think will make you *blush the less*, to his majestys goodness I am ready to trust with such a friend as you to back the cause, he has as good a heart as any man in his own dominions & as much consideration for others, shew him some of the arguments I have used and I am persuaded that after an absence of four years from England he will indulge us in a short visit at home. –

Our new governor arrived here about a week ago, I mentiond to you in my last that we had prepared excellent accommodation for him & all his suite – for the Ladys – put up beds & procured every requisite necessary for their comfort which it is well here to provide before they are wanted, Mr Barnard had told Major Erskine (General Dundass late aid du Camp, & friend) that we meant to request the company of Miss cumings* till his return, you may therefore suppose that we were both surprized and mortified when on Mr B^{S} accompanying the commodore on board to pay an early visit to the new governor he found that the other had taken a boat, boarded the ship before she came to anchor and had in General Dundas's name made a point of his going to a dutch mans house in the first place (the future father in law of Major Erskine as report says)* and to Rondebosh next day, four miles out of town where he requested Miss Cumings might remain under his care till the government house (occupied by Lord Macartney & by himself afterwards) was ready for his reception. – this arrangement did not seem to have been *preferrd* by Sir George or the ladys, but he had given a hasty Assent and did not think he coud retreat. – I was particularly sorry at it, as I had hoped to have begun a little friendship with Mrs Blake* and Miss Cuming by the kindness I meant to shew them and was surprized at my intention being frustrated by Major Erskine & in a manner that appeard too eager to have been accidental. – next morning I waited on all at their lodging house, Sir George received me like *an old friend*, he had told Mr Barnard that I was one of his most esteemd ones & of longest standing, I was glad *to hear it*, who woud not be *Eves contemporary* to be the friend of the *first Man* in the world – of *Africa* at least. – But I own I recollected his *face* at court, better than our friendship in private.

– I found he had kept his health charmingly during the voyage his aid du Camps* – secretarys – his niece – Miss Cumings, all were well, Mrs Blake seemd rather a shewy pretty woman desirous of *pleasing*, & being *civil* which will be well, Miss Cumings I did not see, she had been so much disappointed on her first arrival by finding the general at so great a distance & engaged in war, that it had unfitted her for seeing any body & she declared she woud not appear till his return. – I thought her

*cumings**
General Dundas's affianced. According to Burke's *Peerage* her name was actually Eliza, dt. of Sir John Cumming, Bt., though Lady A. consistently spells it this way. They were married on 22-1-1800.

*says)**
See Letter 24, note 5.

*Blake**
It may be deduced that Mrs. Blake, wife of Richard Blake, the Governor's Private Secretary, was Sir George's niece.

*Camps**
These were Major, aft. Lt.-Col. James Cockburn (24th Dragoons), Major Berkenhead Glegg (91st Regt.) and Capt. John George Tucker (72nd Regt.)

right, the less a woman in delicate situations exposes herself to animadversion so much the better, I had an amiable character of her from the Captain of the ship she came in, I hope sincerely to find her deserving of it as it will be of some importance to *us all* that she shoud be of the *cementing quality* which sweetness & sense can always be if they please. – the paragraph in your letter to me regarding her I shall keep to myself I cannot imagine why the general did not beg Lady Janes protection & adieu to her on her way to this arduous undertaking & *Your Sanction* to the Step, the *Independance* of acting I do not think, shoud have been exerted so fully, on this occasion for her sake, as to the paragraph which conveys your satisfaction in his conduct as far as you coud judge of it, the end of August, and Lord Macartneys favourable report of, and interest in him I shall in justice to you and to Lord M. transcribe it for the general. – it is saying *something* for the liberality of my own mind, and more for the Interest I take in any favourite child of yours (*the Cape* I think is *one*) when I assure you that I shall be better contented to be found *Wrong* by you, and even *scolded* a *little* for having supposed some of the generals measures to have been rather injudicious, than that you shoud think they have esentialy [sic] injured the tranquility of the colony. – how soon he will be able to join his love we know not, peace and war are alternately talkd of, peace I am convinced he *now* wishes to make, but I doubt much if there will be a lasting one, unless the Caffres and Hottentots are kept true by the hope of further benefits – Sir George and the ladys went to Rondebosh the day after their arrival and have resided there ever since, a table is coverd for 18 every day and a company of the *particular friends* of the general & of *Erskine* invited by *him* to dine with the governor, this Mr Pringle *blab'd*, tho sworn to secrecy, how can 18 men be expected to keep secret that they dine together? – Mr Barnard has *never* been invited there; *he sees that* but he takes no notice of any thing, he feels himself the natural friend of Sir George, the *lawfull wife* of the Colony, and any little attempts made to injure him by *the Dollys*,* he will undo, he hopes at *leisure* when Sir George fixes in town, mean time He (Sir George) is taken possession of by the Staff, and by their anxiety to keep Mr Barnard at a distance I suppose they have some view in it which time will develope, General Dundas continues to correspond with Mr Ross & with General Fraser, a paragraph in a letter to the last which was shewn to Mr B. determind him to offer to the governor *Now* what he had *once* meant to have offerd the General on his return – "to be sure says General Dundas the government house in the Castle which Mr Barnard occupys, is the fit one for me as commander in Chief, I gave it up to him only at Lord Macartneys request, but when Sir George Yonge arrives he will make what arrangements he pleases" – Mr B: before this, as I mentiond had determined to offer it to him on his marriage, it is the best House in the place next to that the governor occupys, & his giving it up to us when he had no wife, is a reason why Mr Barnard was glad to put it again in his power when he was begining *un Etat* where a little additional representation might not perhaps be either disagreeable to *him* or to her. – I care little for such things tho where a duty calls on me I fill my place I hope; this letter however shewd that some ideas had been suggest-

*Dollys**
Presumably female favorites, according to contemporary slang usage.

ed to the General of getting us out of our present abode – it will be inconvenient to us in some respects as it is next door to the secretarys office which renders it very commodious to us, and to those who have business to transact being sure of finding Mr Barnard at all hours, I have filled it up myself entirely but I dont mind that if it will make the general and her Happier to have it, he is our Superior as Lieut. Governor and is entitled to it. – Mr B: therefore took an early opportunity to tell Sir George that it was at his service to offer to general Dundas if he preferd it to his own house in the Castle – he told me Sir George appeard as if a millstone had been untyed from his neck – "I am very much obliged to you Sir, very much indeed, I never coud have askd you to give up your house, but I believe the General wishes for it & since you are so good as to offer it to *me*, I beg you may rather have the merit of offering it to *himself*. – " this Mr B declined, the general has behaved too unkindly to us of late to render it *now* natural for Mr B. to pay him a compliment, tho our attachment to his uncle coud lead us to give him up chearfully every point of publick pre-eminence which he is entitled to. – Sir George went on to tell Mr B. that he shoud not be a loser by this conduct as he shoud certainly make him a Handsome allowance for a House in Town. – this Mr B. utterly declined, he did not think government ought to be put to any *new* expence on his account – Sir George said he coud easily *Manage that*, but I am certain Mr Barnard never will accept of any compensation which puts it to a new expence particularly as he sees (*as he is afraid*) a tendency to spending money rashly, which he coud not be authorized by respectfull hints to *restrain* if the first act of Sir Georges administration was to confer an apparent obligation to himself; while government has any *other* House to bestow, *little* or *large* situated so as he may fulfill the dutys of his office he will have no allowance for one, nor even then unless authorised by you – so much for the little politicks of our *Lilliput* court. – How our new folks will like this place I know not, I dare say the aid du Camps wont, at least one of them as I hear he is a little of a fine gentleman & they you know are despisers by trade; Sir George I think must be happy he will like the sort of life a *governor* has it in his power to lead, for my share, I think the transition from debt and Holyrood House to being his Excellency here, and *lookd up to* by everything but the Table Mountain is such an one as requires the snow of 63 years at least to stand! – as to the Ladys I hope they will have their share of Happiness from being made Goddesses of in their different ways, I at first regreted that L^{y} Yonge had not come, I am a *good Subject* and apt to think that one Supreme Queen Bee, is better than any chance of a divided Hive – I hope there wont be any, as both of our new Ladys are reckond good humourd, tho from some little things which have dropd from the friends of the one or the other, I shoud not be surprized if they were distinct powers, & that I, instead of being poor little Holland, ready to be swallowd up by every body, may chance to represent the Armed Neutrality & like old England, while I am least, be greatest, by possessing in my Hands "the ballance of Power" – But I must not begin Talking Nonsense, else I shall lose my opportunity – I shall however very soon resume my pen. – tell Lady Jane her kind letter gave me the greatest pleasure, her pleasing & ever

The Brewery, Newlands, home of Dirk van Reenen

flattering expressions are very comfortable, in truth when corresponding with you it makes me feel the same to her I do for yourself & that is saying not a little, after a habit of – (dare I say it?) almost 20 years. – I dare say she is very glad I cannot boast of this habit with her quite so long. – by the bye, unless you let me come home eer long, I shall grow so abominably old that you will have no great credit in me on my return, but while there may be a few more wrinkles in our faces, if we keep the affections of our hearts well filld out to the social tyes the others will be pardoned by those who love us for something more dureable than a fine skin. – by the bye, again; I tell my sisters that my residence at the Cape has unveild to me a beautifull page in Human nature, for it is not to be told you the attentions, the multiplicity of kind letters that I receive from my friends any where, & even from my *acquaintances* on whom I have *no rights*, all seem united in a league to flatter & support my mind at a distance, in the prosecution of a measure they naturally suppose I consider to be my duty. – I sometimes frighten Margaret by saying they are all so good to me at a distance that I doubt much if I shall go home!

Jan: 5th – when ready to send this off, I was told the opportunity which I had regarded as a favourable one was by no means so good an one as that of sending by the *Regulus* which was expected to sail shortly. – this being the case has remaind open & I will now add the new matter which the last fortnight has presented, with such opinions as I have been able to form, which however premature & therefore possibly unfounded you shall have in the frankness of confidence. – Imprimis – (dare I say it) our new governor I fear is a very – very – weak old soul! he is full of good intentions and *Great* intentions, but how his acts will turn out I am not sure of; he is disposed I see to think that *He* is the man who is to make this a fine & florishing Colony, that no one else at home was thought equal to that task, that *nothing as yet has been done*, he does not perceive the wisdom of our late Governor (I mean Lord M:) in pausing over all measures which were likely to disburse the publick money till he was sure the place was to remain with us, while he permited no wise regulation which cost nothing to remain undigested & establishd. – on the contrary Sir George is for having every supposed improvement done at once, and I fear does not begin with the things most necessary, but with those most connected with his own domestic conveniency. – to Mr Barnard he is Hearty, apparently open, & very flattering in his expressions, he wishes to take credit with him, for what I own I trace to *you*, thro the good opinion of Lord Macartney, that of connecting Mr Barnard by some document in writing, with himself and the Lieut governor in the councils to be held in future on publick measures, a testimony of *Your* opinion of him which I own myself very particularly glad of for *various reasons*, some of which I trace every day more clearly to their source. – Sir George says *he requested you* to put Mr Barnard in that document, Mr B. *has not seen* what he alludes to, but he had an idea of its nature, it will give him the right of speaking out his mind, and of remonstrating with respectfull firmness where he thinks it necessary, & ultimately in expressing his opinion in writing when he can not influence, which he has reason to think may be the best way both with the Governor, & the General for different reasons. – but before we come to grave matters let us have a little Slight Chat on Slight things. – after a weeks residence at Rondebosh the Governor & his family returnd to town & to the House of Mynheer du Wal,* where they *Slept*, while the day time was spent at the Government house in overseeing reparations, improvements, & unpacking of furniture; we see he has a great love of pretty things of that sort. – I coud have told him, that less carving and black Morocco leather instead of Scarlet woud have suited the Cape better but it is needless to put people out of conceit with what they have got. – if Sir George will superintend the reparation of the publick buildings falling to decay (as they do here in a twelve months time almost, if not attended to so rapidly do the rains pierce and burst the clay walls if the smallest crevice gives them entrance) as well as he superintends the reparation of his own Kitchen he will be a *Treasure*, but as a governor is not quite in his place doing so, I dont expect that. – to build a new stair case in the Government house was his first plan, to repair the Government gardens & build a high wall all round them, the 2d – other plans came forth which I shall mention in their place, Mr B. trembled for the wall, it woud not have cost less than 2.000 (needlessly laid out) so he got it undermined, at least he has procured a delay and that he looks on as nearly the same thing. – the Stair case: he tried to influence into an alteration only, it really is necessary, being so narrow & perpendicular in the steps that nothing short of Lord Macartney['s] resolution to do *nothing*, & the beautifull thing called *Habit* which accustomed him to hop up like a Parrot to his Perch, woud have made it practicable for a person with a gouty tendency to mount it. – the reparation of the *government* gardens he begun directly, & planting guards at the gates refused entrance to the Inhabitants till the *Governors* Gardens shoud be put into order. – had he torn the Magna Charta of the place into a thousand tatters he coud not have put the natives into such an Allarm! – for 150 years they had enjoyd the priveledge of walking under the shade of those oaks, tis the only publick walk at the Cape & all ranks of people, the women particularly of each, were furious. – Mr B: heard of the manoeuvre & knowing the sort of effect this woud have (which the civility of ten revolving years woud not have power to wipe away) he hurried off with a proclamation in his pocket, undoing the restriction by leaving the main walk free while the others were reparing, Sir George kept the paper but when he sent it back tho he adopted much he had introduced a foolish rule, to make all persons write down their names every time they enter the gardens (which they do sometimes a dozen of times in a day) in a book at the guard house which they think a great trouble tho they are glad to have the total exclusion remedied – this a way of making private property of a publick benefit – after we had waited as in duty bound till Genl. Frazer our commander in Genl Ds: absence had given the first dinner to the Governor, we invited him here, Sir Roger Curtis,* the Staff & the heads of departments &cc a dinner of 30 people – in the evening I had my Thursday party and being desirous to influence the future invitations of Sir George by shewing him a company composed of any of those supposed to be ill affected as well as those who are attached to Govern-

*Wal**
Arend de Waal.

*Curtis**
Vice-Admiral Sir Roger Curtis, Bt., G.C.B. (1746-1816), C. in C. Cape Station 1799-1801.

ment I wrote notes to many of the most democrate of my beautys & their familys saying that as the new Governor and his family were to be with me in the evening, I wish to present my old friends to my new – the effect was all I coud desire – every one came & I had a splendid assembly, Sir George fell directly in love with the daughter of one of the greatest Jacobins in the place (as it was once *supposed*) tho it is otherwise proved, & flirted as if he had been 25. – on the other hand, having observd that there was a strong tendency amongst the higher Militery powers to exclude the subordinate officers from all share in pleasant dances or partys, I hinted to the Col^s: to bring all their Ensigns & Lieut^s, that they might appear in One *civil* house by way of a precedent, if that was any thing – they thankd me & came, of course there was a handsome company & as many supd as coud find chairs. – I presented my dutch ladys to the governor, and his niece, they were surprized at their number & Smart appearance. – the thursday after Mr B. invited 56 of the principal dutchmen to meet the Governor & Admiral – the Staff also, of course – all came, I again secured my ladys & having foreseen that there woud be a great deal of company I had a Sly provision of fiddlers ready, to give Mrs Blake an impromptu ball, Miss Cumings I was sorry was not of the party, she does not go out yet. – the Ball, being unexpected went off charmingly, Mr Barnard sett Mrs Blake a going, & Sir George had his little lassie again to flirt with. – as to Sir Roger Curtis, in all secrecy be it spoken, he says, that, as Admiral, he reckons a flirtation with Mrs Baumgard* (now that the General is otherwise engaged) is attachd to his Flag: Mrs Baumgard is perfectly of the same opinion she is a good Humoured vain creature, & a very good mother to *her* children, *tho* she certainly does make fish of one and flesh of another. – her husband finds no fault so tis no business of any bodys. – A quiet little English woman (Mrs Pattison) whisperd to me as at supper the two gentlemen were ogling their loves, "How do you think Lady Yonge and Lady Curtis woud like it if they were to see their old boys behaving so?

– Jesting apart, for this is only a jest as yet, I dont see what they can do but coquet, if wives wont accompany Honest men they must run the chance. – Sir Roger seems to be a clever pleasant man, & I hear he is an excellent officer – I believe this is the last party we shall ever have in this house; there has been much shabby Manoeuvering going forwards which has now explaind itself, but I trust that temperance, Silence & proper dignity never asserted till the moment is ripe will put all things to rights in a little time. – without orders from the Governor, General Frazer has moved into General Dundas's house in the Castle – without orders Major Erskine has taken possession of General Frazers, they have circulated it every where that Mr Barnard has received the Governors *commands* "to move off & to make way for general Dundas" & as they conceive this to be a pretty *broad hint*, they wonder he does not *take it* the more so as they have *flitted* their furniture before our windows into their new houses. – every one is anxious to know the *cause of this disgrace*, a disgrace which does not exist, but this and other derogatory reports spitefully circulated and falsely stated, woud be provoking if one did not *rise a little above them*. – Sir George at last is displeased; they have fortunately trod on *his own toes*, while they were meditating only

*Baumgard**
Johanna Elizabeth Baumgardt (b. 1765), 2nd dt. of Daniel van Renen and wife of Johannes P. Baumgardt, collector of land revenue and member of the Court of Justice.

a triumph over Mr Barnard. – Major Erskine invited him into his house yesterday when Sir George was in the Castle yard, "I did not know this was *Your* house Sir" – O yes, General Fraser has gone to live in Genl: Dundas' late House, & that makes room for me" – "Humph – I beg Sir to have the pleasure of seeing you at 2 oclock *today*, and Genl Fraser at the *same hour* – " he passd on – the other mortified, – "dont stir said he to Mr Barnard, make no move, this is a little too much" – Mr B. said, he did not mean it till he had *his* orders; – in the morning, previous to this conversation hearing from all quarters that we had been orderd out of the Castle like a couple of servants who have behavd ill, & thinking it possible from Sir Georges being rather infirm, in mind rather more than in body, that what had passd with Mr Barnard in various conversations might escape his very bad memory, he sent to him a letter the copy of which I shall enclose. – the truth is, that it had been settled by the gentlemen who at present try as Sir George says "to have all their own way" that *we* were to *leave the Castle* & to have no government house *atall*, but an allowance for a house, which was to be that of Mr Du Wals, father to Major Erskines *intended*, and also to a fair lady who smiles on general Fraser. – that General Dundas is not only to have our house but is to keep Rondebosh,* it being convenient for the horses of the Staff to eat the barley its gardens produce. – they had almost persuaded the Governor to put *all* the *publick offices*, the *bank* &c (at present secure & within one court) out of the Castle too, he threw out a hint of this to Mr Barnard saying that Mr Pitt had them all *near himself*, & that he was a very Great Man! – "A very great one indeed said Mr B. but Sir George, the Cape is not England, nor this place the town of London, the expence of getting other offices woud far exceed any benefit that the change coud be of; at least *Pause* till you can look about you. – this was agreed to, but the idea of Mr Pitt having all publick offices within a step of Downing Street is not out of his head yet, nor am I atall sure that Mr Barnard will not be sacrifised thro the whole of this business tho Sir Georges *words* are perfectly *firm* to *him*, but he is an old courtier, they are not therefore to be depended on like Gospel & Major Erskine at present frightens any thing out of him with the name of *Dundas* – I do not think my old friend *Henry* Dundas woud turn me out of doors without giving me another door to enter if he were here. – Money we wont take – one of Sir Georges family who seems to like Mr B. particularly, at a Dinner lately where there was a small company & a little of the *in vino veritas* which very good claret produces, said in Mr B^{s}: ear, "do you see any thing going forwards at our house?" *a Little* – said Mr B. – "the truth is replied the other that certain gentlemen who have taken possession of us, have moved Heaven & Earth to prejudice Sir George both against you and Lady Anne, but they have shot their bolt in vain – have patience, tho they influence at present, things will come round by and bye. – keep my secret & profit by it with discretion." – what may be drawn from all this as far as it relates to Mr Barnard? – exactly this – (like the puppys my eyes see at once after a nine days blindness) that had I been pleased to suspect sooner that Madam Human nature is the same all the world over, whether she is man, or woman whether dressd in scarlet or blew, I might have seen that

*Rondebosh**
Rustenburg, Rondebosch. Baumgardt's farm adjoined it.

from the first *One* description of men, and that is the Staff men in this Garrison, have been envious of Mr Barnard. – Living in the very center of it, in the best house, with the best Salary – with a sort of little eclat from the accident of having a wife to whose train a Ladyship is pinn'd it is not the thousand civilitys & kindnesses we have done them, nor the good dinners they have constantly been receiving from us which has been of any other use than to make them the more angry at his powers of giving them better ones than they coud return. – General Dundas *of himself* I do not think woud have behaved to us quite as he has done, had it not been for a sett of men inferior to himself who have disliked Mr B for no other cause than what I am mentioning, they have over the General considerable Sway, but so long as Lord Macartney remaind General D was in many respects a different man, his Haughty humour was kept in order by the ascendant powers of the other and – the consideration in which *he* held Mr Barnard *awed* their attempts, he gone the day was theirs, and I have not a doubt they have instigated the general to much of what has been improper in his conduct to Mr B. and in particular in that of placing the under Secretary Mr Ross on all occasions before him who being also *pay master* is in some degree one of *themselves*; all this has had no effect beyond *their own circle*, there is not I will venture to say an officer in this Garrison a civilian in the Cape, a man of any description in the place (those connected with the Staff exepted) who does not mark the most perfect respect as well as affection to Mr B – he is literally the Honest Mans friend, the Staff only makes a foe of him, tho a foe he will not condescent to suppose he is made. – I am glad to be able to account for General Dundass conduct he is not an interested man, shabby, or a Gossip by nature & I dare say it has taken them some pains to rouse so *little* a passion in him as Jealousy, the cause over, Mr Barnard out of the Castie which is the great eye sore probably their spite may cease and the generals disdain. general Fraser will *then* have a pleasure which he has wanted ever since Lord Macartney refused him the old cottage of Paradise and gave it to Mr B. In revenging himself as he will suppose it by getting us out of this house, and he is welcome to it; – I never mentiond any thing of his silly conduct on that & subsequent occasions, as I never like to blame any body particularly to *you* whose opinions of people are so valuable *unless* there is an absolute necessity to speak out, but the truth is, he is a silly fellow – very interested – with a gentlemanlike appearance – some of the other officers near General Dundas, are cleverer than he is, but not less interested, the General is entirely Managed by *Erskine* for tho they quarrel when the first lords it too much over him, he is so necessary to the General, that he is obliged to bend to him. – How *his* part of the contrivance of "getting" us *out* of our abode as he calls it will end I know not, the commanding officers of the different Regts I hear are united to remonstrate, but I dare say he will carry the point & establish *his* wife, next door to General Dundas, with *his*. – I have seen Miss Cuming frequently since I begun this letter she is not handsome, but if her qualitys are *real*, her temper good, and her sense equal to the undertaking, I see nothing in her Manners to prevent her being liked, I try to cultivate her, she is not cold to me, nor the contrary, which is just what

I woud have her to be to so new an Acquaintance, I do not like over eagerness in people to please, it generally falls off, and produces disappointment. – a new Hottentot chief is arrivd in Town with a face of a different character from any I have seen before – finely made, Mr B. is taking him to the Governor who said he wishd to receive him with "some State" and askd me what sort of cold collation he woud like. – I told him a good lump of boild beef or mutton and a little brandy, but begd his french cook might not put any of his scavoir faire into the mess, those people dont like any thing high – they dont even eat salt if they can avoid it – one of his train has a curious instrument which I am convinced might make a mans fortune in England, so I have bought it of him for 2 skellins* – a stick with a peg & a bit of Sheeps guts, which he applys to his lips with a strong exertion from the lungs, which produces a sound as loud as any trumpet, he playd the dragoons Music & told me he coud learn any thing I coud teach him by singing* – I think when I return Ill bring him in *My Suite* – I have not heard any thing more of peace or war, I hope we shall have the first, and that no extraordinary calls of *any* kind may demand further cash from our poor Treasury which I fancy must be nearly pennyless, what with 50,000 which The Caffre war must have cost at least, what with Sir George Yonges years Salary for a year, of 10,000, and what with General Dundass for the same year of 10,000, the 3[d] quarter of which he very properly did not draw for, and part of the 4th quarter had not earnd when Sir George arrived, but all of which the governor has made him a present of from the publick funds & I fancy much *new* expence shoud be precluded for some time, Yesterday a person dined here who Mr Barnard was very sorry to see at the Cape, tho glad to offer him an abode in this house had he not been otherwise engaged as he is a Clever and Honest man – the Governor of Batavia* who has unluckily come away at a time when I understand it woud have been fortunate had he staid, but he had left the place before the news had reachd it of the probable conquest of Holland – that man I hear has by Abilitys and Good temper kept the Prince of Oranges flag flying for five or six years over the heads of the most Jacobin garrison – I fear he has not left a governor as Clever as himself, but the Fiscal seems to hope that he will prove true also – our Governor sent to beg a consultation with me on a ball he meditates giving two days after the Queens birthday – he wishd me to draw the line of invitation – I recommended *all the garrison* & every dutch person who had been in the habit of attending the levees or balls in the dutch time, which was making them draw *their own line* – I knew the folks here are Critical respecting ranks, & prowd to a great degree, some of my best female friends are the daughters of a Butcher John van Renin, but they woud disdain to be placed at table with the daughters of another Butcher who sells the ox dead which their father sells alive – some objections being made to this by a dutch friend I highly respect, I closed with him on the point of making out the invitations to the wives & familys of all who had been at the Governors levee the first of the year, I thought this was a way of keeping the door open to all *future* Repentant sinners who might pay their compts on future levee days, and afterwards be invited. – Sir George is disposed to conciliate all, but I per-

*skellins**
A skilling was worth about 2¼ d.

*singing**
Clearly the 'Gora'. See Kirby (P.R.) *The musical instruments of the native races of S.A.* 2nd ed. 1965, p.171-192.

*Batavia**
The visitor was Sebastiaan Cornelis Nederburgh, not a Governor but Commissioner-General with S.H. Frykenius. He had spent a year at the Cape in 1792-93, after which he had been in Batavia. He had left the latter on 9-10-1799 in the *Catharina Anna* of Hamburg, reaching the Cape on 14-12-1799 when he was granted leave to land, Messrs Barnard and van Ryneveld standing security for him. (Cape Archives BO 57, Day book 1799-1803). He later became Chief of the Department of the East Indies under the Batavian Republic.

ceive some of the dutch themselves, are eager to keep off others of their country men by calling them Jacobins, now as to the whole of the people here I look upon the *best friends of government* to be *only* a sett of men who have by accident fallen sooner than the others *on what was for their interest*, for as to *foreseeing* any thing in this strange change of events not even Mr Pitt & you together I dare say coud have pronounced finally on what the event of any thing was to be; – now that all is going well with us, and with them, they are anxious (as they prize attentions to themselves in proportion as they are denied to others) to keep some people at a distance who might put in for a share of the loaves & fishes – these very people Mr B and I wish to have some civility paid to, Sir George is newly arrived & need not enter into part of old politics – "to be sure says my friend they will *all* gladly come in *now* that they *see* the french game is up for them, but is not that very hard on *us* to see ourselves at the same table with a sett of *Rascals* who woud have overturnd us all if they coud? – that may possibly (said I) hurt the pride here and there of an individual, and what you say *may* be all very just, but Sir George has the *instructions of his court*, to shew *General Civility*, you will not find the Enemys of Government treated in *private* with the *consideration* & *confidence* of its *known friends*. – I thought it was best to lay this *general* System of *urbanity* on *your backs* at home, to prevent their backs from being up at Sir George. – I believe nothing but my being a very great favourite woud have made some of them pardon me for having introduced so many Jacobin beautys as I did tother night to Sir George, but I know in all familys women have their sway, & papa comes gently round to visit in the House where his Yonge Vrows are taken notice of. – I hear that at the Levee which was crowded he endeavourd as much as he coud to talk, stand, think, look like his Majesty in some of which points he succeeded in a certain degree, he wishes to make his ball like *a certain one* he told me & hintd at St James, but I fear the two rows of chairs round the room will constitute the only likeness – I said in my last that we woud recommend Representation to Sir George as agreeable to the Dutch, perhaps you fear this advice may agree too much with his natural taste, & influence him to *expence* & *folly*. – No – there is *no call for either*. – Representation in publick days is well here, if attention is also paid in private days to the business of the individual, and *easyness of Access* is Joined. – a Governor will then be both feard & loved – Lord M. was Respected & loved without parade, Sir George *needs* more, for he is not him, oh No – No! – he was repeating a conversation to me he had held with a dutch man of consequence ["]I told him[, "] said he ["]that to Good people this shoud be found a Mild Government, – ["]your Excellency is right said I – but to bad people it shall be a Firm one – your Royal Highness says Justly (I was very near replying) – *Firm* cried he darting out his arm and cocking his eye brow – *Firm* – *Firm* – Oh your Majesty is certainly right!!! –

Jan. 12 – I am sorry I shall not be able to send you the Sequel of what is now pending about our abode, as General D. cannot return I find for some days yet & the ships sail tomorrow – I shoud have been glad to have been able to say whether I am "a man or a mouse" for his decision governs our motions & makes me the Lady of the Castle or of Rondebosh as he pleases unless when he makes his choice of Houses he says like a certain bishop I forgot who – "Baiths best" – In which case I shall live in a wee wee cottage Mr Barnard is building, paradise being too old & crazy to be safe any longer, and Mr B. will ride in every day at eight to his office, which I dare say the military will contrive to get shoved out ot the Castle somehow. – I hear Sir George has had the folly to shew them Mr Barnards letter to him, that they reckon it extremely *Insolent* & take it up as personal affront to themselves that he shoud dare to ask Rondebosh, tho he is giving up his own house – certainly we do not wish for it in *preference* to that we occupy, & if Mr B^{s} office remains in the Castle, at least the House lately inhabited by genl D. might be given him, but this genl Fraser will oppose, & at present they all *Hang together* – this day gives us a list of new appointments which I *leave you to pronounce on* – two under Secretarys are fixed, Mr Blake & Mr Daniel* – the same situations which were droppd by Lord Macartney as an unnecessary expence. – Major Cockburn is appointed Barrack Master general with a salary of 30 sh. pr day* – Col De Lisle* is continued too with a salary of 150 – a new Engineer or Architect for reparations of said buildings (Mr Thibaut)* is appointed – great plans of additional buildings are talkd of – a long list of promotions are made in the 8th dragoons with new people put there too – Mr Tucker aid du camp is made capt lieut – Abercrombie, Genl Dundas aid du camp has got the Troop – General Fraser[s] son a cornetcy – I forgot the rest, but the officers of the Regt are petitioning and it's supposed will succeed in getting reversed whatever seems unjust to his Royal Highnes* – tears start involuntarily into ones eyes on feeling how things *are* & foreseeing how they are *likely to be* – the gentleman who *surround* the governor are full of his praises. – to *himself* & indeed to the world *He* is not the *illiberal parsimonious* man Lord Macartney was, at the head of the publick funds, who woud give no allowance he coud possibly with hold, he acts upon a much *larger* & more *manly* scale – Genl Fraser is sure he is incapable of putting on his spectacles to look at the *dirty Items* of a bill – we conceive a long one to be in his pocket, All flattering up to folly & extravagance this silly old man. – Ross goes to England on the next ships, the Staff are much *concernd* for the *want* there will be in the office of a person to conduct the *publick business*, Genl Fraser & Major Erskine think Mr *Blatterman* a servile but plodding Dutch man,* head desk in the office & husband to Generals Fr^{s}: *Bonne Amie* who is *sister* to Erskines, shoud be introduced into a higher rank there, to fill Rosss place in his absence – nobody *ever* did any business there *but* Ross' – Ross to be sure was the only person *employd* to do business there, by the two generals – dirty people! cannot they say all this boldly to Mr B^{s} face but there is not one of them that has spirit to attack *bravely*, they stab in the dark & I dare not unveil the truth to a man as generously unsuspecting as he is, ready to *resent* where he *shoud* – sometimes (tho I tremble too at the thought) I almost wish something shoud occur to justify Mr B^{s} temperance for calling some of them out, he was once before obligd to tell Genl: Fraser that he heard he had abused him about our little place calld Paradise, that if he thought he had injured him he was

*Daniel**
Samuel Daniell (1773-1811), artist and author of *African scenery*, 1804-05, and *Sketches representing the native tribes, animals and scenery of Southern Africa*, 1820.

*day**
The post was in fact only that of Deputy Barrack Master General but after Yonge's recall there was an inquiry into the receipt of a gratuity of £2,000 in connection with the appointment.

*Lisle**
Lt.-Col. de Lisle, or de Lille, was appointed Barrack Master by Sir Alured Clarke on his taking over the Cape in Nov. 1795. He was described as 'late of Gordon's Regiment'.

Thibaut
Louis Michel Thibault (1750-1815) the celebrated Cape architect. He came out with de Meuron's mercenaries in 1783 and became Capt.-Lieut. of Engineers under the D.E.I. Company.

*Highnes**
It would appear from the Army List that these promotions were not confirmed.

*man**
Engelbertus Lodewyk Bletterman, married to Geertruida Christina de Waal. He was 1st Clerk in the Secretary's Office and Secretary to the Matrimonial Court.

Louis Michel Thibault

ready to give him satisfaction, or to shake Hands with him if he said the report was a false one – the Genl. denied the truth of his Informer, offerd to shake Hands & *gulpd it over*, but has ever since doubly disliked Mr B. – My dearest friend I did not always write you such vexed grumbling letters, but what can I do? – Oh never – never have I felt the delay of leave of absence in the manner I do *now*, never I am sure while I had the idea that our stay might *do good*, but now that I have but too much reason to fear that there is a party *too strong* establishing itself against us at the Government house, I tremble for the ensuing twelve month, if Mr B is improperly treated by the governor in *league with the General* I really fear he will throw up the game and along with me prefer a turnip top where we are loved & respected to a life of oppression & spite, shewn us by the one side, *endured in silence by the other.* – for we are not people who can Gossip & tittle tattle, all must be on *broad ground*, or sea & resignation. – but be assured my best friend *nothing shall be rashly or testily done* – better prospects of amity may open & gladly shall we embrace them. – Still – Still – if we can benefit a Cat, do good to a Human creature, or follow up *Your wishes particularly to Your Satisfaction*, we *will endure*, even with the leave of absence in our *pockets. – Support us However*; – we *need it* & *look to you for it.* My dear Lady Jane I am afraid I shall lose all credit with you for this long *Vile* Epistle, but out of the abundance of the heart, the mouth will speak!

God Bless you both –

Anne Barnard

Jan-13 – two further liberalitys of our Generous Governor 1500 to General Fraser being 5 months Salary as *Lieut Governor* which he has convinced Sir George he ought to draw, while Genl D is absent – and 10 sh. a day to Mr Tucker as an *additional* assistant to Major Cockburn (now Col Cockburn) Col de Lisle, and Mr Thibaut; – how long shall we hold out at this rate? the funds cannot pay even the Sallarys if this goes on – he has wrote to England for a person to be sent out to build more Barracks & other Edifices – he seems wonderfully fond of buildings but never thinks of how they are to be paid – he thinks coal, and mines have been *imperfectly* searchd after by Lord M: & has sent people to explore & to bore for them, the mineralogist who went after the coal gave it as his opinion that the foundation for supposing a vein might be found worthy of the pains of boring was so slight that he wonderd the Search had been so long perseverd in –

Letter 26

Cape of good Hope
Feb 7 1800

If you did not combine a great many other things to me with that of being *A Great Man* I shoud make you a thousand apologys for my last letter before I go on with this, it was full of female detail full of then only *supposed* motives for conducts in others which vexed me, and it finishd I remember, agitated, oppressd & imploring you to stand by us else we were likely to be overpowerd & trampled on by a strong *party* who were taking advantage of the weakness of our old governor. – how all this will *end*, I cannot yet say, perhaps I may see day light in it before the next ships sail, at any rate, I will go on bringing up my account of things as they go on here, so that a few words may finish my letter if a fair opportunity of sending it off occurs. – if you tire of me, or blame me for troubling you with the minutia of things, recollect that it is to *you alone that I open my heart*, that your approbation is to us all in all, in our present situation, that in order to do ourselves Justice I must let you behind the *curtain*, but that while I do so, both Mr Barnard and I are totally *silent* to *all here* from that rigid prudence which hates to be *quoted* for any thing, pretty sure that things must come round *at last*, & the less there has been said on our part, the better chance there will be of sweet blood hereafter!

– I wrote to you that our Governor was to give a great dinner the Queens birth day & a large ball the monday following, – to give fair play to his cooks we proposed he shoud dine with us the day before his dinner to which he agreed –. I hardly expected Miss Cumings woud be of the party as she had not dined out, and was the more surprized & pleased when she came – I hoped it was a desire of living in friendship with me, but as I thought perhaps a little curiosity might mix to see this same House which had been so much talkd of, I shewd her the whole after dinner, the fine pond in the back court, the view from the roof – the number of bedchambers we have made, that she might judge of the conveniency of her premeses *to be*; as it quite satisfys me, I was surprized to hear afterwards, and not sorry, that she did not like it atall; – the bedchambers to be sure are all paved with tiles, no wooden floors above stairs but then they are spacious. – mean time the General wrote that he woud arrive on tuesday morning and marry the lady directly – that a peace was made with the Caffres &cc – of course we expected that monday night she woud spend in her own room *saying her prayers* a little anxious on a thousand points which a four years absence from her lover might justify and too much agitated to be fit for company – I leave *you* to settle from what cause she appeared at the ball however, and danced away all night when she was to be married next morning, & you shall also settle why when the Clergyman &

the general arrived (the wedding taking place on the wednesday) she woud not come to be married, but run off wept, and made great difficulty – the weeping I thought not unnatural, one may cry from attendrisment as well as sorrow, there is also something imposing in a ceremony which agitates the nerves but the running away I did not comprehend. – Sir Roger Curtis however, said it was "All very right" – she was prevaild on at last – the marriage took place, and they went off to Rondebosh immediately. – there let us leave them for a day or two, and talk of some officers who came down from Algoa Bay,* Graaffe Renet &cc – as there is a good deal of variety of account given of that part of the country I thought it not amiss to ask half a dozen of them separately what sort of country that really was which had been plunderd, & what sort the part was from which General Dundas had orderd Genl Vandeleur to drive the Caffres commanded by Congo.* – all united in saying that the first 400 miles after leaving Cape town is barren, sandy, unfertile (I cannot help thinking from being uncultivated) unwooded and ill waterd, the Hollow brooks w^{c} do not deserve the name of rivers being all dry in summer & the grounds parched up by the heat of the sun, exept immediately on the banks of those brooks* – this seems to be the reason that all the dutch assign for this part of the country being skipd over by Settlers, not one of them has ever thought of digging to find water, and yet I have lately seen a variety of instances where this attempt always laughd at as vain by the natives has been attended with constant success – I am convinced this country is full of springs, I wish we had Lady Milbanke* here to twist her wand for them, in that case Saldano Bay woud soon I dare say become the Capitol of this country. – we purchased a bit of ground some time ago, it went cheap from there being no water on it. – A hasty low brook run deep by the edge of it almost dry in summer, Mr Barnard confident of success built a cottage on it where we shall live if we have no Government house allowed us, and in the center of the Kitchen which is a white sandy soil but rich beneath, while digging for clay for the walls, up popd a spring which having remaind there for six months I do not think will now get dry – the dutch stare and think we are very lucky, this bit of ground had always been reckond good for nothing for want of water. – Sir Roger Curtis too, enclosing a piece of ground on the sea shore for a dock yard, found a fresh spring a foot or two beneath the surface, and within the sea mark –

At Graafe Renet the officers all allow that the soil becomes more moist and fertile – there is good pasture too, but inferior to what it is at Algoa Bay, and far inferior to the Auteniquas* & other countrys. – in those more remote districts they described the vegetation to be luxuriant, the grass better than the best field of grass in England because taller & more of it, that their horses & cattle fattend & grew frisky upon it immediately, that there was plenty of large timber there, not in Glens only as at Zwellendam & at Sweet milk valley,* but on the plains – trees featherd down to their roots like old English oaks, and clover breast high near which however it was dangerous for the troops to pass, for fear of having serpents rush out on them whose sting is sometimes mortal tho less frequently so than in Bengal – they planted pottatoes

*Bay**
Algoa Bay.

*Congo**
Cungwa, son of Shaka, chief of the Gqunukwebe.

*brooks**
Doubtless the Karoo.

*Milbanke**
Judith Lady Milbanke. See Letter 11, note 17.

*Auteniquas**
Outeniqua Mts. between George and Oudtshoorn.

*valley**
The Soetmelksrivier flows about 6 miles east of Riversdale, C.P.

here, that best of *fruits*, but they run all to leaf from the richness of the soil & had nothing at their roots. – the return of grain is frequently here 150 fold – I must try to get you a little of various sorts for *Dinaira** – cattle & sheep were there in plenty, Genl. Vandeleur told me, that while he paid the expence of the troops under his command, previous to General Dundas's arrival with the commissary department that the men coud live on half their allowance, a sheep being only a rix dollar. – he does not think the peace with the Caffres will last, no one does. – he said he had pointedly followd his instructions [for] the first part of the business by attacking them, but I saw he wishd it had been let alone – the latter part, viz a peace made before they were conquerd, after having been roused, he much disapproved of together with the terms of that peace, and General Dundass having granted them a new boundary, which was only winkd at before – on these two points I who am the worst of all judges to be sure, and always ready to cede much for peace, am more disposed to think Genl: D. right than Genl. V. – the person grants but little for peace who grants what will be kept whether granted or not. – General Vandeleur says, that in all savage nations peace after Hostility, is only secured by *fear*, & that Genl. Dundas with 800 men might safely have attackd & subdued them, since he with less than 200 stood his ground, tho the force was insufficient to the point he had to carry, of dislodging them from the country they occupied –

As to all that, I do not believe they ever woud have stood a regular ingagement, I believe attempting it woud have only prolongd a war which has tended to no good purpose, and I am therefore of the opinion of the poet who says "tis the first widsom, to be wrong no more" –

I hear the two generals are not on good terms, but I hope not bad enough for it to be laid before *you*, Genl: Vandeleur has fortunately got back his orders and papers which the Caffres had possessd themselves of when they killd his servant.* – the Captain of the band, wears the wheels of his watch in his ears by way of earrings – but what shall we say of my humble friends the Hottentots! one man only of that corps deserted, tho they were brought against their countrymen; the officers describe them as the most faithfull, disciplind and obedient creatures in the world, a band of the servants of the farmers who joind the English certainly were afterwards ready to betray them, (supposing they coud not stand their ground,[)] but inspite of this, Genl. V. holds the *national character* to be *good*, and (where well treated for such a length of time to inspire confidence) attackd to a great degree – I can perceive however from things in the newspapers & in letters from England that there is a good deal of *mistake* about the number of Hottentots still existing in this country, I fancy it is believed there are from 10, to 20,000, & from what I can learn from those qualified to judge I doubt much if there are above 4.000 – 3.000 was the number mentiond to me & Im afraid they are diminishd since* – there is now no longer any fixed residence for these poor people I have heard said, exept the vicinity of the Missionarys where there are not above 300 – the rest are all servants in the Colony, or live in small bands establishing their Craals as I am told where they think they will be least annoyd & ready to move off when they are so – the many other nations which are to be found on piercing

*Dinaira**
Dunira, Perthshire. H. Dundas's estate.

*servant**
This incident probably took place on the occasion described by Cory (*Rise of S.A.* 1:92-93) when a party of Xhosas attacked Vanderleur's undefended camp at Ferreira's Farm, Papenkuilsfontein, 10-8-1799.

*since**
The largest figure seems the most likely. The census return in 1805 stated that 20,000 "Hottentots, half-breeds and Bushmen" were in service but that it was impossible to give an exact count.

into this vast country have each their fixed boundary, but the character of the nations differs as much as their countenances & size do, a Boshie man being as Ingenious Subtle and faithless as I have heard a Hottentot supposed the contrary. – the Caffres are a superior race in size, force, and judgement I fancy to either; – Jacob Van Renin* a Dutch friend of mine started [sic] an opinion to me which as it is curious and certainly not without *some* foundation I shall repeat. – perhaps I may have given it you before, but I dont think I have. – Jacob is convinced from conversations which he had with the natives when exploring the country for the crew of the Grosvenor many years ago, that the Caffres who we have lately been at war with met the English troops with the less fear that they believe them also to be "*Men of the Sea*" – Men, born & bred in vessels, leading a wandering life, without fixed Habitation any where, poor, weak & miserable; – vessels which had been wreckd on their coast have establishd this notion in them, as the crews have always appeard objects of pity, and begging for mercy, from this cause they have got the Habit of despising these Men of the Sea, who by their spys sent to the Cape they find have now got the place from the dutch, and rule it with "a wise old man" for their Governor, now gone away. – General Dundas I suppose they must have reckond *a Man of the Sea* only, else they woud have run from him, but I hope they will now look at Sir G.Yonges *star*, which shines brighter than Lord Macartneys did, & suppose him at once older – greater – and wiser than he –

To return to private matters. – while General Dundas remaind in the country with his new wife, General Fraser, Erskine & the rest of that sett, continued to press the governor to order us out of the Castle, stating that the general wishd very much *he* woud, to save him the awkwardness of doing it when he came to town for the winter. – NB this is February the middle of summer – this hint Sir George totally resisted, he declared his intention of waiting the Generals reply to his offer, and as the General seemd in no hurry to give it, the *suspence* became in some respects inconvenient and in others unpleasant to us. – Mrs Dundas I heard much preferd Rondebosch to the Castle and that the general did so too for the *summer*, it is cool, convenient as to offices and has a most beneficial farm round it, at the moderate distance of four miles of good road from town – if the general liked it better than the governors house, he had still his own of the lieut governors which Fraser for the present has assumed, or if he preferd the governors house in the Castle, he had *Whittebont** besides, as a country house to go to, at ten or twelve miles distance from town where he used to live & which for the present he has lent to Col Hamilton* whose regt will soon move into town – *Any* government house tolerably near we are ready to be contented with and to *evacuate our* own, but as all the other houses in the Castle exept that we live in are the right of *military men*, none but Rondebosch is on the cards for us, if we quit this, which is only preferable to it from its being close to the Secretarys office – to have *no* government House *atall* after a three years residence in one, woud be very mortifying – the pecuniary loss I do not *either name or think of* when compared *to the appearance* it woud have to the *dutch*, who *look at such things* in men of publick situations – it woud tally too much

*Renin**
Jacob van Reenen, 3rd of the name. See *Tour into the Interior*, note p.130. The *Grosvenor* was wrecked on 4-8-1752.

*Whittebont**
Wittebome, an estate in the present Wynberg district.

*Hamilton**
In her letter to Lord Macartney of 25-1-1799, Lady A. describes him as of the 61st Regt., but he was probably Lt.-Col. John Hamilton of the 81st Regt.

with various malicious reports of our staff friends who have endeavord to convince *them* and all others that woud listen, that no gratitude is due to Mr Barnard or me for the pains we are at to entertain and to please them as we are *paid* by Government for every ball and *dinner* we give, and have been allowd while General Dundas was a single man to occupy the governors house for *that purpose*, this woud be a little provoking if I cared much about what was said by those I do not esteem, but it is a shabby way of apologising for the *want* of those civilitys in *themselves* to say we have been paid for those we shew. – most undoubtedly it is the salary of government which pays for all we do, but so does the salary of *every other* servant of government, & I never heard it hinted after you had given an excellent dinner at Wimbledon or Mr Pitt in Downing street that those gentlemen only kept eating houses for the benefit of the State. –

A Hottentot policeman

*nine**
No precise explanation of this term can be discovered. From the use of the adjective 'Scottish' it most probably originated in England, descriptive of a Scottish practice. Mr. D. Murison of the *Scottish National Dictionary*, suggests that it refers to a cold collation with tea or coffee, as it was not customary for gentlemen to drink liquor with ladies at that time.

Mean time, we perceivd from some little words that dropd first from one, then from another of the government House people that the old Boutique had been *pressing their powers* too far, and had begun already to Jar with the new, General Fraser having taken it much amiss that the barrack masters appointment had not been given to *him* & the deputy to his Brigade Major – on the other hand some little inequalitys of manners in general D. to the new aid du camps & others there, had not been relishd by them – to all this we lent a *Deaf* ear, keeping totally apart from the Gossip of what was going on – *complaining of no one* – entering into no discussions – but foreseeing, that the moment woud not be very distant when *Interest clashing against Interest, pride against pride* woud do the business for us much better than we coud do it for ourselves. – already it poped out that the government house people were half sorry that general invitations had been given to two or three gentlemen who had made their table an every-other-day conveniency and whose company they begun to find dull, and censorious. – All this we saw, and smiled at, pleased to find they were cutting their own throats and pleased to draw no weapons whatsoever *against them* but those of good humour – cold chickens – music – & what little agrements this house coud afford, or the lady who tho lazy at the bottom of her heart is not so when any real good purpose is to be effected. – the governor of course was asked to such little evening partys – his family &cc – "How chearfull & gay you all are said he, & Yet I never hear you abusing any body! pray let me see you as often as you *can* at my house, every night there is a Scotch tray walks in at nine,* it is an invention of the advocates, & holds twelve friends – all friends mind me, we must sit too close for foes" – to this Scotch tray we have since often ajournd, and when we enter off moves the other party who appear to be vanishing away *one by one* –

by the bye – I have omitted to tell you that on the Generals wedding day, I sent him a few goodnatured lines & transcribd that part of your letter to me where you mention the kind interest Lord Macartney took in him & how pleased you was to find he had conducted the affairs of the colony so well since his departure. – to this note I have received no reply, he passes my door every day but has never come in, nor taken any notice of it, this I think is carrying pride strangely far, not to condescend to be pleased with so *valuable* a paragraph from you because it came thro me, or perhaps he will not stoop to be pleased with the approbation of *any man.* –

– How often have I not wishd by the bye that he woud give me an opening to tell him *that I have complaind of him to you*, I do not like to feel myself in the room with a person who I have blamed to their friend without speaking out, "I did so" – but he woud only hold me in disdain for supposing he cared what I said of him to you, or any body, and as he has never professd himself my friend, or I his *exept* on being your nephew I believe I do not Owe him the explanation. – Oh how glad I shoud be if he and his wife woud be comfortable with us all! Mr Barnard is a man so unpresuming in his manners & *sought his friendship at first so sincerely* that it is a wonder to me why he shoud Hate him so. – may be *She* will put things right, tho I have my fears on the score of pride, as I suspect that on board of ship she lorded it over the poor Blake, in a way that she is not now disposed to forget. – I believe I am *a witch*, for cross as all has hitherto gone, I fully expect to find myself the *Armed Neutrality* after all, already I have put in a mediating word or two, and shall continue to do so if I find it necessary. –

with respect to more important matters. – Mr B. & I begin to hope (nothing further having been done or proposd *in grande* by the Governor) that his *little* follys will not grow up [to] be *greater ones*. – he has provided for his suite perhaps rather *too liberally* and the department under the barrack master is perhaps *needlessly* swelld by clerks and secretarys, but as this is a matter which regards *his family* and cannot occur again, it goes to no more than so many unnecessary hundreds pr annum – Mr Barnard has frightend him a good deal I believe about the revenue, being possibly unequal to the demands on it unless he is carefull, & hinted that shoud it fail, the *where* to apply next is not pointed out, he thinks this has had effect, in particular there is no longer any talk of *a new sett of publick offices* got. – or more Barracks built, let them repair the old ones first which need it much, old they are not, being scarcely finishd when the place was taken. –

We had a botany Bay Captain dining with us tother day, I beg its pardon, by the bye, for I find Botany Bay takes it ill to be so called, New South Wales I find is its name. – he is carrying a freight of Bullocks from this, about 200 – Mr Hogan a merchant here,* tells me they cost government 150 £ each, before they land them there, & that he has lately had a contract with it for a few which he put on the shore at £36, each, & that a merchant here can afford to do it much cheaper than government can for itself. – this I repeat because you like to hear every thing out of which any usefull hint can be pickd, there was no idea that I shoud repeat it, as it occured only in common conversation. – the captain of the ship whose name is Kent, gave me a very pleasing account of the place and the reformation it works on individuals, most of whom become at last Honest members of the community. – he talks of Barrington* with Enthusiasm of his good conduct – his modesty: his ability & *publick virtue* are now he says as conspicuous as he was conspicuously eminent before in Roguery. – tho his time has been long up he does not mean to return to Europe, but has a humble pride in

*here**
Michael Hogan, a merchant of doubtful morality, later involved with Yonge in illegal slave-trading. See Letter 27.

*Barrington**
George Barrington (1755[?]-1804), Irish "prince of pickpockets", transported in 1790, pardoned 1792. He was appointed Chief Constable of Paramatta, N.S.W., 1796-1800.

An Indian

being the first magistrate where he is respected instead of being pointed at where he can never be forgotten in his *first* character. – he was lately taken ill, all ranks of rogues, Rogues of 2 years – 3 years – 6 years, & those made honest again by the sweeping clause of seven, bewaild him, he left all he had (about 1,500) to the orphans of the place, but he recoverd much to the satisfaction of the governor. –

I often say, that I shoud have much pleasure if I was not a terrible coward in going to Botany Bay & America before I return to England. – it woud be feeling *as an Angel woud* to prefer a visit to Botany bay to seeing my friends – *they* have more Joy it is said over one sinner who repents than over 99 righteous persons. – when I am put to the trial however with *the leave of absence*, I believe I shall prove myself a mere mortal woman & sail on as fast as I can . –

Governor King* & his wife were here on their way to New South Wales, good people I think & apparently well suited to their destination – I have seen them but twice & that in this house – I sent a present of a silk gown to a rogue there, Transported by Margaret & me, the only creature I believe we ever punishd or prosecuted in our lives – but She was too great a thief to let pass – if she is reformd & that is easily found out Mrs King is to give her a few encouraging lines from me & the gown – if she continues bad, I have begd her to give it as a wedding gown to the first young girl of a good Botany bay character who is married after her arrival – apropos to marriage Major Erskine *is* married to Miss Du Wal – Capt Bird* also married to a Miss Bassini – I think *all* will repent by & bye –

Feb 14 – 1800

I am told that the Amelia is to sail in two days now cher ami, and tho very unwell with a bilious complaint which has confined me to my room these three days, I *must* write a few lines in addition to what has gone before, & enclose the Finale of the affair of the House – which I hope will be a Finale & that I shall be able to close my books as to *grievances*, a most uncomfortable stile of writing & one I have regreted I have been obliged to get into with *you*, to whom I woud never express any thing if I coud but contentment, and particular kindness to every one *connected with you*. – I enclose Copys of the letters that have passd between Mr Barnard & the General & leave them to speak for themselves without comment – simply ushering them in, by saying that after having waited a fortnight after the generals marriage for his determination as to what house he chose, during which time the governor often promised to obtain his decision, at last Mr Barnard wrote to his Excellency a letter such as he thought he might shew the General to facilitate the conversation – but the governor declined this, saying he had already "pressd his reply as much as he coud in propriety" but thought Mr Barnard had a fair right to task him to decide & advised him to express his own wishes & sentiments on the subjects whatever they were" – Mr Barnard on this transmitted to Genl Dundas the letter markd N° 1* to which he received

*King**
Philip Gidley King (1758-1808), 3rd governor of New South Wales, 1800-1806.

*Bird**
Lt.-Col. Christopher Chapman Bird (1769-1861), then a lieutenant and Asst. Q.M.G. He was Colonial Secretary 1814-24, under Somerset. He married Christina Buissiné, dt. of Major Buissiné, formerly of the Company's service.

*N° 1**
See Letters 26a-e below.

next day in reply the letter markd No 2 – the implication of this letter being so totally different from what Mr Barnard had reason to understand from the governor were his intentions, as it bore that he (the General) had obtaind *both* Houses from Sir George, but granted us the liberty of remaining in *this* as *his* house, from which *he* had the power of removing us when he pleasd that Mr Barnard amazed wrote to the governor, pressing to know the exact state of the case & begining to suspect, that his Excellency had entangled himself on his first arrival by some hasty promise to Mr Erskine *for* the General, & did not know how to get free so as to satisfy both partys. – Sir Georges reply Ill send, N° 3, rather because it *at first* seems to make *against all I have been advancing*, than because it is *necessary*. – A hint was brought us by the *bearer* that the letter was *calculated* to *be seen by the general* & that he had therefore *chose* to misunderstand Mr Barnard in order to render the doctrines he laid down for *both* less unpalatable to the general – perhaps Mr B. might not (after this) have thought any further correspondence with general Dundas necessary had he not advanced to the Governor that Mr B^s^ note implyd a Right, which he did not think was implyd in it. – but this motive together with the natural reluctance he felt at staying in any house from which (circumstanced as they have lately been) general D. coud conceive he had a right to remove him at pleasure led him to explain his sentiments on the *nature of his Tenure* by N° 4. – & to the governor by N° 5 – . as the old gentleman had been a good deal puzzled and workd, as it appears thro his letter Mr B thought it best to smooth him down a little, but indeed his letter is *very well Judged* as it substantiates fully his own power over all, & *floats slightly over* every thing else which coud create words between the partys. – to his letter to the general (which is strong but I hope you will not think it improperly so) there has been no reply, indeed nothing more can well be said. – I think it likely that he is secretly very angry, but when a man soars too high over the head of another he must not be surprized if the sun melts his wings & brings him down to the fair level – I am sure I wish he were in this House instead of us, surrounded as we are with his staff, & that we were at Rondebosh – I wonder as a military man he does not prefer living in the Castle; for the object of a little Barley corn & vegetables Cannot be an object I shoud think worthy of his attention and the command of *all* the houses of government is a little out of the question – this choice is his own however, & no fault of ours – here *then ends this business* – a little time I hope will make all friends, at present there are no *foes* amongst us, as the general & Mr Barnard speak to each other, and the last has visited the first on his marriage – A *Coldness* I own there is, in consequence of past Slights, but whenever a duty calls to bring them together Mr B: will be found performing it without prejudice and without resentment. – Once more I say Amen – & so be it. –

about two months ago, I mentiond a paper which the governor said he had askd of you to give him, in which Mr Barnards name is joind to Genl. Dundas as a person to be consulted with *occasionally*, we have never heard more of this paper, so it is still in the shade – I had formed perhaps, when I wrote, an erroneous opinion of that paper but I was led to it by the governor himself, who said we shoud all see how highly he was impressd with respect to Mr B. & that he might to give a publick testymony of it – what this testymony is to be we know not, it is long of appearing if there is any such thing –

we are all however *perfectly comfortable* now with the government house people, I think that from the head to the foot they are all very fond of us, and as our good footing shall if possible sway to *General Harmony* I trust all will go on smooth. – I see a considerable alteration for the better since the generals marriage in the attentions shewn to *the world*, dinners have been given to every body, field officers invited, and even Captains who have never been askd there before, civilians too have dined there for the first time, if this is *her* it is well, at any rate it is well judged & I mention it with pleasure. – every chance now being over as I hope of any further misunderstanding between the General and Mr Barnard I begin to regret that I have taken up so much of your time as I have done most disagreeably by my details, that I have ever hurt you (as perhaps I may have done) by reflections on him, or said a severe word in the vexation of my heart which I might have spared, but we have not the gift of *prescience* and as I knew not how things might end with a person of his turn I thought it Safest to write on *ingenuously* as matters occurd. – I conclude this letter in health and full of the kindest wishes that this may find you both well – I sent by the Sir Ed[d] Hughes a pair of living Cape Louries to Lady Jane like the dead ones I sent her before – they are curiositys and were in noble Health when they left me –

God Bless you both my dear friends –

Anne Barnard

Mr B was agitating with himself today when writing to you whether he ought or ought not to say anything to you of what has been lately passing respecting our abode, he hates to bring forwards needless *matter* to you, and yet woud be sorry to suppress any proper communication, I told him I had already said All that was necessary – you will laugh & say – "and more too." –

I send you A very *Imperfect* and *slight sketch* w[c] if I had Time I woud endeavour to compleat, of the Bay here, *not* as you have seen it in common views, but taking in that part of the beach where the *Sceptre* and other ships were lost the 5th of November last, it shews the form & nature of *the shore*, the manner in which dammage is done by the N:West Winds in winter, I have added a South East wind begining to express itself on table Mountain. – when these ships were lost it was the Summer Season – Shew it to Lord Spencer* with my best compliments he will see what a frail creature a Ladyship is, tho A *Man* of war when attackd by one of our Cape winds – not a bit of the wreck is here drawn which my eyes did not see, tho many bits were too small to be traced. – the drawing is rolld up tight and I have sent it to Margaret to have it flattend after its voyage for you – the land is perfectly *like in color and form* But the whole is very *ill done* – admirable pasture country – no corn – calld Brunches Hook or some name like that* –

*Spencer**
George John, 2nd Earl Spencer (1758-1834), 1st Lord of the Admiralty 1794-1801, described as the "organiser of victory".

*that**
As far as is known this sketch has not survived. From the description it would seem to have been drawn from the vicinity of Signal Hill, looking across the Bay and showing Table Mt. and beyond it the Tygerberg. 'Brunches Hook' is not known.

Letter 26a

ANDREW BARNARD TO MAJOR-GENERAL DUNDAS

(Copy)

Castle
4th February, 1800

Dear Sir

I should be much obliged to you if you would let me [know] your determination respecting the house I at present occupy in the Castle, my plans & motions being much suspended in consequence of the uncertainty of my situation.

I applied yesterday to Sir George Yonge (who had ordered me to remain where I was, till he knew your decision from yourself). He informed me that he had offered you your choice shortly after his arrival amongst all the houses belonging to Government after reserving the Garden house to himself, but that you had not as yet given him a reply and requested me to ask it of you myself and to express at the same time whatever wishes or sentiments I had on the subject. As to wishes I have none, but to do what is right, subscribing most fully to your superior right of choice in the first instance & maintaining what I conceive to be my own (with the Governor's permission) in the second. I therefore beg that no delicacy of moving my family may influence you to inconvenience yourself for a moment: shoud you prefer the house I occupy in the Castle to that you at present inhabit in the Country, I shall get my furniture moved with the utmost expedition; in whatever manner you please to determine I should be really obliged to you if you would let me know in a day or two; various inconveniences attending the suspence.

I remain
Dear Sir
your most obedient
humble servant
(signed) A. Barnard

M. Genl. Dundas
&c &c &c

Sir George Yonge, Governor of the Cape, 1799-1801

Letter 26b

MAJOR-GENERAL DUNDAS TO ANDREW BARNARD

(Copy)

Rondebosch
5th Febry. 1800.

Sir

My respect for the Ladies of your family & my desire to contribute to their accommodation have certainly induced me to forego my right to the house which you occupy at present in the Castle, having signified to Lord Macartney my determination upon that head when it was offered me by His Lordship soon after he landed at the Cape, and at the Commencement of his Administration here.

The same polite motive as above mentioned has withheld my claim since the arrival of Sir George Yonge who wished to put me in possession of what in his opinion belonged to the Lieut: Governor & Commandant of the Troops. In reply to your letter of yesterday, I have nothing further to add, than to inform you that as the Governor has vouchsafed to allow me to remain in possession of Rondebosch, it is not my intention to live in Town for the present, therefore you are at liberty to stay in my house in the Castle until such time as it becomes necessary for me to request you to remove from it.

I have the honour to be
your most obedient, and
humble Servant.
(signed) Fras. Dundas

A. Barnard Esq.

Letter 26c

SIR GEORGE YONGE TO ANDREW BARNARD

(Copy)

Government House
6th. February 1800.

Dear Sir

I am favoured with your letter of this days date enclosing a Copy of one you had wrote to M.G. Dundas on the subject of your quitting the house in the Castle, with M. Genl. Dundas's answer to that letter.

From the contents of your letter to me, as well as of M. Genl. Dundas's to you, it appears to me, that you both have labour'd under some mistake, & therefore, though I very much wish to avoid any sort of discussion on the subject, yet to prevent any more misapprehension if possible, I will now endeavour to explain my sentiments upon it.

In the first place then, it is impossible I ever should, nor have I ever meant to acknowledge any right either in you or in M. Genl. Dundas as Lieut. Governor or otherwise either to the Governor's house in the Castle, or to Rondebosch, and whoever occupies them or either of them, can never, from the nature of the thing hold them otherwise than precariously, because I neither have a right, or ever had any intention that either should be held otherwise, and the Tenure in either must depend on my conveniency, or on such circumstances as may arise.

I hope this will be sufficient to explain to you my ideas on this point, to which I have only to add, that on my arrival here I found a letter from M. Genl. Dundas stating his readiness to quit Rondebosch, if I chose it; to which my answer was, that I did not wish him to be disturbed at present: In like manner I offered him the Governor's house, to which he gave no reply 'till his return, when I again renewed the offer, and left it to him to decide, which Decision he communicated to me only yesterday; in consequence as I understood of your application to him for an answer; This Decision I understood from him to be as follows.

That he had so much respect for you and Lady Ann that he was unwilling to desturb you and therefore, as I allowed him to reside at Rondebosch he should not think of accepting my offer at present; but that *your* letter *imply'd* a *right* which could not be admitted, & that in his answer to you he should explain his Ideas on that point. If I may be allowed an opinion in the answer he has sent you, I think his error consists in the supposition that I considered that there existed a right in the Lieut. Governor to occupy the Governor's house, but I do not conceive his meaning to be to wish to remove you.

This is all I can say by way of explanation, and you will allow me to say, I conceive no *Right* exists in either of you. If I chose to leave the Governor's House empty, I may do it, or if I chose it to be occupied, it is not *necessary* that the Lieut. Governor should be the Occupier. But if I chose it should remain empty, or if I offered it to any other Occupier; in either case the Lieut: Governor can only occupy the Lieut. Governor's House.

But at present I conceive that tho' I have offered M. Genl. Dundas the house, yet having Rondebosch, he is, as he assured me, satisfied, and does not wish, as I certainly do not wish, that you should be put to any inconvenience or be removed.

I look upon this matter therefore as being settled for the present; Whenever any other arrangement comes under consideration, then will be the time for determining what is proper to be done, at present there appears to me to be no sort of necessity for going any further.

I am with great Regard
Dear Sir
your most ob^{t} Servant
(signed) Geo. Yonge

To
A Barnard Esq.
&c &c &c

Letter 26d

ANDREW BARNARD TO MAJOR-GENERAL DUNDAS

(Copy)

Castle
6th February 1800.

Sir

I had yesterday the honor of receiving your Letter, and shall so far advert to past circumstances as to say, that when on Lord Macartney's offering you the Governor's house in the Castle, you declined it, to remain in the Lieut: Governor's, giving up the other to me as being larger and more commodious for the size of my family, I at the time thanked you for the accommodation it afforded us; Had you occupied it yourself, I had the refusal of the other house which Government possessed.

When His Excellency Sir George Yonge arrived we both it seems offered back into his hands the Government Houses we then occupied. That of Rondebosch on your part, and the Governor's house in the Castle on mine. What your sentiments are on the subject of your Rights over the last I do not pretend to judge of; my sentiments were what they are still, that I never have had, nor ever wished to *assert* any *Right* over any House of Government except "*with the Governor's Permission*" who when he reserved to himself the Garden House declared himself ready to bestow the others on the Servants of Government, and you being the Person of highest rank in the Colony very properly were allowed the first choice; after you I conceived I had a right or *fair pretension* (if that phrase is closer to Point) to the second choice which the Governor admitted.

I find by His Excellency's reply to a letter I took the liberty of troubling him with yesterday "that you have made your decision to remain at Rondebosch", and "that as no Right exists in either of us to the Governor's house in the Castle", he gives me his permission to remain in it during his pleasure, this being the case I shall take the liberty of continuing to occupy His house while I have his leave, ready to quit it when he orders me, but admitting of no power in any other person in this Colony to remove me out of it –

I am
Sir
your most obedient
humble Servant
(signed) A. Barnard

M. Genl Dundas
&c &c &c

Letter 26e

ANDREW BARNARD TO SIR GEORGE YONGE

Castle
February 1800

My best thanks are due to your Excellency for a letter which comprehends every judicious purpose, and is at once so clear and fully stated, that it cannot fail of establishing things on the footing they ought to be understood, that of your Excellency's pleasure being the only Law respecting the distribution of the Government houses; a point on which I trust you never could have supposed me to be presumptuously asserting any further right than that of Hope, under your sanction, and of a second choice under your permission.

I fully enter into the wisdom of your seeming to apprehend that both the General and I have laboured under a mistake and rectifying it to both; at the present I acquiesce with respect and gratitude to your opinion, that there is no necessity for making any change; I conceive myself with your permission inhabiting *your* house, during *your* pleasure, ready to quit it when you order me, but admitting of no power in any other person in this Colony to remove me from it.

I have the honor to remain
&c &c &c
(signed) A Barnard

Letter 26f

ANDREW BARNARD TO HENRY DUNDAS

The following confidential letter from Barnard to Henry Dundas dates from this time. It is one of the few that we have showing the former's sound views on Cape affairs and warrants inclusion here.

Private

Castle of Good Hope
March the 9th 1800.

My Dear Sir,

My last Letter of the 9th of Feby Ultmo was very short being merely an Introductory one which Mr Nederburg the late Governor of Batavia requested me to give him; it however contained a piece of Intelligence which I was not sorry to have an opportunity of communicating to you. I mean the Capture and afterwards the blowing up of the Preneuse French Frigate by the Tremendous and Adamant. this event puts a finishing stroke to the French Marine in these seas, altho there still remains a number of privateers that have been fitted out from the Mauritius, the Crews of the Prudente and the Preneuse having supplied them with Men in abundance.* – The Diomede Captain Elphinstone arrived here a few Days ago from India, he brings the intelligence of the Arsenal at Manilla having been destroyed by fire, and all the Naval stores consumed, so that there remains no more for the Men of War on that Station, except those they have on board. He also says that the Fiscal and first in Council at Malacca, have been taken into Custody and sent to Bengal, being accused of having endeavoured to stir up an Insurrection amongst the Malay Inhabitants, and attempting to take possession of the Settlement for the present Dutch Directory.

I am Happy to acquaint you that at this place all is quiet at present, and I hope that if timely precautions are taken that it will remain so. no immediate Danger is to be apprehended, as the Hottentots that were at War with us have taken away from the Farmers Cattle enough to last them these Six Months, it will therefore be that time at least, before they begin Plundering again. The Caffres will not molest us unless they are urged on by the Boors that have taken refuge amongst them, so that I trust we shall remain at Peace till a Reinforcement to our Garrison arrives. – To give you an Idea of our Weakness at present, I will tell you a circumstance Sir which most likely you will never learn from any other Pen than mine. – on Wednesday last the Governor desired General Dundas, the Fiscal, the Judge of the Vice Admiralty Court, and myself to meet at the Garden House for the purpose of consulting on the Steps most proper to be taken with respect to the Dutch Prisoners that have been in confinement ever since the first breaking out of the Disturbances at Graaf Reinet. after much consideration whether it wou'd be advisable or not, to bring the matter before the Court of Justice, as there were some doubts that the Members dare not do their Duty, and Convict the Prisoners if they were proved Guilty or to send them at once out of the Colony without any Trial. it was however at last determined, that it was most prudent not to decide on that Subject at present, least if we shou'd adopt strong Measures we might exasperate the Boors that are living with the Caffres, and by that means bring them upon our backs, when we have not strength enough to oppose them. It was my opinion that the Prisoners ought to be tried by the Court of Justice, as it was a matter of consequence that Government shou'd be acquainted with the *real* Dispositions of the Gentlemen composing that Court. This was more particularly my opinion when the Prisoners were first apprehended, as I conceived that where there existed a Court of Law doing Justice in the Name of His Britannick Majesty and that an offence had been committed of which that Court took full Cognizance, that in the first instance the affairs shou'd be brought before them for their Investigation, and Decision, which if Government Disapproved, it was then time enough to take the Law into its own hands and send the Prisoners out of the Colony being certainly very improper Persons to remain in it. I wish that opinion had been followed at the time it was given, as many of the Poor Creatures who have now suffered nearly twelve months imprisonment besides a total loss of all their property wou'd at that time have been released, as there is *little* or *no* proof against them but we dare not release them now, for the same reason that we dare not deter-

*abundance**
The *Preneuse*, frigate, 44 guns, was run ashore on Mauritius on 11-12-1799. For the fate of the *Prudente* see above p. (Introduction to letter 23)

mine in what manner to proceed with the most Guilty.

I observe Sir in the *Copy* of an Instruction which I received from the Governor about a *Fortnight* ago in order to have it entered in my office, that I am desired to sign together with the Governor and Lieutenant Governor all accounts for Extraordinary Expenses that may be incurred, and that I am also at Liberty to make what remarks I think proper on them in a Book kept for that purpose, a Copy of which remarks, if any, are to be transmitted home together with the accounts every Quarter. – I rather regret that that Power is by that Instruction so Limitted (sic), that my observations if any, can only be made on what is done, consequently, they must be too late to *prevent* or *Remedy* the Evil, and cannot well be made without giving in some degree offence to the Governor. – If I may be permitted to offer an opinion to you on a subject which you are so much more competent to Judge of than I can be, but which I am certain your Liberal Mind will not impute to any selfish motive, I wou'd say that if by any future Document or Instruction you shou'd think proper to order, that Previous to any Extraordinary Measure of Expence being entered into, that the opinion of the Lieutenant Governor and Secretary of the Colony, or any other Person or Persons that you may think proper to appoint shou'd be taken. I am persuaded that it might, and in many instances really wou'd be productive of essential Good to the Colony.

I have nothing further particular to trouble you with, but

Have the Honor to Remain
Your Most Faithful
& Truly, Obliged Servt
A Barnard.

R^{t} Hon^{l} Mr Secretary Dundas.
Downing Street
London

A boer and his wife

Letter 27

About the same time as the foregoing letter was written, the Barnards removed themselves from the unpleasant atmosphere of the Castle and Government House to the rural peace of their newly-built cottage, the Vineyard, at Newlands. Their former country refuge, Paradise, had become too delapidated, as Andrew explained in a letter to Lord Macartney on 29 March. The Vineyard was on the banks of the Liesbeeck on the site of the present hotel of the same name.

LADY ANNE TO HENRY DUNDAS

Vineyard –
Cape of good Hope
May 14 – 1800

If you knew how often I have thought of getting on with a long letter to you, how often I have pospond it till I shoud find a better moment, how much I have wishd to write to you happily – gayly – foolishly, and as I used to do, nothing in my letters to disturb or annoy you, but how constantly vile little circumstances have arisen to put it out of my power to do so with *sincerity*, you woud almost pity me – all I have now time to say is that those delays tho all from the best motives have so gone on from day to day that the ships sail the day after tomorrow without my having *wrote a line*, and I have a whole cottage full of company, with my head full of you, and the letters I have to write to you when I shoud be making the agreeable to those who look up to me for attention and amusement –

I certainly coud say in general terms that we are well and defer further particulars, but that woud not be using you like a friend, – I have little doubt that the letters from this place will be full of circumstances which have being [sic] arising here to surprize and agitate a small circle who know not the meaning of *Some things* nor how *others* will *end.* – the bad terms the general & the governor are on, you will learn from various quarters on this I might have *prophecied* almost from the first, but I *hoped* things might turn out better than I expected, the reverse has been the case – the causes of this I will endeavour to give, as far as I am able to Judge, If I can find half an hours leisure uninterupted to detail events – if not, I shall try to give the cream in as few words as I can. – with respect to the *present government*, when I tell you that all who compose it are on the best terms with us, civil & rather flatteringly conciliatory, you will not suppose me biasd by any personal Disaffection to them when I lament the uncreditable *Shade* which some events have lately thrown over it. – I realy durst not sooner (from the fear of being unjust) *breath* even to *you* what has been here loudly *whisperd*, and what has been too frequently *corroborated* by a blush that tinged the poor Governors cheek when pressd by Mr Barnard – that in some late transactions the Hands of Government have not been so clean as they ought to have been –

the Dutch have got this idea of him, with what Justice God only knows, but so strong an exertion of power has lately been made in favour of a merchant he is unconnected with,* giving him not only liberty to import 1,600 slaves, but to land here a *supposed prize Cargo* (afterwards proved by Capt Campbell* in the court of Justice to be a smuggling transaction, not to use a harsher name to it. the slaves realy having been *purchased* at Mosambique) that it is generally believed that a douceur of no small magnitude was given to effect, what had it passd, woud have put from ten to fifteen thousand pounds in the merchants pocket – whose privateer *affected* to have *taken* those Slaves – you will naturally say how happend it that Mr B: who knew how opposite it was to the ideas of Government at home, this of permitting a Slave Trafick to go on at the Cape, how happend it that he omitted to state its impropriety to the Governor. – Mr Barnard actually did so, in the strongest terms – he also told the merchant he woud oppose it, – but found the Governor deaf to all remonstrance or argument, & as a proof of his being anxious to avoid all further conversation or *respectfull* opposition from Mr B. he gave the order for the landing & selling of the Slaves & all the necessary arrangements himself – without bringing them thro the *Secretarys office* as is *customary* – was I to speak my sentiments openly I woud say, that inspite of the mildness of Mr B. and the governors apparent regard for him, I shoud think he stood more in awe on some occasions of the secretary, than the secretary of the governor – unfortunately by the invention of appropriating one day of the week *only* to publick business Mr B: has less constant intercourse with him than he coud wish, and by his letting it be generally understood that all pressing business which cannot wait an approaching wednesday will be done by the governor himself if introduced by Mr Blake his private secretary, there is a door opend by which all sorts of solicitations enter – are replied to – and the business generally settled before Mr Barnard *hears a word of it*. – one thing you may depend on, that every fair, broad, and proper request invariably goes thro the *Secretary to the Colony*, to the governor, every matter of an unsound or equivocal nature proceeds by the other road, whether in hopes of obtaining a hasty consent from an *unexperienced* Governor who will not take time to investigate the matter in question, or whether from other motives I shall not say. – I have sometimes heard Mr Barnard regret that his powers of being of use were so limited, and that it is only after the ill is done his sentiments can appear, but as to all that, you knew best what is fit, if he has not the means of doing good, he is also free from the vexation of dispute with-

*with**
This merchant, Michael Hogan, was concerned with more than one underhand deal. In the allegations later brought against Yonge the latter was accused of receiving £5,000 from Hogan for giving him permission to import 800 slaves into the Colony. (Theal's *Records*, v.3, p.487). The Commissioners afterwards appointed to investigate these charges had no doubt that this was true. Blake and Lt.-Col. Colburn were also implicated. (Ibid. v. 4, p.256-)

*Campbell**
Capt. Donald Campbell, port captain.

out personal advantage. – I can perceive that there seems to be no *hurry* in either the *present* governor or the *past* to send home their accounts. I ask Mr B. frequently when they are to go, expressing my hopes of his being absolved from giving his opinions on past expences from the time Lord Macartney left this place to that when he is required to countersign the papers, but he finds no Zeal, no intentions of sending them up but on the contrary much dislike of business in the Governor, indeed to such a degree that he has never read a proclamation or any paper on the publick business of the Colony previous to his arrival –

with respect to the bad terms he and the General are on together, I cannot posatively [sic] affirm whether the blame is on one side only or whether it is divided. – the general skips over the field officers in the garrison andsends orders to their men without transmitting them thro them in the regular way, to their great disgust – the governor sometimes forgets and does the same in trifles, and while the *first* thinks it presumption in his inferior to be angry, he is offended to the greatest degree with the other for following his example. – the governor reckons himself the Head of the army, as well as of every thing else, the general allows him to be only *nominally* so, and is *displeasd* at him more frequently giving orders respecting the troops than Lord Macartney used to do, who most cautiously avoided *small interferences*, tho he was for *ever in his place* when it was necessary, the *Head of all*. – perhaps the General might not be so jealous of Sir George as he *is* was it not for those around him who having got all they coud from his Excellency on his first arrival turnd their backs on him the first sop in the pan he gave to one of his *own* family. – we saw the growing coolness or rather irritability & conjecturd the first moment woud be seizd that coud for rupture. – an order for moving a manger where 3 horses fed belonging to the Cavalry, to the newly repaird barracks in Col Cockburns department, produced a publick order from the general conceivd in terms so derogatory to Sir George, that Military men stared and feared an arrest woud be the consequence – Sir George tho petrified, behaved well on this occasion by shewing a degree of temperance which wisely gave the general the alternative of asking him pardon, or taking the consequences – he on a little reflection preferd asking pardon, which he did as I am told in the fullest manner to having the matter sent home, and Sir George *Gallantly* saved his credit with the publick in a manner which those who wishd to see the generals pride and Hastyness Humbled called Tame, but which we thought wise upon the whole –

– his Excellency told me that he had promised *You* to check with mildness any "ebolitions" which the Generals particular Temper might throw out, & that he had kept his word. – Since that time I hear there have been new disputes – fresh offence given & taken & I heard today that the Generals aid du Camp Mr Smith* is going home with dispatches, containing amongst other things, complaint of his excellency. – I know not if this is true, I am living out of town at our little country place which we purchased, built a cottage on & call the vineyard, removed from all *party work*, exept *working partys* in our fields rooting up of palmite roots* – & planting of fir trees & coeur Boms* – pottatoes &cc

– I have seen a little of Mrs Dundas – she is I think a judicious woman

*Smith**
Lt. James Carmichael Smyth, R.E., a.d.c. to General Dundas.

*roots**
Palmiet, i.e. *Prionum palmieta*, a woody plant growing in damp places in the Western Cape.

*Boms**
Keurboom, i.e. *Virgilia croboides*, a flowering tree with mauve-pink blossom.

Verloren Vallei, near Elands Bay

& well calculated as far as *I can judge as yet*, to increase the popularity of his House, for which I approve of her, she is extremely attentive to the world and *it* is sensible of it. – I think she has more method and better sense in her proceedings than Mrs Blake who seems to me to have for her society only the girls that the aid du Camps are in love with, and as they change their loves, so she changes her girls – I see more of her than of Mrs Dundas, tho not much, I think she wishes to convert me to her *own use*, but the *Armed Neutrality* will be of no League. – the ladys are as I foresaw on terms of Ice, the gvemnt House people particularly disliking Mrs D – I repeat to each every little civil word I *can*, which is likely to keep them friends in the *Benedict & Beatrice* fashion, & I hope will continue well with *both*, from living *very much* with *neither*. – by the bye (for I must bring out things as I recollect them without arrangement at present) I must take notice to you that in one of my last letters I remember I mentiond Mr Hogan, the gentleman who has lost the lawsuit & cargo of Slaves, in terms which implyd good will and good opinion – the present occasion calls on some little *explanation* of my ideas respecting him – I feel singularly about him, I like *the Man*, tho I think his abilitys (which are *excellent* in my opinion) have too much *Invention & dexterity* in them for a small place such as this, girt in by restrictions, yet holding forth temptations for *interprize*, if the wheels which may counteract them, can only be tyed up from moving – I need not say more for I think you have here his character – he has many friends, is of mild manners anxious to please & to *oblige* – Major Erskine I hear from every body has a share in his privateer, as has his father in law, which was the cause of Mr Hogans obtaining permission from the General, to land Slaves on a *former* occasion; no one however *ever* accused that concession as they have done the late one. – if the Generals government was a haughty & unprosperous one, at least it was I am convinced an *Incorrupt* one as regards *him*, & I believe I may say his suite.

There has been another Strange Higgleday Piggleday business going on – it has ended in one person being *suspended* & two sent out of the Colony – Mr Jessop* is the first, who goes home till the pleasure of administration shoud be known – Mr Moss* & Mr Pontardent* are the others. – I shoud state the matter very ill I dare say if I attempted it in *detail* therefore I shall only say in general terms that the governor having granted a permission to certain merchants respecting shipping of certain goods, of a nature contrary as Mr Jessop thought to the words & spirits of the acts of parliament or council & rights of the East India company, he laid his paw on the goods so permitted to be shipd & sustaind by the opinion of Mr Moss as council, sett the Act of parliament & his own opinion of the Governors powers of infringing it, against the permission & express orders of the Governor. –

Mr Barnard is apt to think that however wrong Sir George *is*, or is *not*, in the first instance Mr Jessop is bound to *obey* that the Governor only is responsible for the *step* if wrong was not this the case every man woud turn lawyer & with the act of parliament in his hand coud Act as suited his own translation of it. – Mr Moss is sent off for the terms in which his opinion is given. – Mr Pontardent for endeavoring to negociate

*Jessop**
Henry James Jessop, chief searcher in the Customs Department.

*Moss**
Peter Mosse, advocate in the Admiralty Court.

*Pontardent**
David Pontardent. According to Andrew B., writing to Lord Macartney, 14-5-1800, he "came out here lately with a passport from the Secretary of State."

a compromise between the partys which woud have purchased Mr Jessops silence – I dont know the respective merits of those gentlemen therefore I dont enter into them, I shall only say that the punishment is a Heavy one on men glad to escape from Home, & earning a livelyhood here – but I conclude there is cause for it, tho I can scarce think there can be enough to send off the last, who acting only as a private friend (as I believe) between the partys, was not bound to any particular rigidity of Maxim as a publick man is, in matters connected with the Laws

– within these few days some of the troops are arrived, in a very sickly state, but they will soon get well here – I am told that Peace is much talkd of at home, I believe in none as yet. – Mr Barnard tells me that you have made "A glorious Speech"* and is to get me the paper – that *you* shoud do so is very *surprizing*!!! – I hear Lord Loughborough* is retiring – I hope his health is not worse than it used to be – my love to him when you see him – Mr B. and I are both well at present, I have however been more liable this year to little attacks than before, & he swears if I go on so he will pack me off to Europe. – Never – Never – unless he packs himself off with me. – I wish however that the *conditional* leave of Absence was in my pocket, it woud do me much good & Harm no one for I realy do not think we shoud make use of it, at least for some time, & woud pine much *less* that we had the power. – I *think* you will send it us back with Mr Ross whose return woud place on the spot (were we afterwards to go home) a person accustomed to the business of the place – in truth ever since Lord M. put every thing in the regulated order he did, there is no sort of difficulty in it –

Mr Barnard tells me that the Trial of the dutch prisoners in the Castle is now taking place,* I am sorry they were not tried at first, a year & a halfs suspence woud have been abridged to misery & much injury avoided to the property of the Innocent confined, as well as to the guilty – but the General coud resolve on nothing, what a sad pity it is that he cannot determine on any thing unless he is in a passion, and then it is a great chance whether it is not the wrong way – "Ill think of it – " – "we shall see" – then business of every kind stands still, or rather *stood still* exept military operations which are fixed at a minutes thought, without consultation with other officers, & off with the men, without shoes or stockings or without their dinner, hundreds of miles! – perhaps I shoud not say this but who will speak out of a person (*Your* nephew) unless such an one as myself? – Why has he not Lord Macartney always over him! tho he eminently disliked him while he staid, he awed him by his superior abilitys & he *now* much prefers him to the present master. I am this morning told by some military men that the generals family expect Sir George will be *recalld* in consequence of representations he is sending home in which case they affirm the general will succeed to the Government as governor; – certainly every good fortune which coud attend the general I shoud rejoyce at, but that which woud make him the *Head*, of (what I have seen *this*) a peaceable & well regulated Society; – he is not (I think) calculated for *civil* life tho he may be a brave officer & an Honest man; but too sure it is, that while he reignd over us disaffection in all the departments feuds & war took place & every sort of personal disgust was given; even in *Ones own heart* in ones own

*Speech**
In January 1800 Napoleon wrote personally to George III making an overture for a general peace. The "glorious speech" by Dundas referred to was made in Parliament in February 1800, opposing the concluding of a doubtful peace with France while the Allies were in a favourable position to force better terms.

*Loughborough**
Alexander Wedderburn, Baron Loughborough, afterwards 1st Earl of Rosslyn, Lord Chancellor, 1793-1801.

*place**
The Graaff-Reinet rebels. (See Andrew B.'s letter of 9-3-1800). They were actually brought to trial before August.

family, where *kind Heartyness* to *him reignd* till forcibly kickd & cuffd out of doors by his Haughtyness & want of common consideration – however I fancy the good folks here need not be afraid of his having again the reins of Government, as however Sir George may be *suspected* of loving a douceur, it requires far broader proof than it is likely ever *can* come forwards; for a *recall* to take place, the more so as Sir George woud be without provision at home; I protest I shoud be very sorry if any thing of the sort were to take place; aid du camps – niece – nephew & his Excellency himself are all very civil to us & I feel great good will to *them* tho I do not think they proceed on good plans. – at first Sir George did me the Honor of consulting me on various things, & I gave my opinion as ingenuously *where I thought it my duty* as Gil Blas gave his to the Arch bishop of Toledo,* of course it had the *same* effect, my councils being sometimes unpalatable I was soon suspended; – I advised him against *A Select* concert on which he had sett his heart, to the exclusion of all in the Cape exept a favourd 50 – (without consultation with me) the *Fiscal did the same* – A droll letter or two passd between his Excellencys house & ours on the subject – he was obligd to give it up he found so many Lions & Lionesses in the way, for tho I offerd to do all he required of me (*and is not that a great deal from every woman*) I told him the effect woud be fatal to the peace of society & the Fiscal did the same – Mr B. thinks he has not quite forgiven me for being in the right, but he is so well bred and friendly in his *manners* to Mr Barnard that he buys me off, tho he certainly acts too much without consultation with him for a man who is totally ignorant of the Interests of the place. – the same conduct however which (along with other things) made the General & Mr B. cool friends keeps him cordial with Sir George – [? ?] they act on being different – the first consulted him on nothing from a disdain of any mans opinion but his own, the last from fearing his opinions woud be contrary to what he is *resolved to do*, when those things happen to be a little tinged, as they often are with the Job here. – Mr B is therefore spared remonstrance, often the cause of coolness, & has less to do than usual, his business by degrees becoming wholly colonial, & in the rotin [routine] way which every wednesday he carrys to the governor and has finishd off if necessary, that does not prevent him however from going *every day at ten* to honor Sir Georges commands – but what with his flower garden – his new stair case – his new fire places, & the arrangement of his furniture and planned improvements of his demesnes his excellency seldom has time to talk on business – Col Cockburn seems to be far more active, and far more a man of business that at first I supposed he woud be, I mention this because I recollect having said that I heard he was only a fine Gentleman – he is I believe the leading spring of the government machine, I mean he has more influence with the governor than any body, I never have seen or heard the least suspicion of its being improperly exerted, I know not why I shoud form any decided idea of him, but if I was calld on to give one, I woud say I take him to be a Man of Honor. – Mr Tucker (Mr B tells me from some things he has seen of his writing) is by no means diverted of cleverness, but he is a vague talker which does him Harm – Mr Blake seems a very dull Honest Stupid man who one wishes

*Toledo**
Lady A. was in error. It was the Archbishop of Grenada, not Toledo, to whom Gil Blas gave advice in Lesage's famous novel *Gil Blas de Santillane* (1715-35). The hero, in the service of the Archbishop, was invited to comment on the latter's sermons and when he did so sincerely was summarily dismissed.

well to without knowing why, & Sir George himself! I shoud have thought him too high minded to be capable of any thing low – perhaps he is not so, & that all is undue deformation, if so I lay on the back of *Strong appearances* all my demerit in repeating what I have repeated – this is the full account of every thing as it now stands – I long to hear from you of all things, you bid me continue to write to you unreservedly which I do in the amplest manner; giving you my thoughts where I think they can be of any use to you, unprejudiced accounts of what is going on in a corner of the world you are interested in, in the full confidence of friendship, often "extenuating" but never setting down ought in *Malice*, tho Many very crusty things I have sett down – How I have filld my paper by the light of the midnight taper – as I have no time in the day I am sitting up at night after I have said good night to all my folks – they live like sparrows in little nests in my thatch roof – Col and Mrs Barlow* he an admirable worthy man & a gallant officer – Dr Patison & his wife – he physician to the navy – Col & Mrs Craufurd our cousins – Mr and Mrs Smith – he storekeeper to the navy* – Mrs Saul our old ship mate, protected by David Scot – a good *Crater*, & young Jain from Colinsburgh close by Balcarres my own old nest – we pig in about two thirds more people than the government house does in whose *Hall* this house coud stand – God Bless all at Wimbledon, Dear Lady Jane first, after your sweet self if it was not for Margaret I shoud not know half enough about you for the newspapers tells me only fibs at least I think it very improbable that the state will consent to your retiring, A Lazy Peer, No longer the Sonorous voice of wisdom giving the law in The house of Commons to John Bull – if however you find such cases *absolutely* fatal to your Health, retire from them in a degree – never However intirely by living in Scotland till such time as the Temple of Janus is shut – then open the temple of Dinaira & let us in I pray into some corner of it when we return from the Cape –

God Bless you again

Anne Barnard

Letter 27a

*Barlow**
Lt.-Col. John James Barlow, 61st Regt.

*navy**
William P. Smith, Naval storekeeper and Clerk of the Cheque.

This letter inspired a reply from Dundas which, has fortunately survived in a copy in the collection in the South African Library. If Lady Anne felt duly humbled by it we have no record. A missing letter dated from the Cape on 27 December 1800, may have made reference to what here follows.

LETTER 27

The text of the General Order issued by General Dundas on 10 April 1800 will be found in Theal's Records of the Cape Colony, *v.3, p.129-30, followed by the stiff exchanges of correspondence between the General and the Governor. The cause was perhaps trivial – the transfer of certain mangers from the cavalry stables at Stikland to Cape Town – but the principle, that all military orders should be given through the Major-General or his deputy, was one of the greatest importance. What might well have given Yonge further offence was the pointed mention of Lord Macartney's administration as "able, upright and prudent." The implication was clear.*

HENRY DUNDAS TO LADY ANNE BARNARD

Copy

Cheltenham,
11th Sept. 1800.

Dear Lady Ann

Within these few days I have received your letter at this Place, and as Mr Wellesley* to whom this letter is entrusted is on the Wing I have not time to trouble you long – You may believe that the Picture you give me of the Settlement where you are is to me a very unpleasant one, and a radical Cure must be immediately applied to it – What that may be I shall decide when I return to London – I cannot however allow Mr Wellesley to go without undeceiving you in some particulars, of which you are certainly inaccurately informed – I know not more precisely than you have told me the Grounds of Misunderstanding between Mr Barnard & General Dundas; for in truth the General has never in any letter public or private given the smallest Hint that such a Misunderstanding did exist, nor should I at this moment have known of it, if your Letters had not progressively put me in possession of the *Fact* that such Misunderstanding did exist – I am perfectly aware that there are irritable parts in the General's Temper, which may at time break out, but I must do Him the Justice to say that I have seen no proofs of it in any part of the public Proceedings which have come before me. With regard to the general order which he published in consequence of the strange Conduct of the Governor, and which you say might have brought an Arrest upon Him, I have only to say that the order appears to me and every Person whatever such a one as His Duty to the King's Commission which he holds rendered it necessary for Him to issue, and my only surprise is that the Proceedings which gave rise to it, and which seem still to continue, did not on his part produce something more violent. I give him great credit for his restraining Himself in the manner He did.

*Wellesley**
The Hon. Henry Wellesley (see Letter 15, note 5) private secretary to the Marquess Wellesley, left India for England on 15-8-1799 and returned thither before March 1801 (*B.N.B.*) So this was almost certainly he.

I am afraid from the Contents of your Letter that you have conceived erroniously of other parts of his Conduct – His Administration when acting as Governor has met with our perfect Approbation – Indeed it would have been impossible to have felt otherwise without giving an indirect Condemnation to the Administration which went before Him, for He has uniformly in point of economy, regularity of Accounts, and civil Government followed without a single Variation the footsteps of Lord Macartney. So much was this case, it was with bitterness of Heart Lord Macartney saw Him superceded; and often has He since urged me to offer the Government to Him again. I can give no stronger Proof of his Feelings with regard to Him; for you will not suppose Lord M. could have wished the Government & Care of his own favorite Child put into Hands not likely to continue the Administration of it with Honour & Credit – There is the thing I am surprized you should have been misinformed upon – I mean that part of your letter which supposes & indeed classes together the present & *last* Government on the question of irregularity of Accounts. Surely Mr. Barnard could have informed you that the Accounts of General Dundas down to the last Hour of his Administration have come home in the most pointed (?) and accurate form, not surpassed even by the accuracy of Lord M. Accounts.

[A Cape Coloured man]

I am ready to make every allowance for every unpleasant Circumstance you may have felt in any Communication which Mr Barnard has had with the General; but I am sure your own Candour must feel how impossible it is for me not to set you right in several material particulars in which you have been misinformed. Don't imagine however from this that in the Consideration of this unpleasant business, or in the Decision I shall form upon it I mean to act on the Principle of a *Partisan* for a near Connexion of my own – That circumstance is more likely to operate against than in favor of General Dundas; but if in a general and radical reform of the Government of the Cape, I should ultimately think it necessary to make no Exception, I can assure you that Disapprobation of any of his Conduct civil or military will not form any ingredient in the grounds of my Decision – With best respects to Mr Barnard I remain

Signed
Henry Dundas

Letter 28

A happier tone is apparent in the next letters. Even if the maddening Governor was still there, there was at least a rapprochement with the Major-General and his wife.

LADY ANNE BARNARD TO HENRY DUNDAS

Cape of Good Hope –
Vineyard June 1 – 1800

– I wrote to you so very lately my dear Friend, that is to say by Capt Smith* who saild about the 20th of last month in the Minerva that it is hardly to be supposed I can have much to say at present, however, this may arrive before him if he is detaind at St Helena & I feel so *delighted* to have a page or two with you free from any grumblings or vexation that I seize the pen with the greater Alacrity – perhaps with additional Alacrity from having had yesterday a visit that gave me satisfaction. – Mrs Dundas, not alone, but accompanied by the General. – I was happy Mr Barnard was at home; whether he came of himself or whether She brought him we shall not inquire too closely, but as I rather suspect the last, I must say, it is this trait in her conduct as yet which particularly pleases me, that I think she sways him to conciliation and right things, instead of keeping him aloof as his men friends did – this is not her character with the other party; I mean, the Government house people, but I must *Judge for myself* and I lean to the opinion of her being Temperate, civil and judicious – if she continues so I shall strongly wish to call her *Friend* instead of acquaintance, and shall be delightd if thro her means, some little faults in his temper may be wholly *smoothd over*, if not eradicated which woud be of solid use in a character which has not one mean or dishonorable point in it, tho many very *Sharp* ones impossible to avoid being hurt by. – he is really a little of a character! it is impossible he can have *wholly* forgot what has been passing between him and Mr B: but he enterd the room yesterday and conversd in common conversation with Mr B. as a man woud do, who had no notion that another had any cause to resent any part of his conduct. – I rubbd my eyes and fancied I had been asleep – however, such is the power that old impressions have over me, such the Good will I have always felt for his own sake as a Dundas & such the double, triple portion as so near a connection of yours that when I lookd at him I said to

*Smith**
Capt. K. Smith, H.E.I.C.S. *Minerva.*

The Theatre in Hottentot (now Riebeeck) Square, now St Stephen's Church. This sketch closely resembles that by Samuel Daniell in his 'African Scenery', 1804,

myself "O what a pity that you cannot be good humourd and friendly with us all without interruption, and how vexd I am that I have felt myself necessitated to Growl at you to Your Uncle without telling you I have" – if I see any thing like heartyness however continue, *tell him I will*, nothing shall keep me silent but *Fear*, and if that fear blows bye & kindness is allowd to grow again I will make a clean breast with him shake hands & begin again on a new score. – to me the Joy and comfort of Society consists in loving & being beloved by those one lives amongst whether Britons or Hottentots; I see Slights with difficulty, as I look for none; but seeing I feel, with that *deep vexation* which I am convinced drives a nail in my coffin. – such a frame of mind (when it takes place) is too painfull for me not to be ready to throw it off, & to forgive – aye – from the very bottom of my heart whenever I can find a loophole to be happy again. – & this is just the position I stand in now. – I long to read "upon my soul you are good people I believe after all" in the eyes of those abominable scarlet Coats who have so workd us, coud I find that sentence in *every pair of eyes round me* I shoud not mind staying here as much longer as you woud think for the benefit of the place, but ill us'd by the above folks for a length of time, my *heart* died within me at the prospect of remaining fixed here where it was quite Frozen & chilld up with cold looks. – Now, Ill begin again (sanguine fool that I am) to hope better things – to give all another fair trial and also (aided by Mrs Dundas if she will help me) try to cement better together the Head & shoulders of the Body Politic viz the Governor & the General, than they have been of late.

You will think I have been reading my bible lately as I perceive I am making the statue of Darius out of the component Materials here. – in that Statue the *Head* was made of *pure Gold** – I know not how far the allusion holds true with Sir George, it has been thought, *as I told* you that Gold was *in his head*, perhaps from being so long at *the Head of the Mint** – but if his head had been made of Gold, I think L^{y} Yonge woud have tried to melt it before now, in such a case the woman who adds heigth [sic] to her husbands head certainly 'exalts his horn' – when it is a golden one – but I am talking nonsense – if Mr B. & I coud get this same golden head and silver shoulders to Jar less, and *fit better*, it woud be very comfortable to us *the pedestal*, which being composed of a little of the *Inferior metals* as well as a *mixture* of the equal, is not strong enough to bear much fighting. – as yet Mr Barnard has, without appearing in it, been of some little *use*, by becalming advice when the Governors eye brow was cockd, and I woud fain hope there will be no more wranglings now, till the return of Mr Smith the Generals aid du camp with a good scold I hope to both of them – I declare I think they might be very happy here in their departments if that foolish thirst for Supremacy, & inattention to the thing below them (I talk of military matters) did not step in. –

– for the last four months as I told you, I have remaind constantly in the country "like a mouse in a mill" till the Ladys shoud get *righted* in their *Births* [sic] as they say of ships, and why not of Ladyships – but I shall shortly go to town to pay my mite to Society now that I perceive it begins to live for me. – I believe it is a pretty policy on some

*Gold**
Lady A. must have been thinking of the great statue in Nebuchadnezzar's dream interpreted by Daniel. (*Daniel* 2:31-35).

*Mint**
Sir George Yonge was Master of the Mint from July 1794 to Feb. 1799.

occasions to make oneself *scarce* – by the bye there is a new scheme with which the governor is *bit* and which (like the affair of the *Select concert*) will probably fall to the ground from its not being on a *well Judgd plan* – tis a *Theatre* – all boxes – no pit – each box to cost 24£ pr an, & to hold 6 subscribers, for 12 nights only, consequently it is on too dear a plan to suit the pockets of subalterns and yet they look for the performers from amongst *the military.* – we have a box of course, but take no subscribers, giving away our tickets as we please to our friends – 32 boxes are subscribd for, but large as this sum is for this small place it is found too little to repair an old pottery belonging to government for that purpose – which by estimate (the scale of Sir Georges ideas being always too much *en grande*) woud cost 2.500£* –

this idea of a theatre was grounded on a little piece got up by Doctor Somers physician to the army,* in the military Hospital which Hospital his wife who is a fine spoken woman will not call *Hospital* but *Sea lines* – Ill *send you a ticket* to her play.* – it was really very well however upon the whole the piece was one of Footes calld "Taste"* – the doctor himself acted Lady Bentweazle, in a very Lady Bentweazle like manner – Major Clegg was Carmine – Capt Amory the Alderman – and Col Barlow was inimitable in Puff. – I had an old shilling paris plaister horse, which acted the Equestrian Statue of *Marcus Aurelius* – the *figure only* wanting of *the Marquiss* & a large bronze venus in paper out of my stores, was dug *out of the Herculaneum* for the occasion. – the Doctor spoke an ode, rather as I thought *of* than *to* the passions, and Mrs Somoner [Somers] spoke a prologue of her own composing. – Altogether it was very good innocent fun & much more harmless than horseracing drinking or any other amusement that coud be introduced to bring people together in such a place as this. – Sir George, enchanted with the intertainment, instantly begun to invent a mode for continuing it, arranged the plan of this theatre & brought forth the bantling scheme, a *full grown arrangement.* – we all subscribed to it tho we here saw the difficultys likely to present themselves – no sooner was this first point gaind, and a prospect had of a sufficient number of Male performers, than the gentlemen actors declared half off, unless *Ladys* woud join in the cause – this idea was secretly one of Sir Georges too – and thus supported he came forwards with All his power & all his *persuasion* to prevail on *us all* to assist – Mrs Somers – a pretty Mrs Kelso* and one or two other Ladys hinted themselves ready to act – if *I* woud or if Mrs Dundas or Mrs Blake woud – the last said, she woud if I woud, (knowing that I coud not) the other said nothing; I told the Governor frankly that if he had a Theatre in *his Own house* and laid his commands on me to do any thing to prove my desire of contributing to his entertainment that I was ready, providing the part given me was sufficiently *Insignificant,* but that I had neither *Talents* nor *Memory* for more. – as to acting on any theatre where *money* was to be paid for admission or *any* theatre exept one in *His* house, I whisperd my fixd refusal – but every one is at me on the score of my being *able* to sing – *able* to act, I make no doubt that I *coud* if I were to try, But I am very sure that I *wont*, and that if I coud suppose I was to start forwards the first of actresses, it woud not make me the *less* resolved against what it is *want of sense to propose to*

*2500£**
Yonge ordered the building of the first South African theatre in what is now Riebeeck Square. It was opened after hs recall in October 1801 however. The building still stands having become a church in 1839.

Lord Wellesley wrote to Lady A. from Fort William on 2-10-1800: "... Your lofty twaddler's order in council for the arrangement of his playhouse is incomparable. If I could disclose his most secret dispatches to me, how I should amuse you!"

*army**
Dr. Edmund Somers M.D., Physician and Director of the General Hospital for the Forces. (*African Court Calendar 1801.*) Writing to Lord Wellesley on 14-9-1800 Lady A. said of him: "Tho a very good Comedian is a very bad physician from having his faculties in a total state of Inebriation every day after dinner." In the same letter she commends the Head Surgeon to the Navy, Dr. Isaac Wilson.

*play**
The ticket has survived and reads:

"Attica in Africa./ ----/ Sea Lines/ Monday Evening, 9th June, 1800, at Seven./ -----/ (*Not Transferrable.*)/ ---- [Seal] /*Lady Anne Barnard = E.S.*" The name and initials are handwritten.

me. – whether this matter will fall to the ground altogether or whether the Governor will fit up a little Theatre in his own house, (which in point of expense woud be a twopenny matter) I cant tell, if he does the last, all the ladys are ready to join me in offering to do something, to dance a cottillon [sic] between the acts, be chorus – or orange girls – or any thing to prove their good humour – but we are in great hopes that the trouble this woud give him (which he is not fond of taking exept in his *own way*) will prevent our offers from being accepted of – we have had many female recruits from the arrival of the 34 & 22^{d} Reg^{ts}, some of them acquisitions of Society – Col Dickins* was an old Westminster schoolfellow of Mr Barnards and has married a woman reckond to be well bred & pleasing but she is I believe ten years older than I am *if that is possible.* – it seems to have been the way of that *class* to marry Charmers of the *Upper forms*, however if it answers as well in her instance as in another I know of, she has no cause of regret. – I am much pleasd with the arrival of this *Colleague* in Seniority, I before stood unrivald, now, I am a chicken by comparison – they live at our house in the castle, or to speak more accurately at the House *we occupy there*, till they can fix themselves – Genl Dundas has lent the lieut governors house to Col & Mrs Hamilton & lives in town this winter, so we shall have a good female society in the Castle – there is a Col Mercer* & his wife who have been lately staying with us in the country also, her Name before Mariage was Miss *Clarinda O grady*, she is rather handsome but the *longest* woman I ever saw in all my life and wears a pair of seven leagued boots with which she steps across a room of any dimensions. her Col: is four inches taller than her they measure 12 feet seven together. – it is the fashion to laugh at Clarinda here, as uncouth and unpolishd, but Mr B. and I have an odd tendency to like her ingenuous bluntness, and if on further acquaintance it proves to be *Honest frankness* I shall prize it as a large web of a *rare* coarse stuff the pattern of which she gives one the first moment one is in her company. – she was married but a month before *she Stepd across the sea* in her boots – there are four or five other ladys, but the two I have mentiond are the principal ones. – All bring me a quantity of Fibs about you – your insisting on retiring – your peerage – your pension – . and give me many long conversations on the subject between you and his Majesty – I believe nothing I hear; exactly as I hear it, but I believe in that tiny quantity of truth which makes a *basis* of falsehood – you wont desert the house of Commons till you have made a peace or till there is one found in some degree equal to fill your place, and where is he hid at present? – every one here is full of approaching peace, I do not credit that either, I wish I did, It woud give me a delightfull vista of Hope of seeing home before I die. –

I have letters yesterday from Lord Wellesley Alias Mornington he writes in health & in spirits – says he is often prowd sometimes melancholy – that he affects to be happy but sighs for Home tho he does not conceive he has any chance of returning till every thing is fixd where he is on a firm & permanent foundation. – the large pension that I hear has been voted to him will add further Joy and astonishment to that *thunderbolt* of prosperity which has almost at once struck him,* he has a mind

*"Taste"**
Samuel Foote's play *Taste* was his earliest, first performed in 1752. A bitter satirist, his most famous play was *The Mirror* (1760). He built the Haymarket Theatre in 1767 and was known as "the English Aristophanes".

*Kelso**
Wife of Major Robert Kelso, 22nd (Cheshire) Regt.

*Dickins**
Lt.-Col. Richard Mark Dickens, 34th (Cumberland) Regt.

*Mercer**
Lt.-Col. James Mercer, 22nd Regt.

*him,**
After the conquest of Mysore and the defeat of Tippoo Sultan, the H.E.I. Co. voted Wellesley a pension of £5,000 p.a. for 20 years. The Crown honoured him with a Marquisate in the Irish peerage. This was a great disappointment to him but try as he might he could never achieve a loftier title.

to taste all his power & I really think a heart to make the best use of it – knowing him as intimately as I do, I had a great *latent wish* Rather than *a hope*, to hear of some *wee bit Title* being in his patent to gild over the disgrace of Illegitimacy to his eldest Son who I am told is *promising* & amiable to a *great degree.** – nothing short of *such a deed* as L[y] Welleslye [sic] has done, coud I dare say draw such a mark of the Royal bounty [crossed out] favour, but I declare it does not strike me as being so strong an one, as the Title given to Lady Cecil Hamilton.* – I am sorry for that poor girl – married to a different sort of man I dare say she woud have behavd better. – I hear *Margaret** is to be married to him and have wrote her a letter of *condolance* "Sister Anne, Sister Anne" woud be very sorry to see her married to such a blew beard – I must however say that if he were to propose it to her I shoud think it the wisest thing he ever did in his life for his family, and if She were to accept, I shoud think – . – She had better let it alone. –

The weather here begins to be very bad, it rains *seas*, but I wish to remain here till we can get this little place quite furnishd & comfortable in case of our remaining another season in it, which I woud fain hope woud be the extent of our stay – will it, do you think? – I suppose this will be a gay winter at the Cape – a subscription ball – a concert – besides three houses to give good things – the governors – General Dundass & ours – I tell the two ladys* that I am entitled to be lazy now that such dutys devolve more regularly on *them*, but as I before said, I shall still pay my mite to publick & private chearfulness. – I hear the governors society seems very young just now. – I fancy he takes himself for King David by his fondness for having a little girl of fourteen or fifteen on each side of him. – half a dozen of such compose the evening partys and they dance & he dances to a handorgan, the little girls laughing, (I cannot say in their Sleeves as there is nothing now but bare elbows) Col Cockburn is generally in love with from six to twelve of them at a time & as he is very inconstant the governor has a good chance of seeing all the young beautys the Cape affords at his house in a short time – he takes care however to let all understand that he *is a flirt*, & cant think of marrying without the consent of Sir George who he intends *never* to consent, so all is above board – Sir Roger Curtis has given over the chase of the fair Baumgardc [sic] * I fancy she wont like this, she never was left before for any other person, tho often when her Swains went home, but report says he has attachd himself to another frigate more to his mind & as I often see him riding at anchor, gallantly escorting on horseback a pretty married woman, we are inclind to believe it. – thus you have all my Cape news – one piece still remains, but it is no scandal – I believe you will in due course of time have a little relation in the generals family – it appears to be so, and Im glad of it – & now having finishd my 7th page –

God bless you both

Your ever Gratefull &
affect friend –
A Barnard

*degree**
Wellesley had no legitimate offspring. The eldest of his 5 children was Richard Wellesley who became an M.P. in 1810. The Marquis made every effort to obtain a title for him but without success.

*Hamilton.**
Lady Cecil Hamilton was the daughter of Canon George Hamilton, son of the 8th Earl of Abercorn. By Royal Warrant of 1789 she was given the precedency of an earl's daughter. This is described in Cokayne's *Complete Peerage*, v.1, p. 7n, as "a most unusual proceeding". She afterwards married, as his second wife, her cousin John, 9th earl of Abercorn. It is suggested that she had been his mistress and that he had persuaded Pitt to obtain the rank for her, against the King's better judgment. They were divorced in 1799, she marrying Capt. Joseph Copley.

*Margaret**
This can only be Lady A.'s widowed sister Lady Margaret Fordyce. She did not remarry until 1812. Abercorn married again in 1810.

*ladys**
Presumably Mrs. Blake and Mrs. Dundas

[*sic*] *
Baumgardt. See Letter 25, note p.213.

June 5th

No Sure! is it possible that a leave of Absence to Mr Barnard is actually sent to us by your own dear self!! this piece of news comes in two letters to me by the Triton, but it comes unsupported by any thing from yourself, from my sisters, or from our friendly peer Lord Macartney – I must not therefore quite believe in it till I see it, tho the manner in which it is mentiond carrys the face of Truth in it. – well! – (with a sigh) if it is so we will receive it by some ship not yet come in, and will thank you for it with all our Hearts and Souls – it will make our future *voluntary* residence here the more cheary and light that we may shorten it at pleasure, as *Health* or any very strong compulsatory reason may Govern – but *as things at present stand here*, neither Mr Barnard nor I shoud reckon we behaved Handsomely to *You* if we availd ourselves of it *now*. – from a *variety* of reasons, Mr Barnard has cause to suppose that he *Has* been & *May* be of use in more *respects than one*, not always perhaps to the extent he coud wish, but still to a considerable degree, composd as the government here is, at present, and ill assorted as the Jarring Individuals are to eachother, he thinks that he shoud ill repay your goodness if he permittd personal gratification to take the lead of duty; indeed the justice of his sentiments on this point silences every feeling I shoud have *even* if I saw your presumption to go home laying on the table. – "that which we *ought* not – that we woud not do" – this Is all I need say –

Nothing can exceed the satisfaction I have in one or two of my letters today, some of them are from the Norths & announce to me the approaching marriage of my brother John with Charlotte.* – I woud rather that any brother of mine had married her than any other girl in England with six times her fortune as I look on the connection with such good and pleasant people as the Norths, as containing a whole Host of Comforts & additions to our *fire side Happiness* thro life. – every thing else must sink on the comparison with this. –

June 25

More ships are come in – but no more letters for *Poor me*. – I suppose all that I am now most desirous of receiving are gone to India to be returnd to me from England about a year hence – Somebody I forget who, says "philosophy is a fine horse in the stable but apt to tire on the road" – have I not need my dear good soul of a stout palfry of that Kind at present? – but I will not repine, they'l come when we shall feel ourselves more at liberty to act upon them, mean time I hope we shall receive duplicates – by the bye Ill send you a duplicate of this letter if I can find an hour to transcribe it. – my Grumbletonians I never have sent duplicates of because if they are lost, let them go – but of this I will – write me a few lines I pray my dear friend on the receipt of it, as it is possible this leave may never reach us atall if it is gone on to India. – write them *kindly* & in charity with me pray, forgiving me for all my

*Charlotte**
Lt.-Col. the Hon. John Lindsay married Charlotte North, youngest daughter of the 2nd earl of Guilford (formerly Lord North, the prime minister) on 2-4-1800.

Impertinencys, else I shall sail home (even if you permit me to sail) in bad spirits & may perhaps jump into the sea in the blue devils –

I find I have said nothing of another gale we have had equal to that in which the Sceptre was lost, which has stranded six or seven small vessels. – our fleet is at Simons Bay so it has not received any dammage – if we have sufferd by the winds in this bay which has allways been supposed dangerous at certain seasons, at least the English skill in navigation has cause to hold up its head upon the proof of small vessels going all the year round to Bays which none before dared to enter into, and this at a loss, not much greater than what an equal number of such vessels might have sufferd in the channel. –

The first agricultural meeting took place a few days ago,* – the Governor President – the Lieut Governor vice president – Mr Barnard woud not step forward as the other vice president declining his chance of election to that *dignity* in favour of some *dutch* gentleman whose knowledge of the country – climate & usages of the farmers is better qualified to take the lead. 4,000 dollars was subscribed to the plan the first meeting – & more I believe daily comes in so the governor for once has reason to be pleased with His scheme, which to the truth is the only one which has any reference to the real improvement of the country – poor soul he seems to have proceeded hitherto in the idea that laying out its funds on superficial matters is *improving* the place. –

the 34 & 22 Regts landed with a Heavy loss of men from a fever which raged on board, it is supposed from the number of diseasd lascars employd as seamen – the Surat Castle, & Scal[e]by Castle were very well appointed as to provision but those on board the Minerva, arrived half starved – all are better now in health, but I am afraid that several five young officers have fallen under this malady – I do not say this in my letters home for fear of making relations unhappy without cause – since I begun this the *Mercers* have left us & I find he has had a slight stroke of an apoplexy, so Mr B. is gone to fetch them here again that I may nurse him up once more on his long legs –

this page is like a newspaper – N: B. the governor is resolved to have one here – if it arrives as the printing of an Almanach did in the dutch time it will be droll – the printer made a fortune of *two shillings by it* each of the 4 districts took *one* at 6 pence – all the inhabitants read or copy out of that one* –

*ago**
Officially styled the Board of Agriculture, Arts, Sciences &c.

*one**
A single leaf of the Almanack for 1796, printed by Johan Christian Ritter, South Africa's first printer, survives in the S.A. Library. It may be presumed that this was the almanack referred to by Lady A. Barrow states that its reputation sufferd from the incorrect reference to an eclipse of the moon.

Letter 29

Cape of good Hope –
Vineyard
Novr 9 – 1800

I wrote to my dear friend so very much at large about two days ago by the Schooner which carryd Capt Tucker and the addresses from this Colony to his Majesty on his providential Escape,* (which all ranks & colors here rejoyce at I believe most sincerely) that I shoud not trouble you again so soon, was it not that I daily see the great use there is in slight recapitulation of subjects, as too many of my letters have gone to the bottom or gone to france for me not to have gaind the Experience that "a Tale twice told" is not the bad thing at a distance it is by the fire side – In short hand therefore let me say that in my last I thankd you with the overflowings of a gratefull heart for the leave of Absence you had sent the Governor for Mr B: that the best testymony he can give of his value for your approbation & of his being deserving of your confidence is, that eager as we are to see home again he has declined making use of it at present, tho pressd by his Excellency to carry home the addresses, which however shewing a point of view for Mr B. to stand in (a conquerd Colony seldom being so soon a loyal one) he thought woud be a step less for the real advantage of *the place* than if he remaind here, at least till the return of Ross who knows the business of the Colony, and will carry it out (as we trust) in all respects more as it was done in *the old time* than it woud have been done had there Remaind in the Secretarys office no *check on measures* – . I very grievously feel the disappointment My dear Sisters will sustain when they learn that we cannot have a Hope of leaving this before next May or June but I fear I do not think we can so soon – as I doubt much of his being back by that time – Heaven grant he may & that I may see you all again well – mean time credit me a little & Mr B. a little for our remaining here even when His Excellency makes it *Neat* for us to go, & credit us, without allowing one single atom or alloy for any *bye view* – *motive* or *cause* for our stay beyond that of *fulfilling our duty* – advantage, have we none, or benefit thro it which we woud not *equally enjoy* in England thro your *leave of Absence* – one thing Mr B will *certainly do*, the example of which was sett by his last master, I mean Lord Macartney, & the propriety of which, in the *present administration* strikes him strongly he will request an oath to be administerd to him, by which he will declare himself never during his stay to have drawn advantage or accepted of gain – present – fee or reward beyond his Sallary from any person whatsoever or for any purpose –

we are in daily expectation of a little General from Mrs Dundas, we do not see a great deal of each other but are very well indeed when we meet, & He & We, much better than some time ago – we dined at his

*Escape**
An attempt was made on the King's life at the Drury Lane Theatre on 15-5-1800 by a madman, James Hadfield. The letter referred to has not survived.

House lately, and there were some very sulkly faces on seeing us so well together – we think that as his wifes influence increases the influence of one or two of his male friends diminishes and that the effect is good

the best piece of news which we have here at present is the taking of two frigates which are reported to have been taken off the coast of Brazil by Capt Elphinston* with two millions worth of dollars on board – the prize will be an immense one if it is what we hear – he is a fine young man and the world will rejoyce over his good furtune – there is a Capt Alexander* also who will be a Croesus thro the capture he made some time ago of Tippoos Ambassadors to the directory, tho they secreted the presents they bore, yet it seems the papers taken at Seringapatam has given such a *clue* to find them out that Lord Wellesley in his Just way had ajudged the presents to belong to Alexander, I suppose however this intelligence must have reachd England before now –

I believe it is fortunate for you that I was broke off & have not only time to seal my letter as I might have swelld it a little – I hope that some opportunity will occur soon of writing again & I still more hope that I shall hear soon from England that Ross is well & likely to keep to his first resolutions of returning by May next – there are a dozen of subjects which I will not come on atall at present but shall leave to a future day – remember Me most kindly to Lady Jane, & accept of my cordial and gratefull Blessing

Anne Barnard

*Elphinston**
Capt. the Hon. Charles Elphinstone, son of the 11th Baron Elphinstone and a nephew of Admiral Lord Keith. He later took the additional surname of Fleeming. He also rose to the rank of Admiral.

*Alexander**
Thomas Alexander. Commanding the *Braave* some months earlier he had intercepted the *Surprise*, French man of war, bound for Europe with the two ambassadors mentioned. He achieved the rank of Rear-Admiral of the Blue in 1819. (Marshal. *Royal Naval biography*.)

The months of December 1800 and January 1801 were overshadowed for the Barnards by the sickness of the Craufurd's little girl Sarah, whom Lady Anne looked upon as a grand-daughter. It was believed to be a severe attack of chicken-pox only which afflicted her but after weeks of worry and alternating hopes and fears, the little one died on January 21st. Lady Anne reported the sad event to Wellesley in a letter of that date. It is ironical that in the same letter she records that "The doctor [Somers] *? will be comforted that his bottled up disease (the fine name of which I forget, but its vulgar name is cowpox) has just arrived here in proper preservation – 6 people have been inoculated & none have since caught it."*

At last in February arrived the welcome news of Yonge's recall and Lady Anne took the first opportunity to express her approval.

Cape of good Hope –
vineyard
Feb. 16 – 1801

Thanks to some Anxious reason Lord Wellesley has for sending off a quick sailing vessel as I hear to England with orders not to be an hour beyond three days at the Cape, for the opportunity it affords of writing a few lines to my dearest friend; – on the 27th of Decr I wrote you much at large;* but an Event too important to this Colony has taken place (or at least a well authenticated report of it) for me to be silent at present. – nothing can exceed the wisdom of this recall of Sir George* – a measure infinitely Judicious by its strength and its untemporising desicion which came at once like a thunder bolt on the discontented Dutch who were begining to talk lightly of a government which had sent them such a head, and made several of them break out into a sort of astonishd gratitude & respect for the care manifested of their interests at the wide distance of 6000 miles and which had prompted at once so firm a step as the change of the governor – a change grounded on not above the 4th part of the improper things which have since taken place to have grounded a change upon. – to say the truth transported as both Mr B. & I were when the news reachd us, we were (at least *I* was) very much astonishd at the right *radical reform* which you had administerd to the evil. – Sir George has always lulld it so into my ears, that, of his being a particular favourite of the King – How much *his majesty* has

*large**
This letter has not survived.

*George**
The official notice of the recall of Sir George was dispatched in January 1801 and was only received on 19 April. Yonge announced the handing over of the Government to Major-General Dundas in a proclamation of 20 April. As late as the 16 April however he was writing to William Huskisson that he understood from a private letter – having had no official dispatch – that he was to have a successor. Col. Cockburn, a.d.c., writing to his sister Polly on 22 March, acknowledged an undated letter mentioning the appointment of Lord Glenbervie as the new Governor which had arrived on 1 Feb., though this seems remarkably quick. Doubtless it was by the same mail that the Barnard's received the intelligence however.

Writing to Wellesley on 23-4-1801, on receipt of the news of Pitt's resignation (announced on 3-2-1801 but only effected on 14-3) Lady A. said: ". . . lucky it was for him and the place I suppose, that the ship which should have arrived first did arrive first, for if it had arrived two days later very possibly Sir George might have objected to the order of a man no

Continued overleaf

made it a *point* that he shoud *accept* of this government, that I had feard such a part of this might be true as woud influence you to more consideration for *the MAN* than his conduct deserved, and I had rather expected something of a council along with him for this reason than for any other, there seems not a doubt even to my addle pate, that the present method is the best, as he woud not have submitted to collegues in judgement, but while we all rejoyce in his foolish faulty reign being over that he is succeeded by Douglas* is a matter of real gladness to the Colony, and to us such a hoard of foretasted comfort as will render the portion of time we spend here one of agrement, instead of pennance. – Somehow the High character of Douglas for wisdom has pre-establishd itself here; partly in consequence of many people on this place knowing that he was *originaly* talkd of as to succeed Lord Macartney. – had Douglas stepd into the government immediately after he quitted it, altho it might have done very well, it could not have done half so well for his interests or for his popularity as it will do *now*, Lord Macartneys strong abilitys which appeard even in common conversation & lay of course within the reach of every bodys Judgement, his agremens, and his L'Usage Du Monde were so acknowledgedly suited to his station, that few men coud have succeeded to him however able, who might not have lost on the *comparison* – but With this poor man between, who possesses nothing but civility, the bow of a long apprentiship at court and a star, Douglas will step forward like a diamond who has had at his back a foil, which had he chosen it *himself* coud not have been a better one, and there will be even a considerable advantage to the place in his being accompanied by Lady Katherine,* as every Hive is the better for a *Queen Bee*, and this place has never had a supreme one entitled to give *the Law* to female society with Judgement, Sweetness & power a[s] Katherine has, & will have, from her excellent nature & excellent temper, and good sense. – Certainly it so happens that *whoever* or *whatever* has been the worse for our poor old governor, Douglas & Lady Katherine will owe him *a vast deal* – he has been for them a most *active overseer*; – instead of finding a dirty old house with a perpendicular Stair case, up which Lord Macartney hopd, Gout and all, like a parrot to his perch, he will find, rooms well painted & prepared with paper of my Lady Yonges *own choosing*, I leave it to you to determine whether She, or Sir George has shewn most *taste* in some of the leading features of *their choice*. – an excellent Stair case the fellow of Lady Buckingham* in S[t] James Square; – instead of gardens productive only of weeds, his are now full stockd with every thing – fish ponds, made at an expense – we shant talk of that now. – but every thing which Douglas coud have *wishd for*, but woud have *grudged* to have given himself out of the *publick purse*, Sir George has provided & *nothing to pay* – at least nothing by the *new* administration, this is I think being in *luck*, nor let the great Saving of *patience* be forgotten – & of *constitution* employd in *Scolding* – & the sad employment of time in being the overseer of workmen. – all this Sir George has savd to Douglas, & if he is not gratefull to *him* I am sure he will at least be *thankfull* for the trouble he has abridgd to him – I have not a doubt that He, and She will like this place very much, they are at a time of life when they do not resign much by the pleasures of a

longer minister, if he had I suppose the general would have been violent and the military called out to act, so God knows to what lengths the matter would have gone." Since Pitt did not actually hand over the seals of office until March however, the fear may have been groundless.

*Douglas**
See Letter 2, note 2.

*Katherine**
Lady Catherine Anne, eldest daughter of Lord North and hence sister-in-law to Lady A.'s brother John. (See Letter 28, note 17.) She married Sylvester Douglas, later Lord Glenbervie, in 1789.

*Buckingham**
This comparison presents an interesting problem. The solution would seem to be that the house referred to in St. James's Square, London, was No. 33 at the corner of Charles St. on the east side of the Square. This house was built by Robert Adam in 1770-72, for the Earl of Buckinghamshire. In 1801 this was Robert Hobart, the 4th Earl, who had married Eleonor Agnes daughter of Lord Auckland. The "Great Stair" was in an almost square two-storied compartment where the stairs rose to the first floor by three flights against three walls. This part of the house was redesigned in April 1805 by Sir John Soane and the staircase moved further

Continued opposite

London life & where they taste some new ones in an african life, particularly thro the choice pleasure of finding themselves of solid use in a large society – no official accounts are as yet received from home – at first Sir George was I believe very much thunderstruck, he said next day to Mr B. that he coud not comprehend *what* part of his conduct coud have given displeasure at home; that to be sure he had no reason to believe in a report, which came *unauthenticated*, but that Lady Yonges letters gave him some cause to put faith in it, however as nothing now makes much impression on his *memory* I dare say he will soon believe he has had an ugly *dream of recall* only, he currently talkd here the other day (at a dinner to which he had in a fit of graciousness invited himself and a large party) of what he was to do *three months hence*; I hope he will not in the mean time do any thing difficult to be *undone* afterwards, some fears of this kind I fancy made Genl Dundas ask to have a conference with Mr Barnard tother day, who from *every Cause* was Happy to have it, and they there *laid their heads together* how to prevent some things from taking place which woud put Douglas to the trouble of undoing, which is better avoided. – Mr B. told the general how earnestly & reiteratedly he had argued against these and various other matters, not only by conversation but by pen and ink, perhaps in too strong a manner for civility, but not stronger than the necessity of the case demanded. – the genl: approved – I own myself very much pleased to see Mr B. standing almost the only person who has neither askd nor obtaind any favour from Sir George nay, who tho pressd and solicited to name but his wishes whether for grant or land or any thing else has never been tempted into acquiescene however glad he might have been to have obtaind such a grant from a more respected hand. – I shoud really be glad to learn for certain whether poor Sir George has actually lodged in his own pocket any of the douceurs returnd for favours conferd – by much the larger part of society here believe he has, but some are of a contrary opinion & I am apt to Class with those who think that his greedy secretary, using a female influence which it is supposed has power over him, has prevaild on him to do many things for *their* benefit which I trace to the weakness of a very old man for the person about him. – I suppose something must clear this up in the course of a little time. –

with respect to our motions, we shall not leave the Colony for some months after Douglas's arrival as our stay will not be unpleasant to ourselves, & for a time of use to them. – I trust they will come to us, till Sir George can evacuate the government house – selling off of things requires a few weeks – this over Mr B: will ask him to remain with us till he sails, poor man he is good natured tho weak & one feels a pity for those grey locks which he might have laid down with Honor & peace at the bottom of the table mountain if he had had a sett of more disinterested people about him, but those round him can make him do any thing – Ill give you a whimsical instance – a person in the corn board lately establishd here somewhat on the plan of *Josephs* in Egypt, as granarys against Scarcity – complaind sadly yesterday that Sir George orderd the board to occupy, & pay rent for the warehouses underneath the playhouse, instead of remaining in the premises they had already

back. (*Survey of London*, v.29, p.205-10, v.30, plate 186.)

The foregoing suggestion is based on the assumption that Lady A. wrote "Lady Buckingham" for "Lady Buckinghamshire" – an understandable error. It must be borne in mind however that close by on the south side of Pall Mall stood the substantial Buckingham House, rebuilt for the 1st Marquis of Buckingham by Soane in 1792-95, of which the great staircase is described as the most striking internal feature. This stair however consisted of a single central flight leading to a landing from which curved and parallel flights returned to the U-shaped landing gallery on the first floor. This however is far different from the stair installed in Government House, Cape Town, by Yonge. (*Survey of London*, v.29, p.363, v.30, plates 225-227.)

taken – altho they have remonstrated by letter, stating that they have 3000 square feet *more* in space, at 360 rix dollars *less* rent – but all his favourites & household are subscribers to this same play house, So the board is orderd to take the Store houses – N:B. we never woud subscribe to this same plan – nor has General Dundas. – The threat of the weather at present is very great, every body is annoyd by it, but me – the thermometer is 104 at Cape Town in the Shade – at our country house there is ten degrees of difference – the 61- Reg[t] or part of it embark tomorrow, the last troops that have come out have all landed much more Healthy than the former ones, probably from having excellent accomodation* – I will now release my Dearest friend with every deep & kind wish for his Health & happiness & that no ailings may destroy the fine tenor of good Health which has been habituel to him – & with kind love to Lady Jane, remain

Yours most truly
Anne Barnard

Mr B. just now shewd me a note of the governors, displeasd at his having purchased for Government a cargo of rice without his order – poor man he has given him direcutions [sic] a dozen of times to buy it – & once or twice before The Fiscal & others – I mention this as a proof how much his memory is failing him – we are all reduced to brown bread & that on allowance – the Harvest which lookd fair has faild – the crop having only one side of the ear filld – this is a sad disappointment & unexpected even to the farmers –

*accommodation**
In her letter to Wellesley of 21-1-1801, Lady A. wrote: "2 of our late Regts to be sure are but tall infants scarce old enough to carry their firelocks but the 91st is become a very steady good Regt. of late, by the Renovation of Youth which the death & discharge of most of the old men has produced."

The foregoing was the last letter from the Cape found among those in the Melville Castle collection, but this was still eleven months before Lady Anne was able to leave for home. The following five letters have been gleaned from other sources. The first, to her old admirer William Windham, Secretary at War, 1794 1801, is in the British Museum (Add. MSS. 37915/136-40).

Letter 31

LADY A.B. TO THE RT. HON. WILLIAM WINDHAM.

Cape of Good Hope –
Vineyard –
Feb 21 1801

"Rest – Rest – perturbed Spirit' * – I have heard those words applyd somehow or another before, but I forget where, or by whom – no matter – I will apply them now, it is *My* turn, & to the Secretary at War. – Rest – Rest Mr Scretary, [sic] be at ease, and fear nothing no longer expect my arrival with dread, no more feel the stings of conscience reproaching you for letters unanswerd; I am *not* on the Seas (Alas!) on my way home, on the contrary, *here* I am, and your letter of the 13th of october, last lays before me – . had You wrote to me oftener, or answerd me more regularly, you woud have given me *more* pleased moments, by those additional certaintys that I was not forgotten, but I did not think I *was*, even in your silence, and if you *had* been regular, you must have changed your *nature* & I wish to see *no more changes now*, all that you ought to have changed for, I believe you are now, & I believe every change has increased your Happiness, Your worth & Your respectability – change so far, as to be excessively good to me when I return, and pardon all the many changes which five years at the bottom of the Table mountain must have produced on a couple of poor cheeks which had never much to recommend them, exept some smiles & a certain air of Happiness which I am not sure if you ever saw much of; therefore they will not have lost so much to you as they may to some others who I cared less about then, & care less about still. – I merely write a Hurried line to you now Cher ami, to acknowledge your letter, & to put you at ease, for I have but a moment allowd me to write & seal – I never write on affairs in *Europe*, as my antidiluvian [sic] notions must be as old before they coud reach you as the notions of Methusalems wife woud be, but I must congratulate Myself *to* you, on the piece of great luck before me in the arrival of the Douglas's viz Glenburvies. [sic] – now that there is no longer any call for that *beautifull degree of prudence* I shewd, when I wrote to you last, by *underwriting* so much as I then did, what we all thought of Sir George here I may frankly say, that his recall is a very wise & an almost a *necessary* measure, poor man he *means* no harm, on the contrary he means to make this a flourishing looking place

*Spirit**
Hamlet, Act I, sc. 5.

by the same sort of method that some pretty women in bond Street &c – mean to appear rich & in good head, by taking the last guinea in the poor pocket to buy a new bonnet – with one of our last colonial guineas he has built a play house – by the bye I fib. this is a subscription, but I might have said a *suite* of *fishponds* which is fully as foolish a way of spending money within 50 yards of the sea; the botanical garden lately divided & subdivided by Myrtle hedges for the gentle choristers of the woods, is now divided & subdivided, for the gentle choristers of the waters – Frogs – for as yet there is no fish in them – & I suppose Douglas's cook if a true born briton, will make those *Sans Culottes** suffer in fricassees for their presumption. – Sir George has certainly been very volage* of the publick money, & fame has whisperd some very naughty things of him, which upon the whole I do not believe in their Haughtiest extent, as I impute most of what is unsound, to have arisen from the influence of greedy people who encircled him thinking more of what Was to procure douceurs to *themselves* than of what it was for his honour to grant. – I cannot suppose he has actually accepted of the dirty *hard thing* called money – *paper currency* you'll say may make a difference, certainly it *woud* if a bribed man was to carry off his douceur in the *new pence* you have sent out to us, which by the bye are calld *doublechees** here & go for two pence each, they are sad promoters of gaming amongst the Slaves, being a sum so suited to a Slaves fortune; to be sure they are very heavy – N. B. if you happen to have any poor protegé coming out here, you may put him on a way of making ten pounds by bringing ten pounds worth of such pence (the allowance passengers have) when they reach this they become of exactly Double their value* – but this is departing from my Subject – all sorts of people rejoyce at present over the coming of Douglas, he has a pretty character, I mean a *good* character already establishd here, from the circumstance of having been originally named as the Successor to Lord Macartney whose memory here will always have the words "Wisest, best" annexd to it; – the Hot headed General, followd by the weak headed Sir George, has so doubled the value of the wise old Lord as the *Sheep skin chiefs* called him. – the recall of Sir George has astonishd the Dutch, & impressd them with an awe & gratitude to that Government which they had begun to despise, but which now marks so much care of their welfare as to lead it to redress the instant the necessity of it is spyed, thro the long telescope of 6000 miles of mental vision, to talk in the Eastern way. – I own however that I feel a little commiseration for the poor old foolish King Lear who has permitted his Conrads & his Gonrades* to wax him out of all his Knights & out of his situation which is worse – he might have laid down his grey locks here in peace & honor free from care and gilded with supremacy which he likes, but for – those around him – that, will do without names – Douglas & L[y] Katherine will owe him the comfort of their first wintersmonth, he has made every thing so perfectly commodious for himself, sparing no expence, that had they sent him before as a *skillfull overseer* to *superintend* every thing previous to their arrival they woud not have found it half so clean or so nice – rooms were painted & paperd chimney pieces in all – new stair cases – Kitchens – Larders – poor soul! when He

*Culottes**
A French republican of the poorer class.

*volage**
Giddy or foolish. (*Fr.* Voler = to fly.)

*doublechees**
The Dutch "dubbeltje" is to-day the small silver 10c coin, the equivalent of two stuivers.

*value**
The Cape was chronically short of currency. Writing to H.D. in Jan. 1801, Yonge stated that "All the specie in this Colony consists in foreign Coin, viz. Spanish Dollars, Pagodas, Rupees and some Dutch Florins." A year earlier he had announced (Procl. 14-1-1800) that "a Copper coin, weighing one English ounce, and stamped with the profile of His Majesty on the one side and of Britannia on the other, will be issued to the Garrison at the rate of Two pence or Two stivers for each Copper, and that the same shall pass current in the Colony, and is to circulate at the aforesaid rate of two Stivers." (Theal's *Records*, v. 3, p.31.) In Jan. 1801 however he was writing that "the foregoing copper does not get much into circulation being hoarded, like all the rest of the Specie, except what is so much diminished and depreciated, as to be reduced greatly below its Denomination, and this debased Specie almost all that remains in circulation, the rest being hoard-

Continued overleaf

Gateway to a Cape Dutch homestead

vainly shewd me all tother day, I coud not Help thinking on the short livd tenure he had of them, but this he seemd to have totally *forgot*, his memory & feelings being deadend & Hunted by time – perhaps they are so often *called upon* when the man is a *minister*, that like certain Brass knockers we see in London they are worn out by the extraordinary rip raps of a high station. "Say for thou canst, what is the memory of a Secretary at War" – A very bad one, I know you will answer, for when yours was at its brightest (& brighter every memory must be in youth than in maturity) you was not contented with it – I wish my pen woud write a little more distinctly but I will not mend it, else I shall go on too long – I am very sorry to find Mrs Byng is not well – your letter leaves me in doubt – "she is (you say) at present in a situation that she likes, yet" &cc. now, what sort of situation is that? – I hope it is Not the situation Home the poet describes Lady Randolph to have approved of*

I never heard from any of the Byngs, but I wish them all truly well for all that; – you woud receive a long letter from me about the begining of last november, I know it reachd England in safety as I have had replys to others by the same envoyance – it woud please but fidget you sadly as you saw by it I had received none from you, & you woud begin calculating how soon the present incumbent now on my table woud reach me – I hope Cecy* will make it up to me in face to face kindness for her Silence to a poor absent Hottentot who merits much from her, but imputes nothing unkind to her, Bad as appearances are – I know there are spells & cantropes* cast over some things & I am more willing to blame the angels of darkness than Angels of my own Hue – but while I am now dipping my pen in ink to conclude, I have said nothing of return! – that will depend on the arrival of Douglas – of Ross the Deputy Secretary, &cc some months after Lord Glenburvies landing we shall certainly remain for our satisfaction, for his benefit in some degree too, for Mr B. certainly can be of use to him in various ways at the first setting off – & for the winding up of our own little concerns, which includes our *Venducie** of goods & chattles, our country house, which I wish we coud transport instead of selling &cc – but when I return to you all & give up my fat mutton tails & Bonti Buck* flesh for you, You must feed me, for I [?_] back to ill gotten gains & secret purse to pay for English Beef at *1-6* pr pound, which quite frightens a poor householder who has it here for 3 pence, & who consumes a sheep & half a day & a qr of a bullock! – adieu – I *will* not take another sheet

god Bless you! –

ed, or clandestinely exported, by every ship that comes here in Defiance of the Laws. The general currency is supplyd by Colonial Paper which is also bad, as to be much depreciated and daily loses its value, besides being counterfeited." (Ibid. p.392-3.)

*Gonrades**
Goneril and Regan, Lear's cruel daughters.

*of**
One of at least two Mrs. Byngs could have been referred to here, Either the Hon. Mrs Bridget Byng (d. 1823), wife of the Hon. John Byng, later 5th Viscount Torrington, author of the *Torrington diaries*, whom she married in 1769, or her daughter-in-law Elizabeth, wife of her eldest son George, afterwards 6th Viscount, married in 1793, who was one of 13 surviving children.

The allusion to "Lady Randolph's situation" is somewhat obscure but is certainly taken from John Home's poetic drama *The Tragedy of Douglas*, first performed in 1757. From this one would presume that the "situation" was motherhood, Lady Randolph being made to say that soon after her husband's death in battle "I found myself – As women wish to be who love their lords." If this is correct, the younger Mrs. Byng was clearly meant. She had lost her only son in infancy in 1796.

*Cecy**
Windham's wife, Cecilia (Forrest), younger sister of Mrs Bridget Byng.

*cantropes**
Cantrips (Scots) = witches' tricks.

*Venducie**
Vendutie = public sale.

*Buck**
Bontebok – *Damaliscus dorcas.*

Letter 32

The next two letters are the last known to have been written to Dundas from the Cape, though there must have been more. They are respectively in the Cape Archives and the Africana Museum, Johannesburg.

LADY A.B. TO HENRY DUNDAS

Cape of good Hope –
Vineyard
April – 24 – 1801

I *ought* not to write to you my Dearest of Friends by the present opportunity, as I believe it is not supposed to be a very safe one for various reasons, but the vessel may very probably reach England so long before any other one can, that I cannot resist trusting a few lines to it with all the chances against their reaching you. – they shall go for nothing with me, as I shall take the very first opportunity of writing again. – what extraordinary, & unlookd for events the last three or four days have produced! – when almost hourly expecting Lord Glenburvie [sic] (having understood that he was to sail about Christmas) some ships arrived a few days ago charged with dispatches, in which Sir George has his Majestys lease to return home & orders to resign the government into the hands of genl: Dundas till Lord Glenburvies arrival – this was complied with next day, sorely I believe to the mortification of himself & his family. – but poor foolish Man he has brought it all on himself & has no one else to blame, the day after, the General was sworn in, & mounted the throne of the Cape accordingly. – twenty four hours had not elapsed before another ship arrived which having touched at Lisbon brought newspapers later than the date of her sailing, & those newspapers brought us the unwelcome news that Mr Pitt & Yourself* had retired from the Administration. – the first being succeeded in office by Mr Addington. – a piece of news so unlookd for, so astonishing, and so melancholy – so fatal I might add to the interests of poor old England I never heard! he and you out! – "twas as the living Pulse of Life Stood Still & nature had a pause – an awfull pause, but I hope not "prophetic of her end! – Living in the country alone – this intelligence sent me without comment, Mr B in town & busied beyond the power of returning to me, I had but my own conjectures for it, and however false or unfounded I will launch them in the confidence that you will not be angry

*Yourself**
Pitt's government resigned on 14-3-1801 over the Catholic Emancipation issue which was strongly opposed by the King, and not over the question of a dubious peace with Napoleon, as Lady A. and many others it seems imagined. Pitt, Lord Grenville and Dundas (Lord Melville) resigned their offices, though Pitt agreed to support the new ministry under Addington, the former Speaker, and Dundas continued to control his department for some months. The new cabinet was very weak but lasted until April 1804 when Pitt was again called upon to form a government. The Treaty of Amiens was however effected in March 1802.

– viz that this step of Mr Pitts & of yours can only mean a *Temporary* withdrawing from publick affairs while a measure is ceded to by your party which neither he, nor you individually can approve of – a shabby – unsound – & unstable peace which administration is overborn into from publick Clamour, *Scarcity* and the accumulation of Taxes to carry on a war which John Bull is resolved to put an end to *right or wrong*. – I fear – I fear – that this time two years the peace which I conclude is thought of today will not be worth a penny – ! if this is all an Ideal situation so much the better – and if Mr Pitts retiring and your retiring is in consequence of some *less* important reason so much the better again – but I cannot help thinking that nothing short of such a motive as that of stepping back while *that* is done from *Necessity*, which it is against Your principles & his principles, and publick needs to approve of, woud make either him or you retire at this Arduous moment. – Oh who is there Capable to Manage the Huge concern of protecting the interests of the world, of the Human race & of all that is worth living for but Yourselves! I hope in God I shall hear of you both being in your places again, three months hence, if I dont, I shall press Mr B. to creep into a Hovel at the foot of some mountain, remote from French invasion, where with half a dozen Hens and one chanticleer I may eat my egg in peace, and lay my head under the sod when my time comes, unfleeced by villains, because unenvied and unthought of. – It is with no small anxiety & impatience we shall expect the next ships – not a letter accompanys these papers to any creature here, the ship bringing them (as I mentiond) from Lisbon. – I hope it will not be long before we hear the reasons assigned for the changes talkd of – many things I hear are in the papers, but on Yours & Mr Pitts all the others hinge must hinge – Amongst other conjectures which have passd across my mind, that of this place being very probably given up is one – who know[s] but it may be made a point of, & I suppose it will be granted if peace *must* be made coute que coute.* – Meantime *Here we are still*, & no endeavour shall be wanting as far as the small power Mr B. is vested with goes to carry on the Government under the direction of General Dundas according to the old system of our good old Lord, the General has seen so strong an instance in the Sir George, of the want of wisdom there is in departing from the regular rules *in All* its various Branches which he laid down, that I greatly hope he will in every point *now*, act on the same plan; Mr B. is full of Hope, it will be well worth his while to realize it. – as to the arrival now of Lord Glenburvie I protest I think he has got amongst the *Cambrian Mountains* & I do not look for him here for longer than I choose to tell you, if ever – six months hence, I think (if he comes at all) that he will find himself at the Cape, mean time I shoud not be much surprised if Sir George found his successor in town on his arrival, *He* leaves this place about ten days hence I believe in a merchant ship which carrys him to St Helena there to take his chance of getting on – his effects are to be sold next week, & all the fine furniture which was chosen with so much care will now have the chance of falling into the hands of the Vrows here. – whoever is his successor will find the Government house in most excellent repair tho I fear the Treasury not over rich. – I hear Mr Ross our undersecretary is married & very sick, so ill

*coute**
Coûte que coûte = whatever the cost.

that he is obliged to delay his return, How glad I am that amidst all these changes & dilemnas Mr B has the comfort of thinking he is doing his duty by standing to his post while his remaining can be of any solid use. – I hope that whoever comes out here & whoever possesses the power of granting leave at home will consider us, when the time comes that we think we may fairly & reasonably claim the indulgence but *three times thrice* do I hope that it may be from your hand we draw that & every other comfort which friendship can confer. – this is all I shall say now – my kind love to Lady Jane & my cordial Blessing to Yourself if a *Statesman* when we return we shall attend your levee speedily – if a Farmer at Denaira [sic] say *Come* & I think you will not be long without a visit from Gratefull hearts who must ever thank you for Solid Kindness & I believe for cordial Regards –

God Bless you –

Anne Barnard

I hear the Governor leaves the government house in a couple of days, and (foolishly enough) is to reside with Walker and Robinson, [sic] Merchants* to save whom he has made so many Stretches of power, Had his Government Sickend and died in the natural way on the arrival of Lord Glenburvie [sic] Mr Barnard and I had meant to have given him the honor of war & invited his body to remain with us after the Soul and Sinews of his greatness was gone, but this unnatural Death in some degree alters the case, we think that we coud not *now* ask him to reside in our house without appearing to favour & stand by one disapproved of at home by the higher powers, & on the worst terms with the general – on these grounds we have *not* given the invitation; – I am glad to be absolved from it, it woud have been a *tax* on me to have had him & his family for a month perhaps, but I shoud have done it from a mixture of weakness & Humanity, if there had not been a solid reason against it. –

*Merchants**
Messrs Walker and Robertson were involved in certain doubtful trading practices connived at, if not actually shared, by Yonge. Writing to Wellesley on 21-1-1801, Lady A. said:

' . . . a ship has lately been taken, trading with the spaniards, belonging to his [Yonge's] Firm, Walker & Robinson [sic] & some very naughty papers on board, settling future trading transactions – two others are on the seas engaged in the same negociations one of them the Lady Yonge, & she is supposed to be sir Georges own ship – every one is anxious to catch her Ladyship, who is off without papers of any kind being lodged in Mr. B.s office or any information that she was in existance – Mr B. was up the country when she sailed – he is pursuing the matter but cannot get a sight of any paper. Walker & Robinson [sic] say Sir George has them – Sir George that he knows nothing about any papers – mean time as all eyes are on the look out for *her* we suspect that something is fabricating in the charter party way to save her in case of her being taken."

The Lutheran Church, Strand Street

Cape of good Hope –
May 23 – 1801 –

I wrote to you my Dear Friend on the 24th of last month, but as I am not sure of the conveyance, I will send you a duplicate, and tho I pin this to my first page, it ought to be rather joind to the last, but if you have got my former letter tis only putting my duplicate in the fire. – I have reason to expect that this letter will go in the Lady Yonge, a ship which carrys home Sir George and his suite,* I believe there are many people who woud not venture to send letters by this conveyance as it is supposed our poor late Governor had an ugly trick by saying "Seal by your leave"* – if he opens this he will not be surprised that I felt a *little* fearful, if he never opens it, he will not be angry at my suggestion, as he will not know I have made it. – since I wrote the foregoing pages, I hear what constitutes a small alleviation to me for his foolish conduct about those people he has tried so much to favour, I hear their House (Wells & Co=) since bankrupt, payd the whole of Sir Georges out fitting, & that from having receivd no part back they have been distressed – it is not wonderfull therefore that he shoud have endeavourd to do all he coud for them [&] disappoint the expectations of the farmers themselves – I dined lately at the generals – all well – the boy a fine little fellow – all smooth – Mr B. dans son assiette* – business passing as at first, thro his office, all uncomfortableness of manners passd away & forgotten – as we returnd home "Ah Nanny, said Mr B. if I had always been treated by the General as I am now, I coud have done business with him, with pleasure all the days of my life" –

Amongst the various odd court martials which this place has afforded, there is one gone home or will go in the present ship which I think will have more chance of being read thro than most things of that sort are – tis A captain Towers,* married lately to a Miss Ironmonger, a pleasant well bred woman who every body pitys – I fancy he is Broke by the court martial, for "shamefull & scandalous conduct" as I hear the charge is laid, unbefitting an officer – I thought the punishment *heavier* than the offence deserved which I understood at first was selling at a profit a quantity of articles of merchandice he had brought with him, but I have since heard that there is more against him than this, – what I at present introduce the subject for, is the droll evidence which Sir George Yonge I understand has given on the subject of a Horse, which has been a beast of great note in conversation here, whether he accepted it as a present from Capt Towers, or *not*, whether it was sent him by *Government* or *not*, whether the Horse ought at this moment to belong to him – or Mr Ducat* – or who – no one can make out, but certain it is that hearing Sir George had sold the Horse for a large price, Capt Towers wished to have the Horse again to put the advantage in his own pocket,

*suite**
Yonge sought a passage by a warship but this was refused by Sir Roger Curtis and he was obliged to go by a merchant ship, in fact the *Lady Yonge*, belonging to Walker and Robertson (see Letter 32 note 3), embarking on 29-5-1801. This vessel was cited in the report of the Commissioners appointed to investigate the charges against Yonge in 1802. (Theal. *Records*, v.4, p. 272-4.) The ship was delayed some time at St. Helena where she arrived on June 16, waiting for a convoy.

*leave"**
Sir Geo. had Malvolio in mind, perhaps – "By your leave, wax!" (*Twelfth night*, II, v.)

*assiete**
Out of sorts.

*Towers**
Capt. James Towers, 8th Light Dragoons. Strangely enough he does not appear to have been cashiered, his name remaining on the Army List until 1805.

*Ducat**
See Letter 35, p.276.

& a correspondence by words & writings took place, not much to the credit of either – Sir George when he gave his evidence I think was not aware that it wd read as ugly for him as for the other – I long to see the Douglass and trust that will be soon now – I think they will be contented & Happy here after the first disappointment of finding this short of the Garden of Eden, & bare at the first Coup D'oeul – Adieu my Dearest friend I will now release you[,] accept of my kindest & cordial love & gratitude,

share it with Lady Jane &
God Bless you

Anne Barnard

I find Capt Towers is only suspended from rank and I believe pay, till the Duke of Yorkes pleasure shoud be known – I am glad of it, tho a shabby fellow, tis hard to be ruined for mere shabbyness – the horse still continues a very combustable matter in conversation according as party runs, & in that resembles the Trojan Horse – My Lady Yonge that fair Helen will be able to throw light on the beast by saying *Who* sent it to Sir George – all here believe that when Capt Towers asserts that he made it a present to him – he tells the truth tho he meant afterwards to avail himself of an Equivocal expression of his Excellencys to get back his money –

Genl Dundas & a large party of officers have just been breakfasting with us after a military manouevre – I tell them tis a very thieving manouvre to eat up my half pound of bread at a mouthfull, & scold them for not keeping each their loaf in their pocket as is the fashion here at present – however I compromised with them for nice cakes – Ham & turkey –

Letter 34

The following letter (British Museum Add. MSS. 37915/178-79), again to Windham, shows the writer in a purely personal vein.

LADY A.B. TO THE RT. HON. WILLIAM WINDHAM

Cape of good Hope
Nov 20 – 1801

Have you any creeping sort "of Feels" about you, any sensation in your Thumbs which might give you reason to think that "something evil this way comes"! – some one very glad to return I know is likely ere long to lend her course to Europe, "the days of our pilgrimage are accomplished" five long years have we been away no call of duty at present remains to keep us and many – many tyes call us back – the Captain of Hindostan offers us a passage – we accepted with joy, doubts have been thrown over her sailing but I hope they are groundless* – if so, a month hence we shall be leaving this, and after making all reasonable allowances for accidents – delay at St Helena – delay from probably being the convoy to vessels from it home I think by the end of March or first of April (an akward day too to return on) we shall be landing at Portsmouth. – I do not *think* it will be a great while before I see you! – prepare yourself to *pardon me* for [crossed out]

The devastations which five years have contrived to make even where there was little left to steal away – I am not become a *witch* because I have no broomstick but as I have before told you more than once, I am really a *very ugly old Lady*, keep this in your mind, and that I have a *right* to look ten years older, since you saw me last, while *you* have only *a right* to look *five*, as you have gone thro no change of climates: – this Stipulated for all will go well after the first halfhour when looking on each other, each reach in the pair of eyes adressd to them – what a pity that time has Not felt as kindly to you as I do! – you say you are fat, and Cecy* thin, I shall endeavour to make myself convinced of this, but "I cannot find it in the bond" – Mr Barnard too who from being younger than any of us has less right to grow old, shews his five years also, in two or three little odd ways, and has got a soupçon of the

*groundless**
The Barnards were not to sail in the *Hindostan*. See Letter 35. The Peace of Amiens altered everything. The ship, incidentally, was H.M.S. *Hindostan* (4th rate) (Capt. Samuel Mottley), not the East Indiaman of the same name.

*Cecy**
His wife Cecilia, daughter of Cmdre Arthur Forrest.

Bishop which I am rather vain of – I am certainly not ill – but yet it is right for me to return as I am not the Stout creature I was – Enough of Ego – all I shall say is, that as we are now on the verge of life – on the brow of the hill & every step on is decent, let us feel it alike our pleasure, our duty and our wisdom to lend each other the arm of friendship while decending into the vale – I am convinced that each step you take, which might have been a tottering one unsupported, that You thank Heaven which led you to ask the gentle Cecy to accompany – I was beginning a train of thinking & conversing in the above sentence which I feel woud have led me on when I ought to conclude, so I have scratchd it out and will only add my kindest love to her bad as she is, and to the Byngs & Julia* when you see them – I shall not I believe write more, as I begin to see a prospect of a pleasanter method of conversing, but many times before I see you shall I give up the point and look only for a watry grave! I am too great a coward to sail often – I have a thousand things I wish to write on, but all shall stand till we meet! god Bless you Windham – keep you – & Cecy & all those I love till I can return to the joy of cultivated Society, this, against all rule, does not improve here – but I have not time to develope the why –

Adieu – Adieu – A last adieu I hope in *writing*

Yrs ever –

AB

*Julia**
The Hon. John and Mrs. Byng (see Letter 31, note 7). Julia was presumably Juliana Forrest, elder sister of Cecilia Windham.

Donald the tailer and my Lady's greatcoat

Letter 35

For Wellesley however there was still some Cape gossip to retail. B.M. Add. MSS. 37308/354-58.)

LADY ANNE TO THE MARQUIS WELLESLEY

Cape of Good Hope
Dec 12 – 1801

I have so much to say to you my Dear Lord, that I do not believe the half of it ever will be said, but I shall begin and matters shall pop forth "as whims & fancys may govern" or as accident awakens recollection – first let me thank you for your last cordial Comfortable, charming & most respectable letter – I say respectable because it developed a sett of such beautifull, bright admirable motives for a conduct which I never mistrusted to have excellent ones for its basis (tho I did suspect them to be virtue overstraind) that I again thank you for having thought me worthy of such an explanation – I shall not *soon forget* it – with respect to the grounds on which you have acted between the army and your honorable masters, tho *many* men coud have acted differently, I do not think a right good one woud – you have owed & will owe your army much, as long as the name of Wellesley exist, & you have paid your debt to it like a Prince* – I am much rejoyced however that there is a part of the boon of your masters which having been offerd in a better form,* you have not disdaind because conscious virtue tho she lives like a cameleon upon air a long time, like a cameleon dyes at last of "*Starvation*" – I think the 3^{d} part of that which you rejected will be vastly sweeter to you in your Growling den than The whole coud have been, clogd with any objection be it ever so little, but you woud not take any boon with the soupcon of a blame – with respect to that den I protest I do not see it as impossible that you may beckon us into eer long – it will depend I suppose on how you are treated at home, and your *company* is so very *Fishy* that there is no guessing how they are to be pleased with any thing – quantitys of reports have reachd us here so very extraordinary that I shoud be ashamd to repeat them, however I believe it is better I shoud, (having said so much), as supposition is al-

*Prince**
The magnitude and able handling of military matters in India by Wellesley made him very popular with the Army but less so with the Directors of the East India Company. His conduct of political affairs, such as the deciding of the succession in certain principalities and the appointment of British Residents and the like, did not always meet with the approval of the Court of Directors who refused to sanction them, although time showed that he was acting in their interests.

*form**
Wellesley refused the offer of £100,000, made by the Government as his share of the prize money after the capture of Seringapatam.

ways ready to paint stronger than is the truth – it woud not be easy to go much beyond what we have heard, exept by guillotining your Excellency in Effigie – as by the mouth of a certain *party* here you are *posatively recalld*, as being too proud, too expensive & too successfull in all your undertakings for them to have any chance in catching you in a Hobble* – in short your conquests have been too large – your reforms too large – your schemes too large – your house too large, & your pride & presumption on all you have done much too large & therefore it must be diminishd – but I doubt if this is in their power to do – Seriously many such absurd storys have come out here from England, caught up here by a party who are not attachd to you & who Hawk about such tales in a provoking manner, thro your letter however, I see there is a *Jealousy of you* in the hearts of *Massa*, & was it not that the world woud cry out Shame upon it I think it not impossible that he woud try to *offend you in resignation* in order that a man more anxious to swell the present gains & less extensive in his hopes from the *future* might be put into your place –

I think by the color of all the late intelligence that your Egyptian speculation will have proved by this time as Successfull as your other ones, and that we Shall have driven the French out of Egypt* & I hope we shall be as prosperous in England & that Lord Neilson [sic] may have swept the Sea clean for me before I walk over the channel, I shoud be sorry to find myslf in France instead of England; but this is begining on the broad side of my story – the High Twaddler being recalld, the government for the present in the *hands of* a man whose hands are as clean as his head is Hot, there seems to be no present call for our staying longer here, the more particularly so, as Mr Bs office is (as I have mentiond to you in a former letter) so compleatly a synacure that exept to ask the general *every* day *for his commands*, & to be told he has none, I do not know that they have any further communication together, he has confirmd Mr Bs leave of absence for a *year*, which leave commences the day of our embarkation – perhaps I may have mentiond in my last that a manoeuvre was attempted to get a division of business made in the office by which Mr B woud have kickd himself Downstairs to be a Joint Secretary instead of *The* secretary, but that did not succeed & he has been displeasd ever since – skipping him more over if possible than before, lately he has made a most noted skip, marking a disrespect to him for which we are very *much obligd to him* – an order has come out from home to inquire into the conduct of Sir George Yonge – & 5 commissioners have been named by the General. Your friend *Mr Pringle* one – his private secretary Mr Barrow another – General Vandeleur – Mr Bukley* and the Fiscal* – but not my Lord & Master – we are both glad for the business is an unpleasant one & is not of a nature to be satisfactory in any way, for it will fail of coming up to the expectations Govt have from it & will not therefore be of use to either party – poor Twaddle was foolish – extravagant partial – injudicious & given to winking at the conduct of his Satelites, but I do not believe or at least I must doubt whether any gain came into his Own pocket, the quantity woud not have been worth his pocketing, and the small scale of this place & prying curiosity of its idle inhabitants woud

*Hobble**
Hobble = scrape.

*Egypt**
Wellesley sent a force under General David Baird to help Abercromby against the French in Egypt – the so-called 'Red Sea expedition'.

Bukley*
Edward Buckley, civil paymaster.

*Fiscal**
Willem Stephanus van Ryneveld.

have made it impossible to escape unknown. – the commission however pursue every opening to detection with eagerness and the General is equally keen; tother day on Mr Duckets refusing to answer a question respecting the share one of the Van Rhenins had in a certain contract (which he said was a question wholly belonging to his own private affairs) the general sent him to the Tronk an indelible stain which our free born English farmer will resent I suppose as long as he lives – he afterwards made a slight sort of excuse to the commission for refusing the question, which they were glad to accept of to let him out again* –

with respect to other points in Society the fermentation it is in here, is now become such that I coud cry if it did not go a point beyond that & make me laugh – we have had two duels – one horse whipping – a general – a major – & two captains sent to coventry by their Regts – five court martials now going on – calumnys large & little – without end – Ross's new wife an Innocent well behavd little soul has had her name brought forwards by garrison wit very unfairly – and I have been accused not only of being 'A Thief' – but of having *two sons* here – I wish I coud make them prove their words – inshort we need a sensible steady man of Dignity & good temper to put the place to rights most extremely, the General has not head to do it, and his wife who I really was much disposed to like proves to be the Queen of the tea table & that which tea infuses – I leave you to turn over in your mind what that is – but come we now to the fifth act – fame has it that a new governor is appointed for this place, & Lord *George* Seymour* is the man! first we heard Lord Robert,* but I find that contradicted & Lord George posatively rested on – it surprises me, he is not the *sort* of man I shoud have thought likely to be sent here, he is too Supine, and a bit too much of the fine gentleman, yet I think I recollect some one to have told me that he has good *dormant* abilitys which if rousd woud not be found deficient. – I knew him pretty well a great many years ago; before he was married, I fancy that matrimony has developd his character favourably – but still I do not think him the right man for this place, & wish I had either seen Lord Glenburvie here or Col Fullarton* or your brother Henry* if he woud have accepted of it – here goes another groundless report, at least I hope in god it is so – I was told tother day that he (Henry) was so ill that he was on the point of leaving Bengal – and I have also been told that Lady Anstruther was leaving it on account of her health – what you say of her *Sweetness* makes me tremble for her life as she cannot be dans son assiette if she is so – . now let us come to the agreeable – who have we to thank but *you* I am certain and Mr Wellesley for the favourable impression which our new minister has received of Mr Barnard – Lady Hardwicke mentions Lord H:* having had a conversation with him at court, of Mr Addingtons* seeking in which he expressd his Sense of respect and approbation of Mr Barnards character – I am so sure that you too are at the bottom of this, by some channel I cannot directly trace it to, that my heart overflows with gratitude to you both, for having represented in the fair colors it deserves, a mind so really worthy, a head so unostentatiously sound & a heart so sincere as his, I am so sure that I guess right that I can only say I am very *Much* pleasd & gratified & obliged to you both

*again**
William Duckitt (1768-1825), agriculturist, appointed by Henry Dundas in 1799 to introduce modern farming methods into the Cape. At this time he held the government meat contract in partnership with the brothers Jacob and Sebastian van Reenen. Charges against him were neither proved nor disproved. (See *D.S.A.B.* v.1, p.258.) He remained at the Cape during the Batavian Republic's régime.

*Seymour**
Presumably the 7th son of the 1st Marquis of Hertford. He had no special claim to fame.

*Robert**
2nd son of the Marquis of Hertford. He was M.P. and clerk of the crown, King's Bench, Ireland.

*Fullarton**
Col. William Fullerton, Colonel of 23rd Dragoons, which he himself raised. 1st Commissioner of Trinidad, 1796-1803.

*Henry**
See Letter 15, note 5, and 27, note 1.

*H:**
See Letter 2, note 4.

*Addingtons**
Henry Addington, afterwards Viscount Sidmouth (1757-1844), Speaker of the House of Commons, 1789-1801, Prime Minister, 1801-

LETTER 35

My Dear good friends & that was you to be in the inside of his thoughts I believe you woud find [Page left unfinished, doubtless due to the arrival of important news. Ed.]

Decr 15 –
Cape of good Hope
[1801]

I must pin on what ought to be the end of my letter & make it the begining – What news has reachd us yesterday! A Peace! * it cannot be a thunderbolt it was so unexpected – I know now how You will regard it, nor how it is regarded in England – *here* people think it a bad peace – but all the servants of Government *lose* by it, & that of course sways their opinions – General Dundas calls it a *shamefull peace* – Mr B. and his wife, at first thought it seemd to be a peace made at an odd time when all was going triumphantly for us, but on thinking it over cooly, we fancy it is a *necessary* one, & an *indispensable* one – Mr. B. says it is *not* disgracefull to England as she proves herself the saviour and guardian of all the European powers – but we fear much that it will not be a *Lasting* peace, but a cessation of hostilities to give the french time to thunder on us with redoubled force – nothing can be so *long*, or so *black* as the faces here – every individual loses in some way, the dejection is therefore general, the staff are in despair, Local power had swelld the importance of low and haughty Scotchmen into intemperance & despotism – all had married dutch wives thinking their greatness & situations were to last for ever, all of course feel they must switch directly back to their level with the awkward circumstance calld an uneducated wife & family – they also grieve to be sent to India which is *not in fashion* here, or Ceylon which is less so – the civil servants lose their places which is bad & all having purchased Houses & estates furnishd the houses &cc these must be sold at, I fear half their value – to return to England with a pretty claim on Government only, in their pockets – we had fortunately sold our country house – very cheap but for more than we shoud have got now, we shall lose above the half of our little remaining property from the great quantity of everything which the market will on this occasion be overstockd with – it woud have been fortunate for us if we had returnd to England when we had our leave first, but the publick Duty required Bs stay while Sir George was here, otherwise the late arrangements, particularly those under Lord Hardwicke Mr B might have crept in with a good effect – if government consider this & are kind to us, it is well – we shall not tease them about it, "a dinner of Herbs" without solicitation being sweeter than" a stalled ox with long attendance, & anxious expectation – B & I can rub thro the world without being rich as we are wealthy in a prodigeous stock of contentment, with no inconvenient vanity so if the 3500 pr an. salary is over, we shall say "for what we have receivd" &cc & live on a tiny little scale instead of a more liberal one – . unfortunately however there is an

*Peace**
The preliminaries of the Treaty of Amiens between Britain and France were signed in London on Oct. 1, 1801. Britain thereby surrendered all her conquests except Trinidad and Ceylon.

end of our going home in the Hindostan it will be sent with troops I believe – probably to Ceylon if to India[.] if you see Capt Motley he will tell you all about us,* we have not known him long, but he is a Hearty worthy man I believe, & very obliging – I am delighted in Fred; Northes* account that Ceylon is to be kept – he has been much pleased lately with approbation of his conduct from home which he had been anxious about –

the Dutch here rejoyce – because they do not see an insh before their noses. and the present pride of having the place restord. to Holland prevents them from foreseeing the future woes before them & the contributions which will be levied on them to *maintain themselves*, which they have no nothing to pay for at present – the Fiscal is in a state of great dejection he has been the uniform friend of the English & I hope our Government will do something for him – I imagine *He* looks forward to many dreadfull events here after the English abandon the place, faction, suppressed for the present amongst the Dutch will run higher than ever, & the Caffres & obnoxious party will meet with no levity – Hottentots too, half emancipated will be brought back to their former subordinacy with great difficulty – I expect that this country will get into a desperate State when we evacuate the place & in particular I fear my poor Hottentot friends will cease to be treated as human creatures but be shot as in former times like beasts of prey till they are perhaps extirpated – there is the same insurrections going on as before up the country – more troops have been sent, as there has been no proper regulation or mild firmness in any of the measures, or consistence. of course things must get into disorder – I presume the troops will remain there till the arrival of the new people, we may expect to see the Dutch flag flying I suppose in a month, I shall be glad to be here when the governor arrives & when the port is open to all nations* – I have seen different changes here & I shoud like to be witness to this greatest of all, & to see the panorama of this new Drama where persons – politics – manners will all be different from what has before appeard on the Stage

– the Crawfords are in the country – the child has been sick but is better, he has had a fall from his horse but has got well – she is to lay in a couple of months hence – what the destination or fate is to be of the Regt we know not – no one knows any thing – the frigate w^{c} brought the news came off in haste & was but two months on its passage – I wish they may go on to India – you will be glad to see them – but how much longer will you be there? not above a year now I hope – pray when you return do not leave behind you any part of that regard which I am most Happy to think you feel for us, the older one grows the more dearly precious the affections become, to bestow them unboundedly where one is sure they are well placed & to cultivate them carefully in those who are estimable & return them I call *wisdom* – feeling as I do to you & to Henry I cannot be without my value to you, & hope my time will come when we may have the benefit of a share in your society – *B.* is to write to *him* – my next shall be to him pray tell him so with thanks for his last letter & the assurance that he shall have the Humours of the Cape eer [sic] long in its new State & both of you shall have volumes when we reach England – I have not patience to begin on matters at

*us**
See Letter 34.

*Northes**
Hon. Frederick North, afterwards 5th Earl of Guilford, was Governor of Ceylon, 1798-1805.

*nations**
The Cape was handed over to the authorities of the Batavian Republic only on February 21, 1803.

home – I hear the Hardwicks please in Ireland – I also hear that L[y] Clare has made some attempts to introduce friends that are not likely to be welcomed at the castle – Lady *Westmeath* (married to Bradshaw) being residing with L[y] C; left her card for Lady Hardwicke who *returnd it** – I did not believe this, but the letter from Ireland was red [sic] to me; I think I shoud have never invited her but not taken so strong a measure as *returning* the card – however it was thought *right* it seems. I fear it will make some bitter enemys, but perhaps there is no avoiding that, do what one can – God Bless you both – I know not if I have mentiond in my letter that there is a rumour here of the Queen of the winds* being on her way home for her health! I hope it is not true –

ever Yours truly –
Anne Barnard

*it**
Lady Clare was the wife of John Fitzgibbon, 1st Earl of Clare (d.1802), and Lord Chancellor of Ireland. He was most unpopular in some quarters in that country. The social inacceptability of Lady Westmeath (née Marianne Jeffreys) who was his niece, however, would have stemmed from the fact that she was the divorced wife of George Nugent, 7th Earl of Westmeath. She had married the Hon. Augustus Cavendish-Bradshaw a month after the dissolution of her first marriage in 1796, so to style her 'Lady Westmeath' was unnecessary courtesy.

The above letter was written from the Cape eight weeks before Lady Anne sailed for home in the Scarborough *(Capt. J. Scott), a ship of 418 tons, on 9th January 1802,* reaching Gravesend on 11th April. Sad to relate, she was alone, as it had been decided that since the Cape was to be ceded to the Dutch in the terms of the Peace of Amiens, Andrew Barnard should stay behind and see the government satisfactorily handed over. This was a lengthy, drawn-out operation, and only on 19th February 1803 did Acting Governor Francis Dundas receive official orders from London to hand over authority to the Commissioner-General de Mist of the Batavian Republic. This took effect on 21st February and on the 1st March Lt.-General J.W. Janssens was installed as Governor.*

*1802**
*(*Lady A. to Lord Macartney, 27-12-1801.)*

*winds**
? Lady Anstruther. See Letter 17.

"Johnson's bay about 20 miles distant from Cape Town". [unidentified]

Letter 36

Thereafter for a short term our scene moves once more to Dublin. Soon after Andrew Barnard returned home, he and Lady Anne set out for Ireland that he might visit his elderly father and she her sister Elizabeth, wife of the Earl of Hardwicke, Lord Lieutenant. Bishop Barnard had seriously upset his family by his announced intention of taking as his second wife Jane, daughter of John Ross-Lewin of Fort Fergus, a young woman only 25 years old.

The state of Ireland was still unsettled. After the quelling of the rebellion of 1798, Pitt had given fresh hope to the Catholics by promising them political emancipation on the establishment of Union with Britain. The Union of the Parliaments indeed came into existence in January 1801 but Pitt had not reckoned on the King's almost fanatical anti-Catholicism which caused the former's resignation and the Irish Catholics' frustration at a further postponement of emancipation.

When the Barnards arrived in Dublin at the beginning of August 1803 a fresh, though long planned, insurrection had broken out only a week before which cost a number of lives, even if it only lasted a few hours on a summer evening. The leader, young Robert Emmet, son of Dr. Robert Emmet, physician to the Viceroy, was caught and imprisoned two days later. For much of the information supplied in the annotation to the following letters, we are indebted to Michael Macdonach's The Viceroy's post-bag; correspondence hitherto unpublished of the Earl of Hardwicke, 1st Lord Lieutenant of Ireland after the Union. *(London, J. Murray, 1904.)*

Dublin –
Castle –
August 10th 1803

This is by no means the first letter which I have wrote to my Dear friend, & permit me to say to my two Dear friends, for I hope it is to both, since my arrival here, which was on Sunday a week – viz nine days ago – . I have filld pages on pages with accounts, opinions such as a *woman* forms – and details of all sorts which when finishd I have found sometimes eroneous – sometimes beneath sometimes above the truth, till vexd & allarmd at myself for being on the verge of sending off what from my residence at the Castle might acquire an importance which otherwise it woud not merit, I have been silenced by listening to the blame which has fallen on such as have filld the English papers with rumours without probing their truth to the bottom before they sent them off for *gospel* – so much as an excuse for my silence to my Dear friend, to whom I have so constantly been in the habit of expressing my thoughts unreservedly, on entering this disturbed country – now that the appearance of quiet gives me a right to talk of the past *effort* as over, I will no longer check my pen but tell you how matters stand, as far as I can Judge of them in a general way, without attempting details on which I get too much *variety of statement* to be able to form a true Judgement – tho the English papers I hear are full of riots &c in the distant countrys the Truth is, that since the night of the Tumult & murders, which I think was on the 23^{d},* there has been no risings of the people, appearances here are at a distance to cause any fresh allarm to signify! – it is however allowd by all voices, that it is eminently necessary to keep a vigilant watch – as the snake (tho it has had a knock on the head at present, & is awed from rising) lays still conceald in the grass, ready to bite whenever the occasion seems favourable, and that time I suppose will be on the first appearance of invasion – I heard a wise man say that he thought it not unlikely that before any invasion took place the french who are assuredly at the bottom of this woud insist on another attempt being made to try what they had to depend on – but I do not agree in this – however that may be, This country has lost in Lord Kilwarden* an honest man who has served it more esentially by his *death* than he coud have done by his life, by proving the necessity in time, of stronger powers being given to the government here incase of exigence & by uniting every one in the Sense of danger & in preparations to face it. – the spirit of Loyalty (coud one fully put faith in it) seems to be gaining with the call for it – 50,000 yeomanry are armd, beside the 10,000 army of reserve, & the distant countrys assert there [is] as great a number of volunteers ready as the government please to have – Lord Roden* was here yesterday, he had rode without a servant thro several countrys without allarm & said they all appeard busy & industrious – but as I said before, there is policy in rebellion *appearing* to be intirely gulld, whether there is Truth in it or not – every day brings in some prisoner who has been endeavoring to escape out of the country and who is guarded by dragoons, I fancy there is a great deal of evidence collected, it is painfull to see the post chaise which contains them enter the Castle & take them to the place from which perhaps they may never return, a Catholick may be very wrong yet excuseable from his religion & the instigation of his priest but I feel no lenity for a protestant Rebel – this leads me to think of a reply made tother day by a Catholick whose papers had been examined, but nothing found against him – "after all, said the gentleman who fell into conversation afterwards with him, You Catholicks have been at the bottom of all this" – "No replyd the other, if the Catholicks had, it woud not have been conducted in this bungled manner, but Ill tell you who has been at the bottom of it, your own administration, you have bribed a sett of

*23^{d},**
This is correct. The revolt, to establish an Irish Republic, under the leadership of Robert Emmet, was planned for that night with the intent of seizing the Castle and the Arsenal. Emmet must have realised that there was little chance of success without outside help.

*Kilwarden**
Arthur Wolfe, 1st Viscount Kilwarden (1739-1803), Chief Justice of the King's Bench (Ireland) from 1798. According to the *Annual Register* for 1803, he had lived in constant fear for his life since the rebellion of 1798. He was butchered by the rioters in Thomas St., Dublin, through which he was passing with his daughter and a nephew. The former only was spared. It is said that Kilwarden was mistaken for Lord Carleton, Lord Chief Justice, a much harsher judge.

*Roden**
Robert Jocelyn, 2nd Earl of Roden (1756-1820).

poor fellows with 200,000 to make a rebellion of it to accomplish certain points & you have succeeded in all your views from it" – the real matter I *fancy* (for no one I see knows exactly) was that part of the rebels from the country who had arrived to join those in town, had got drunk after their journey, and some difference of opinion in the method of proceeding amongst their leaders had encouraged some of them to attack, considerably before the hour that was appointed – all turnd out, tho melancholy – fortunate – the murder of Lord Kilwarden & his nephew which arose from no grudge at *him* but merely because he was the first *Lord* who came in their way, diverted their purpose from the castle, which carried, things might have ended more fatally and had they proceeded to the phoenix park* what a collection of Hostages might they not have possessd themselves of, I dare say to get as many as possible will be the future plan – tis B: Ps* & I dare say will be adopted here – mean time there is no timidity in the castle, all are well & now in good spirits – I plainly see that Lord & Ly H: and their family round them, will remain here at their post whatever the situation of the country is – both are firm minded people with a strong sense of Duty & tho she has sometimes the nervous fears of a woman, she has a virtuous courage about her which is stronger than fear – I was so allarmed for her situation, that of the girls & my poor Margarets* that terrified as I was by finding the whole statement of facts at Holyhead & many letters advising me against crossing, that I determined to go, to try to get them away if the rebellion continued, which I supposed was the case or at least to embrace them once more which I had not done since my return from the Cape & then to leave them if they were determind to remain – the event rewarded us for tho it is rather an *anxious* visit for the *future*, there is no cause for *present* fear – Lady Hardwicks seems to think they are in less Danger surrounded by their guards than all of us are in England, an Enemy so near our coast & no guards, but *I do not* quite agree with her there – John & Saundie are more loyal & less savage than Paddy,* when fully allarmed for *their own*, the two first will guard it like Bulldogs, but the moment of danger is the moment I fear when Paddy will think he has the best chance to get *back his own* which usurpers are withholding from him, Heaven preserve us all my dear friends to meet in quieter times, in peace & happiness – mean time I woud fain hope to see you ere long if nothing cross happens to prevent it – we shall certainly go to Scotland, as I shall not be happy till I have paid my visit to my mother – from thence I shall write to you if not before, in case there is any thing worth communicating to you from hence – Rumour has said & I fancy not without foundation that Before the late Tumults Lord C – s* had offerd his services as Commander in chief here – I shoud not be surprised to see him here still – the present good man I fancy is excellent in all his meanings, but I doubt if his State of Health renders him equal to the present exigence – where the nerves have been shaken, decision & L'esprit de L'Apropos is not to be expected; amongst all your various powers, that is one I have heard you eminently extolld for, that while other men take *time* to *consider* what is best to be done, *Action* with you follows the flash of *decision* – by what I learn from the military who take the liberty of talking a good

*Park**
The great park on the west of Dublin, the largest in Europe. It contained also the viceregal lodge, now the President's residence.

*B:Ps**
i.e. 'Bona Parte's' (Napoleon's). He was believed to have promised the revolutionaries assistance by an invasion.

*Margarets**
The Hardwicke's had four daughters, all of whom married well.

*Paddy**
i.e. the Englishman and the Scotsman compared with the Irishman.

*C–s**
Gen. Charles Marquis Cornwallis. He had been Lord Lieutenant and c. in c. of Ireland in 1799 and was now Constable of the Tower of London.

deal on the present subject, *that* is not the case with respect to the commander in chief, who certainly *Had* intelligence given him by Lord H: in ample time to have prevented the mischief which took place – *perhaps all is for the best*, and that had the attempt which was made, been *prevented*, it woud only have pospond [sic] it to a moment when it might have ended more fatally, another view is, that many people woud *then* have doubted the existence of that generally rebellious spirit amongst the lower classess which it is so necessary to be impressd with, in the highest degree – I find Lord H: has been much blamed for want of intelligence & vigilance – to *You* My Dearest friend I shall express myself perfectly unreservedly and perfectly ingenuously: – secretly as the plans of the rebels are *now conducted*, (by french policy it is supposed) he certainly *had* intelligence of what was going on, & re-iteratedly so – he certainly has for three months been pressing for some further powers *in case of Exigence* – he certainly has been vigilant in *keeping his eye* on *suspected persons*, & keeping also *Emissarys* to mix in the councils of the disaffected & to gain him *intelligence*, but while he has done *all the right things*, I rather think that both he & my sister have been more convinced of the Loyalty of the Country than the experience *of others* have justified, perhaps the testimonys of publick affection to *themselves* have renderd them less believing in the rebellious discontents at other things – with respect to want of *vigilance* & *readyness* on the day of the tumult, he sent for General Fox* before dinner & in a well explaind conversation, laid open the plans of the rebels & his reasons for believing in them, that he fully expected the attempt to be made *that evening*, and entreated him not to let a moment elapse in having the troops in a state of readyness – the other left him possessd of the facts, to provide for what was expected – went home – sent for the commanding officer at the barracks (Sir Ch. Asgill)* desired him to have the men prepared, & to *wait there* till he joined him *in person* – seemd bewilderd & lost – the other went – remaind there half an hour – an hour – two hours – three hours – no General Fox – no orders – in the mean time people had persuaded the general that it was unfitting for the commander of the troops to go in person on such an occasion, & perhaps it might, but he had totally forgot that he had *tyed up* Sir Ch: A^{s} hands from *stirring till* he came – at last the time growing dreadfully critical, & no reply being sent to Sir Ch: when He sent to know what was become of the commander in chief, *without orders* he sent a party of men which in reality was the saving of the Castle which but for the interruption which the murder of Lord K:, made to the attempt, woud have *probably* been *surprised*, nor woud the unprovided state of the men afforded the proper resistance – I know not who is in the ordinance nor do I know (as I have not askd) whether it is under the commander in chief or is a third department – I only narrate the *facts* as I hear them & leave you to judge of them in your mind, I fancy that after Lord H: had had the conference with G. Fox & the others necessary to be consulted with, he did not conceive they coud be so tardy in doing their business, & being at the phoenix park perhaps it fell less within his knowledge that it was *not done*, but too surely it was not, & that genl Fox had certainly lost his powers of decision altogether – to

*Fox**
General Henry Edward Fox (1755-1811), son of the first Baron Holland, c. in c. Ireland, 1803.

*Asgill**
Major-Gen. Sir Charles Asgill, bt. (1763? -1823), c.o. of the garrison in Dublin.

blame the poor man ill – languid – one day confined & another day not, is not possible but one may pity him, and think him really not fitted to his present situation – I find however that under the general word, *Government*, Lord H: has been much disapproved of, which to those who do not know the circumstances is not unnatural, blame must have reached the Higher powers in no inconsiderable degree, as there came yesterday a message from the King, thro Charles Yorke,* expressing his disapprobation of the idle reports which had been spread & *his* "perfect reliance on the vigilance of His government" – You see my Dearest friend how impossible it is for me to write to you without expressing myself under the confidence of friendship & this necessarily leads into the details I had forsworn in the *first page*, for fear of being wrong in any statemet, & even on the spot it is not easy to be *accurately right* amidst the variety of repetition – but at present I believe all I am telling you is *as true* as I am sure it is *safe* in your hands you will naturally be curious to know the carte du pays, & you have it –

This letter has remained in my possession for two or three days I was uncertain whether to send it by London or Scotland – a mail coach was fire at two nights ago which was going to Limerick & the guard much wounded: – Mr B: my Lord & Master is returnd from thence he has spent four or five days there, in endeavouring to get his father disuaded from the very idle plan of marrying a girl of 25 at the age of 76 – if she had good character & a fair sett of tolerable connections neither his son or I woud oppose, every man however late in life is justified for trying to improve his Happiness by honorable means, but this is a most dishonourable & uncreditable step – Mr B who is the best son in the world professd himself ready to give up part or All of his expectations from the Bishop of what is *unsettled*, if by *money* she coud be induced to give up a scheme which coud be from interest only, but she prefers being the Bishops widow with a patchd character to being a miss without any patch, & as she has convincd the poor old bishop that she is dying for love of him, he is resolved not to let her die – one cannot do more – so one must banish the idea & the sorrow if possible – we dined at the Chancellor's* yesterday – the only place we shall dine at while here, as I wish to spend all my time with my sisters – *He* has made a *steady* choice & both man & wife seem the Happier for each other – Lord Hardwicke & all the masculine part dine tomorrow at genl Fox they are on perfect good terms – I have never heard *him* say a word of what I have mentiond to you as such subjects are *never* agitated by him, or *before* him, but they are not the less founded in the fact for that – I have said nothing of the extreme eagerness all over the country amongst the gentlemen of it to have the trials over & the punishments take place, they do not conceive how the powers now sent, apply to the future, & that the past enormitys must be judged by the old rules; – but the assizes being nearly over this will not be long delayd – I hope to be gone before this begins – I do not like the feelings which this must produce, & feel that perfect want of confidence in the country, which neither makes me happy in it; nor happy to leave those I loved behind in it – but I assure you *tho* I am here I am by much the greatest coward of the three sisters – L[y] H: separates; she says she is a Cheafull vigi-

*Yorke**
The Rt. Hon. Charles Yorke (1764-1834), Lord Hardwicke's half-brother. Secretary at War in Addington's Cabinet, 1801-Aug. 1803, then Home Secretary, 1803-4.

*Chancellor's**
Sir John Mitford, 1st Baron Redesdale, was appointed Lord Chancellor of Ireland on the death of the Earl of Clare in Jan. 1802, an office he held until 1806. Though a very able man he was strongly anti-Catholic.

lant – brave coward[.] that Margaret is Heroick – & that I am a resignd, desponding coward; – but I think if I had not a little bit of firmness as well as a great bit of affection I woud not be here *now* for I shoud "have turnd my back front my Jewel" & gone off to Scotland from Holyhead – if your daughter Mrs Strange* is with you, my kind love to her – tell Lady Melville I do not write to her, because I *do* when writing to you – *read me* – *Burn me* – & give me a few kind thoughts till we meet – I believe I have said the same things over & over, but my letter has been wrote with many interruptions at Different times & as I shall may be burn it if I read it over, as unworthy of your acceptance I believe it is safer *not* to read it, But to say at once God Bless & preserve you

ev^{r} Yours –
AB

August 14th

I am this moment returnd from an inspection of the Yeomanry corps by Genl. Fox which took place in Stephens Colledge green* this day after church – when L^{y} H. went to see the corps she did not apprehend the enormous crowd that was assembled for the sight – every window of every house was filld as full as it coud hold & every street was lined three & four deep thro which we happend to pass – the Lord Lieut^{s} carriages of which there were three with a large retinue of servants aid du camps &cc were admitted only – the yeomanry cavalry were all drawn up in the green – the different corps headed by their officers – while the infantry surrounded the place but in the outside of the Hedge w^{c} was a pity – the quantity of people was great even in the inside of the green, & the scene altogether was awefull & affecting to a great degree, considering that it was not troops collected from all parts of the country – bound by one sentiment & one tye to face the common Enemy – but troops, men of this country, enrolling themselves to deffend us from themselves perhaps – nor was one certain whether the scarlet cloath [sic] coverd the Heart of friend or foe – the Statue of King William on horseback with his arm extended was along with its Massive pedestal all hung round with groupes of black guards who were eager by being raised to see the sight, & the attitude of King William pointing his finger to the dangerous mob which encircled him was very striking – One back guard [sic] more daring than the rest mounted the horse & got before the King putting his own hat on his head & runing to take the reins into his own hands – I shoud have liked to have known the name of the fellow who clamberd so high for an eminence which being attended by ridicule I thought markd the seditious spirit of the rider who had he simply wanted to *see* might have rode *behind* his Majesty instead of *before* – My sisters however told me that the lower ranks of people had *pleasanter countinances* than the last time they had seen a crowd assembled when they wore an air of Malignity & *mock civility* – L^{y} H: says whenever an Irishman seems *curious* all is right –

*Strange**
Dundas's second daughter Anne, the widowed Mrs. Drummond, married James Strange. See Letter 21, note p.183.

*green**
Lady A. seems to have confused College Green and St. Stephen's Green. The former, adjoining Trinity College, is only about 200 yds long while the latter ½ mile southward, is twice the size, and from the description of the scene more likely to have been the one used in this case.

when he is thinking of mischief he disdains to even look at the object of his displeasure – genl Fox walkd round the line – people thought he shoud have rode – but the poor soul *coud not* ride having had *entre nous* a boil, which has confined him to his room for a day or two – I was glad to see about 5 or 6000 men in the service of Government who had not been embodied above a fortnight or thereabouts so well appointed – well sett up & military in appearance – this is but an *inspection* – Lord Hardwicke will probably review them soon in the phoenix park – Adieu once more if I put this in a cover it will be too thick, so I will sacrifice my respect in appearance to finish & send off as it is – adieu –

truly yours

Turkeys going to Cape Town

Letter 37

Dublin Castle –
Sepr 9th [1803]

I am *ashamed* to send you this *stupid – ill wrote hurried* letter; but if I try to correct it I shall burn it – I believe it also repeats many *things* I may have said before –

Sepr 10 –

As I think that (retired as you are, amongst your own mountains, surrounded by your own friends – your own faithfull Highlanders, eating your own mutton & drinking your own ale) you will not be sorry to know what is going on in this agitated country separated from our *native* land by so little, I take up my pen to give my two Dear friends a little of such Irish news as is on the cards at present – & I will begin first with what is in some degree the *continuation* of what went before – you have probably heard before this time that we are to have a new commander in chief here; it has been notified to Genl: Fox that he is to return, but tho his successor is not yet *officialy* named it is now pretty generally believed to be Lord Cathcart* – Genl Fox I fancy is not sorry to leave this – he says he did not wish to come, that his health was infirm that he wishd for quiet "I did not think it woud *do*, said he, & – it has *not done*" – I am not sure of that, what he left *undone* has thro its error produced very benificial consequences I shoud suppose, as the Calamity seems to have Electrified Ireland very thoroughly & given an additional shock by the grasp to England, so if Fabius* conquerd by delay, the delay of Genl Fox in his operations on the 23^{d} may be said to have done the same, as it has conquered much drowsy napping, by proving how necessary it is for the *loyal part* of the two countrys to awaken & *arm.* – the report of Lord Cornwallis's coming here was one which gained great credit – I fancy he woud have been eminently *desirable to Lord H:* who feels most sensibly his very Handsome conduct to him, but it appears to be no longer on the cards, & I fancy this arises from some fear that – but you are so much better qualified to make your own *just conjecture* than I am authorised to trouble you with my *silly ones*, that I shall only give you the *facts* talkd of *here* as far as I know them – I have heard the point of Lord Cornwallis coming or *not* coming here, a good deal discussd amongst the *uninformd*; many people thought he was the *very best man* that coud be sent, others thought him rather too unpopular amongst the Yeomanry to be a fit one, one sett of men mantaind [sic] that his noble name – abilitys –

*Cathcart**
William, 10th Baron, afterwards 1st Earl of Cathcart (1755-1843). Lieutenant-general. He was C. in C. of the forces in Ireland, 1803-05. His 3rd son, Sir George, was Governor of the Cape, 1852-53.

*Fabius**
Quintus Fabius Maximus, Roman general and consul, known as "cunctator" or "delayer".

knowledge of the country together with the position he was placed in as an apology for some things which might have renderd him unpopular to them when here last, woud in a *weeks time* conquer *every objection* and make him find all smooth – another sett said – that if there shoud be any rub, any thing to turn out ill, woud it not be a great *responsibility* on the shoulders of administration & one which might render it eligible to have a new person to fill this station, against whom no prejudice coud be intertaind – such were the battlings of private conversation in private societys, Lord H: certainly woud have been *happy* to have had him here – but it appears that the NO – S have carried it – & it, as I before said, seems generally believed that our Cousin Lord Cathcart is to be the man – . pray Heaven he may prove in All respects as equal to the Exigence of the times as our hearts can wish – he is talkd of here as active – intelligent spirited – & not unexperienced, I am sure he will find in Lord H: a man eager to be on the very best terms with him & to act with Unison & friendship – I hope Lady Cathcart* will come also she is amiable & sensible I believe & Lady H: is very partial to her – as yet nothing is known here officially – but I suppose it will end so – I hope his Journey (if he comes) will not be long delayd for shortly his presence here will come to be very material as the *nights begin to lengthen.* – As he is I believe a good deal of the martinet he will find some little attention to the *Toylette* of the military necessary, Fox used to be so too I believe, but he has strangely dropd that system, encouraging the wearing of plain cloaths &cc – I can give you no stronger instance of the want of military appearance in himself, than his finding fault with not having been properly salueted one morning, when riding past, the fact was, he was in a brown frock, a round Hat, & was mounted on a Pye balld mule, so no one observd him till he was past. – Honest good humoured man, I hope he will be restored to Health soon when he finds peace & time to attend to it, as yet he cannot mount a horse; I mean since his last illness here –

Lord Hardwicke reviewd the different corps two days ago – above 5,000 in the phoenix park – they made a very respectable appearance – the commanding officers all dined here after in S[t] patricks Hall w[c] (together with the good dinner & sumptuous service of plate) made another very good appearance of a different sort – the trials & executions of those of the poor faulty & deluded wretches, whose guilt *cannot* admit of *doubt*, are now taking place, several have been Hanged in the eye of a great concourse of people who have *shewn* no disposition to question or to rescue – there is however in spite of oneself many circumstances which daily take place while such solemn scenes are going forwards to freeze the blood & sometimes to awaken pity for Youth & talents so perverted! – yet when one recollects *what* the *aim* of the rebel one was pitying went to, it stops it short, or *ought* to stop it. – a young man of the name of Redman* was one of the rebels first taken, he was good looking – clever – & has some property – he was agonised with despair at his condemnation, & offerd to give evidence of all his [sic] knew if his life might be spared – & if he had *first* leave to see a still more noted rebel of the name of Emmet, who had been taken after him – this was refused – Government already knowing all he coud

*Cathcart**
Elizabeth, daughter of Andrew Elliot, Governor of New York.

*Redman**
Denis Lambert Redmond, a coal factor and rebel leader.

tell; & His consequence with his party renderd it necessary for him to suffer by the laws of his country, as it was in *his* House the artfully conceald pikes were found – on the morning of his execution he left his council at breakfast – retired to his room & shot himself but 4 balls faild of their effect, they were flattend on the skull which was fractured but not so as to preclude recovery – he had wrote one Haughty letter which breathd the words of Pierre "I have deceived the Senate" & another to a young woman to whom he was attachd but whose mother had objected to his marrying* – we suspect that it was an idea of preserving his property to his family which made him take this step – & setting aside Religion, the motive partook of virtue – but his recovery subjects him to all he feard, for whenever he is well the poor wretch will atone for his crimes at the gallows – when talking incoherently he exclaimed O Emmet – Emmet to what have you not brought me! – Emmet is the son of a physician & is also clever, I believe I mentiond him in my last – & also the reply of the young woman who was taken at the same time with him & who wore green ribbonds in her Hat,* the rebellious color – if I told you of it before, skip this over – it certainly had point in it, – the point of the *pike* you will say – "why said my informer does so pretty a woman as you bear this badge of sedition?" – She coldly answerd "you cant help the color Sir do what you will, it *grows every day.*" – the life of Emmet will also be a short one – he is to be tryd next wednesday – but the most important person of all was taken yesterday the famous general Russell* on whose head one 1000£ reward was placed – there remains now but one leader of any consequence that is not taken – I *fancy* it will appear that the rebellion has rather been a conspiracy than a rebellion as it does not appear to be so *extensive* a matter as was at first supposed by the world, I am glad to find that the blame which was at first very generally thrown on Lord Hard: for supposed want of information, vigilance, & for an improper degree of *Security* is now applied where it is more due, I have not till *lately* had the *means* of knowing how *very compleatly* he was informd of every thing, nor did I till lately know that it was absolutely owing to the under secretary of State the guards were doubled on finding the commander in chief had given no orders, perhaps I shoud not repeat this as he had no *right* may be to take that precaution where he took it, but it was a lucky one –

I think we shall leave this for certain the middle of next week, but we shall spend a week at my Brother Balcarres house in Lancashire* before we go on to Scotland – he has been here the last ten days & left us last wednesday – I must now conclude else I shall lose the post & there is none tomorrow –

evr Yours affectionately
A Barnard

*marrying**
Sarah Curran, daughter of John Philpot Curran, Master of the Rolls of Ireland, who disowned her. She and Emmet were said to be betrothed. She married Capt. Henry Sturgeon not long afterwards however.

*Hat**
Presumably Anne Devlin, faithful servant girl who refused to divulge Emmet's whereabouts. She was eventually released.

*Russell**
Capt. Thomas Russell, Emmet's chief lieutenant, who styled himself "General of the Northern District". He was caught hiding in a house in Parliament St., Dublin, where he had come in the hope of rescuing Emmet. He was executed at Downpatrick.

*Lancashire**
Haigh Hall, Wigan.

Letter 38

Dublin Castle –
Sep[r] 13 – [1803]

What! another letter you say! no – not another *letter*, but a dozen of lines or so – I wrote you a very scrambling epistle three days ago which I had not time to look over or revise in any way, & I find that tho *that* does very well when one is treating of common chit chat, on occasions such as the present one sometimes tells fibs from ignorance & sometimes from hearing things imperfectly & repeating like a parrot without knowing the meaning of what is said, which makes accounts that are read by a wise person sometimes appear both *silly* & *impossible* – & conversation since, makes me recollect having wrote something about the under secretary (Mr Marsdon)* & of his having got the guards doubled on the 23[d], it struck me at the time as an odd thing for him to have *orderd*, not being a military man, but I since find, it was only that he had prevailed on General Fox the morning of the 23[d] to double the guards at Chapel Izard, [sic] * the road leading to one very suspected part of the country, he (Mr Marsdon) being present at the conference which Lord H: held with genl: Fox at the phoenix park on this subject previous to his taking him to town in his carriage for the purpose of making other arrangements which arrangements never were made. – tho this seems to be a small deviation from the fact, that of his having at his own Hand sent for more guards, or prevaild on the commander in Chief to grant them by stating the danger of having so few, yet I think it proper to put it right to you My Dear friend as I might injure Mr Marsdon in your opinion by my Inaccuracy. – I find there is a paper (Cobbits)* in which there is a desperate attack on this man, I never read political papers, & not having been here when the riots took place, I am not yet versed in all the progressive circumstances necessary to be known, to judge how false the statement of facts is. – I hear however that four gentlemen whose names are mentiond there as having complaind of him for having disregarded with Haughtyness the intelligence they offerd him, have wrote to him disdaining having ever used words so foreign to the truth – I think it probable that Mr Marsdon will prosecute Cobbit without delay, & then I presume many things will come before the publick which woud be rather agreeable to my friends here, as whatever blame is fairly due, will then fall fairly where it ought, according to the facts – as to Mr Cobbit, I do not see what interest he can have in attacking this same Mr Marsdon so violently but I see how he may have been *misled* into doing so, Mr Marsdons publick situation is the object of a good deal of envy amongst his countrymen, particularly to a certain class of men who have some abilitys & less good luck than he has experienced in his rise in life, they have transmitted this abuse of the administration here. to get individually at him, as I hear

*Marsdon**
Alexander Marsden, under-secretary for Ireland.

*Izard**
Chapelizod – a village on the R. Liffy, west of Phoenix Park.

*Cobbits**
William Cobbett's weekly *Cobbett's political register*, 1802-1835. At first Tory, it became radical in 1805. Marsden's actions on 23-7-1803 appear to have been only what one would expect to be done in the circumstances.

Lord H: and General Fox are scarcely named in the business – enough of all this – let it be between ourselves, as *these* are subjects which even if I understood them, which I do not I woud not wish as a woman to enter on exept in *gossip* to a very dear friend who will pardon all follys & inaccuracys –

Since I wrote to you totherday there is a very singular story in circulation here, which I fancy is not without foundation, that the daughter of Curran the famous councellor, has been in correspondence with Emmet (now to take his trial) & that her love letters found on him & mixed with politicks will go hard to condemn him* – no one believes that Curran her father knew of this correspondence – he some time ago changed his doctrines, & professd himself determined to be Loyal for the future as it *was most for his interest* he said, as he had a rising family. – he was to have been council for Emmot, but on this discovery, has declined it, & will not see his daughter – there *sounds* to be duplicity in this, yet people do not suspect any, or that he has had any knowledge of the matter, on the contrary deep mortification appears – the young man is said to have behaved extremely well – but we shall hear more of this on wednesday – but they press us so much to give them another week, that we have consented & shall leave this for Haigh by Wiggan next tuesday where we shall stay a week & go on with our own horses to Scotland – I shall let you hear from us from time to time without expecting a reply as I coud not give you any fixed place to write to me at exept in Edinburgh – & I shall also let you know what time we coud come to you for a few days *incase* it woud be convenient to receive us –

pray are we to have any invasions this summer or autumn? I begin to fancy that B. Parte* will put on his boots & in a general way fall on the *least prepared* spot that belongs to us – the west Indies. – Egypt – or India, incase we chance to be too ready to receive him in England Scotland or Ireland – My kind love to your sweet wife & to Mrs Strange if with you –

ever yours – sincerely
Anne Barnard

*him**
Lady A.'s information here recorded seems to be accurate in most respects. (cf. MacDonagh, M. *The Viceroy's postbag*. London, 1904, p. 342-54.)

*Parte**
Bonaparte

Letter 39

Holyhead –
Sep[r] 21 1803

Having wrote you So much of trials – rebels – & interesting matters of the painful, allarming & Horrid kind (the only matters that I had to write of almost while in Ireland) I think you will like to know the conclusion of Emmets Trial & the manner in which he quitted his busy & turbulent carreer at 23 years of age I believe* – Monday last was the day appointed for his Trial – the court was crowded at a very early hour, it began at 9 o clock & lasted till 8 in the evening – many men carried there with them, a considerable mixture of compassion for his youth & perverted talents, but this sentiment did not remain with them. – the proofs of his guilt were so clear, that at his *own desire*, his council [sic] did not make *any deffences* [sic]* – some extracts only of the letters I mentiond were read, & the name was withheld, I clearly see in delicacy to her father Mr Curran who is but lately become the friend of government, & has so much ability to do harm, that I believe it is *prudent* to bind him by gratitude if possible – the behaviour of the young man during the trial was cool – firm – & manly – after he was found guilty he spoke at considerable length, but it was thought in a daring & improper manner – avowing his principles & glorying in them – I do not however think his speech *reads* ill – to be sure it is daring & impetuous but I think *sincere*, & the speech of a republican & an Enthusiast who from Infancy has imbibed a sett of false doctrines, which an ardent & ambitious mind has confirmed, & an ill placed attachment has rivetted – I enclose to you a copy of his speech, taken in a sort of Short hand, but not well taken – after sentence was passd, he was by a mistake taken to Newgate* & lodged in a miserable cell, which being discoverd by Mr Wickham* he sent a strong party of dragoons & removed him to his former prison where he was comfortably accomodated till the next day, when he was to be executed – he expressd himself sensible of this mark of attention, to the officer on guard, who repeated this and a great deal more to me, & he also in a conversation with the attorney general Mr Ogrady* enterd more at large into his views & plans than he had done the Day before – he regreted that he had been stopd short in the speech he made both on his own account & on that of administration – that he had wishd as far as *he* coud to have exculpated them from any charge of remissness in not having sooner detected a conspiracy which from its closeness he knew it was impossible they coud have detected sooner than they did, he woud have born handsome testimony to the Justice & mildness of the present administration of the country, & in plain & direct words he avowd that the reason he hurried on the conspiracy *prematurely* was that he saw the minds of the people *were begining to be gained over*, they were losing a *part of their energy* &

*believe**
Emmet was born on 4-3-1778, so he was actually 25 years old at his execution on 20-9-1803.

[*sic*] *
His counsel were Leonard MacNally and Peter Burrows. The former is said to have been a government spy and actually to have betrayed Emmet. He was the author of the song "The Lass of Richmond Hill".

*Newgate**
Dublin, of course, not London.

*Wickham**
Rt. Hon. William Wickham, Chief Secretary for Ireland, 1802-04.

*Ogrady**
Standish O'Grady.

were almost contented with their *Chains* – that he had never taken an oath in his life to any government, nor swore any oath but to live & die a united Irishman – more was said, but this is the cream I *believe*; a few hours after he wrote a letter of thanks to Mr Wickham to the same effect – I forgot to add that he reiterated his abhorrence of the french – their principles – their government – & he said he had been *eager* to make *his* push, before the invasion which *they* meditated, woud make it *theirs* – he disdaind private views of ambition or interest, but shewd a mind burning with a fire, which flashd only to mislead, being self misled – I do not believe that Miss Curran requested to see him, if she had, she woud not have been permitted; the conduct of Redman had renderd it necessary that he shoud be searchd in court to prevent his concealing the means of Self destruction – he was handcuffd – many letters were found on him w^{c} were not exposed – & a locket of hair & small bunsh of valerian – he said to the Jailor "for Heavens sake do not take *these* from me – let me have *them* to the last" – they were returnd to him! – next day at one oclock, he was taken to the place of execution in a hackny coach, at his own request – he conversed with ease & calmness with two protestant Clergymen* who accompanied him, he being a protestant & when he arrived at the place seemd much disappointed at ~~not~~ being permitted to Harrangue the populace, giving reason to suppose that his intentions might fairly be *trusted* – but the experiment was one of too much danger – he was not allowd to speak* – & finding he coud not prevail, calmly & at once advanced to the Halter – he had before he left prison requested to have the sacrement, declared himself to have lived & to die a Christian, sincerly sorry for whatever he had done that was wrong, but dying in the firm persuasion that he had in the present instance acted up to what was *his duty* according to every principle which from early Infancy had been installd into him – this request of partaking of the sacrement (which was granted) but at the same time acknowledging *no repentance* for his conduct, produced a very warm dispute at his Excellencys table where opinions were so equally *divided*, that a Bishop being on the side against the administration of the sacrement coud scarcely turn the scale. – I will not venture into a subject so far above me, but one thing I *may* venture to say both with respect to Emmet & the two Clergymen that I believe our great Creator who looks into our Hearts will judge our motives rather than our actions – our actions vary, as countrys – Habits – tenets of faith & moral laws settle it, but the motives of Hearts are of all religions, customs, & where they are sound & pure in their own Tribunal, conscience, I do not believe the Great Judge of all will punish the person whose judgement only, is wrong – & therefore may we not forgive the Clergymen? – & perhaps when we do, find an extenuation for Emmet? – *dont tell*, if this is not orthodox –

and now I close – you will perceive this is dated from Holyhead, we are on our way from Ireland to Lancashire & Scotland & ultimately to you – but I am not ready to say *when* – certainly not before a month – as we travel with our own horses – perhaps a trifle less agreeable but particularly suited to Mr Secretarys who have no sallarys at their backs & of course whose wife must be patient on the road – I find patience

*Clergymen**
The Rev. Messrs. Gamble and Grant. The former was prison chaplain, the latter of Island Bridge.

*speak**
He uttered one sentence: "My friends, I die in peace with sentiments of universal love and kindness towards all men." (MacDonagh, op. cit. p.407.)

very easy in general, but not when my friends are at my Journeys end – if I have any chez vous – Miss Wortly* &c make my love to her, & to your daughter, & to the Dear Lady Jane a large share & the half of this letter –

yrs ever
Anne Barnard

Lord Norburys* address to Mr Emmet after the Jury had found him guilty of High Treason and the substance of Mr Emmets speech –

"You have been found guilty Robert Emmet what have you to *say for yourself* Why the sentence of the law shoud not be passd on you?"

"My Lord. – With respect to the Trial I have had & the verdict pronounced – *Nothing* – I acknowledge the Justice of both, and was I only to suffer Death, and that all shoud die with me, I woud not take up a moment of your time, but with respect to some of the charges this night stated, I have much to say. – I have been charged with being an *Emmissary of France* – Hear the Declaration of a dying man, I say it is *False*, I never was an Emmissary of France, I acknowledge that the provisional Government treated with France, and at this moment an Ambassador from this country is at Paris to obtain a Treaty signd before an Expedition shoud sail, to get for this country such a constitution as *Franklin obtained for America*, I have no faith in Treatys, my object was to obtain for the *people* their *rights*, to restore what had been *wrested from them*, to act with the people *against the government* to obtain it, but *not* as it was construed to night by *Foreign aid*; so contrary was my plan that I accelerated the Attack of the 23[d] *least* the French shoud arrive; – Hear the declaration of a dying man – my views were *not* formd upon Ambitious motives, I had no desire for Emolument or Agrandisement, I sacrifised Idols dear to my heart to obtain for the people their rights, I now lose my life for it. – read our Proclamation my wish was to effect this without bloodshed I declare as a dying man I did *not* wish to spill Blood" – Here Lord Norbury interrupted him and said –

"Mr Emmet if you have any thing in law to advance or any thing in mitigation of the dread sentence, the court is ready to hear you, but know inconsiderate and unhappy young man, that since the fatal verdict has been pronounced that instead of employing the short period you are allotted in this life, in making some attonement for the Crimes you have been guilty of, you have on the contrary given way to a heated Imagination & *confessd* greater crimes than you are charged with, I wishd unhappy Young man to have addressd you in this hour of your distress in a different manner, & to have exhorted you to make as much attonement to your God as the short period you now have woud admit, for the numberless lives you have to answer for, & the valuable & Loyal blood which your desperate plans has occasioned to be spilt aided by an outcast a Bricklayer, a cast cloaths man & a Baker – was this the provisional Government that in fourteen days we were to surrender ourselves to or meet the Punishment of Traitors? Mr Emmet the court cannot waste any more time in hearing expressions that must astonish &

*Worthy**
Probably Mary Stuart-Wortley, sister of James Archibald Stuart-Wortley-Mackenzie afterwards Lord Wharncliffe (See Letter 10, note 4.) She married the Rt. Hon. William Dundas, M.P., H.D.'s nephew, in 1813.

*Norburys**
John Toler, 1st Baron (later Earl of) Norbury (1740-1831), Chief Justice of the Common Pleas of Ireland. He was famed for his jocosity in court and his "bon mots", even when a man's life was in the balance.

cause Indignation in the heart of every one within these walls" – "My Lord it is true that you are the Judge, & I the culprit, but my Lord you are but a man. – so am I, I claim nothing as a culprit from a Judge, I only desire that my dying request may be granted, & that this may pass with my life, that when I meet the cold grave, no Epitaph may be written on my Tomb, – Future times will record the work that I began" –

"Mr Emmet if you [have] nothing in Extenuation of your guilt to say it is my painfull Duty to pass the sentence of the Law upon you, and in so doing it is a painfull task to me – I know your family, some held high situations in this country, I knew one of them an ornament to his country, he was snatched away before he had an opportunity of watching over those great talents you possess, which if applied to good purposes might have raised you to the first situation in this country; you have been born & highly educated here, & if you now look round you, you will see probably many of the noble & loyal youths you have been educated with arrayd in armour to oppose that wicked & unnatural rebellion, of which you are the Essence" "My Lord I was not the framer, on my return to this country I was solicited to join the provisional govt, I desired & took some days to consider of it" "You are not now to impeach others" – "My Lord I do not mean it, but I state the truths as I shall shortly appear before God, that I was *not* the author, but joind in it because the sentiments it professd were congenial to my own; from the age of *ten* these sentiments were *mine* and will go to the grave with me to join the people against their Government for the redress of their grievances, and were it to be done to morrow I woud act as I have done, – but Hear my last declaration, *I Hate French principles*, & Hate *the French*, I see they have paid no respect to treatys, was I in Switzerland I woud join the *people* against the French, I woud do the same Here, and woud be one of the foremost to fight against them. – these are my Sentiments – for these I die – My ministry is come to a close! –

Conclusion

The close of the Barnards' lives was less happy. Returning from Ireland they settled at Wimbledon but a change of ministry brought no new appointment for Andrew. When however, after the resumption of hostilities with France, Britain again occupied the Cape in January 1806, he was asked to accompany the new governor, Lord Caledon, in his old capacity. Doubtless this was in no small measure due to Lord Macartney who had spoken most highly of him to Dundas. Barnard agreed to go for six months, in spite of uncertain health, leaving Lady Anne behind in England. On the voyage out in H.M.S. *Antelope* he was most unwell but seemed much better on arrival at the Cape on May 21st 1807. The following October however, while on a journey inland with the Governor, he became seriously ill and was obliged to remain at a farm where he died "of a bilious fever" on the 27th. He was buried in the cemetery in Somerset Road, Cape Town, and his tombstone bore the inscription: "Colonists . . . he sought the welfare of your country and loved its inhabitants."

A heartbroken Lady Anne, courageous none-the-less, returned to her sister Margaret's house in Berkeley Square for the next five years. In 1812 Lady Margaret remarried but died only two years later. Windham had died in 1810 and Henry Dundas in 1811, his latter years clouded. On the formation of Pitt's new government in 1804, he had taken over the Admiralty but in 1806 was impeached for the misappropriation of public money during the time he had been Treasurer of the Navy in 1782-83. Pitt stood by him nobly but in the Commons the Speaker's casting vote had gone against him. This blow helped to hasten Pitt's untimely end and he did not live to see his friend's reinstatement the following year. Melville however retired from public life and spent his last years on his Scottish estate. Lady Anne herself lived on, her loneliness cheered by the friendship of such men as Sir Walter Scott, until her death on May 6th 1825.

Index

Page references in *italics* indicate illustrations.